Approaches to Teaching Grass's *The Tin Drum*

Approaches to Teaching
World Literature

Joseph Gibaldi, series editor

For a complete listing of titles,
see the last pages of this book.

Approaches to Teaching Grass's *The Tin Drum*

Edited by

Monika Shafi

The Modern Language Association of America
New York   2008

© 2008 by The Modern Language Association of America
All rights reserved
Printed in the United States of America

For information about obtaining permission to reprint material from MLA book
publications, send your request by mail (see address below),
e-mail (permissions@mla.org), or fax (646 458-0030).

Library of Congress Cataloging-in-Publication Data

Approaches to teaching Grass's The tin drum / edited by Monika Shafi.
p. cm. — (Approaches to teaching world literature)
Includes bibliographical references and index.
ISBN: 978-0-87352-811-5   (hardcover : alk. paper)
ISBN: 978-0-87352-812-2   (pbk. : alk. paper)
1. Grass, Günter, 1927– Blechtrommel.   2. German literature—Study and
teaching (Higher).   I. Shafi, Monika.
PT2613.R338B55315 2008
833' .914—dc22   2007037791

Cover illustration of the paperback edition: Drawing by Günter Grass
on a book jacket of Die Blechtrommel.
© Günter Grass, 1959; © Steidl Verlag, Göttingen, 1993.

Published by The Modern Language Association of America
26 Broadway, New York, New York 10004-1789
www.mla.org

CONTENTS

PREFACE TO THE SERIES

In *The Art of Teaching*, Gilbert Highet wrote, "Bad teaching wastes a great deal of effort, and spoils many lives which might have been full of energy and happiness." All too many teachers have failed in their work, Highet argued, simply "because they have not thought about it." We hope that the Approaches to Teaching World Literature series, sponsored by the Modern Language Association's Publications Committee, will not only improve the craft—as well as the art—of teaching but also encourage serious and continuing discussion of the aims and methods of teaching literature.

The principal objective of the series is to collect within each volume different points of view on teaching a specific literary work, a literary tradition, or a writer widely taught at the undergraduate level. The preparation of each volume begins with a wide-ranging survey of instructors, thus enabling us to include in the volume the philosophies and approaches, thoughts and methods of scores of experienced teachers. The result is a sourcebook of material, information, and ideas on teaching the subject of the volume to undergraduates.

The series is intended to serve nonspecialists as well as specialists, inexperienced as well as experienced teachers, graduate students who wish to learn effective ways of teaching as well as senior professors who wish to compare their own approaches with the approaches of colleagues in other schools. Of course, no volume in the series can ever substitute for erudition, intelligence, creativity, and sensitivity in teaching. We hope merely that each book will point readers in useful directions; at most each will offer only a first step in the long journey to successful teaching.

Joseph Gibaldi
Series Editor

PREFACE TO THE VOLUME

"A writer, children," reads a famous and often quoted line from Günter Grass's novel *Aus dem Tagebuch einer Schnecke* (1972; *From the Diary of a Snail* [1973]), "is someone who writes against the passage of time" (141). This statement defines memory work, recollection of the past, as an author's premier task while simultaneously highlighting the writer's responsibility to the present moment and the future. The brief sentence could serve as a leitmotif for Grass's brilliant oeuvre and its extraordinary influence on postwar German literature. Almost all of his narratives evoke his home town of Danzig, and numerous texts explore the lower-middle-class milieu of his childhood, particularly its susceptibility to fascism. Grass's own, albeit brief, fascination with Nazi ideology and above all the horrors of Auschwitz have been the traumatic experiences compelling him to write and speak out. Loss, shame, and guilt as well as the continuous attempt to understand the causes of Germany's horrendous twentieth-century history are thus some of the dominant themes of his vast opus.

Grass's stupendous career began dramatically in 1959 with the publication of his first novel, *Die Blechtrommel* (*The Tin Drum* [1962]). A work of epic proportions and complexity, *The Tin Drum* brought instant fame to the thirty-two-year-old author and won him the 1999 Nobel Prize in Literature. To this day, Grass continues to be identified to an unprecedented degree with his first hit. An immensely successful and highly provocative novel from the very beginning and hailed as inaugurating an innovative postwar German literature, *The Tin Drum* has established itself in the past five decades as one of the most important narratives of twentieth-century German literature, and its protagonist, Oskar Matzerath, has achieved iconic status.

The story of Oskar Matzerath, who at age three decides to stop growing in order to avoid the path of bourgeois mediocrity, using his drumming skills and glass-shattering voice to pursue an artistic career instead, is widely regarded as *the* foundational text of contemporary German literature. The novel's continuing fascination obviously hinges to a large extent on Oskar, the drumming dwarf narrator, and on the riotous account of his life until his thirtieth birthday. In his presentation speech at the Nobel Prize ceremony, Horace Engdahl described Oskar as "a completely original creation: an infernal intelligence in the body of a three-year-old, a monster who victoriously approaches mankind with the aid of a tin drum, an intellectual with infantility as his critical method."

Oskar's preposterous stories and adventures offer a stunning tour de force through German history of the first half of the twentieth century, and Grass's depiction of the rise of fascism, the Nazi regime, and postwar restoration built on denial pioneered subsequent debates on guilt and memory. *The Tin Drum* details the loss of home—according to Grass, the experience from which all his writing emanates—while fictionally re-creating the city of Danzig. Brilliantly adopting and mocking a wide range of European genres and literary traditions, such as the picaresque novel, the bildungsroman, magical realism, as well as the grotesque and parody, it dazzles readers with its artistic bravura and linguistic virtuosity.

The Tin Drum has also been a hugely popular novel, translated into dozens of languages with over four million copies sold worldwide. Its success was reinforced by Volker Schlöndorff's 1979 film adaptation *Die Blechtrommel*, which won an Oscar for best foreign film. For many years, Grass has been seen both in Germany and abroad as the preeminent German author, and his influence on other national literatures has been attested to by writers as diverse as Nadine Gordimer and Salman Rushdie (see Hermes and Neuhaus).

At American and British universities and colleges, *The Tin Drum* figures prominently in a broad variety of undergraduate and graduate courses that includes survey courses as well as comparative literature and film studies seminars, which are taught either in German or in English. These classes cover a wide spectrum of topics in literature, history, and cultural studies, ranging, as respondents to the survey reported, from comparative literature courses on modernity, magic realism, and fiction of the Second World War to undergraduate seminars on the (postwar) German novel, German films, and film adaptations of literary works. The novel also figures in courses on the Holocaust or on such topics as fiction and power, images of state and society in German culture, and memory and identity in twentieth-century German literature. And of course there are graduate seminars that focus either exclusively on Grass's oeuvre or discuss *The Tin Drum* in German literary, historical, and narrative traditions.

The novel's status as one of the canonical texts of postwar German literature, however, has not diminished its challenge and confrontational appeal. *The Tin Drum* continues to spark new scholarly debate—particularly with regard to its representation of race, ethnicity, and gender—and its baroque proportions and visual intensity exercise an unabated fascination among scholars, teachers, and students.

This volume seeks to address both *The Tin Drum*'s role as a watershed literary landmark in postwar West Germany and the debate regarding its depiction of German, Polish, Jewish, and gender identity. Schlöndorff's film, in which Grass actively participated, shares many of the novel's entertaining and radical features. It, too, has become a classic in German film history and is often taught in classes on German or European film. This volume therefore devotes an entire section to the teaching of Schlöndorff's film, and several of its essays discuss how to harness the film's visual power when teaching the novel.

The very same qualities that have earned *The Tin Drum* a place in the canon of world literature pose some formidable challenges in the classroom. Chief among them, as indicated by the results of the survey for this volume in the MLA series Approaches to Teaching World Literature and by the essays that follow, are the sheer size and complexity of an almost eight-hundred-page novel that plays with a daunting array of styles, genre traditions, and linguistic registers and that aims to shock and provoke. How to guide students through the historical periods and conflicts covered in *The Tin Drum* and how to teach the novel's complex narrative structures are two core questions informing the organization and topics of this volume. Following the guidelines of this series, its goals are to present teachers with background information and critical approaches, highlight dominant themes as well as formal and linguistic elements, and provide different ideas and strategies on how to teach those features. Although the essays can most certainly be read in a selective manner, the volume adheres to a certain progression. It moves from what are commonly considered to be the most fundamental areas—namely, history and narrative—to more specific though no less important subjects, such as race and gender, and it concludes with three essays devoted to the analysis of Schlöndorff's film.

The Tin Drum covers the time span from 1899, the year in which Oskar's mother, Agnes, was conceived, until Oskar's thirtieth birthday, in 1954. Without some basic knowledge of German and Polish history of the first half of the twentieth century, which most students do not have, the work simply cannot be understood. The volume's opening essay, by Julian Preece, an overview of some of the novel's most fundamental historical and narrative constellations, thus includes a dual dateline of pertinent historical events and their fictional representation in the novel. Students also need to recognize, as Todd Kontje argues in his essay, the novel's inherent ambiguity regarding historical and fictional representation. They should learn to assess critically the literary techniques and traditions Grass employed in his pursuit of recollecting and depicting the past. The question of how to evaluate his account of National Socialism in *The Tin Drum* has in recent years been the focus of intense scholarly debate. Beginning with Patricia Pollock Brodsky's essay on forms of resistance in *The Tin Drum*, this discussion is also taken up in the essays by Dagmar C. G. Lorenz and Peter Arnds. Together with Timothy B. Malchow's examination of Oskar's corporeal modes of memory and West German remembrance of the Nazi past, these essays provide instructors with succinct analyses of the novel's representation of history as well as with teaching suggestions, including model questions and select text passages, on how to disentangle the nexus of history, fiction, and memory.

The essays in the next section, "Narrative and Reading Strategies," analyze Grass's brilliant narrative devices, specifically his choice of a dwarf narrator. Teachers can find ideas on how to structure the first class meeting through the "title exercise," which Irene Kacandes demonstrates in a step-by-step approach, or consult the essays by Sabine Gross and by Alfred D. White for insights into the supreme unreliability (and linguistic skills) of Oskar Matzerath. Katharina Hall shows how *The Tin Drum*'s two other narrators introduce alternative perspectives that can allow for a more comprehensive picture of Oskar. While most essays provide some information about course contexts and levels, Jane Curran outlines how to cover the themes of fiction and history in an advanced undergraduate or graduate class. Elizabeth C. Hamilton explores the importance of stage and performance and includes an appendix with detailed classroom exercises and assignments on this topic. It is well known that Grass is not only an extremely prolific author but also an accomplished visual artist who has always insisted on the close relation among his different artistic media. The interdisciplinary nature of his oeuvre has attracted widespread attention, and Richard E. Schade explains how this connection can be used to teach *The Tin Drum*.

The third section addresses Grass's representation of race and gender. Whereas Lorenz criticizes Grass for his inadequate depiction of Jewish characters and the Holocaust, Arnds contends that the novel rescues outsider figures from their appropriation by Nazi ideology. Barbara Becker-Cantarino and Teresa Ludden both focus on Grass's representation of women and the novel's patriarchal gender discourse, but their arguments are based on different methodological approaches. A brief but succinct gender critique is also offered by Kontje. In addition to providing teaching exercises and contexts, these essays lend themselves particularly well as topics for student presentations and debates.

The film adaptation of the novel is used, as the results of the survey indicate, by most instructors when teaching the novel, and the volume's final three essays provide pertinent topics and teaching ideas for Schlöndorff's film, ranging from the depiction of childhood (Brockmann), the role of narrative desire (Anderson), to the use of sound and image (Setje-Eilers). Though based on the film, the authors' arguments can also be applied to the novel, such as Stephen Brockmann's discussion of childhood and its appropriation by Nazi ideology. A comparison between novel and film lends itself as a topic for classroom discussion, and the essays, specifically Susan C. Anderson's and Margaret Setje-Eilers's, suggest ideas for how to focus such a debate.

Part 1 of this volume, "Materials," offers a basic road map to the vast territory of scholarship on Grass and his first novel. Grass's avowed intention in all his writing is to activate readers' critical spirit, and the same intention guides the present volume, which aims to help teachers as well as students read and interpret *The Tin Drum* with greater clarity, understanding, and joy.

I thank the contributors to this volume for their expertise, erudition, and enthusiasm. It was a privilege to work with this group of devoted teachers and colleagues, which includes some of the most respected Grass scholars and whose commitment to German literature and culture is unsurpassed. Their patience with my editing queries or suggestions deserves special recognition. I also acknowledge the contribution of the survey respondents, many of whom also wrote essays for this volume, for sharing their pedagogical insights and Grass knowledge. I am further grateful to the readers and consultant readers who gave so generously of their time. The volume benefited tremendously from their insightful comments and wonderfully detailed reading. My sincere thanks to Joseph Gibaldi for suggesting this project and for his continuous support and patience in seeing it to fruition, as well as to the editors of the MLA for their help and guidance. Friends and colleagues at the University of Delaware shared valuable insights, read drafts, and gave support. I would particularly like to acknowledge Margaret Stetz, Mary Donaldson-Evans, and Richard Zipser. The help and goodwill of graduate students who ran library and Internet searches and organized computer files were crucial, and I am grateful to Christina Wall, Jocelyn McDaniel, and especially Heike Gerhold, whose superb work was crucial in the final stage of the project. Finally, I need to speak of my family—my children, Miriam and Karim, and my husband, Qaisar, whose wisdom, kindness, and enduring love sustain me. The three of them keep me grounded and balanced, making my life forever rich and exciting. To them I happily dedicate this volume.

Postscript, September 2006

As the manuscript of this volume was nearing completion, Günter Grass revealed that as a seventeen-year-old he was a member of the Waffen-SS. He first disclosed his membership in an interview with *Die Frankfurter Allgemeine Zeitung*, detailing the circumstances of his military service in his new book *Beim Häuten der Zwiebel* (2006; "Peeling the Onion"), an autobiographical account of his youth and young adulthood. Grass had never hidden his early Nazi allegiance and service in Hitler's army or pretended to have questioned, let alone resisted, Nazi ideology. But his long silence about his membership in the Waffen-SS and the reasons for it sparked an intense debate both in Germany and abroad. The explanations Grass offered—"It weighed on me. My silence all these years is one of the reasons why I wrote this book. It had to get out, finally" ("Warum" 33; my trans.) or "I was only now able to do it and who wants to judge, may judge" ("Es war" 67)—seemed vague and evasive to many critics and invited all the more speculation about his motives and the impact his belated confession would have on his career and on his moral and political authority.

Many were outraged and accused Grass of hypocrisy, opportunism, and shameless self-promotion; some came to his defense; and a few analyzed the surprise disclosure in the context of his oeuvre, his generation, and West German society. Shame, guilt, ambition, fame—each in itself a complex and powerful force—entangled in a biography and story that appeared in more than one way to represent postwar Germany. "Grass Is Germany," declared one headline (Steinfeld).

As the editor of this volume, I pondered if and how this recent development would affect the arguments presented in it. More specifically, would this latest Grass debate alter the pedagogical reasoning, the methodologies, and exercises presented here? The brilliance of Grass's first novel, its place in the canon of world literature, and the need for a pedagogical guide to it are not in question, I decided. Grass's confession raises many moral, political, and historical issues, but it does not diminish his literary accomplishments. This book is designed to enable students to develop their own understanding and interpretation, be it regarding *The Tin Drum* or its author's life and behavior. Grass's revelation most certainly adds an interpretative layer and a further biographical context for *The Tin Drum* as well as for his other novels. The work of rereading Grass, of comparing his fictional and autobiographical accounts of Danzig and adolescence under Nazism, should produce exciting new scholarship for years to come. In the framework of this volume, such new perspectives could give rise to new and productive teaching exercises.

Assignments might range from giving oral presentations on Grass's membership in the Waffen-SS to staging a debate based on opposing responses to his revelation to creating a mock call-in radio show in which a few students act as literary experts and the others make up and "phone in" questions related to the affair. It might also be useful to conclude lessons on *The Tin Drum* with a brief lecture on Grass's silence and ask students if this knowledge affects their interpretation of the novel, especially their understanding of Oskar Matzerath. Such discussions should show students how alive and astringent the German engagement with the Nazi past continues to be and how Oskar's struggles with memory, guilt, shame, and fear reverberate with Grass and the nation he has come to represent.

MS

Part One

MATERIALS

Editions and Translations

German Editions

Grass's *Die Blechtrommel* is available as volume 2 in the ten-volume *Werkausgabe* edited by Volker Neuhaus; it contains useful maps of Danzig. The novel is also volume 3 in the sixteen-volume *Werkausgabe* edited by Neuhaus and Daniela Hermes. Paperback editions of *Die Blechtrommel* have been published by Luchterhand, Fischer, and dtv. Respondents to this volume's survey favored the dtv paperback, but the older Luchterhand version came in a close second, and many suggested that any cheap edition would do. Since currently only the dtv edition is available, it was the obvious choice for this volume, and all quotations from the German text are based on this paperback (first published in 1993, with a fifteenth printing in 2005). Its jacket features Grass's famous drawing of a small person with stark blue eyes holding an oversized red drum.

English Translations

Respondents use the Vintage paperback edition in the translation of Ralph Manheim, which was first published in 1961 by Secker and Warburg in Great Britain and then in 1962 by Pantheon in the United States. The 1990 Vintage edition, currently the only paperback version available, is used for this volume. In a few instances, some contributors modified or commented on Manheim's translation in order to restore or point to nuances that were lost in translation. The cover of the Vintage edition does not show Grass's compelling image, but both depictions of Oskar can be used, as Irene Kacandes points out in her essay in this volume, as a starting point for discussion.

Further Readings for Students

Respondents were divided on the question of whether to assign additional readings to students. Many felt that Grass's novel, "already formidably long and challenging to many," did not warrant the extra burden of secondary sources. Others, however, named a surprisingly large number of historical and theoretical materials, which are too diverse to summarize easily. Most frequently cited was John Reddick's discussion of *The Tin Drum* in The Danzig Trilogy *of Günter Grass*, a by now classic interpretation and an eminently readable, extensive, and well-structured analysis of the novel in the context of the trilogy. Patrick O'Neill's *Günter Grass Revisited*, which provides an updated, comprehensive outline of Grass's life and career, and Alan Frank Keele's *Understanding Günter*

Grass, which explains plots and themes in their literary, historical, and mytho-logical contexts, were also often recommended. Respondents included titles by Neuhaus, Germany's foremost Grass scholar. Among them are *Günter Grass: Die Blechtrommel* (in the series Erläuterungen und Dokumente ["Explanations and Documents"]) and his study *Günter Grass* (in the series Sammlung Metzler), which offers a concise yet detailed overview of Grass's major narratives as well as a brief presentation of his main stylistic features. The extensive bibliography and index in the latter work make, according to one respondent, "an excellent introduction." Other recommendations were Hanspeter Brode's *Günter Grass*; Rolf Geißler's *Günter Grass: Ein Materialienbuch* ("A Book of Materials"); and David H. Miles's *Günter Grass*, which provides a comprehensive and sophis-ticated interpretation of the novel, including a discussion of Grass's ingenious adaptation of literary traditions and forebears. Following the nuts-and-bolts approach of the series Meisterwerke kurz und bündig ("Masterpieces Short and Concise"), Heinz Gockel's *Grass' Blechtrommel* surveys the novel's main themes and literary traditions, its reception, and its film adaptation. For bio-graphical background, some respondents suggested Keele's chapter on Grass in the *Dictionary of Literary Biography* (vol. 75; "Günter Grass") and Grass's Nobel Prize speech (*Nobelvorlesung*), a very personal account of his biographi-cal and literary development.

Respondents who did not recommend additional readings advised using visual materials in *Power Point* presentations or bringing in maps of Danzig, photocopies of headlines from the *New York Times* of 1 September 1939, or images of German nurses taken from Klaus Theweleit's study *Male Fantasies*. One respondent has students do Internet searches on topics such as the battle for the Danzig Post Office or the history of Danzig.

The Instructor's Library

Biography

The two most recent biographies of Grass are Michael Jürgs's *Bürger Grass: Biografie eines deutschen Dichters* ("Biography of a German Poet"), providing useful information about Grass's youth and the history of the writing of *The Tin Drum*, and Claudia Mayer-Iswandy's *Günter Grass*. Whereas Jürgs foregrounds Grass's biography and politics, Mayer-Iswandy emphasizes literary analysis. Her book also contains numerous pictures of Grass and his artwork. A more theme-based overview is Neuhaus's *Schreiben gegen die verstreichende Zeit: Zu Leben und Werk von Günter Grass* ("Writing against the Passage of Time: On the Life and Work of . . ."), because Neuhaus interprets Grass's entire oeuvre as shaped by the topic of guilt and atonement. Two other brief biographical studies are Heinrich Vormweg's *Günter Grass* and Ute Brandes's *Günter Grass*. Although opposed for many years to the idea of writing his autobiography, Grass often commented (before 2006) on his biographical and literary development and elaborated specifically on the role Danzig and his lower-class background have played in his work. In addition to his Nobel Prize speech, the brief essay "Rückblick auf *Die Blechtrommel* oder Der Autor als fragwürdiger Zeuge" ("*The Tin Drum* in Retrospect; or, The Author as Dubious Witness") as well as the interviews and essays in his *Fundsachen für Nichtleser* ("Findings for Nonreaders") provide ample biographical information. Theodore Ziolkowski's "Günter Grass's Century" provides a succinct but superb overview of Grass's literary and political development, complete with a selection of images from Grass's graphic oeuvre. This article would also lend itself as background reading for students.

Background Studies

Respondents to this MLA volume's survey recommended for the most part books that focused on the novel and Grass's creative use of literary traditions. The most frequently cited of these titles appear above in "Further Reading for Students." Die Danziger Trilogie *von Günter Grass: Texte, Daten, Bilder* ("*The Danzig Trilogy* . . . : Texts, Dates, Images"), edited by Neuhaus and Hermes, contains a very useful collection of materials (interviews, interpretations, maps, a glossary) as well as several insightful essays. Respondents recommended only a few explicitly historical references, since most studies on Grass and *The Tin Drum* include information on the historical periods depicted in the novel. Among such references were Mary Fulbrook's *A Concise History of Germany*, which gives the historical context "simply and straightforwardly"; Joachim Remak's *The Nazi Years*, a collection of source materials; Carl Tighe's *Gdańsk: National Identity in the Polish-German Borderlands*, which contains the chapter "Günter Grass and Disappearing Danzig"; Robert G. Moeller's *War Stories: The Search for a Usable Past in the Federal Republic of Germany*; and Anton Kaes's *From Hitler to Heimat*. Similarly, respondents mentioned only a few general literary studies, such as Siegfried Mandel's *Group 47: The Reflected Intellect*, which describes the development and nature of Group 47 and its influence on Grass.

Critical Studies

The scholarship on Grass, particularly on *The Tin Drum* and *The Danzig Trilogy*, is impressive, and instructors can consult many book-length studies, chapters, and articles to familiarize themselves with the topics and traditions that the novel addresses. Given this large and continuously growing body of criticism, the following suggestions do not present an exhaustive or definitive body of Grass scholarship. Instead, they hope to offer to time-strapped teachers a choice of sources and analyses regarding the interpretations and controversies that both the novel and the film have generated since 1959.

Julian Preece's *The Life and Work of Günter Grass: Literature, History, Politics* is an eminently readable and erudite analysis of Grass and his oeuvre that includes a brief but sophisticated discussion of the novel. Patrick O'Neill's "Implications of Unreliability" provides another excellent explanation of Oskar and his principal narrative trait, unreliability, and of the literary traditions inspiring it. A similar focus characterizes H. E. Beyersdorf's short essay "The Narrator as Artful Deceiver: Aspects of Narrative Perspective in *Die Blechtrommel*," which offers a close reading of select passages. Dieter Stolz's *Günter Grass zur Einführung* ("Introducing . . .") contains a twenty-page essay on *The Tin Drum* that interprets Oskar as poet and fool. In his brief, elegantly written chapter "A Post-realist Aesthetic," Michael Minden summarizes pertinent aesthetic and narrative issues, stressing the similarities between Grass and Oskar. Sabine Moser's *Günter Grass: Romane und Erzählungen* ("Novels and Narratives") analyzes Grass's literary and political views as well as *The Danzig Trilogy* and his other major novels. This book presents a well-structured chronological survey of distinct phases in Grass's oeuvre.

Beginning with Hans Magnus Enzensberger's renowned essay "Wilhelm Meister, auf Blech getrommelt" ("Wilhelm Meister Drummed on Tin"), which situated *The Tin Drum* in the tradition of the bildungsroman, many scholars have further investigated Grass's skillful manipulation of literary legacies. Among such studies are Bruce Donahue's "The Alternative to Goethe: Markus and Fajngold in *Die Blechtrommel*," which reads Oskar as a parody of Goethe and his classical ideals; Miles's "Kafka's Hapless Pilgrims and Grass's Scurrilous Dwarf: Notes on Representative Figures in the Anti-bildungsroman"; and Rolf Selbmann's brief but useful summary of Grass's subversive use of bildungsroman traditions. For a superb study on the genre itself, readers should consult Todd Kontje's *The German Bildungsroman: History of a National Genre*. Detlev Krumme's *Günter Grass:* Die Blechtrommel provides commentary on the novel that also contextualizes it in German literary, historical, and social traditions. Werner Frizen, in "*Die Blechtrommel*—ein schwarzer Roman: Grass und die Literatur des Absurden" (". . . a Black Novel: Grass and the Literature of the Absurd"), discusses how the novel's portrayal of *Kleinbürger* ("petit bourgeois figures") engages with the images and epistemology of absurd literature in a way that extends well beyond the novel itself.

At the core of *The Tin Drum* are the topics of history and of historical representation, and much criticism delineates the complex interplay among history, fiction, and memory. Judith Ryan's chapter "The Revocation of Melancholy: Günter Grass' *The Tin Drum*" in her influential study *The Uncompleted Past: Postwar German Novels and the Third Reich* examines the novel's depiction of evil and fate, particularly Grass's critique of Thomas Mann's *Dr. Faustus*, whose structure *The Tin Drum* reverses. Readers wishing to examine the topic of guilt in Grass's oeuvre will find Thomas Kniesche's article "'Das wird nicht aufhören,

gegenwärtig zu bleiben': Günter Grass und das Problem der deutschen Schuld"
useful ("This Will Not Cease to Remain Present: Günter Grass and the Problem of German Guilt"). For a specific discussion of guilt in the context of *The
Tin Drum*, they could consult Klaus von Schilling's *Schuldmotoren: Artistisches
Erzählen in Günter Grass' Danziger Trilogie* ("Engines of Guilt: Artistic Narra-
tion in Günter Grass's *Danzig Trilogy*"). David Roberts's "'Gesinnungsästhetik'?
Günter Grass, *Schreiben nach Auschwitz* (1990)" ("'Aesthetics of Persuasion'?
Günter Grass, *Writing after Auschwitz*") develops a detailed analysis regarding
the connections between guilt and Grass's aesthetics. Ruth K. Angress ("Jewish
Problem") as well as Ernestine Schlant have criticized the novel's depiction of
Jews and the Holocaust as severely lacking. Peter Arnds, on the other hand,
in the 2004 study *Representation, Subversion, and Eugenics in Günter Grass's
The Tin Drum* argues that the novel's unique stylistic blend amounts to a multifaceted subversion of Nazi racial ideology. Katharina Hall, in her book *Günter
Grass's* Danzig Quintet: *Explorations in the Memory and History of the Nazi
Era from* Die Blechtrommel *to* Im Krebsgang, extends the time frame of this
discussion, for she traces Grass's depiction of the Nazi regime, the Holocaust,
and German wartime suffering from 1959 until 2002. Older scholarship on the
topic of history and guilt frequently cited by respondents include Ann L. Mason's *The Skeptical Muse: A Study of Günter Grass' Conception of the Artist*
and Frank-Raymund Richter's *Günter Grass: Die Vergangenheitsbewältigung
in der* Danzig Trilogie ("Coming to Terms with the Past in . . ."), which outlines
the manifold thematic and formal links and parallels in *The Danzig Trilogy*, offering a still very useful discussion of the trilogy's narrative complexity.

Among the numerous articles and book chapters dealing with select themes
or figures, respondents cited William Cloonan's *The Writing of War* (sometimes
also recommended for students). It contains a short chapter on *The Tin Drum*
that takes as its starting point the novel's focus on fear and the different coping
strategies the characters develop. Rainer Scherf, in *Das Herz der* Blechtrommel *und andere Aufsätze zum Werk von Günter Grass* ("'The Heart of *The Tin
Drum*' and Other Essays on the Work of . . ."), offers an autobiographical reading
of the novel. An important dimension of Grass's *Danzig Trilogy* is the Christian
legacy, the focus of Neuhaus's article "Das christliche Erbe bei Günter Grass"
("The Christian Legacy of . . ."). Another crucial area is Grass's representation
of gender. While the gender discourse in the novel *Der Butt (The Flounder)*
has extensively been examined, no major study has focused exclusively on *The
Tin Drum* or *The Danzig Trilogy*. For a brief overview of Grass's portrayal of
women, readers can use Barbara Garde's "'Die Frauengasse ist eine Gasse,
durch die man lebenslang geht': Frauen in den Romanen von Günter Grass"
("'The Frauengasse [literally, "women street"] Is a Street a Man Travels All His
Life': Women in the Novels of . . ."). Those who would prefer a more extensive
analysis can consult Mayer-Iswandy's "*Von Glück der Zwitter*": *Geschlechterrolle und Geschlechterverhältnis bei Günter Grass* ("On the Happiness of the
Hermaphrodites: Gender Role and Gender Relation in . . ."). The classic study

on Grass's use of myth is Edward Diller's *A Mythic Journey: Günter Grass's* Tin Drum. Glenn A. Guidry's "Theoretical Reflections on the Ideological and Social Implications of Mythic Form in Grass' *Die Blechtrommel*" argues that myth can function in a progressive manner.

Several studies trace the novel's complex and far-reaching reception. Among these are Franz Josef Görtz's Die Blechtrommel: *Attraktion und Ärgernis* ("Attraction and Annoyance"); Gert Loschütz's *Von Buch zu Buch: Günter Grass in der Kritik* ("From Book to Book: Günter Grass in Criticism"); Heinz Ludwig Arnold's discussion of *The Danzig Trilogy* in *Blech getrommelt: Günter Grass in der Kritik* ("Tin Drummed . . ."); and Timm Boßmann's *Der Dichter im Schussfeld: Geschichte und Versagen der Literaturkritik am Beispiel Günter Grass* ("The Poet in the Field of Fire: History and the Failure of Literary Criticism in the Example of . . ."), depicting in a somewhat polemical manner Grass's reception by West Germany's professional literary critics. Grass's reception abroad is the focus of *Günter Grass im Ausland: Texte, Daten, Bilder zur Rezeption* (". . . Abroad: Texts, Dates, Images"), edited by Hermes and Neuhaus.

Film

Instructors who would like to read up on Volker Schlöndorff's film adaptation will find useful the chapter on *The Tin Drum* in *Volker Schlöndorff's Cinema*, by Hans-Bernhard Moeller and George Lellis. Schlöndorff's Die Blechtrommel: *Tagebuch einer Verfilmung* ("Diary of a Screen Adaptation") contains the journal that the director kept while filming the novel as well as helpful background information on the film, the novel, and the novel's reception. Critical issues in film adaptations of novels are explored in Richard Kilborn's "Filming the Unfilmable: Volker Schlöndorff and *The Tin Drum*" as well as in David Head's "Volker Schlöndorff's *Die Blechtrommel* and the 'Literaturverfilmung' Debate," which also discusses the role of film adaptation in the New German Cinema. Carol Hall's "A Different Drummer: *The Tin Drum*: Film and Novel" offers a very brief account of the film and its production.

Pedagogical Tools

Neuhaus's *Günter Grass:* Die Blechtrommel, in the series Oldenbourg Interpretationen mit Unterrichtshilfen (Interpretations with Teaching Aids), gives a basic outline of the novel's main topics and features as well as some brief guidelines and ideas for teaching the text. Neuhaus also edited *Günter Grass:* Die Blechtrommel, in the series Reclams Erläuterungen und Dokumente. It provides an extensive glossary, documents pertaining to Schlöndorff's film and the novel's reception, and Grass's own comments regarding the novel's inception. Walter Jahnke and Klaus Lindemann's *Günter Grass:* Die Blechtrommel is a pedagogically based introduction to the novel. Instructors teaching the film might wish to consult Die Blechtrommel *Volker Schlöndorff*, a volume of teaching ideas prepared by the Goethe-Institut Nancy in the series Sequenz: Film und Pädagogik ("Sequence: Film and Pedagogy").

Günter Grass Archives

Located in Bremen in northern Germany, the archive Günter Grass Stifung Bremen collects and documents audiovisual work of and about Grass. It also researches Grass's literary, graphic, and political work as well as its national and international reception. The Günter Grass-Haus in Lübeck collects Grass's manuscripts, sculptures, and graphic art.

Audiovisual and Electronic Resources

No other contemporary German author has generated such a wealth of audio recordings and films. In addition to a DVD recording of Schlöndorff's film *Die Blechtrommel*, the instructor can choose from numerous audiocassettes. The entire *Blechtrommel*, read by Grass himself, is available from Deutsche Grammophon, and Recorded Books offers a reading of *The Tin Drum* by George Guidall. Fred Williams read it for Blackstone Audiobooks.

Googling Grass's *The Tin Drum* opens a labyrinth of close to ten thousand sites, most of which are of little help to the instructor or the student. The sites listed under "Grass Archives" and "Grass Biographies and Resources" after Works Cited provide useful information about the author and his oeuvre.

Part Two

APPROACHES

Introduction

Zugegeben: ich bin Insasse einer Heil- und Pflegeanstalt, mein Pfleger
beobachtet mich, läßt mich kaum aus dem Auge; denn in der Tür ist ein
Guckloch, und meines Pflegers Auge ist von jenem Braun, welches mich,
den Blauäugigen, nicht durchschauen kann.   (9)

Granted: I am an inmate of a mental hospital; my keeper is watching me,
he never lets me out of his sight; there's a peephole in the door, and my
keeper's eye is the shade of brown that can never see through a blue-eyed
type like me.   (15)

This is the well-known opening sentence of Günter Grass's first novel, which
catapulted the young author into fame and inaugurated a distinctive postwar
West German literature. On its publication in 1959, *The Tin Drum* was both
hailed as a unique masterpiece and vilified as pornographic and slanderous, the
subject of rapturous reviews and of lawsuits. This extremely polarized reception has followed almost all Grass's numerous prose works. Both as author and
as outspoken, politically active citizen, Grass continues to challenge literary,
moral, and ideological taboos.

As can be expected from a work of such scope, originality, and flamboyant
verbal artistry, no single interpretive approach can do justice to its wealth of
ideas, themes, forms, and allusions. Since the 1960s, *The Tin Drum* has thus
"assembled around itself an entire army of analysts, interpreters and exegetes"
(O'Neill, *Acts* 97) whose critical weaponry has been directed, among other targets, at the text's treatment of literary traditions and influences; its episodic form
and narrative strategies—a main topic in this area is the figure of the narrator,
Oskar, and the question of his reliability; the wealth of its Christian, mythic,
and literary motifs; and the role of objects. Many studies have focused on the
novel's engagement with German history, specifically the Third Reich and the
postwar period; its depiction of social milieu; its importance in postwar German
literature; and its wide-ranging influence on other authors.

Together with the novella *Katz und Maus* (1961; *Cat and Mouse* [1963]) and
the novel *Hundejahre* (1963; *Dog Years* [1965]), *The Tin Drum* belongs to the
so-called *Danzig Trilogy*, a haunting requiem to Grass's lost home, the city of
Danzig. Some respondents to the MLA questionnaire for this volume have designed graduate classes on the trilogy or read the novel, and this is a frequent
practice, in conjunction with *Cat and Mouse*. Respondents have also paired *The
Tin Drum* with texts ranging from Thomas Mann's *Dr. Faustus* (1947) to novels
by writers of the Group 47 such as Heinrich Böll, Martin Walser, and Siegfried
Lenz or taught the novel in the context of seminars on the Holocaust (see
Lorenz's essay in this volume). Increasingly *The Tin Drum* is also matched with
Grass's novella *Im Krebsgang* (2002; *Crabwalk* [2002]), in which the memory

of German wartime suffering is linked to characters from *The Tin Drum* (see Malchow's essay in this volume).

For the most part, respondents advised against reading only excerpts from the three-part novel, but most focus the discussion on book 1. To help students with the massive amount of text, some instructors give minimum reading requirements or assign individual chapters for students to report on. Assigning chapters is particularly useful to cover book 3. While the following essays allude to or explicitly deal with almost all the novel's forty-six chapters, those most frequently referred to from book 2 are "Die Polnische Post" ("The Polish Post Office"), "Fünfundsiebzig Kilo" ("165 Lbs."), "Die Ameisenstraße" ("The Ant Trail"), "Desinfektionsmittel" ("Disinfectant"). In book 3 the chapters "Madonna 49" ("Madonna 49"), "Im Zwiebelkeller" ("In the Onion Cellar"), "Am Atlantikwall oder es können die Bunker ihren Beton nicht loswerden" ("On the Atlantic Wall, or Concrete Eternal") and "Dreißig" ("Thirty") are often pointed to. The amount of class time devoted to the novel obviously depends on a number of different factors (syllabus, student preparation, class format, etc.), therefore no general guideline can be established. When the book is read in German, instructors recommend spending anywhere from nine to sixteen one-hour sessions; most use more than four two-hour sessions for the novel. When the book is taught in large English lecture classes, respondents on average suggested two fifty-minute lectures.

For homework, most respondents rely on oral presentations on individual chapters or select background material and assign essays and term papers. Weekly position papers, peer-critiqued papers, and poster sessions, particularly for undergraduate students, were also recommended. Instructors using Schlöndorff's film often assign topics that involve the comparison of selected scenes from the novel and the film. Some also reported using Leni Riefenstahl's *Triumph des Willens* (*Triumph of the Will*) or Helma Sanders-Brahm's film *Deutschland bleiche Mutter* (*Germany, Pale Mother*) in order to have students compare the representation of power, ethnicity, or disability in these films. Overall, teachers hoped, as the results of the survey indicated, that students gained insights into the interconnection between history and fiction and became aware of the novel's literary and stylistic traditions. They also wanted students to grasp Oskar's moral and narrative ambiguity and critically evaluate Grass's depiction of the petite bourgeoisie and fascism and, in the process, realize, in the words of one respondent, "that creativity can yield strange, wonderful, and unconventional results."

Modes of History in *The Tin Drum*

Julian Preece

Die Blechtrommel is a multivoiced narrative, part parodic antibildungsroman, part novel of the artist as young man (the Romantic *Künstlerroman*), part picaresque adventure and fake confession. The novel's rich mixture of literary styles ranges from poetic montage to Nietzschean philosophical reflection to mock Balzacian realism. It is also a displaced autobiography, which is the reason Günter Grass knows his material so well and has never quite succeeded in bringing another narrative voice to life, after Oskar Matzerath, in so compelling a fashion. Grass is saying: This is how I, who am also an artist and inventor of stories, who was born in 1927 to shopkeeper parents three years after my narrator, and who had to make my own way under the Nazis (whose creed and propaganda I believed until I was seventeen), wish my life had been. Indeed, in so many ways, this narrative is the story of his life. *Die Blechtrommel* is a glorious counterexample to anyone who has said that a novel about writing novels can be of interest only to other novelists. Its spirit is comic: as the narrator, Oskar loves puns and wordplay; as a main character, he enjoys playing roles, such as fool, trickster, prophet, lover, and rebel. That he is a mimic, forever imitating other ways of speaking and writing, accounts for the variety of genres he parodies. It explains, too, why he is so unsure of his own identity and why the story he unfurls does not have a unitary meaning: part of his failed quest is the inability to find sense, truth, and certainty.

Teaching this novel, whether in the original German or English translation, is rewarding but also presents problems. The first problem is the sheer length of the text, which can be off-putting for students. Students must be given time to absorb it. As Grass divided the novel into reasonably self-contained episodic chapters, one approach is to assign individual students specific chapters, or perhaps groups of chapters, to prepare for presentation and discussion in class. That way the class as a whole has a chance of reading the novel in, say, a fortnight. The approach also fosters a sense of communal effort and teamwork. Some chapters from different books of the novel work particularly well when studied together, as it were in isolation from the rest of the text. For instance, grouping "Die Tribüne" ("The Rostrum"), "Bebra's Fronttheater" ("Bebra's Theater at the Front"), "Im Zwiebelkeller" ("In the Onion Cellar"), from books 1, 2, and 3 respectively, enables discussion of Oskar as performer from the prewar to the postwar period. "Fernwirkender Gesang vom Stockturm aus gesungen" ("The Stockturm: Long-Distance Song Effects") and "Glaube Hoffnung Liebe" ("Faith, Hope, Love") present the two Jewish characters, Sigismund Markus and Mariusz Fajngold, whose roles in the life of the Matzerath family can be compared profitably. There are many other possibilities. Because there is a wealth of critical and secondary material on *Die Blechtrommel* and many chapters or articles address a specific topic or aspect, asking students to prepare an item from the bibliography to present to the rest of the class can also be a useful exercise and serve a similar function.

For all the novel's literary artistry, recent German history of the Nazi period stands at its heart, and in this essay I focus on the particular representation of history in *Die Blechtrommel* and Grass's unique ways of narrating and accounting for it. History determines the very shape and form of the work. It is divided into three books, which cover the prewar period (1899–1938); the war itself, from the German invasion to the fall of Danzig to the advance of the Red Army (1939–45); and the postwar austerity and reconstruction in West Germany (1945–52). Oskar writes the novel in the years 1952–54. His frequent interruptions; the interventions of his friends Klepp and Vittlar, who are typically deracinated, modernist intellectuals; the commentary of his male nurse, Bruno, also a part-time artist; and the occasional references to contemporary political events all show how Oskar manufactures literary and historical meaning in the telling of his life.

Grass challenged both groups and individuals who preferred to forget or whose versions of what happened averted the truth, which is why he upset readers in various countries. Russians objected to the unheroic behavior of the Kalmucks who liberated Danzig, shooting the defenseless Alfred Matzerath and gang-raping Lina Greff (as Soviet soldiers raped German women in all the German territories they liberated). Poles were angered by Jan Bronski's cowardice at the Polish Post Office, the defense of which had entered the annals of Polish nationalist history as a glorious episode, and by the appearance of Polish partisans who raid the train that transports Oskar and his surviving family to the West in June 1945 (Gesche 68–77; Tighe 268–88). Conservative West Germans used language that had been current during the Third Reich to object to the novel's treatment of religion and sex (Arnold and Görz 262–81, 303–27), while Communist East Germans decried its nihilism (Wittmann). German disapproval really had more to do with how Grass links Nazism to ordinary folk. He not only undermines the East German heroization of the working class, he also contradicts various self-serving myths that informed discussion of Nazism in the West: that the Germans suffered as much as their victims, that their crimes were either exaggerated by the Allies or committed only by a minority and out of sight of the rest of the population, and that Hitler had tricked the German people by not stating his real intentions.

Grass's home city of Danzig has given Grass a rich source of historical material over his long writing career. In his later work *Im Krebsgang* (2002; *Crabwalk* [2002]), he develops an incident, the sinking of a former passenger liner ferrying refugees to the West in January 1945, that he mentioned in *Die Blechtrommel*. In *Hundejahre* (1963; *Dog Years*), published after *Die Blechtrommel*, he turned his attention to the concentration camp at Stutthof a few miles along the coast, and he writes of the suburb where he grew up: "Langfuhr war so groß und so klein, daß alles, was sich auf dieser Welt ereignet oder ereignen könnte, sich auch in Langfuhr ereignete oder hätte ereignen können" (261) ("Langfuhr was so large and so small that everything that happened in the world or could have happened also happened or could have happened in Langfuhr" [trans. mine]). By telling the story of Langfuhr and Danzig, Grass is telling that of Germany as a whole.

Up to September 1939 and again from January 1945, when Danzig fell to the Red Army, the city was to some extent at the center of events (Brode, *Zeitgeschichte*). Its rich ethnic mix of Germans, Poles, and Kashubians[1] included an ancient Jewish community, to which the toy-shop owner Sigismund Markus belongs in *Die Blechtrommel*. Because Danzig occupied a peripheral location, where resentment against the post-1919 settlement, which separated the city from the rest of Germany, seethed among the majority German speakers, it is more revealing of the mentality throughout Germany, manifesting it in a more direct, extreme form, which in the end proved typical. A former Hanseatic city, Danzig had been German for more than six centuries when it was made into an independent city-state by the Treaty of Versailles, which concluded World War I. Reclaiming Danzig and the Polish Corridor that surrounded it, a region that linked newly independent Poland to the Baltic coast, was one of the reasons Hitler went to war. Indeed the first shots of World War II were fired in Danzig, when two warships began shelling the Polish Post Office in the early hours of 1 September 1939.

Like the realist novels of the nineteenth century, of which Thomas Mann's *Buddenbrooks* (1901) is the greatest German example, *Die Blechtrommel* is a document of social history. Grass gets exactly right the details of how people lived, what they wore, what they ate, what music and books they liked, how they spent their leisure time, and how technology (the radio, the newsreel) changed their lives. He places his characters very precisely in the context of historical forces that ultimately threaten them all but that they often also embody or typify (Reed). The gay vegetarian greengrocer Herr Greff, for instance, whose interest in strangely shaped potatoes is matched only by his passion for the company of Boy Scouts, exemplifies trends in thought (his liking for mystical literature) and behavior (his cult of the body beautiful) that underpinned Nazism (Arnds, *Representation* 49–76). The characters are typical of their social class: represented are the peasantry, the urban working class, the shop-keeping *Kleinbürgertum* ("petite bourgeoisie"), and religious and national groups (Catholics, Protestants, Jews, Germans, Poles, Kashubians). The members of the adulterous triangle at the center of Oskar's early life can even be said to stand allegorically for Danzig, Germany, and Poland. Agnes Matzerath, née Bronski, thus represents the doomed city-state and is courted by the no-nonsense Protestant Rhinelander Alfred Matzerath (Germany) and the impractical romantic Catholic Jan Bronski (Poland). Alfred Matzerath embraces Nazism because of the excitement of running with the crowd, participating in mass activity, and being part of the great new era, like millions of other Germans; Bronski dreamily wanders to his death when he joins the ill-fated attempt to defend the Polish Post Office on the day war breaks out; Agnes loves Bronski but marries Matzerath and is ultimately crushed by their competing demands.

Oskar is the most typical and representative character of all. Although he casts himself in opposition to his parents' corrupt world and its dreadful deeds, his emotional and material needs, his selfishness, at times quite callous, make him part of the venal adult world, whether he likes it or not. His drum, which he is given by his mother on his third birthday, when he decides to stop growing, signals his allegiance to art, creativity, and thus independence from ordinary life. But the drum is a martial instrument that beats out a marching rhythm; Grass is aware that Adolf Hitler was known as "the drummer of the national cause," because he "drummed" up passions and his supporters paraded behind him in step to his rhythm (Kershaw 157). From behind the bars on his hospital bed, Oskar uses his drum to beat out the insistent rhythm of his story. He has to tell it right through to the end, when the past catches up with him and he is released back into the world on his thirtieth birthday, a full two years after he began writing. He has found there is no hiding place from the ghosts of his past and the guilt that he acquired as a consequence of surviving. In this respect, he does what the other characters in book 3 and West Germans generally refused to do: he remembers and records what has happened. For all his well-advertised slipperiness, his continuing to be disturbed by his memories shows that he possesses more moral integrity than most of the characters he writes about.

Oskar indicates that his story will be embedded in historical reality when, four pages into the text, he begins his narrative proper with a sentence of classical simplicity: "Meine Großmutter Anna Bronski saß an einem späten Oktobernachmittag in ihren Röcken am Rande eines Kartoffelackers" (12) ("Late one October afternoon my grandmother Anna Bronski was sitting in her skirts at the edge of a potato field" [18]). On the next page he pinpoints the date: "Man schrieb das Jahr neunundneunzig" (13) ("The year was 1899" [18]), thus beginning his story portentously on the eve of the new century. What happens on this Kashubian potato field at the edge of Danzig when Grandmother Bronski shelters a Polish arsonist on the run from the Prussian police is a prelude to the action that will begin with the hero's birth in 1924 and accelerate once the Nazis seize power in the Reich in 1933. The grandparents' encounter is pregnant with historical meaning; as a result of it, Anna soon finds herself expecting Oskar's mother. It is a coming together of the elements earth (Anna Bronski, who represents warmth and security) and fire (Joseph Koljaiczek, representing violence and revolt), a binary opposition of the type Oskar loves first to construct, then to undermine. The episode presages conflict between Prussians—that is, the German speakers in charge of the region—and Slavs—that is, the Poles and Kashubians who made up most of the population in this part of rural West Prussia. By starting his story with his maternal grandparents, Oskar suggests his preference for the Slavic side of his family, though because he is an inveterate survivor who knows when to change sides, he will betray his "Polish father," Jan Bronski, in 1939 as unfeelingly as he betrays Bronski's German counterpart, Alfred Matzerath, in 1945.

Koljaiczek is a terrorist advocate of Polish nationalism, a cause that triumphed when Poland regained its independence in the wake of German defeat in World War I, only to be crushed once more at the beginning of World War II. When the police get on Koljaiczek's trail again in 1913, he enacts an escape that will become familiar to Grass's readers: he dives out of trouble and swims to freedom. Whether he drowns, as seems most likely, because he is never seen again, or miraculously escapes to Buffalo, where he makes a fortune in fire insurance, as is rumored by some (thus moving from one extreme to its opposite, as characters often do in Grass's fiction), is left open. There is always more than one version of what happened, because history is told according to who is doing the telling, a lesson readers will encounter many more times before they are through with the book.

Different individuals or groups tell different stories, depending on what gives them comfort in the present. It is more pleasant for Koljaiczek's relatives to think that he got away and made a fortune in America. It is because past events matter that these different versions are invented: each party has an interest in establishing ownership of the past, which can give control of the present, whether on a personal or collective level. *Der Butt* (1977; *The Flounder*), Grass's third major novel, which delves into the beginnings of German and Slavic settlement on the Baltic coast, represents his most sustained engagement with this theme. In *Die Blechtrommel* there are different versions of the deaths of a number of characters close to Oskar: his mother; both his putative fathers; Roswitha Raguna, the dwarf actress who becomes his great love; and finally the nurse Dorothea, for whose murder he is arrested and charged. He also revises his account of how he came to tumble into his father's grave: did he jump or did he fall when Kurt, whom he claims is his son and not his father's, threw the stone at his head? We get used to Oskar's ostentatiously correcting himself, giving the impression that he lied the first time around and has decided to tell the truth with a second account. We have no way of knowing, however, which version is to be trusted. At the end of book 2, Oskar passes the pen to Bruno, who then narrates the long journey from Danzig to Düsseldorf in an overcrowded goods train. Through liberal use of the subjunctive, Bruno stresses in each paragraph that he is only writing down what Oskar claims happened and that we should take the details of his story with a pinch of salt. He does not tell us anything new or that we would not have learned from Oskar himself.

The point about the different accounts of the deaths of Jan and Alfred is that Oskar is directly implicated each time and has an interest in offering an account that puts his role in the best light. Jan Bronski would not have gone to join his colleagues to defend the post office had Oskar not wanted to see the caretaker Kobyella to have his drum mended. When the Germans appear in triumph, Oskar's instinct is survival, as he tells us in the second account, because he does what millions of European civilians did when confronted with the triumphant invader: he ingratiates himself with the German soldier, runs to seek protection from him, and points accusingly at his father/uncle. He pretends to cry and

> wies auf Jan, seinen Vater, mit anklagenden Gesten, die den Armen zum bösen Mann machten, der ein unschuldiges Kind in die Polnische Post geschleppt hatte, um es auf polnisch unmenschliche Weise als Kugelfang zu benutzen.   (318)

> pointed to Jan, his father, with accusing gestures which transformed the poor man into a villain who had dragged off an innocent child to the Polish Post Office to use him, with typically Polish inhumanity, as a buffer for enemy bullets.   (246)

Oskar repeats the gesture at the end of the war when he jabs the pin of Alfred's Nazi Party badge into his hand as the Soviet soldiers approach, causing his German father to panic, put the open badge into his mouth, choke, and get riddled with machine-gun bullets.

The past stays alive after the event is over. Grass shows that it is not merely what happened, when, how, and why it happened—though he provides all that information—sometimes relegating it to an apparently insignificant subordinate clause; it is what the past means for the present that is of paramount significance. This is why a psychiatric hospital is the only appropriate place from which Oskar can tell his terrible story: any emotionally or ethically sensitive individual would be destroyed by what Oskar has gone through. Oskar feels there is poetic justice in his incarceration for a murder he has not committed, because he has other deaths on his conscience. For this reason the third, postwar book, which is sometimes thought to be less exciting than the first two, is just as important: it depicts individuals from the perpetrator nation struggling to make sense of their survival. With the exception of the opportunist Bebra, a propaganda impresario under Goebbels, then an entertainment entrepreneur as the West German *Wirtschaftswunder* ("economic miracle") begins to take off, they remain prisoners of the past even if they refuse to think about it or express their feelings openly.

Grass's approach to historical events is characterized by variety and experimentation. Halfway through book 2, in the summer of 1944 on the eve of the Allied landings in Normandy, there is an episode told exclusively through dialogue with no narrative commentary. Five French nuns collecting mussels and shrimp for evacuated children in their care are mowed down by German machine guns because the heavily fortified beach is off-limits to civilians. Reporting this atrocity through dialogue is a distancing technique or *Verfremdungseffekt*, which makes the impact of these deaths all the more powerful; it also reflects the witnesses' and participants' wish to look away from what is happening. The postwar smugness of what Grass calls the neo-Biedermeier (after the period 1815–48, of authoritarian politics and artistic conservatism that followed the German wars of liberation against Napoleon) is already anticipated during wartime. The concrete experts who built the fortifications along the Normandy coast are already looking forward to reconstruction contracts once the fighting is over. The postwar attitudes of West Germans are anticipated, too, in the behavior of Oskar's colleagues in Bebra's circus troupe, who not only fail to intervene to stop the shooting but close their ears to it. In 1944 they play a record to drown out the gunfire, a record that was not released until ten years later: the Platters' song "The Great Pretender." This deliberate anachronism is another indication that the attitudes of pretense and denial that characterized the 1950s were already in place by the end of the war. The characters deny what they are doing as they are doing it, not just afterward. Oskar returns to the bunker with Maler Lankes, in 1944 still Obergefreiter Lankes, and finds the officer who gave the order still at the scene, obsessively measuring the concrete installations. But neither Oskar nor Lankes can get the image of the nuns out of their heads: repression has only limited success.

There is also documentary history in *Die Blechtrommel*. To report the execution of Jan Bronski, Grass slightly alters a document that was sent to his own aunt (Gesche 120):

Geschäftsstelle des Gerichtes der Gruppe Eberhardt St.L. 41/39-
Zoppot, den 6.Okt.1939

Frau Hedwig Bronski,
auf Anordnung wird Ihnen mitgeteilt, daß der Bronski, Jan, durch kriegsgerichtliches Urteil wegen Freischärlerei zum Tode verurteilt und hingerichtet ist.

Zelewski
(Feldjustizinspektor) (321)

Court-Martial, Eberhardt St. L. Group 41/39

Zoppot, 6 Oct. 1939

Mrs. Hedwig Bronski,

You are hereby informed that Bronski, Jan has been sentenced to death for irregular military activity and executed.

Zelewski

(*Inspector of Courts-Martial*) (248)

The barbarity of the action screams through the linguistic formulations: the preemptory "Frau Bronski" (instead of "Sehr geehrte Frau Bronski" ["Very Honored Frau Bronski"], as formal letters begin in German to this day) and "Zelewski" make explicit the absence of human feeling or respect; the use of the passive voice and the phrase "auf Anordnung" ("directed by," which is not translated) distance individuals from responsibility; "der Bronski, Jan" is a deliberately disrespectful designation of the executed man. It is clear, too, that the widow was not informed of his trial, if indeed one took place at all; she was also not informed of his sentence until after it had been carried out.

In his account of the siege of the Polish Post Office, Grass was treading on different territory, because this historical sequence had already entered the history books and what happened was contentious. Images of the captured post office employees were shown first, as Oskar remarks, in a German propaganda newsreel film, "der später in allen Kinos gezeigt wurde" (317) ("that was later shown in all the movie houses" [245]). When Grass returned to Gdańsk to research the episode, he discovered that both the official accounts—that written by the Nazis in wartime and that written by the Poles after the war, according to which there had been no Polish survivors—were not true. It had suited both sides to write out the survivors, those who had eluded their captors and lived to tell their tale, which Grass now includes. He brings them to life in book 3, in the fantastic, Kafkaesque episode when they are rearrested by German revanchists who want to make good their failure in 1939 by executing them in the early 1950s. This is history as recurring nightmare, which indicates the persecutors' refusal to accept what has happened: that Nazi Germany has lost the war. Life can be stranger than fiction, but in this instance fiction tells a more accurate story than the official records.

One method of rooting a private life story in historical reality is to insert references to well-known people and events into the account of a character's progress. At the beginning of the second chapter, Oskar lauds, for example, his drum for providing him "was an Nebensächlichkeiten nötig ist, um die Hauptsache aufs Papier bringen zu können" (23) ("all the incidentals that I need to get the essential down on paper" [25]) and resumes his account of his grandfather's escape from the gendarmes with what seems an inconsequential allusion to the Boer War in South Africa, in which Germany supported the Boers in their struggle against the British: "An jenem Oktobernachmittag des Jahres neunundneunzig, während in Südafrika Ohm Krüger seine buschig englandfeindlichen

Augenbrauen bürstete" (23) ("That afternoon in the year 1899, while in South Africa Oom Kruger was brushing his bushy anti-British eyebrows" [25]). But who decides what is "incidental" and what "essential"? Because the name of the leader of the Boer revolt against British rule gets into the history books, does that make him more important than Joseph Koljaiczek? The reference to Ohm Kruger appears flippant but establishes that other conflicts than those between Germans and Slavs will determine the outcome of the novel.

Similar references to textbook history punctuate the story. There are links between the microhistory of the Matzerath family and their neighbors in the Labesweg and the macrohistory of grand and often faraway events, because so many of the characters will be sucked up by the events and fall victim to the force of history that they embody and express. Up until the end of the second book, when Oskar has his vision of the simultaneity of world events from the top of "the diving board" in the courtroom, followed by his hectic narrative of Danzig history after the city's fall to the Red Army, these references tend to make sense. Meaning begins to break down in the autumn of 1941, when Oskar, now aged seventeen, continues the sexual apprenticeship he began with Maria in Lina Greff's bed but, like the Wehrmacht stuck in the mud at the gates of Moscow, makes little progress. He compares his sexual activity with an image of the wheels of military vehicles spinning in the mud, which he saw in a movie theater. The comparison is quite absurd; there is no connection. The stalled German advance simply accompanied his sexual advance like so much background music. All Oskar knows about the invasion of the Soviet Union is what he hears on the radio *Sondermeldungen* ("special communiqués") and sees in the *Wochenschau* ("newsreel"). These references show *Die Blechtrommel*'s limitations as a historical novel: at this stage of the war, the place for the narrator to be is the Eastern front, not Frau Greff's bed. Grass recognizes that and gets Oskar out of Danzig the following year, when Oskar goes to France with Bebra to entertain the troops.

Whatever the immediate location, the narrative of *Die Blechtrommel* is never more than a step away from the destruction that resulted in the deaths of millions, including many of Oskar's family and neighbors. There are twenty-three deaths of named characters reported in the novel: young men who are killed on the battlefronts from Crete to the Arctic, civilians who perish on the home front. Oskar attempts to encompass millions more, such as children who died in the evacuation from the Red Army and the Jews who were murdered in the extermination camps. He commemorates Jewish victims twice: in the narration of Kristallnacht, when Sigismund Markus commits suicide to elude his persecutors, and through the story of Mariusz Fajngold at the end of book 2. Markus and in particular the chapter "Glaube Hoffnung Liebe" ("Faith, Hope, Love"), which is narrated part as fairy tale, part as literary imitation of a musical fugue, have received much critical attention (O'Neill, "Musical Form"). Oskar interweaves Markus's story with that of the trumpeter Meyn, a former Communist, now member of the Nazi militia, the SA, who is commended for his behavior in ransacking Jewish properties on 9–10 November 1938, then reprimanded for his cruelty to his pet cats. Underlying both stories is the "leichtgläubiges Volk" (261) ("credulous nation" [203]) believing in the "Weihnachtsmann" ("Santa Claus"), who would bring them happiness and answers to all their problems but who turned out to be "der Gasmann" (262) ("the gasman" [204]), who brought nothing but the stench of death. Gas is an appropriate metaphor: as it enters every household through the pipes to be used for cooking, so every person is implicated in the extermination of the Jews and the Nazis' other victims in the gas chambers. Oskar tosses up the words "faith," "hope," and "love," which he sees written on a banner held up by nuns on Kristallnacht, "wie ein Jongleur mit Flaschen" (261) ("as a juggler plays with bottles" [203]), rearranging them to see how these precepts of Christian civilization from Saint Paul's First Epistle to the Corinthians can make sense in the context of murderous persecution.

The chapter is a stylistic tour de force and remains the most memorable account of the first modern pogrom in western Europe. The later, briefer section featuring Fajngold is less well-known but no less remarkable. Fajngold's entrance is preceded by three pages of Danzig history—from the time the area was first settled; through the Middle Ages, Renaissance, and the eighteenth-century partitions of Poland; right up to the end of World War II. It is an account of conquest, invasion by more powerful neighbors, and fighting among ethnic and linguistic groups. Oskar calls it "ein zerstörerisches und wiederaufbauendes Spielchen" (520) ("a little game of destruction and reconstruction," which is not translated on 395), since each new conquering force burns the city to the ground before setting about a rebuilding program. The range and perspective appear impressive, but this is history as parodied ideology, a reordered regurgitation of textbook facts that were originally assembled to legitimize nationalist claims to the city. Oskar stops when he gets to the present, because this time something unusual has occurred: "Merkwürdigerweise kamen diesmal nach den Russen keine Preußen, Schweden, Sachsen oder Franzosen; es kamen die Polen" (523) ("This time, strange to say, no Prussians, Swedes, Saxons, or Frenchmen came after the Russians; this time it was the Poles who arrived" [397–98]). The development is remarkable because the Poles up to this point have tended to be the objects rather than the subjects of Danzig history:

> Mit Sack und Pack kamen die Polen aus Wilna, Bialystok und Lemberg und suchten sich Wohnungen. Zu uns kam ein Herr, der sich Fajngold nannte, alleinstehend war, doch immer so tat, als umgäbe ihn eine vielköpfige Familie, welcher er Anweisungen zu geben hätte.   (523)

> The Poles came with bag and baggage from Vilna, Bialystok, and Lwow, all looking for living quarters. To us came a gentleman by the name of Fajngold; he was alone in the world, but he behaved as though surrounded by a large family that couldn't manage for one minute without his instructions.   (398)

The Poles who arrive in German Danzig, which is soon to become Polish Gdańsk, now take the place of the German-speaking Danzigers, who are obliged to move to the West. The refugees have either fled the Red Army or made way for the Polish refugees who were moved from the east, from prewar Polish territories now ceded to the Soviet Union. Wilna (Vilnius) is today the capital of Lithuania, and Lemberg (Lwów in Polish, L'viv in Ukrainian) is the capital of the western Ukraine; both were part of interwar Poland. Only the eastern city of Białystok remained Polish after 1945. Through the phrase "zu uns kam" Oskar connects his own microstory with the macroevents of the Second World War, having just established their place in a chain reaching back more than two thousand years. Grass through Oskar is a teller of stories, and stories must have human characters who possess names and destinies that readers can follow. The problem for a storyteller, when it comes to the Holocaust, is that all destinies were suddenly ended, irrespective of merit or desert, which takes away the possibility of a meaningful ending, thus removing the basis for stories. Yet Grass internalizes the monstrosity of the Nazi crime and has Fajngold speak to the ghosts of his past, the dead members of his large family, which makes his every utterance an act of mourning and commemoration. His own survival is in no way redemptive or meaningful.

Fajngold's jumbled recollection of working as a camp disinfector includes an account of the revolt at Treblinka. Grass thus contradicts the cliché that the Jews were passive victims: Fajngold appears to have survived because he fought back and escaped over the wire. The rhythm of the passage is insistent and repetitive, the tone sober, but it is no less a prose poem than the celebrated chapter "Faith, Hope, Love" at the end of book 1:

> Vom Bilauer erzählte er, der dem Desinfektor eines Tages im heißesten August geraten hatte, die Lagerstraßen von Treblinka nicht mit Lysolwasser, sondern mit Petroleum zu besprenkeln. Das tat Herr Fajngold. Und der Bilauer hatte das Streichholz. Und der alte Zew Kurland von der ZOB nahm allen den Eid ab. Und der Ingenieur Galewski brach die Waffenkammer auf. Und der Bilauer erschoß den Herrn Hauptsturmführer Kutner. Und der Sztulbach und der Warynski rauf auf den Zisenis. Und die anderen gegen die Trawnikileute. Und ganz andere knipsten den Zaun auf und fielen um. Aber der Unterscharführer Schöpke, der immer Witzchen zu machen pflegte, wenn er die Leute zum Duschen führte, der stand im Lagertor und schoß.   (543–44)

> He told me about Bilauer, who one hot day in August had advised the disinfector to sprinkle the camp streets with kerosene instead of Lysol. Mr. Fajngold had taken his advice. And Bilauer had the match. Old Zev Kurland of the ZOB had administered the oath to the lot of them. And Engineer Galewski had broken into the weapons room. Bilauer had shot Hauptsturmführer Kutner. Sztulbach and Warynski got Zisenis by the

throat; the others tackled the guards from Trawniki Camp. Some were electrocuted cutting the high-tension fence. SS Seargent Schöpke, who had always made little jokes while taking his protégés to the showers, stood by the camp gate shooting.   (413)

In this passage, two sentences lack verbs (which Manheim puts into the English translation), as if the grammar has broken down because the subject cannot be contained within the conventional rules of language. Agents are detached from their actions, because their hold on life is tenuous and their actions ultimately make no difference. The missing verbs also give the retelling a ritualistic dimension.

All those with Jewish names in this scene apparently escaped. To say that their escape was atypical would be an understatement. Treblinka was one of the three extermination centers constructed solely for the purpose of killing Jews (the others were Sobibor and Belzec). There are no narratives of escape and survival associated with these camps. Grass implicitly acknowledges this, as no sooner do the names appear in the novel than they disappear again, leaving no trace. They are the names of ghosts that vanished from German life along with the Jews; by recalling the victims in this passage, Grass turns them fleetingly from statistics into individuals. The account is in reported speech: Oskar is passing on what Fajngold told him as Oskar lay in his bed, feverish after the bump on his head that he sustained at his father's funeral. The story is true, Oskar believes Fajngold, and nothing is in the subjunctive mood, which would usually be employed in such situations to suggest doubt. Like Oskar's vision from the diving board in the courtroom or like his nightmare of the infernal merry-go-round, both of which also come at the end of book 2 as the war enters its most bloodthirsty, final phase, the sequence is narrated as a broken dream but rooted firmly in historical fact.

Grass also presents history through symbol, in chapters such as "Karfreitagskost" ("Good Friday Fare"; see Schade's essay in this volume), and through allegory, especially in "Niobe," which concludes Oskar's series of parodic critiques on those Germans who claimed after 1945 that they had been somehow seduced or tempted by irrational forces into becoming involved with the National Socialists (Stern). There are moments in *Die Blechtrommel* when the action coincides directly with historical developments. The chapter "Niobe" begins, "Im Jahre achtundreißig wurden die Zölle erhöht, zeitweilig die Grenzen zwischen Polen und dem Freistaat geschlossen" (235) ("In '38 the customs duties were raised and the borders between Poland and the Free City were temporarily closed" [183]), and continues to explain that herrings pile up at the port and begin to stink while politicians hold crisis meetings. Relations between Danzig and Poland deteriorate at the same rate as the fish rot, and Oskar's friend Herbert Truczinski, whose back shows the scars of many an interethnic brawl at the dockside bar where he works, decides that he has had enough.

Oskar played the role of tempter himself for a while, waiting in dark doorways for passersby to pause at shopwindows to gaze at the goods on display before expertly cutting a hole in the glass with his piercing voice and watching his victim succumb to the temptation of theft. He sits beneath the podium at the Nazi Party rally and makes the assembled masses dance to his own tune instead of the one played for them by the Nazis, thus mocking the idea that the audience at such a meeting is hypnotized into doing the bidding of the actors on stage—an idea that Thomas Mann explored in his novella *Mario und der Zauberer* (1929; *Mario and the Magician*). In the party rally scene, Oskar demonstrates his oppositional spirit and refusal to run with the crowd, brilliantly rendered by Volker Schlöndorff in his film as a parody of Leni Riefenstahl's *Triumph des Willens*.

At birth, Oskar noticed how a moth was beating or drumming its wings against the forty-watt lightbulb that lit up the room in which he was born. The image is important enough for it to supply the heading for the chapter "Falter und Glühbirne" ("Moth and Light Bulb"), for it anticipates the behavior of several characters in book 1 who are irresistibly attracted to a deadly force. Herbert is the best example. In an embrace as bizarre as it is passionate, the former barman, who risked his life to keep the peace among his international clientele, impales himself on a five-hundred-year-old wooden statue of a half-naked woman that originally adorned a sailing ship as its figurehead (see Becker-Cantarino's essay in this volume). Herbert gave up his job because of his frequent and increasingly serious injuries, a sign that relations between peoples are breaking down. The episode in the museum that follows is even less credible than Oskar's disruption of the Nazi Party rally, because the idea that it represents, that the German working class became fatalistically enamored of Hitler and thus was powerless to resist his charm, is ridiculous and false.

History in *Die Blechtrommel* is uncertain. That Oskar is sometimes unsure of its meaning contributes to the fact that he himself can be impossible to pin down. He disrupts the party rally as much in imitation of the Nazis as in opposition to them, and during the war he puts himself on Goebbels's payroll by joining Bebra's troupe. In the fledgling Federal Republic he achieves fame and fortune as a pop star who exploits his fellow citizens' need for emotional release by encouraging them to relive their childhood and youth. Yet he shows sympathy for victims, such as Sigismund Markus or Roswitha Raguna; his two fathers; his "poor mama"; or the deranged Schugger Leo, that holy fool who is fascinated by death and cemeteries.

Oskar is perhaps above all an ambitious narrator who wants his experience to be somehow all-encompassing and all-inclusive, not merely representative. This impossible ambition is one reason that he is defeated in the end by his story, when he is found innocent of Nurse Dorothea's murder and finds himself on the threshold of the freedom he dreads. Had his version of events not been overturned this one last time, he could have retreated to safety. Far better to barricade himself behind the bars on his bed in the secure, secluded hospital than to face the world with all its messy contradictions. When it comes to the recent history of Germany, *Die Blechtrommel* asks questions rather than answers them. Oskar could have asked along with Grass's next narrator, Pilenz in *Katz und Maus* (1961; *Cat and Mouse*) "wer schreibt mir einen guten Schluß?" (111) ("Who will write me a good ending?" [trans. mine]). Oskar does not have one himself.

NOTE

¹ Grass's family on his mother's side were Kashubians. Grass presents them usually as standing between the Poles and Germans, who were both more powerful.

APPENDIX
Chronology of Events

1899–1902 Boer War in South Africa. Agnes Matzerath, née Bronski, conceives in October 1899.

1914–18 World War I, between Germany and Austro-Hungary, on one side, and Russia, France, and Britain, who are joined by the United States in 1917, on the other. Alfred Matzerath is wounded fighting for the Germans, while Jan Bronski is repeatedly declared unfit for military service. Grass himself had uncles fighting on both the German and Russian sides.

1915 Battle of Jutland in the North Sea, between British and German fleets. Eels in *The Tin Drum* are said to have been especially fat that year, because they fed off the flesh of the drowned sailors.

1917 Gregor Koljaiczek is an early victim of the flu epidemic, which claims more victims in 1918–19 than the war itself.

1919 By the Treaty of Versailles, which concluded the war between the Western Allies and Germany, the independent state of Poland, which had not existed since the late eighteenth century, when its territory was divided among Germany, Austria, and Russia, is reconstituted. The Polish Corridor, linking the otherwise landlocked country to the Baltic Sea, surrounds the predominantly German-speaking city of Danzig, which has become a free state under the jurisdiction of the League of Nations, the forerunner of the United Nations (to be created at the end of the next world war). Poland has control of the post office in the city center, where Jan Bronski begins work.

1923 Agnes Bronski and Alfred Matzerath marry in the year of the inflation, which has weakened the already unstable German republic and also affected Danzig: "da man für den Gegenwert einer Streichholzschachtel ein Schlafzimmer tapezieren, also mit Nullen mustern konnte" (49) ("when you could paper a bedroom with zeros for the price of a matchbox" [44–45]).

1924	Birth of Oskar in September. A period of relative stability for the Weimar Republic begins.
1927	Oskar engineers his fall down the cellar steps to account for his refusal to grow.
1929	Wall Street Crash in October plunges capitalism into worldwide turmoil.
1931	The Weimar Republic is in seemingly terminal crisis. Oskar's first (and only) day at school.
1933	On 30 January, Adolf Hitler is appointed Reichskanzler by President Hindenburg.
1934	Leni Riefenstahl films *Triumph of the Will* at the Nazi Party rally in Nuremberg. Alfred joins the party, replacing his picture of Beethoven with one of Hitler above the family piano.
1935	Oskar begins drumming under the rostra of various political organizations, including the Nazis, an activity he claims to continue until November 1938.
1937	In April, German planes of the Condor Legion bomb the Basque town of Guernica on market day during the Spanish Civil War, inspiring Picasso's famous painting named after the town. Agnes gives up the will to live in "Good Friday Fare," which takes place that same month.
1938	On 9–10 November, Jewish businesses and places of worship throughout Germany, Austria, and the nominally independent Danzig are ransacked by Nazi thugs. Sigismund Markus commits suicide to elude his persecutors, thus depriving Oskar of his favorite source of new tin drums.
1939	The first shots of World War II are fired in Danzig. On 1 September, 4:45 a.m. (a time made infamous in Hitler's speech announcing war to the German people), the battleship *Schleswig-Holstein* begins bombarding Polish targets in the city. Jan Bronski is lured into the Polish Post Office by Oskar, who needs his drum mended. Bronski is captured and shot by the Germans.
1940	In June, France is conquered by the Germans, and British troops are evacuated at Dunkirk.
1941	The German invasion of the Soviet Union, which begins in June, is halted at the gates of Moscow in December. Birth of Kurt Matzerath, son of either Oskar or Alfred, also in June.
1942	In October, Greff commits suicide after hearing the news of the death of Horst Donath on the eastern front.

1943   In February, the victory of the Soviets at Stalingrad marks a turning point in the war. In June, Oskar accompanies Bebra's theater troupe to France.

1944   In June, Allied landings in Normandy open up a front in the West. Oskar's love, Roswitha Raguna, is killed by a stray American shell.

1945   In January, Danzig burns and falls to the Red Army. Alfred is shot by a frightened Kalmuck soldier. In June, Oskar, Kurt, and Maria are evacuated to Düsseldorf in West Germany.

1945–48   The black market thrives until the currency reform of June 1948 introduces the Deutsche Mark into the three western zones of occupation. The Soviet Union responds by blockading West Berlin. Oskar and Kurt deal in a variety of goods to feed their family. For Grass the Biedermeier period, which Oskar anticipated on the Normandy beach in 1944, begins as the economic miracle gets under way.

1949   The Federal Republic (West Germany) and the German Democratic Republic (East Germany) come into being. Oskar plays jazz for the Rhine River Three and performs in the Onion Cellar.

1952   Oskar is arrested in Paris for the murder of Nurse Dorothea.

1954   Oskar is released after he has finished his novel, on his thirtieth birthday.

The Tin Drum as Historical Fiction

Todd Kontje

In this essay I explore ways in which Günter Grass represents history in the fictional world of *The Tin Drum*, with a particular focus on three techniques. The first involves his refusal to demonize the Nazis or to idealize their victims. Second, he represents history as it is experienced at the individual level, by people who have only a limited knowledge of the larger picture. Third, he reminds us that even the most comprehensive overview of historical events must leave out many or indeed most of the things that are taking place simultaneously around the world. I introduce broad themes as illustrated by particular incidents and characters in the novel, instead of offering an exhaustive analysis of the entire text. Students are encouraged not only to look more closely at these specific examples but also to use the general concepts as guidelines for the investigation of other events and characters in Grass's fiction. My larger goal is to inspire students to move beyond the rather vague sense that *The Tin Drum* is "about" the Second World War, and to consider more precisely how Grass depicts the origins of German fascism, the experience of the war itself, and—most important—the ongoing difficulty of coming to terms with the past in postwar Germany.

Historical fiction has a history of its own, and Grass signals his stance toward literary tradition through his protagonist's choice of reading material. Soon after his disastrous first—and last—day of public school, Oskar Matzerath decides to pursue his education in a less traditional venue. After trying in vain to find guidance first from his putative father, then the drunken trumpet player Meyn, and finally the greengrocer Greff, he finds what he is looking for in the apartment of Gretchen Scheffler: books. "Auch schlechte Bücher sind Bücher und deshalb heilig" (111) ("Even bad books are books and therefore sacred" [90]), decrees Oskar, and he proceeds to detail the contents of Frau Scheffler's random collection. Among the books he finds a well-worn copy of Felix Dahn's historical novel, *Ein Kampf um Rom* (1876; *A Struggle for Rome*). In the mood for stronger stimulus, he soon becomes absorbed in the unlikely pair of Goethe and Rasputin, but the heroes of Dahn's novel are not entirely forgotten. Soon after his mother dies, Oskar returns to the home of Gretchen Scheffler and builds his eclectic knowledge of world history by reading Dahn's fiction together with a few other unrelated texts. We learn years later that the disaffected youths who roam the streets of Danzig in the final year of the war "riefen . . . sich mit merkwürdigen Namen an" (478) ("gave each other weird names" [364]) such as Totila, Teja, Belisarius, and Narses, all taken directly from the pages of *A Struggle for Rome*.

Today's English-speaking reader is unlikely to be familiar with Felix Dahn (1834–1912), whose work was widely admired by his late-nineteenth-century contemporaries, reviled by twentieth-century modernists, and yet still read by generations of readers that included the young Günter Grass (Schwab 1065–69).

Dahn taught the history of Germanic law at the universities of Königsberg and Breslau, and his scholarship informed literary works sometimes known by the derogatory term of the *Professorenroman* ("professor's novel") (Mews 28). *A Struggle for Rome* is a sprawling epic set at the time of the *Völkerwanderungen* ("migrations of [Germanic] peoples") of the sixth century CE that pits noble Goths against treacherous Romans and decadent Greeks of the Byzantine Empire. It features vividly drawn characters, intrigue, passion, and occasionally lurid violence.

But why would Grass allude to this novel on several occasions in *The Tin Drum*? That Gretchen Scheffler should find it among the favorite books of her brother, Theo, adds an element of realism to the novel, for Dahn's fiction is just the sort of thing that might appeal to a boy who grew up to become a sailor and died at sea. At the same time, the reference to Dahn's work establishes an intertextual relation with the genre of the historical novel fully in keeping with the literary self-consciousness of a work that also plays with the genres of the picaresque novel and the German novel of education or bildungsroman—despite Oskar's coy claim that he is simply going to tell his own story and dispense with the literary fireworks of experimental fiction.

In his standard work *The Historical Novel* (1962), Georg Lukács dates the emergence of the genre to the Napoleonic era. In earlier periods, authors had of course set their works in the past, but they told timeless tales about the human condition portrayed by characters clad in arbitrary historical costumes. Only the mass experience of revolution and war produced "specifically historical" novels in which "the individuality of characters" derived "from the historical peculiarity of their age" (19). While novelists such as Sir Walter Scott and Felix Dahn set their works in the distant past, Grass depicts much more recent events, yet like the earlier novelists he combines in his work actual historical figures and events with fictional characters. Oskar begins his story by drumming up the memory of a rainy day in October 1899 and continues until he is arrested in Paris in early September 1952, on a false accusation of murder. Shortly thereafter, while incarcerated in a mental hospital, he begins to write his novel, which he concludes on the eve of his thirtieth birthday in early September 1954 (Neuhaus, *Günter Grass* [1993] 23–25). *The Tin Drum* thus depicts the years before, during, and immediately after the Second World War, a period of German history marked by unprecedented crimes against humanity and catastrophic defeat.

At this point, Dahn's *A Struggle for Rome* offers an illuminating contrast to the depiction of history in *The Tin Drum*. Dahn's Gothic heroes also face catastrophe toward the end of the novel, as they are vastly outnumbered and backed onto a narrow ridge on Mount Vesuvius. Here they will fight to the death, and when the last warrior has fallen, the women and children plan to leap into the volcano. As it turns out, Nordic allies show up in the nick of time to rescue the survivors, but the Goths had been cheerfully resigned to their fate and prepared to perish as one in "glorreichem Heldentod" (1034) ("glorious heroic death" [trans. mine]) rather than surrender to their foes. To Grass, who experienced the Second World War as a seventeen-year-old veteran with fragments of shrapnel in his shoulder and haunting memories of his less fortunate comrades hanged for their unwillingness to die for a hopeless cause (*Autor* 316), such tragic-heroic resolution to the fate of the *Volk* could only seem demented folly. When the young Grass was confronted with the magnitude of German guilt while in an American prisoner-of-war camp, he reacted at first with disbelief and then with growing shame and horror (Jürgs 56–58). Since that time the man who was indoctrinated with Nazi ideology in his youth has devoted his career to the cultivation of doubt, skepticism, and the desire to inspire critical distance rather than blind enthusiasm among his readers. To such an individual any mystification of the people's destiny remains anathema, and Grass has repeatedly declared himself opposed to the Hegelian philosophy of history and its implicit glorification of the state (*Angestiftet* 175; *Schriftsteller* 93).

How, then, does Grass represent history in *The Tin Drum?* He begins by refusing to idealize individuals or the experience of war. Readers of Grass's *Katz und Maus* (1961; *Cat and Mouse*), the novella published two years after *The Tin Drum*, will remember the satirical portraits of young veterans who return while on furlough to their former high school to entertain students with tales of adventure and heroism in battle. Grass must have had similar experiences, for in a subsequent interview he recalled that a certain Dr. Littschwager had led his own high school class in a reading of Ernst Jünger's *In Stahlgewittern* (1920; *Storm of Steel*), a memoir of the First World War that, while unstinting in its graphic depiction of the horrors of trench warfare, nevertheless describes combat as a strangely exhilarating baptism of fire. Grass goes on to note that at the same time he was reading Erich Maria Remarque's *Im Westen nichts Neues* (1929; *All Quiet on the Western Front*) together with his uncle in the privacy of his home, a novel that presents a decidedly less heroic perspective on the Great War (*Autor* 313–14). He claims that the contrast between Jünger and Remarque made a strong impression on him in his youth, and in fact many years later he devoted the sections on the First World War in *Mein Jahrhundert* (1999; *My Century*) to a fictive encounter between the two authors.

In *The Tin Drum*, Grass tends not to represent war at all: for the most part it happens in the background while people go about their ordinary lives. The major exception is his depiction of the battle for the Polish Post Office that signaled the beginning of the Second World War. Here again, heroism is hardly the order of the day. Jan Bronski returns with extreme reluctance to join his coworkers in the besieged building, not out of loyalty to the cause of Polish resistance but because Oskar desperately wants a new tin drum. During the attack, Bronski fires off his gun in panic and hopes for a flesh wound that will keep him out of the action before drifting into a fantasy world during a game of skat with the dying Kobyella. By the time he is being led off to be executed by the victorious Nazis, Bronski is smiling stupidly, blissfully unaware of his surroundings, conscious only of the queen of hearts that he clutches in his upraised hand while dreaming of his former lover.

The corollary to Grass's injunction against idealization is his refusal to demonize his enemies. In comments first published in a 1969 issue of the German
news magazine *Der Spiegel*, Grass spoke of his annoyance with a complacent
literature of resistance that had become the norm before the publication of *The
Tin Drum*, *Cat and Mouse*, and *Hundejahre* (1963; *Dog Years*):

> Meine Kritik galt zuallererst der Dämonisierung des Nationalsozialis-
> mus, und wenn es mir gelungen sein sollte . . . die Dämonisierung ein-
> zudämmen und das kleinbürgerliche Detail aufzuwerten, bin ich schon
> zufrieden.   (*Autor* 68; see also 104, 212)

> My criticism targeted above all the demonization of National Socialism,
> and if I succeeded . . . in stemming the tide of demonization and giving
> greater value to the details of petit-bourgeois life, then I am satisfied.
>   (trans. mine)

He may well have been thinking of novels such as Alfred Andersch's *Die Kirschen
der Freiheit* (1952; *The Cherries of Freedom*), *Sansibar* (1957; *Zanzibar*), or
Anna Seghers's earlier novel *Das siebte Kreuz* (1942; *The Seventh Cross*), all of
which portray escaped prisoners, resistance fighters, or deserters from an evil
government and thus tend to encourage readers to identify with the persecuted
against a clearly defined enemy.

On a loftier plane, Thomas Mann's *Dr. Faustus* (1947) ponders the proclivity
of the German people to enter into a pact with the diabolical powers of National
Socialism. While Mann was one of the most visible and outspoken opponents
of Hitler's Germany, his work grew out of a tradition of nineteenth-century Romantic thought that was still willing to speculate about the spirit or essence
of the German *Volk* in ways that Grass emphatically rejected (Mason 48–49).
Mann's novel focuses on an elite group of artists and intellectuals in the Weimar
Republic who dabble irresponsibly in the sort of irrationalist, antidemocratic,
vulgar Nietzschean ideologies that paved the way for the National Socialist take-
over; Grass concentrates on the stale air of the lower-middle-class milieu of his
own childhood, a world of shopkeepers and artisans who struggle to make ends
meet and fall into fascism through a combination of personal character flaws
and historical accident (Koopmann; Preece, *Life* 34–46).

The greengrocer Greff, for example, seems to embrace many of the manly
virtues central to fascist ideology (Mosse, *Image*): he enjoys physical fitness and
the lean, hard bodies of the adolescents that he leads on vigorous hikes or to icy
plunges in the Baltic Sea. Yet it is not only the inaccurate weights in his shop
that arouse the suspicions of the authorities, for Greff is a little too fond of the
boys while remaining utterly indifferent to his slovenly wife. He commits suicide out of a combination of grief for the death of one of his former favorites
and because he has received "eine Vorladung vors Gericht . . . der Sittenpolizei"
(414) ("a summons to appear in court on a morals charge" [317]). As an indi-

vidual, Greff hovers between the ridiculous and the pathetic, but his personal foibles are symptomatic of the inconsistencies of a state that places the highest possible value on a militarized form of masculine camaraderie but that cannot tolerate even a hint of homosexuality.

Oskar's legal father, Alfred Matzerath, provides a second, more important example of a character who captures the complexity of life in Nazi Germany instead of serving as the embodiment of evil. In some ways he is a rather sympathetic figure: he makes his first appearance as a merry cook from the Rhineland who quickly becomes one of the nurses' favorites when wounded in the First World War. He loves his wife in his own rather inept way and tolerates her infidelity to the point that he claims that he does not care whether or not he is Oskar's biological father. Oskar, for his part, finds it unexpectedly difficult to say good-bye to Matzerath when Oskar prepares to leave town with Bebra's troupe, and on his return, Matzerath "empfing mich wie ein Vater und nicht wie ein mutmaßlicher Vater. Ja, er . . . kam auch zu echten, sprachlosen Tränen" (455) ("welcomed me . . . like a true, not a presumptive, father . . . to the point of shedding real, speechless tears" [346]). Yet this same person had been one of the first to join the Nazi Party in 1934. He assembles his uniform with pride, hangs a picture of Hitler on the wall of his apartment, and religiously attends the Sunday morning party rallies. As Oskar describes it, however, Matzerath's early entry into the party had nothing to do with ideological zeal; it reflected only his desire to be one of the gang: "immer zu winken, wenn andere winkten, immer zu schreien, zu lachen und zu klatschen, wenn andere schrien, lachten oder klatschten" (195) ("he always had to wave when other people were waving, to shout, laugh, and clap when other people were shouting, laughing, and clapping" [152]). Thus when Matzerath warms "seine Finger und seine Gefühle über dem öffentlichen Feuer" of religious objects looted from a burning synagogue on Kristallnacht (259) ("his fingers and his feelings over the public blaze" [201]) or when, after some hesitation, he signs the letter that will commit Oskar to the Ministry of Public Health and almost certain death, it is not out of deepseated malice or conviction but because it seems the socially appropriate thing to do. This by no means excuses his actions, but it does provide a portrait of a Nazi as a vacillating follower rather than as a demonic leader.

Oskar confirms the general impression that the more important a character is, the more conflicted—that is, the less capable of being fit neatly into a single ideological or moral category (Mason 41–49). He begins the novel with a reference to his blue eyes, a symbol of guilelessness in the popular imagination, whereas the Nazi Party member Alfred Matzerath has eyes as brown as his shirt, "Kackbraun . . . Parteibraun, SA-Braun . . . Evabraun . . . Uniformbraun," as Grass puts it in *Hundejahre* (256; *Dog Years*) ("shit brown . . . Party brown, SA brown . . . Eva Braun, uniform brown" [167]). Yet the crowds that gaze, "jubelnd . . . in jene blauen Augen" (*Blechtrommel* 325) ("jubilantly into the blue eyes . . . of Adolf Hitler" [252]) when he enters Danzig in his black Mercedes confuse any clear link between eye color and political allegiance. In fact, as Klaus Theweleit has observed, Hitler's "eyes were as brown as they come" (2: 130), but people saw what they wanted to see in the hypnotic gaze of their Aryan leader. The colors of Oskar's red-and-white drum could indicate sympathy for Poland, which Oskar denies, but they could also refer to the colors of the Nazi flag. Oskar entertains the Nazi soldiers in occupied France, but he also disrupts a party rally by drumming waltzes under the rostrum. He betrays Bronski to the Nazis, but he also causes Matzerath to choke to death on his Nazi insignia. His refusal to grow could signal a childlike innocence in a world full of unprecedented evil, but it also indicates a failure to take responsibility for his actions in a way that was symptomatic of many in the postwar period who indulged in a brief bout of collective guilt during the hard times so that they could say to themselves, "Machen wir es jetzt ab, dann haben wir es hinter uns und brauchen später, wenn es wieder aufwärtsgeht, kein schlechtes Gewissen mehr zu haben" (570) ("Let's do our stint now; when things begin to look up we'll have it over with and our consciences will be all right" [436]).

Just as Grass collapses contradictory characteristics into a single character such as Oskar, who is both a Nazi collaborator and a potential victim of Nazi violence, so too does he condense the global conflicts of the Second World War into the local confines of the city of Danzig. German armies from the west sweep into the city at the beginning of the war, only to be driven out by Russian soldiers entering the city from the east at the end. Religious and political conflicts take place on the intimate level of the family, as the rivalry between Alfred Matzerath and Jan Bronski over Oskar's mother is also a clash between the Protestant Nazi and the Polish Catholic postal worker. The Jewish shopkeeper Sigismund Markus urges Agnes to flee the city on the eve of the war, while the concentration camp survivor Fajngold takes over the family business when they are expelled to the west after the war. Oskar's grandmother remains behind as a member of the local Kashubian minority whose history pre-dates the conflict between Germany and Poland by many centuries.

Thus Grass implodes events of world-historical significance into the microcosm of Danzig, the intimate world of Oskar's German-Polish-Kashubian family, and the conflicted allegiances of individual characters. At other times, however, he explodes this claustrophobic setting by introducing seemingly random references to events taking place in other parts of the world. In such passages Grass follows the lead of his mentor Alfred Döblin (1878–1957). In an essay about Döblin written in 1967, Grass notes that in comparison with Thomas Mann, Bertolt Brecht, and Franz Kafka, the expressionist writer has been largely neglected ("Über meinen Lehrer Döblin"). Döblin is even less well known in the English-speaking world, with the possible exception of his novel *Berlin Alexanderplatz* (1929). In this novel about the life of an ex-convict set in the waning years of the Weimar Republic, Döblin depicts a series of unsavory characters in a gritty urban milieu in a way that anticipates the petit bourgeois figures that populate Grass's fiction. Grass is particularly interested in Döblin's representation of history and devotes a considerable portion of his essay to the discussion of *Wallenstein* (1920), Döblin's novel about an indecisive general during the Thirty Years War. Students of German literature are more likely to be familiar with Friedrich Schiller's historical drama about the same figure (*Wallenstein* [1798–99]), which draws in turn on Schiller's major historical treatise, *Geschichte des dreissigjährigen Kriegs* (1791–93; *The History of the Thirty Years War*). As Grass describes it, Schiller set out to provide a clearly organized overview of the war; he wanted to draw connections between disparate events and explain their meaning. In contrast, "Das alles zerschlägt Döblin mehrmals und bewußt zu Scherben, damit Wirklichkeit entsteht" (*Deutschen* 76) ("Döblin repeatedly and consciously smashes such coherence to bits, so that reality emerges"; on Döblin's influence on Grass, see Böschenstein; Durzak; and Trappen).

In *The Tin Drum,* sudden allusions to distant parts of the world disrupt the narrative continuity and encourage the reader to reflect on their possible significance. For instance, the second paragraph of the second chapter of *The Tin Drum* consists of a single long sentence that sums up the contents of the first chapter: "An jenem Oktobernachmittag des Jahres neunundneunzig, während in Südafrika Ohm Krüger seine buschig englandfeindlichen Augenbrauen bürstete, wurde . . . meine Mutter Agnes gezeugt" (23) ("That afternoon in the year 1899, while in South Africa Oom Kruger was brushing his bushy anti-British eyebrows, my mother Agnes . . . was begotten" [25]). The elided portions of the sentence contain details about the location, the grandmother's four skirts, the rain, and the constables—but who was Oom Kruger, and why does Oskar allude to South Africa in the midst of a description of the Kashubian potato field?

Paul Oom ("Uncle") Kruger (1825–1904) was a South African statesman and president of the Dutch-speaking republic of Transvaal. In the late nineteenth century, the Dutch Boers or farmers sought to maintain their independence from British South Africa until the British provoked the Boer War in 1899. After initial successes the Boers were ruthlessly repressed, although they retained a certain degree of autonomy in a unified South Africa according to the terms of the Peace of Vereeniging of 1902. The Boer struggle for independence inspired popular enthusiasm throughout Germany (Parr). Among the many intellectuals who championed the cause of the underdog Boers against the evil British Empire was none other than Felix Dahn, who wrote a poem that placed their cause in a long tradition that extended back to his own favorite theme of Gothic resistance to Roman imperialism. Dahn and his fellow enthusiasts contrasted what they portrayed as the organic connection of the Boers to their native land with the amoral aggression of the rootless British armies. Germany's anti-British feelings ignited by the Boer War were rekindled in 1914 and again in 1939, inspiring "a veritable Boer-Renaissance" during the Nazi period that included the big-budget propaganda film *Ohm Krüger* (1942) (Parr 262).

But in *The Tin Drum,* the reference to Oom Kruger does *not* signal an upwelling of German patriotic sentiment. Oskar's grandmother Anna is portrayed as being rooted to the soil of her native Kashubia. She shelters the Polish sympathizer Koljaiczek, who is fleeing from German constables. Hence the passing reference to Oom Kruger inverts a cause that allied German patriots with Boer underdogs against British imperialism into an alliance between the Kashubian peasant and the persecuted Pole against the encroachment of the *German* Empire. Thus the seemingly superfluous reference to Oom Kruger conjures up a network of global alliances and enmities that places local conflicts in partitioned Poland into the larger context of the rivalry between Germany and Great Britain in an age of empire.

A more sustained example of the way in which Grass juxtaposes the local and the global occurs in the chapter "Sondermeldungen" ("Special Communiqués"). In this episode Oskar surprises the nearly forty-five-year-old Matzerath and his seventeen-year-old employee Maria in flagrante delicto on the couch. Since Oskar has also just had sexual intercourse with Maria and she soon becomes pregnant, the chapter raises themes of fatherhood that are central to Oskar's conflicted identity, together with broader issues of paternal authority gone astray in Nazi Germany. Like most chapters in *The Tin Drum*, "Special Communiqués" is structured as a frame narrative in which Maria, now a successful postwar businesswoman, visits Oskar in his mental hospital. In a gesture symptomatic of his refusal to grow up, Oskar tries to play their old sexual game with the fizz powder, just as he had done in the earlier scene after Matzerath stormed out of the house, but Maria has forgotten their former ritual or perhaps repressed the memory. Afraid of Oskar's weird obsessions and sexual aggression and uncertain whether she should stay in his room or run away, she hesitates and then turns on the radio.

The special communiqués that are broadcast over the radio give the chapter its name and thus invite speculation about their function in the text. Listening to the radio serves as a substitute for communication between people who are unable or unwilling to listen to each other, "denn der scheußliche Kunststoffkasten muß einen Teil unserer Gespräche während der Besuchstage ersetzen" (368) ("for it is the function of that execrable plastic box to replace a part of our conversation on visiting days" [283]). At the same time, the special communiqués introduce information about events in the larger world beyond the sordid details of the Matzerath family. Maria visits Oskar on 5 March 1953, the date of Stalin's death, which has been reported on the radio that morning. The events narrated within the main body of the chapter take place in the midst of the Second World War, as the radio broadcasts news of German U-boats torpedoing Allied ships in the Atlantic.

At first there would seem to be little or no connection between the events in the political world and the private lives of the individuals. Maria absentmindedly whistles whatever tune happens to be on the radio, whether it is a popular waltz or the song "Sailing against England," seemingly oblivious to the fact that one is a mindless ditty and the other a piece of political propaganda. Yet it soon becomes evident that the radio does in fact provide information of direct relevance to the characters' lives, or at least it encourages the reader to look for links between the private world of the family and the public events that surround them. For instance, Oskar urges Maria to open a second branch of her business during the early years of Germany's postwar *Wirtschaftswunder* ("economic miracle"), because he has heard on the radio that the good economic times are likely to continue.

During the war years, connections to the larger political world are far more ominous: Maria's younger brother sends postcards from the front that hang on the walls beside the bed where Oskar claims that he impregnated her. In the bitter spat that follows what was unsatisfying sex for Maria on the couch, Matzerath sarcastically suggests that she should "sich doch einen Fremdarbeiter angeln, den Franzos, der das Bier bringe, der könne es sicher besser" (376) ("get her hooks on one of the foreign laborers, the Frenchie that brought the beer would surely do it better" [288]). Matzerath's offhand insult indicates casual awareness of the French prisoners of war condemned to compulsory labor in Nazi-controlled Danzig, and it evokes the familiar racist stereotype of the foreigner's sexual prowess (Preece, *Life* 39).

In a passage in which Oskar imagines what the neighbors thought about the unusual marriage of the middle-aged Matzerath to the teenage Maria, he suggests that they must have considered little Oskar lucky to have a stepmother who treated him so well, even though he really belonged in a mental hospital. As noted earlier, Matzerath does eventually sign the papers that commit Oskar to almost certain death, but when enraged, even the otherwise benevolent Maria calls Oskar "eine verfluchte Drecksau, einen Giftzwerg, einen übergeschnappten Gnom, den man in die Klappsmühle stecken müsse" (378) ("a loathsome pig, a vicious midget, a crazy gnome, that ought to be chucked in the nuthouse" [290]).

The incidents reported in this chapter provide a good example of how Grass represents history in *The Tin Drum*, as individuals go about their ordinary lives only partially aware of the ways in which they are affected by the events reported on the radio. Yet the radio also introduces information that has no clear political significance: it is already March but will soon be getting colder, says Maria, who has been listening to the weather reports. While the war rages, the radio continues to announce the water level of the local rivers, a natural event that would occur regardless of who was in control of the city of Danzig. Earlier, during a lull in the battle for the Polish Post Office, Oskar suddenly becomes aware of the gathering silence as the "absterbendem Gebrumm einer vom Sommer ermüdeten Fliege" (299) ("the buzzing of a fly tuckered out from the summer heat died away" [232]). At the end of the war, Grass names an entire chapter after the ant trail that Oskar watches crawling across the basement floor beneath the family shop. It is a moment of great political significance that marks the beginning of the end of the war, a moment also of great personal trauma, as a half dozen Russian soldiers burst into the cellar, rape Lina Greff, and then shoot Oskar's choking father. Through it all, Oskar remains fixated on the trail of ants toward an open sugar sack. The dying Matzerath collapses across their path, but the ants are undeterred and soon find a new route, "denn jener . . . Zucker hatte während der Besetzung der Stadt Danzig durch die Armee Marschall Rokossowskis nichts von seiner Süße verloren" (519) ("for the sugar . . . had lost none of its sweetness while Marshal Rokossovski was occupying the city of Danzig" [395]).

One of the best examples of the way in which Grass combines significant events with trivial details in his representation of history in *The Tin Drum* occurs earlier in the same chapter. The members of the Dusters, including those named after the heroes of Dahn's *A Struggle for Rome*, confront the authorities to answer for their crimes. As each boy takes his turn in front of the tribunal, Grass likens his position to that of a youth who dares to ascend to an impossibly high diving platform and then hesitates to take the plunge. Finally, urged on by the sinister figure of Lucy Rennwald, each boy does jump; each confesses to his membership in the gang accused of having set fire to a training submarine and caught vandalizing a church while conducting a Black Mass. Only Oskar, the Christ figure in this blasphemous ceremony, refuses to jump. In a clear reference to the Gospel according to Matthew (4.8–10), he resists the temptation of the diabolical Lucy Rennwald and looks out from his lofty vantage point and observes "da lag mir die Welt zu Füßen und nicht nur Europa" (505) ("not only Europe but the whole world" [384]). A list of what he sees follows, which includes snapshot images of the various theaters of the war in different parts of the world: Americans and Japanese on the island of Luzon, Mountbatten in Burma, aircraft carriers in the Pacific, and Russian generals leading their troops into Eastern Europe. Yet Oskar also notes other events taking place on that day in January 1945: a tailor in Stockholm sews buttons on a suit, a widow in Lima teaches her parrot to talk, a streetcar driver in the town of Haparanda gets off work and begins preparing dinner for himself and his fiancée, rain falls in Ireland, and a woman burns milk in Panama. "So blieb es auch nicht aus, daß der Faden des Zeitgeschehens, der vorne noch hungrig war, Schlingen schlug und Geschichte machte, hinten schon zur Historie gestrickt wurde" (505) ("Inevitably the thread of events wound itself into loops and knots which became known as the fabric of History" [385]).

The inclusion of random details in Oskar's panoramic vision represents the third of Grass's varied techniques for representing history in his fiction. In these examples, Grass reminds us that even the most comprehensive overview of historical events must leave out many or indeed most of the things that are taking place simultaneously around the world. The combined effect of these various techniques is to create the impression of a vivid realism that rejects ideological mystifications or the vagaries of myth. Yet one need only scratch the surface of his novel to discover that it also contains a mythic substratum. To grasp the significance of this aspect in his historical fiction, we return for a final, brief glance at *A Struggle for Rome*.

Dahn's monumental historical novel about larger-than-life heroes and villains participates in the mythmaking that was central to the project of nineteenth-century nation formation (Geary). Dahn joined forces with other popular writers such as Gustav Freytag and Georg Ebers in an effort to create the impression that there was a clear continuity from the Germanic tribes who struggled to free themselves from the Roman Empire to the members of the recently unified German nation that sought to make its mark in the modern world. That Grass should borrow the names of Dahn's Teutonic heroes for a gang of anarchic teenagers as the "thousand-year Reich" teetered toward total destruction offers a sarcastic commentary on the heroic nationalist mythology that propelled Germany into the war and provides further evidence of the novel's realistic depiction of history. Yet a novel narrated by a character who remembers precisely the details of his birth, voluntarily stunts his growth, and feels a close affinity to Tom Thumb clearly has ties to the marvelous world of the fairy tale as well, and a recent critic has in fact identified the paradoxical combination of naturalist precision and a "wild surrealism" as the defining feature of Grass's entire oeuvre (Øhrgaard 141).

The mythic aspects of *The Tin Drum* emerge most clearly in Grass's depiction of women (see Becker-Cantarino's essay in this volume). Nearly two decades later Grass would publish the controversial novel *Der Butt* (1977; *The Flounder*), which at least superficially condemns men for having made a mess of world history ever since they broke free of the tutelage of Aua, the mythical three-breasted matriarch who stilled their desires and kept them in a kind of protective custody. According to the talking fish captured by a group of modern feminists, man's escape from the ahistorical realm of the primal mother figure has resulted only in war and destruction, not progress. A similar critique of man-made history already informs *The Tin Drum*, where a series of quasi-mythical earth mothers offer men food, warmth, and shelter from the storms of a world at war (Diller; Jahnke). The novel opens with the image of Joseph Koljaiczek's finding refuge beneath the skirts of Anna Bronski, and Oskar will repeatedly seek out the same sanctuary. In fact, Oskar wants to crawl back into his mother's womb as soon as he is born, and even on the eve of his thirtieth birthday he clings to the womblike safety of his hospital bed.

What Oskar fears is not so much a return to historical reality as the persecution of the Black Witch. Such a fear is paranoid on the realistic level of the novel but fully consistent at the level of myth: the female figures that give birth to the men and foster their development also embody destructive forces that hasten their demise, both womb and tomb or, as one of Oskar's favorite authors describes the realm of "The Mothers" in the second part of *Faust*, a site of constant "Gestaltung, Umgestaltung" (Goethe, *Werke* 3: 193 [line 6287]) ("formation, transformation"). The dual aspect of the female figure on the mythical level, in turn, informs Oskar's attitude toward the actual women in the text, who oscillate between nurturing mothers and castrating harpies, nurses who wear white and vixens who delight in sending men to their doom. Sometimes the same female figure can switch without warning from one aspect to the other, in keeping with Grass's tendency to make his most important characters the most complex and conflicted. Maria, for instance, who "hieß nicht nur Maria, sie war auch eine" (338) ("wasn't just called Maria; she *was* one" [261]), soon sheds her saintly status to become the "behaarten Dreieck" (348) ("hairy triangle" [268]) that Oskar bites, punches, and tries to stab with an open scissors. Oskar's mother, Agnes, turns the violence against herself: for years she gives free rein to an indiscriminate sexual appetite that wanders from Alfred Matzerath to Jan Bronski to Gretchen Scheffler, but the sight of lascivious eels devouring a dead horse's head transforms her desire into a self-destructive gluttony that takes her to an early grave.

Viewing women as either angelic virgins or demonic prostitutes is hardly unique to Oskar; it is central to the "male fantasies" of the protofascist members of the paramilitary bands that roamed unchecked in the early Weimar Republic, and perhaps to men in general in patriarchal society (Theweleit). For precisely this reason, it is ironic that these fantasies should emerge in the imaginative universe of *The Tin Drum*, which portrays ordinary Germans who become entangled in historical events that they only partially understand. Grass works to refute the notion that the Nazis were alien embodiments of evil and resists any suggestion that the Germans were their innocent victims. The terrifying image of the Black Witch, however, and her various manifestations as female figures that inspire fear and loathing on the part of the protagonist suggest subliminally that the men who make history are actually in the thrall of feminine forces that hasten their destruction.

The suggestion grows stronger in Grass's subsequent works. In *Cat and Mouse* and *Dog Years*, Lucy Rennwald evolves into Tulla Pokriefka, whose face is also described as an evil triangle, who reeks of glue and is associated with death, and who commits vicious acts of violence for no particular reason: "Aber warum? Na darum!" (*Hundejahre* 209) ("'But why?' 'Because!'" [*Dog Years* 248]) (see Neuhaus, "Belle Tulla"). Tulla resurfaces in *Im Krebsgang* (2002; *Crabwalk*), where she stands accused of having abetted her grandson's slide into neo-Nazi circles and anti-Semitic violence. Nor is Grass alone among postwar writers in suggesting that there is something fascinating and female about German fascism (Sontag; Byg). One of the most popular German novels of the 1980s, Patrick Süskind's *Das Parfum* (1985; *Perfume*), portrays an evilly charismatic, Hitleresque figure who exerts control over the crowds only when he is bathed in the scent of a woman, while Bernhard Schlink's international blockbuster *Der Vorleser* (1995; *The Reader*) portrays a sadistic SS guard as a beautiful seductress (Metz). *The Tin Drum* already provides the paradigm for this mixed message about twentieth-century German history. On one level the work stands as the first and perhaps still most important postwar German novel that attempts to come to terms with the past—refusing excuses, trying to show *wie es eigentlich gewesen* ("how it really was")—but on another level, it suggests that beneath the crimes of male history there lies the essence of fascism as a femme fatale.

Resistance in the Borderlands:
Outsiders and Opposition in *The Tin Drum*

Patricia Pollock Brodsky

Much has been written about Grass's fascination with outsiders and misfits. Likewise it is common knowledge that he thematizes the borderland culture of his Slavic ancestors, though little analytic work has been done to evaluate this aspect of his work. Finally, there has to my knowledge been no discussion of antifascist resistance in Grass. These motifs are central to the development of the book's main theme, the German denial of the Nazi past. When I teach *The Tin Drum*, I foreground these three elements, thus bringing a new dimension to the discussion of the novel.

Six decades after the end of the Third Reich, debate over the twelve Nazi years still dominates German intellectual life. Quite recently arguments raged about the nature, purpose, and even necessity of a Holocaust memorial in Berlin. Among the other subjects on which Germans still disagree is the antifascist resistance. While it is clear that there was a significant resistance movement in Germany, carried out by such disparate groups as left-wing labor, Catholic youth, and conservative officers, it long remained controversial: Was the resistance an act of heroism or of treason? With others of his generation, Grass thematized the Third Reich and the early cold-war years. He confronted his readers with uncomfortable questions about collaboration and guilt, which were later taken to the streets by the generation of 1968, children dissatisfied with their parents' answers or with their refusal to answer.

At the center of Grass's Danzig novels is his depiction of the *Kleinbürger*, the lower-middle-class Germans who formed the backbone of the Nazi movement. We see in the microcosm of Danzig their hopes and rationalizations; we see the wedge driven between neighbors and between family members by ideology. Despite their individual quirks, Oskar's family and neighbors as a group represent ordinary dwellers in a provincial city on the margins of the Reich whose lives are transformed by National Socialism. The theme of resistance in *The Tin Drum*—to fascism, autocratic rule, or national oppression—has largely been ignored, in part because like much else in the novel, it is obscured in the equivocations of Oskar's narrative. Thus the search for examples of resistance in the novel requires our engagement with the essential ambiguity of Oskar's world.

The context in which I most often teach *The Tin Drum* is an upper-level course offered in English and entitled The Antifascist Tradition in German Letters. The seminar-sized class of ten or twelve attracts students from across the disciplines. Students take two exams and write a final paper, in which comparative or interdisciplinary topics are encouraged. (Papers have included a dramatic monologue by a Jewish actor about to be deported and a study, which will probably develop into a master's thesis, of Brecht's musical collaborations.) Texts vary but have typically included Bertolt Brecht's *Fear and Misery of the Third Reich*, Anna Seghers's *The Seventh Cross*, Heinrich Böll's *Billiards at Half-Past Nine*, Horst Bienek's *The First Polka*, Jurek Becker's *Jacob the Liar*, Christa Wolf's *Patterns of Childhood*, and Siegfried Lenz's *The German Lesson* and *The Heritage*. We also read Carl Zuckmayer's memoir *A Part of Myself*.[1] Poetry includes works written in the concentration camps. Unfortunately the reading list is increasingly determined by what is still affordably available in English translation.

To approach Grass from the angle of the resistance requires considerable preparation: discussion must be grounded in the historical context. I begin with an overview of German history, lecturing on such concepts as self-image, patriarchy, honor, and fate, from Tacitus's *Germania* to medieval chivalry to the rise of Prussia. Focusing on the target years, I talk about the stab-in-the-back myth (*Dolchstoßlegende*); the concept of lebensraum; and the principle of *Gleichschaltung* ("enforced alignment"), by which everything from education to hygiene to musical performance was regulated by party dictates. Careful juxtaposition of supplemental materials provides a kind of alienation effect, which encourages discussion. Students watch a film on "degenerate art" and examine works by Nazi artists, including Hitler; excerpts of recorded speeches by Hitler are compared with scenes from Charlie Chaplin's *The Great Dictator*; anti-Semitic caricatures from *Der Stürmer* or Nazi schoolbooks are juxtaposed to drawings by Käthe Kollwitz and satirical montages by John Heartfield. I have shown *Das Beil von Wandsbek* ("The Ax of Wandsbek"), a film based on Arnold Zweig's 1943 novel about the Nazis' betrayal of the little man, and Conrad Wolf's autobiographical East German film about a young German serving in the Red Army, *Ich war neunzehn* ("I Was Nineteen"). Among the most popular means of contextualizing the lectures and readings have been guest speakers—for example, a Holocaust survivor and a former member of the Hitler Youth. Face-to-face with living participants in the history described by the authors, the students are deeply struck by its reality, perhaps for the first time.

We discuss the nature of resistance and examine historical examples. The approach to texts is roughly chronological. Thus in the second half of the course, when the time arrives to read and discuss Grass, the students not only have some idea of what fascism and resistance were about, they also know that however difficult it was, German resistance did occur. Students are eager to see how Grass portrays a history now familiar to them.

Most resisters are created by their situation. People find themselves in opposition to a government because of definitions that have been imposed on them. The Nazis' ever-growing list of undesirables—Jews, Slavs, Sinti and Roma, leftists, pacifists, asocials, homosexuals, people with disabilities—constituted a pool not only of outsiders and victims but also of potential resisters. Grass draws from this pool in portraying the possibilities of resistance. In this essay, I describe some approaches to resistance in *The Tin Drum* and show how it is supported by the Slavic and outsider motifs. The examples given are not meant to be exhaustive but should suggest productive ways of reading the text.

A point that I raise early in my course is that antifascist resistance continues to be relevant so long as sympathies for fascism persist. Art can serve this function in two ways: by thematizing resistance and by embodying it. As a young prisoner of war, Grass, like many Germans, refused at first to believe the stories of the camps and other Nazi crimes. Only radio broadcasts of the Nuremberg trials convinced him (Jürgs 57). With his resulting shame and his distrust of postwar denazification, his thematics began to take shape. In 1956, he left Germany for Paris, where he wrote *The Tin Drum*, a book full of unpopular truths challenging the postwar culture of strategic forgetfulness (Brode, *Zeitgeschichte*). Thus not only does Grass's novel portray resistance but the very fact of his writing it was an act of resistance against pervasive denial. Years later, in a 1996 speech, he noted that a writer his age is "not free in his choice of material, too many of the dead are watching him as he writes" (Jürgs 58).[2]

Having established that the book in itself is an act of opposition, class discussion moves on to its contents. Answering the question, "Is Oskar a resister?," is as difficult as any other attempt to pin down Grass's protagonist. Just as Oskar's contradictory nature is symbolized by his equal attraction to his masters, Goethe and Rasputin, so he has a foot in the camp of both the Nazis and their opponents. In his protagonist, Grass presents a disturbing mixture of impulses and behaviors. Oskar can be seen as a potential victim and an opponent of the Nazis or equally as an opportunist and collaborator. Each example of resistance or opposition in which he is involved is immediately undermined by his actions or words. He is a most untrustworthy narrator. We know that he is writing his life story from his bed in a mental hospital, and he readily admits to lying to his keeper, Bruno. On the other hand, Hanspeter Brode argues that by writing his memoirs, Oskar is facing his guilt in ways that the other characters, and his audience, do not (*Zeitgeschichte* 93–96). Thus we must weigh both his reported acts of resistance and his commentary on them.

If victimhood leads to opposition, Oskar ought to be a resister. His stunted physical growth and supposed mental retardation make him a prime target for Nazi eugenics laws. Such an abnormal child, socially unproductive and an excess consumer of increasingly scarce goods, is an embarrassment to the healthy German community. Sooner or later he must come to the attention of the euthanasia program, the "mercy killing" of the physically and mentally disabled from 1939 on that prefigured the final solution. And indeed, in the chapter "Die Stäuber" ("The Dusters"), father Matzerath receives a letter from the Ministry of Health demanding that Oskar be turned over to them. His dead mother's protective shadow, and perhaps a lingering sense of fatherly affection, prevents Matzerath from complying. But pressure from the authorities increases, and the second time an official approaches Matzerath, Matzerath signs the committal order. By then it is too late, however, for the post office is no longer delivering mail, and the city is about to fall into the hands of the Russians.

Oskar's reaction to the threat of committal is a personal campaign against the Nazi world that leads to what seem to be acts of resistance. Plagued by nightmares of smiling doctors with hypodermics, "Oskar sang damals viel," Oskar says (475) ("In that period, Oskar sang a good deal" [362]), using his glass-shattering voice to proclaim his continued existence. His nighttime forays attract the attention of the Dusters, a group of asocial youth who attack Hitler youth and soldiers home on leave; steal weapons, munitions, and gasoline from military sites; and plan an attack on a government office. They invite Oskar into their ranks after a serendipitous air raid allows him to display his talents: he breaks all the windows in a chocolate factory that caters exclusively to the German air force, while the local antiaircraft batteries (or Oskar's voice) succeed in bringing down an Allied bomber. On the basis of this ambiguous display, Oskar is made their leader. His miracle weapon is used against party headquarters and military patrols. The Dusters seem to be modeled on real antifascist youth groups such as the proletarian *Meuten* ("packs") of Leipzig; the middle-class Swing Boys, whose resistance took the form of modish dress and decadent music; or the *Edelweißpiraten* of Cologne, who committed sabotage and aided deserters and escaped prisoners.

Yet Oskar undermines any connection to these historical resistance groups, and the rumor that "Verbindungen zwischen der Stäuberbande und den Edelweißpiraten in Köln am Rhein bestanden hätten, daß polnische Partisanen . . . unsere Aktionen beeinflußt . . . hätten . . . muß . . . ins Reich der Legende verwiesen werden" (490–91) (". . . the Dusters had connections with the Edelweiss Pirates of Cologne or that Polish partisans . . . exerted an influence on us . . . is pure legend" [373]). He even gratuitously denies any connection with the 20 July 1944 assassination attempt on Hitler. He describes how the Dusters broke up because of politics. That Communist dockworkers tried to enlist them in underground activities led to a split along class lines; the working-class Dusters expressed an interest, but the gymnasium students rejected all politics, declaring, "Wir haben überhaupt nichts mit Parteien zu tun, wir kämpfen gegen unsere Eltern und alle übrigen Erwachsenen; ganz gleich wofür oder wogegen die sind" (491) ("We have nothing to do with parties. . . . Our fight is against our parents and all other grownups, regardless of what they may be for or against" [374]). Thus their antifascist acts are reduced to self-indulgent adolescent anarchy. Oskar's own agenda is to establish himself as "Nachfolge Christi" (484) ("to . . . walk in the footsteps of Christ" [369]), with the Dusters as his disciples.

The chapter "Die Tribüne" ("The Rostrum") also seems to place Oskar firmly in the ranks of the resistance. Here he first meets the clown Bebra and is warned of a coming "Zeit der Fackelzüge und Aufmärsche vor Tribünen" (145) ("era of torchlight processions and parades past rostrums" [115]). In this chapter Grass makes extensive use of historical detail about the party organization in Danzig, introducing rival politicians and presenting a vivid picture of political life. After Matzerath joins the party in 1934, Oskar develops the habit of going to the Nazi rallies.

That Oskar long interprets the hunchbacked party official Löbsack as a messenger from Bebra speaks for his ambivalence concerning the Nazis. But Oskar's experience resembles that of many Germans who mistook the new party for an answer to their personal problems. Oskar sees in Löbsack an outsider like himself who has succeeded in finding a niche on the rostrum. He soon realizes that Löbsack, like any other adult, regards him as a child, not a secret comrade. Oskar's alienation is completed when he approaches the Nazi reviewing stand from below, literally discovering the underside of Nazi spectacle. Using his drum as a weapon, he seduces the drummers and trumpeters on the stage above him away from their military rhythms into the playful strains of a Viennese waltz. As the crowd begins to dance in the aisles and the officials fume, he switches to the Charleston rhythms of "Jimmy the Tiger." The spell of the political rally is broken, and the crowd disperses, dancing.

This is Oskar as antifascist pied piper; just like the Swing Boys, he sabotages the rally with music declared decadent by the party. He expressly relates his actions to the resistance when he says that the SS and SA spent an hour searching under the reviewing stand for "einen Sozi womöglich oder einen Störtrupp der Kommune" (155) ("perhaps a Socialist or a team of Communist saboteurs" [122]). But his role as *Blechtrommler* ("tin drummer") also allies him symbolically with the Nazis. Hitler was popularly referred to as *der Trommler*. A poem published in 1934 began "Eine Trommel geht in Deutschland um / und der sie schlägt, der führt . . . " (Brode, *Zeitgeschichte* 49; "a drum is making the rounds in Germany / and he who beats it, leads"). A poster by John Heartfield with the caption "Gold schlucken und Blech reden," literally, to swallow gold and talk tin (i.e., nonsense), connects Hitler with tin as well.

Oskar undermines his own image as a resister in the very next chapter, "Schaufenster" ("Shopwindows"). He is at pains to discourage the reader from considering him a resistance fighter merely on the basis of "sechs oder sieben zum Platzen gebrachten Kundgebungen, drei oder vier aus dem Schritt getrommelten Aufmärsche und Vorbeimärsche" (157) (" . . . it would never occur to me to set myself up as a resistance fighter because I disrupted six or seven rallies and threw three or four parades out of step with my drumming" [124]). He insists that we see in him simply an eccentric who drummed up a little protest for private reasons. As if to underscore his apolitical agenda, he lists all the other events that he disrupted with his drum: " . . . Roten und den Schwarzen, . . . Pfadfindern und . . . Vegetariern" ("Reds and Blacks, . . . Boy Scouts . . . Vegetarians"). He declares firmly, "Mein Werk war also ein zerstörerisches" (158) ("Yes, my work was destructive" [124]). Oskar's political drumming may begin as a protest against a Nazi rally, but it soon loses any antifascist impulse and eventually becomes outright collaboration, as he dons a miniature uniform and joins Bebra's traveling company, entertaining the troops in occupied France. Like the Dusters, Oskar feels the need to reduce his actions to a kind of selfish anarchism. He does not want to be associated with the idea of resistance.

There are several possible reasons for this reluctance. One is his deeply divided personality, which he never lets us forget. He clings to both Rasputin and Goethe, fearing surrender to either. He is genuinely attracted to both the demonic and the humanistic. On another level, his enormous ego and his survival instinct prevent him from allowing others to predict or define him. But another possibility is suggested in the narrative frame of "Schaufenster," when he holds forth bitterly about the cheapening of the term *Widerstand* ("resistance"), which has become fashionable in postwar Germany. He has only contempt for writers of the inner emigration, which he considers facile and spurious, or for those who boast of having been resistance fighters, for example, just because they once had to pay a fine for forgetting to close the blackout curtains (157; 124). Grass understood and deplored the calculation that led some Germans after the war to claim victim status or to concoct for themselves a heroic history as resisters. He felt a duty to the truth: "too many of the dead [were] watching." He could not allow his protagonist to lay self-serving claim to motives and achievements that he himself viewed with deadly seriousness. Perhaps such claims would run counter to what Oskar is attempting to do by telling his life story: through his confessions, to shame his fellow Germans into facing up to their past as well. Oskar's frequent disclaimers seem to undermine resistance itself, but his refusal to accept the label "resistance fighter" may really be a sign of respect for the truth and for actions that lie beyond his cynical and anarchic reach.

Aside from the stunted misfit Oskar and the asocial Dusters, a number of other outsiders should be examined as possible sources of resistance. The word *Jew* appears only twice in the novel—once referring to the toy seller Sigismund Markus ("beim Juden" [172], significantly omitted by Manheim) and once in the combination "Judensau" (260) ("Jewish Sow" 202]), scrawled on the window of Markus's shop during the vandalism of Kristallnacht. Yet two important and positive figures in the novel are Jews, Markus and the camp survivor Fajngold. It is Markus who provides Oskar with drums and who consents to watch him while Oskar's mother, Agnes, goes to meet Jan Bronski in a nearby rented room. In some ways he fits the Nazi stereotype: he rubs together his "weißgelblichen Hände" ("his yellowed white hands"), and he *mauschelt*—speaks a recognizably Jewish German. Yet Markus is tolerant and generous; he accepts Oskar's peculiarities as "das natürlichste Geschehen" (132) ("took [them] perfectly for granted" [106]).

On the day described in the chapter "Fernwirkender Gesang vom Stockturm aus gesungen" ("The Stockturm: Long-Distance Song Effects"), Oskar finds Markus kneeling before Agnes, begging her to come with him to London or, if that cannot be, urging her at least, "[S]etzen Se . . . auf de Deitschen" (133) ("bet on the Germans" [106]) rather than on Bronski and the Poles. Markus warns of the rise of the Nazis and the coming destruction of Poland, but nothing he says suggests a desire to resist or for Agnes to do so. In fact, his suggestions to her are purely pragmatic: to flee to England with him (taking Oskar along) or to distance herself from those he foresees will be the losers in the coming conflict.

Yet indirectly Markus plays a role in the development of the antifascist motif, in a fashion that also partially redeems Oskar from his self-portrayal as cynical observer. The final pages of the chapter take us back to Oskar the chronicler, in the asylum. Oskar evokes the historical partitions of Poland and suggests that cold warriors are planning new aggression. He remarks that whenever his memory takes him back to that day in Markus's toy shop, he finds himself "seeking the land of the Poles" with his drumsticks and perhaps with his soul. The image refers to a scene in Goethe's *Iphigenia auf Tauris* (1787), where Iphigenia yearns for her lost home, "das Land der Griechen mit der Seele suchend" (5.7) ("seeking the land of the Greeks with her soul"). Oskar connects memories of Markus with the loss of his homeland, which leads in turn to an incantation based on the Polish national anthem, "noch ist Polen nicht verloren" (135) ("Poland is not yet lost" [my trans.]).[3] Oskar's variations on the *Polen verloren* theme betray the depths of his feeling for Poland and express a clear condemnation both of the German deeds predicted by Markus and of the vengeful plans of Germans in the early 1950s, who will seek "das Land der Polen mit Raketen" (135) ("go searching for Poland with rockets" [107]).

Markus's subsequent appearances in Oskar's memoirs confirm his prescience, though Markus could not have foreseen the details. When he attempts to express his condolences at Agnes's burial, he is roughly hustled away by two Nazis; Markus, the Jew, is unwelcome at the ceremony. Oskar slips away to speak with the toy dealer, referring to Markus and himself, significantly, as "der Hüter meiner Trommeln und ich, der Trommler, womöglich sein Trommler" (214) ("the keeper of my drums, and I, the drummer, possibly his drummer" [167]). This is a rare example of human connection for Oskar. In the final important scene containing Markus, the chapter "Glaube Hoffnung Liebe" ("Faith, Hope, Love"), Oskar becomes in fact Markus's drummer, playing his requiem. The chapter, built around a repetition and variation of the formula "es war einmal ein . . . " (there once was a . . .), is a fugal fairy tale. It focuses on the trumpeter Meyn who lives in the attic of Oskar's building, plays wonderfully on his trumpet, joins the SA, slaughters his four cats one afternoon in a fit of depression, and is kicked out of the SA for cruelty to animals, despite his exemplary service during the Kristallnacht. One of the victims of the pogrom is Markus. Oskar finds the old man sitting at his desk, dead by his own hand, while around him SA men like Meyn smash windows and defecate on toys. Markus has offered the only resistance he is capable of, by depriving the Nazis of a victim. But his death inspires a protest from Oskar, for whom this powerful scene is a turning point.

Oskar realizes that the events presage "Notzeiten" for the "gnomhaften Blechtrommlern, wie er einer war" (261) ("hard times were in the offing for gnomelike drummers like himself" [203]). A rapid crescendo of "es war einmal" weaves together the actions and fates of Oskar, Meyn, and Markus. Oskar's cry of personal loss—he has been deprived of his source of drums—is at the same time a cry of protest against the fascists, who have robbed life of all joy and innocence: "Es war einmal ein Spielzeughändler, der hieß Markus und nahm mit sich alles Spielzeug aus dieser Welt" (264) ("There once was a toy merchant, his name was Markus, and he took all the toys in the world away with him out of this world" [206]). The chapter ends with a German fairy-tale formula: "Es war einmal ein Musiker, der hieß Meyn, und *wenn er nicht gestorben ist, lebt er heute noch* und bläst wieder wunderschön Trompete" (264; emphasis added) ("There once was a musician, his name was Meyn, and *if he isn't dead he is still alive*, once again playing the trumpet too beautifully for words" [206; emphasis added]). The formula suggests that the criminal Meyn may be thriving even now, playing his horn at the service of Nazis new and old.

Through the other major Jewish character, Herr Mariusz Fajngold, Grass evokes the Holocaust and Jewish resistance directly. Just as Oskar connects Markus in his memory with Poland, Fajngold, who is clearly Jewish, is also identified by Oskar as a Pole, one of the many liberated Poles who after the Soviet conquest of Danzig made their way westward, occupying dwellings and pushing out the Germans. Matzerath's grocery store is taken over by Herr Fajngold, a man whose entire family died in the camp at Treblinka but who addresses them constantly as if they were alive. He survived only because he was assigned to the disinfection crew.

Fajngold, though traumatized, is a man without thoughts of vengeance. He runs interference with the Russians, helps Maria and Oskar bury Matzerath, and makes room for Maria, Oskar, and Kurt when they are displaced by a large Polish family. And he may have saved Oskar's life by releasing him from a feverish nightmare. Oskar began to grow, painfully, at Matzerath's burial; from a doctor he had heard about a shipment of four thousand children who died because there was no room on the ferryboats to bring them across the Vistula to safety. Oskar hallucinates that he is trapped on a fiendish merry-go-round with the four thousand children, all begging it in vain to stop. He is released from this nightmare because "Herr Fajngold beugte sich und stoppte das Karussell. . . . [E]r desinfizierte mich" (542–43) ("Herr Fajngold bent over me and stopped the merry-go-round. . . . [T]hat is to say, he disinfected me"). The man, who had lost his children to the Germans, steps in with his "cloud of Lysol" [412] and his kindness and liberates the suffering German child.

While conscientiously disinfecting the apartment each day, Fajngold tells Oskar about his job at Treblinka. He describes the prisoners' uprising and his own escape into the woods. His reminiscences become a memorial, as he recounts the names of all the living and the dead whom he has disinfected. Thus a tale of actual historical resistance is related as an aside, "während er spritzte . . . " (543) ("while he sprayed" [413]). Twice the motifs of victimization and resistance are embodied in a kindly Jewish man who is in turn irretrievably associated in Oskar's mind with Poland. And in each case, the man is tied to Oskar's own vulnerability: Markus's death robs the world of joy; Fajngold's skill restores Oskar to health.

Like the Jews, Slavs possess outsider status, both in Nazi ideology and in Grass's novel, and the Slavic theme is the next major motif I examine. Poland and Germany have a long history of conflict, from the Teutonic Knights through the partitions of 1772, 1793, and 1795. Slavs were second on the Nazis' list for mass extermination, right after the Jews. They too were considered subhuman. The General Plan East, coauthored by Himmler about the same time as the final solution in early 1942, envisioned the deportation to Siberia of thirty-one million "racially undesirable" Slavs, to be followed by colonization of the de-populated areas by Germans. Fourteen million people would be spared, to be employed as slave laborers in the German colonies (Madajczyk). In the 1930s, the academic discipline of *Ostforschung* ("research on the east") attempted to prove that the dominant ethnic and cultural influences in Central and Eastern Europe were Germanic, not Slavic. Scholars cranked out propaganda and jus-tifications for official Nazi racial policies (Burleigh 22–32). Poland was the first country to be attacked militarily in World War II. In the light of these facts, Grass's extensive use of Polish motifs and the borderland setting of his novel take on a deeper meaning.

At least seven of Grass's novels center on Danzig, now Gdańsk, and the Baltic region. Danzig is, of course, his native city and as such is connected for Grass with the realm of childhood and with inevitable loss. Now part of Poland as a result of the war, it is doubly lost to him. During Grass's childhood it was an independent city-state thanks to the Treaty of Versailles, with parallel German and Polish institutions (e.g., the Polish Post Office). In *The Tin Drum* German and Polish cultures collide on many levels, reflecting the more general dual-ity that informs both Oskar's character and the novel. Although Grass insists that he did not set out to create types (Personal interview), he does draw on national stereotypes when constructing some characters, as in the juxtaposition of Oskar's German father, the jovial, insensitive Nazi from the Rhineland, and Oskar's Slavic Uncle Jan, elegant, weak, and sentimental.

The most important confrontation of Germans and Poles takes place in the symbol-laden chapters "Die polnische Post" ("The Polish Post Office") and "Das Kartenhaus" ("The Card House"). The Nazis chose the post office as one of the first targets of the war because it represented the official Polish presence in Danzig. Seeking a postal worker, Kobyella, who has sometimes repaired his drums, Oskar lures his Uncle Jan, also a postal employee, into the post office just before the attack begins. He cannot know that it will cost Jan his life. While the Poles organize their defenses and prepare for battle, Oskar and Jan find themselves in what was once the nursery of the postal director's apartment. Among the toys there are "Ein noch unverletztes Schaukelpferd, . . . eine Rit-terburg voller umgestürzter Bleisoldaten . . . Puppenstuben, in denen Unord-nung herrschte" (293) ("An unharmed rocking horse, . . . a medieval castle full of upset tin soldiers . . . doll's houses with disorderly interiors . . . " [228]). In these details, Grass turns the nursery with its scattered toys into a meta-phor for Poland (and for Oskar's ambivalent attitude toward it), with its famous

cavalry still intact, its historical defeat of the Teutonic Knights, and its legendary "polnische Wirtschaft." (Literally, the phrase means "Polish housekeeping,
Polish economy." One popular German stereotype of Poles was sloppy, inef-
ficient, and undisciplined people, an image belied by both the postal workers
and the cavalry.)

The fabled Polish cavalry appears at several crucial junctures. Having betrayed Jan to save himself and his drum, Oskar lies delirious in a hospital in paci-
fied Danzig. He fantasizes about the cavalry—gallant, graceful, frivolous, and
doomed. Leading the attack on German tanks is "Pan Kiehot"—Don Quixote.
Oskar is both attracted by the Poles' Romantic idealism and disgusted by their
stubborn and suicidal impracticality. The cavalry reappears near the end of the
novel, just in time to rescue a one-time defender of the post office from Nazi
pursuers who have finally caught up with him in Germany ten years after the
war. Once again drumming Poland's national anthem, Oskar conjures a ghostly
squadron of uhlans who scoop up both the Pole and his pursuers and ride off to
Poland, "hinter dem Mond" (761) ("beyond the moon" [575]). This triumphant
act of antifascist resistance is paired with a warning: though the uhlans save
the Pole, they take the Nazis too, suggesting that Poland has not seen the last
of fascism. The description of Poland as "hinter dem Mond" echoes an idiom
suggesting someone old-fashioned, out of touch with reality. Threatened by the
rockets of the German revanchists, Poland may be part of a dead or dying world,
perhaps finally "verloren" despite Oskar's repeated assertions.

Like the national anthem and the cavalry, the colors of the Polish flag, red
and white, are put to symbolic use. The main red-and-white image is, of course,
Oskar's drum. Oskar himself remarks that it bears the colors of the Polish flag
and at one point declares himself willing to use his glass-shattering singing talents in the Polish cause. But predictably, he later tries to distance himself from
Poland, and from the Pole in himself, as from a taint of foolhardy altruism.
Angry that the defenders of the post office have bled all over his drum, he asks
with undisguised hostility, "Was hatte meine Trommel mit dem Blute Polens
gemeinsam!" (291) ("What had my drum in common with the blood of Poland?"
[226]). Though fascism is condemned, Oskar both loves and scorns the Poles;
his drum evokes their bravery, but he despises their spilled blood.

One final important piece of the national puzzle is the small Slavic people
called the Kashubians, resident in eastern Pomerania and west Prussia. Grass
himself is Kashubian on his mother's side, a heritage bestowed on Oskar through
the Bronski-Koljaiczek side of the family. Two generations back, the family of
Grass's mother had already moved to Danzig and become urbanized and Ger-
manized. Grass also has affectionate memories of his family's frequent visits
to the Slavic-speaking Kashubian relatives in the villages (Personal interview).
Clearly the Kashubian part of his heritage and childhood means a great deal
to him.

Historically, Poland has regarded minorities like Kashubians, Sorbs, and Ma-
surians as Poles, their languages as mere Polish dialects. The official German at-

titude reflected larger policy issues. In the 1930s, Slavic minorities were treated as independent nationalities, in order to fragment Polish identity and to undermine Poland's claims to much of its territory. The minorities did see themselves as separate from Poland, but this did not mean that they universally supported the Germans. A more aggressively propagandistic approach was promulgated in 1939. The fact of historical Kashubian opposition to the Poles was to be emphasized, but the term *Slavic* was to be avoided. Suggestions were made that the Kashubians were really Germanic and that the less valuable elements among them—that is, those who insisted on their Slavic identity—could be eliminated through sterilization. Ultimately a ban was imposed on public discussion of the very existence of these minorities. The goal was to smooth the "path to German self-consciousness" for these minority peoples (Burleigh 207–09).

Grass's Kashubian figures are sometimes connected with the antifascist theme, but they also constitute a third element. This can be confusing for readers unfamiliar with their history. As members of a minority culture, caught between German and Polish demands, Kashubians were faced with hard choices, and subsequently their resistance had a different focus. Oskar's Kashubian grandfather Josef Koljaiczek thus becomes a symbol of Polish opposition by setting fire to a number of Prussian-owned sawmills. The red flames devouring the white-painted mills evoke Poland's flag, and people gather around the fires and sing hymns to the Virgin Mary, patron saint of Poland: "in ganz Westpreußen boten . . . Sägemühlen und Holzfelder den Zunder für zweifarbig aufflackernde Nationalgefühle" (26) (" . . . throughout West Prussia . . . sawmills and woodlots provided fuel for a blazing bicolored national sentiment" [28]). Later, when he is recognized as the Polish firebug, he disappears under a raft of logs in Danzig Harbor. Various versions of his fate persist, but Oskar's denouement of choice is that the indomitable Kashubian escaped to Buffalo, where he made a fortune in lumber and matches, and surrounded himself with the Polish-singing Phoenix Guard, named after the legendary bird that rises from its ashes.

Grandpa Koljaiczek is explicitly connected with Polish nationalism and anti-German activities, but Oskar makes it clear that he is, in fact, a Kashubian. Koljaiczek's first act of arson occurs after he is punished for painting a fence red and white. The sawmill master tears two boards from the fence and "zerschlug die polnischen Latten auf Koljaiczeks *Kaschubenrücken* zu soviel weißrotem Brennholz" (26; emphasis added) ("smashed the patriotic slats to tinder over Koljaiczek's *Kashubian back*" [27; emphasis added]). Koljaiczek, faced with the choice of loyalty to Poles or Germans, violently embraces the Slavs.

Similarly Jan—like Oskar's mother, Agnes, a child of the oft-evoked Kashubian potato fields—exhibits ambivalent identities. Oskar describes Jan in terms that could be applied equally to the Kashubians between their powerful neighbors: "So klein und gefährdet . . . zwischen den Gesunden und Platzeinnehmenden . . . " (63) ("small and frail amid these robust occupiers of space" [55]). As tensions in Danzig grow, he takes a public stance and seals his fate by choosing to work at the Polish Post Office. Jan becomes a Polish citizen and sends his son to a Polish school (after his son was kicked out of a German day-care center and Oskar left in solidarity with him). Jan's decisions seem consistent with his identification with Poland. When Oskar forces him to return to the post office, one expects him to accept the role of defender and resister. But though he has rejected what the Germans stand for, he does not want to endanger himself for the Poles. During the heroic defense of the post office, he hides in the mail room, and his death at the hands of a German firing squad is an accident, the result of Oskar's egotistical betrayal.

Agnes, caught in the love triangle between the German Matzerath and the voluntary Pole Jan, likewise faces an either-or. Though she follows Markus's advice and "bets on the Germans," she is opposed to Matzerath's involvement in the party and resists his purchasing the "kackbraunen Reithosen und Stiefel" (146) ("the shitbrown riding breeches and high boots" [116]). Agnes could be compared to Danzig itself, courted by both Germany and Poland, playing along with both, ultimately destroyed in the struggle.

The position of the Kashubians between nationalistic Poles and anti-Slavic Germans is best expressed in Anna Koljaiczek's soliloquy at Oskar's bedside after Matzerath's death. Earthy Grandma Anna is a symbol of warmth and safety, the opposite of the terrifying Black Cook. Oskar continually longs to return to the protection of Anna's skirts, which are in turn always associated with the Kashubian potato fields. Anna understands that the Kashubians are caught between two hostile forces. She says:

> So isses nu mal mit de Kaschuben, Oskarchen. Die trefft es immer am Kopp. . . . [W]eil unserains nich richtich polnisch is und nich richtig deitsch jenug, und wenn man Kaschub is, das raicht weder de Deitschen noch de Pollacken. (547)

> Yes, Oskar, that's how it is with the Kashubes. They always get hit on the head. . . . [B]ecause we're not real Poles and we're not real Germans, and if you're a Kashube, you're not good enough for the Germans or the Polacks. (416)

The historical expansionism of the Poles cannot compare with the criminal acts of the Nazis, but for those who recognize themselves as outsiders and targets, either choice is dangerous and ultimately futile, since the powerful are not prepared to accept them anyway. Significantly, Anna's monologue causes Oskar, for the only time in the novel, to address her in Polish as *babka* (548; "grandmother"). But his admission of his Slavicness comes too late: Anna leaves him behind, and the next paragraph foreshadows a turning point in his life: "Anfang Juni fuhren die ersten Transporte in Richtung Westen" (548) ("At the beginning of June the first convoys left for the West" [416]). Against the backdrop of the scene with his grandmother, Oskar's turn westward reflects all that he is losing and that he was unwilling to embrace before.

The approach to *The Tin Drum* outlined here can make the book accessible to students in several new ways. It focuses on duality, a key structural element, but also on outsiders who are forced to choose between two unacceptable options. It emphasizes Danzig's location at the intersection of two cultures and Grass's own roots in those cultures. It emphasizes resistance, an important historical element that broadens the scope of the Third Reich theme. By examining major characters simultaneously as outsiders, resisters, and people with ties to the east, readers can gain striking insights into the world of *The Tin Drum* and proceed to Grass's other works armed with a new way of reading.

NOTES

[1] The original German titles, with the German and American translation dates of first publication, for these works are Brecht's *Furcht und Elend des Dritten Reiches* (1957; 1983), Seghers's *Das siebte Kreuz* (1942; 1987), Böll's *Billard um halbzehn* (1962; 1975), Bienek's *Die erste Polka* (1975; 1978), Becker's *Jakob der Lügner* (1969; 1990), Wolf's *Kindheitsmuster* (1976; 1980), Lenz's *Deutschstunde* (1968; 1971) and *Heimatmuseum* (1978; 1981), and Zuckmayer's *Als wär's ein Stück von mir* (1966; 1970).

[2] All translations except from *Die Blechtrommel* are mine unless otherwise noted.

[3] Ralph Manheim's translation of *The Tin Drum* is not always dependable. A case in point is the fugue on the Polish national anthem (in Polish, "Jeszcze Polska nie zginęła"), which fails to convey Grass's intricate incantatory prose. Manheim translates "Verloren, noch nicht verloren, schon wieder verloren, an wen verloren, bald verloren, bereits verloren, Polen verloren, alles verloren, noch ist Polen nicht verloren" (135) (literally, "Lost, not yet lost, lost yet again, lost to whom, soon to be lost, Poland is lost, all is lost, already lost, Poland is not yet lost") as "Poland's lost, but not forever, all's lost, but not forever, Poland's not lost forever" (108). Not only does he gratuitously add "not forever" but also his omission of some of Oskar's phrases mutes the implied threats and weakens the importance of Poland for Oskar by omitting his quotation ("Polen verloren, alles verloren").

"Even Wallpaper Has a
Better Memory Than Ours":
Personal and Public Memory in *The Tin Drum*

Timothy B. Malchow

Oskar Matzerath both fascinated and baffled me when I was a student in Robert Warde's memorable course The Novel at Macalester College. From my undergraduate perspective, Oskar was a sort of Teutonic Johnny Rotten. Much like the punk-rock icon and lead singer of the Sex Pistols, Oskar embodied a shrieking irreverence, a taboo-breaking assault on bourgeois sensibilities, and an agonized mix of condescension and arrested development. But what exactly did this character have to do with Nazi Germany, that pathos-filled period I knew through Hollywood films like *Sophie's Choice*, the *Holocaust* television miniseries, and childhood readings of Anne Frank? Especially perplexing was that Oskar, a witness to the historically momentous rise and fall of the Third Reich, had memories focusing on such seemingly arbitrary objects as a toy drum, nurses' uniforms, a severed finger, and a character from a children's song.

Students reading *The Tin Drum* for the first time may need help in coming to terms with the apparent disjunction between Oskar's bizarre personal memories and public memory of the historical period reflected in the narrative. They will also likely require information about how Germans in the 1950s, when Grass wrote the novel, remembered the Nazi past. This essay focuses on guiding students through an investigation of Oskar's distinctive mode of remembering and its relation to 1950s West German public discourse about the Nazi era. The suggested approach should work in a variety of settings, as long as students have the linguistic proficiency necessary for close reading, analysis, and comparison of specific passages. Thus, in the American context, appropriate venues might be undergraduate or advanced secondary literature courses in which the novel is read in English translation as well as courses for graduate or advanced undergraduate students capable of reading the German original. Students should have regular reading assignments and be encouraged in student-centered discussions to develop individual and collective readings of the text. The instructor's role might be to help identify important themes and related passages, pose leading questions, and provide missing information. The questions listed in this essay in conjunction with specific passages may be utilized as written homework, small group work, the basis for whole class discussion, or any combination of these assignments. It is understood that the theme of personal and public memory is one focus among many as students read the novel.

As an exemplary and extremely influential work exploring the tensions between personal and public memory of the Nazi era, *The Tin Drum* surely belongs in a course titled Literature and Memory of the Nazi Past. This topic has been, inevitably, a central concern of German-language authors over the past half century. The broad range of relevant texts, many of which are available in translation, includes documentary dramas, such as Peter Weiss's *Die Ermittlung* (1965; *The Investigation* [1966]); novels exploring the intricacies of remembering and narrating, such as Christa Wolf's *Kindheitsmuster* (1976; *Patterns of Childhood* [1984]) or Jurek Becker's *Jakob der Lügner* (1969; *Jacob the Liar* [1975]); dramas concerned with continuity between the Nazi past and the postwar present, such as Thomas Bernhard's *Vor dem Ruhestand* (1979; *Eve of Retirement* [1979]); memoirs, such as Ruth Klüger's *Weiter leben: Eine Jugend* (1992; *Still Alive: A Holocaust Girlhood Remembered* [2001]); and prose representing a younger generation's struggle to comprehend the legacy of the past, such as Uwe Timm's *Am Beispiel meines Bruders* (2003; *In My Brother's Shadow: A Life and Death in the SS* [2005]). Finally, Grass's own *Im Krebsgang* (2002; *Crabwalk* [2003]) explores the changing status of memory in the new millennium, a point to which I return.

Memory is a central theme of *The Tin Drum*. The narrative, after all, covers the historical period between 1899 and the 1950s, its main characters moving eventually from the potato fields near Danzig to West Germany. Yet in a narrower sense, the novel is set in a West German mental institution between 1952 and 1954. Everything else is conjured up through the act of remembering, to which the first-person narrator, Oskar, repeatedly draws attention. As students begin to read the novel, it will be helpful to point out that the first few pages establish the asylum cell as the site of remembering and that nearly every chapter of the first book either begins or ends there. Once aware of the important tension between the remembered past and the present of the narration, students should be able to identify numerous passages in which memory is a theme.

Oskar's viewpoint determines how he remembers. Having rejected the "Welt der Erwachsenen" (71) ("grownup world" [60]), he emphasizes aspects of his perspective that set him apart from it. His allegedly complete "geistige Entwicklung" (52) ("mental development" [47]) at birth resembles that of a young child. His narrative focuses on sensory perceptions, such as visual impressions and smells, and highlights random associations and resemblances among things. Generally oblivious to abstractions and causal relations, his narrative viewpoint treats his sensory perceptions and mental activities so literally that a personification of objects and body parts, bordering on the animistic, predominates. Indeed, his perspective involves an "Entäußerung des Psychischen in die Dinge" (Just 119) ("externalization of what is psychological into the realm of things" [trans. mine]). Thus, he attributes his memories to the objects in his environment: "Heute weiß ich, daß alles zuguckt, daß nichts unbesehen bleibt, daß selbst Tapeten ein besseres Gedächtnis als die Menschen haben" (247) ("Today I know that everything watches, that nothing goes unseen, and that even wallpaper has a better memory than ours" [192]). This passage continues with a list of miscellaneous objects that might bear witness to the past. Because Oskar attributes memory to objects outside of himself, and because he is subject to incessant sensory perceptions of the objects in his environment, memory is an irrepressible onslaught for him. All his senses are so involved in memory that it is an overwhelming corporeal experience through which the events of the past are perceived in the present.

To facilitate the analysis of this mode of memory, the instructor could provide information about Grass's aesthetics as students approach the end of book 1, in which they will encounter not only the personified objects mentioned above but also Agnes Matzerath's remembering organs (207; 161) and the remembering scars on Herbert Truczinski's back (230; 179). The notion that objects themselves have a compelling power is related to the aesthetic principle of *Gegenständlichkeit* ("concreteness"), which Grass learned while studying art under the sculptor Karl Hartung in Berlin during the mid-1950s. At the root of this term is *Gegenstand*, the German word for "object." As Grass remembers, Hartung advocated principles for practicing artists such as "[h]ingucken, nicht auswendig fummeln" ("look, don't fiddle about from memory") and "[l]ieber etwas totarbeiten, als eine Scheinlebendigkeit auf Podesten zur Schau stellen" (qtd. in Neuhaus, *Schreiben* 53) ("better to work something to death than to display the semblance of life on a pedestal" [trans. mine]). Viewed this way, good art is handiwork in which details have precedence over abstractions.

In *The Tin Drum*, seemingly tangential details are central to the memories that Oskar obsessively recounts. The narrative highlights his childlike perspective and avoids a treatise on the politics of memory even though Grass clearly objected to many of the ways in which West Germans referred to the Nazi era during the 1950s. In fact, he has spoken out against the use of overtly political discourse in literature: "Die Dinge müssen sich darstellen: Es ist die Aufgabe des schreibenden Künstlers, daß er auf seine Mittel vertraut und mit dem deutenden Fingerzeug möglichst sparsam umgeht" (Grass and Zimmermann 70) ("Things must represent themselves: it is the writing artist's task to trust in his means and to point his finger as sparingly as possible" [trans. mine]). Moreover, Grass believes there is a direct connection between the power of objects to represent themselves and his attempt to counteract the repression of memory of the Nazi era specifically. Referring to his initial interest in concreteness, he states:

> Es ging auch um das Wahrnehmen oder Übersehen der Wirklichkeit in einem Land, das geschlagen, geteilt war, dessen zu verantwortende Last Völkermord hieß und das dennoch oder deshalb im Begriff war, alles zu verdrängen, ich sage, gegenstandslos zu machen, was die Vergangenheit heraufbeschwören und die Flucht nach vorne behindern konnte.
>
> (qtd. in Neuhaus, *Schreiben* 54)

> It was also a matter of perceiving or overlooking reality in a country that was defeated, divided, and burdened by the responsibility for genocide and that was nonetheless, or therefore, poised to repress everything, I say, to render everything irrelevant [literally, "objectless"] that could conjure up the past and prevent the flight forward.   (trans. mine)

Grass's ongoing conviction that objects can elicit a confrontation with the past is evident in how he referred to the memory of the Shoah three decades after the publication of *The Tin Drum*:

> Das wird nie aufhören, gegenwärtig zu bleiben; unsere Schande wird sich weder verdrängen noch bewältigen lassen; die zwingende Gegenständlichkeit dieser Fotos—die Schuhe, die Brillen, Haare, die Leichen—verweigert sich der Abstraktion; Auschwitz wird, obgleich umdrängt von erklärenden Wörtern, nie zu begreifen sein.   ("Schreiben" 236)

> That will never stop being present. Our disgrace can be neither repressed nor overcome. The compelling concreteness of these photographs—the shoes, the glasses, hair, the corpses—resists abstraction. Though surrounded by words of explanation, Auschwitz can never be comprehended.
>
> (trans. mine)

Here, as with Oskar's perspective in *The Tin Drum*, the distinction between the past and the present is obliterated by the power of images and objects. There is an indefinable remainder, an ineffable quality, to the central trauma that Germans experience when confronted with the past through the presence of objects. Words cannot capture it. Once equipped with an understanding of Grass's interest in how objects convey what words cannot, students will be in a better position to investigate Oskar's narrative and the ultimate loss for words in which it culminates.

Book 2 contains ample opportunities for students to analyze Oskar's corporeal mode of memory more closely. These include his sexual encounter with Maria at the beach (346–49; 267–69) and his discovery of the hanging body of the greengrocer Greff (412; 315). Both passages illustrate that selective memory is impossible for Oskar. In the former, he does not locate sexual desire within himself, as a subjective response to external stimuli, but rather experiences it as a force exerted by objects and body parts in the world, which bring about disconcerting and alienating reactions in his body. Sexual compulsion acts in concert with memory, forcing him to experience things that, by association, prevent the repression of the past. The latter passage reveals that Oskar experiences his memories, even in the postwar present, as a physical sensation. Traces of the past persist in the present and cause specific pains in his body. These are inescapable because even the slightest association, such as the mention of hanging laundry, can evoke them.

Students could compare these two passages and consider what they have in common and what they show about how Oskar remembers. Some helpful questions might be, What forces Oskar finally to remember what he would rather forget in the first passage? What role do the senses play in this memory? What does the passage imply about his ability to repress unpleasant aspects of his past? Why does he begin the second passage by describing Greff's hanging body but end by referring to his own body? In both passages, what is the connection between Oskar's memories and his body? What other passages in the novel imply such a connection? This discussion should help students recognize that Oskar's memories are triggered by sensory perceptions and entirely irrepressible, especially when he would prefer to forget them.

By the time students read in book 3 about Oskar's stay in a clothes cupboard in Sister Dorothea's room in postwar Düsseldorf, they should be conversant with his corporeal mode of memory (647–53; 492–97). Here, while fleeing from a personified lightbulb, Oskar sees a belt that evokes an irrepressible string of associations. When he attempts to vanquish the unpleasant memories by focusing his mind on Dorothea and masturbating, the force of this activity expels him from the cupboard, thus thwarting his attempt to find refuge. A fruitful exercise could involve asking the students, Does this passage seem to refer directly to any others? Does it remind you of others? Which ones and why? How do objects mentioned here—such as the black belt, the lightbulb, the cupboard, or the Red Cross pin—connect this passage to others in the novel? How does this passage typify Oskar's mode of memory?

With some prompting from the instructor and time to develop their ideas, students should be able to link the postwar cupboard passage meaningfully to several other moments in the novel. The most obvious connection is to the grotesque description of eels emerging from a severed horse's head on Good Friday, 1939, to which the narrative compares Dorothea's black belt directly (190–93; 148–51). Also, Oskar's failed attempt to repress his guilty memories sensually and sexually evokes the aforementioned encounter with Maria (346–49; 267–69). Furthermore, the lightbulb that Oskar sees on falling out of the cupboard suggests the lightbulbs present at his birth, establishing the cupboard unequivocally as a surrogate womb (52–55; 47–49). If reminded that Oskar describes his goal as "die Rückkehr zur Nabelschnur" (229) ("to get back to the umbilical cord" [179]), students may be able to list other places where Oskar has sought a return to the womb (see Ludden's essay in this volume). An important one is the space beneath the four skirts of his grandmother, Anna, with whom he associates an elusive return to his origins and the ability to forget (159–60; 125) (275–76; 215) (459–60; 350). Indeed, Anna emerges as a central agent of the idiosyncratic cosmology that Oskar creates around his longing to escape from traumatic memory. Her polar opposite in this cosmology is the *Schwarze Köchin* or Black Witch (776; 586), whom Oskar mentions in the cupboard passage (650; 494) and whom he finally characterizes in the novel's last scenes as the hidden force behind everything that he has experienced (778; 588). The Black Witch personifies the central feature of his memory, his subjection to an overwhelming and inescapable sense of guilt and trauma. A discussion of the cupboard as one of many places of refuge from which he is invariably expelled while attempting to escape his memories will help students understand the significance of the opposition between Anna and the Black Witch as it develops in book 3.

A central passage to include in the postwar cupboard discussion is the account of Oskar's first stay in a cupboard on Good Friday, 1939 (199–204; 155–59). Here, Oskar is overwhelmed by the afternoon's traumatic events, including his mother's vomiting at the sight of a man catching eels and the ensuing family argument after Matzerath has bought and cooked them. Oskar seeks solace by climbing into a bedroom cupboard in his family apartment and focusing on remembered impressions, including smells and colors, which he associates with the nurse Inge. As in both the postwar cupboard passage and the sexual encounter with Maria, he cannot control the flow of associations. Instead the personified images are in control, finally metamorphosing into the frightening Black Witch and denying Oskar the comfort he has sought. The similarity between the eels and Dorothea's belt provides a link between the events of Good Friday, 1939, and the postwar passage, and Oskar describes this directly. The red crosses and cupboards mentioned in both passages also imply an unexamined connection, casting the latter passage as an unconscious and compulsive reenactment of the former one.

The revisiting of the first cupboard passage (199–204; 155–59) will help introduce the question of the relation between memories and narration, which becomes increasingly important in book 3. To this end, students might focus on Oskar's failure to recall the elusive hue of Inge's comforting Red Cross outfit, which has grown in his imagination:

> bis ein die ganze Sicht bewohnendes Rot einer Leidenschaft Hintergrund bot, die mir damals wie heute zwar selbstverständlich aber dennoch nicht zu benennen ist, weil mit dem Wörtchen rot nichts gesagt ist, und Nasenbluten tut's nicht, und Fahnenstoff verfärbt sich, und wenn ich trotzdem nur rot sage, will rot mich nicht, läßt seinen Mantel wenden: schwarz, die Köchin kommt, schwarz, schreckt mich gelb . . .   (200)

> until a red occupying my entire field of vision provided the background for a passion which then as now was self-evident but not to be named, because the little word "red" says nothing, and nosebleed won't do it, and flag cloth fades, and if I nonetheless say "red," red spurns me, turns its coat to black. Black is the Witch, black scares me green . . .   (156)[1]

Oskar links the refuge he seeks, both in the remembered past and in the narrative present, to a visual impression that can be captured neither in words nor in images. To help students understand this passage and relate it to the rest of the novel, the instructor might ask, What does this passage imply about the relation between memory and words? Does memory operate apart from language for Oskar? Does Oskar express frustration with words or suspicion of them in other passages? Such questions could lead to a discussion of how Oskar implies from the beginning that the written words of his narrative are somehow attributable to his personified tin drum, without which he would be "ein armer

Mensch ohne nachweisliche Großeltern" (23) ("a poor bastard with nothing to say for my grandparents" [25]). In another passage, he accuses his pen of lying and proceeds to correct what it has said (318; 246). In general, the narrative of the novel presents itself as something secondary, as a mediated expression of the more primary sensations that make up his corporeal memories. His growing suspicion of words culminates in the novel's final passage, where he implicates language itself—"[a]ll words"—as the realm of the Black Witch, declaring, "[Oskar] hat keine Worte mehr" (779) ("Words fail me" [588, 589]). Significantly, in this final passage, Oskar again relates cupboards to the Black Witch. When the narrative ends in fragments, these include a reference to the first cupboard passage: "Wort, Mantel wenden ließ, Schwarz" (779) ("[B]lack words, black coat" [589]). Students will be better able to appreciate the novel's climax if, in the context of the postwar cupboard passage, they begin to discuss the relations among Oskar's corporeal memories, his futile attempts at evading memory, the slippery nature of language and narrative, and how his grandmother and the Black Witch become manifestations of these themes in his imagination.

The novel's skepticism toward language extends also to moments in which the narrative satirizes 1950s West German discourse about the Nazi past. The satire suggests a more sophisticated analysis of postwar society than Oskar evinces elsewhere, so one might read these passages as ironic insertions by the text's implied author. To help students identify and analyze such satirical moments, it will be useful to provide some background about the early 1950s in the Federal Republic of Germany. Relevant historical studies are Jeffrey Herf's *Divided Memory: The Nazi Past in the Two Germanys* (1997; esp. ch. 8) and Robert G. Moeller's *War Stories: The Search for a Usable Past in the Federal Republic of Germany* (2001). During this period, the policies of the chancellor Konrad Adenauer reflected a desire to downplay the role of everyday Germans in Nazism, to seek amnesty for Nazis, and to "leave the Nazi past in the past rather than to seek justice for Nazi crimes" (Herf 275). Adenauer's rhetoric of "totalitarianism" drew parallels between the Soviets and the Nazis, enabling Adenauer to advocate integrating former Nazis quickly into West German society as a bulwark against the Soviet threat (297–300). Polls conducted in 1952 indicate that fifty-eight percent of West Germans "approved unrestricted opportunities for former members of the Nazi Party" (274). Grass clearly sympathized with the oppositional German Social Democratic Party (SPD), which promoted more open discussion of the past and judicial action against Nazi war criminals.

Reference to former Nazis in public life, and to the rhetoric that enabled this development, appears at the end of book 1, in the chapter "Glaube Hoffnung Liebe" ("Faith, Hope, Love"). Having compared the Germans' earlier acceptance of the Nazis to a childish belief in Santa Claus, Oskar suggests continuity between the Third Reich and the Adenauer era by proclaiming, "[I]ch weiß zum Beispiel nicht, wer sich heute unter den Bärten der Weihnachtsmänner versteckt . . . " (263) ("I don't know, for example, who it is nowadays that hides under the beards of the Santa Clauses . . . " [204]). The subsequent image of

West German butchers selling sausages alludes allegorically to public servants with dubious pasts and to politically motivated postwar narratives about the Nazi era. These sausages are filled with the flesh of unnamed victims and with words from unidentified dictionaries. Oskar suspects:

> Es sind dieselben Metzger, die Wörterbücher und Därme mit Sprache und Wurst füllen, es gibt keinen Paulus, der Mann hieß Saulus und war ein Saulus und erzählte als Saulus den Leuten aus Korinth etwas von ungeheuer preiswerten Würsten, die er Glaube, Hoffnung und Liebe nannte, als leicht verdaulich pries, die er heute noch, in immer wechselnder Saulusgestalt, an den Mann bringt. (264)

> It is the same butchers who fill dictionaries and sausage casings with language and sausage, there is no Paul, the man's name was Saul and a Saul he was, and it was Saul who told the people of Corinth something about some priceless sausages that he called faith, hope, and love, which he advertised as easily digestible and which to this very day, still Saul though forever changing in form, he palms off on mankind. (205)

Postwar producers of rhetoric are equated with dishonest butchers, and both are presented in the guise of a hypocritical Saint Paul. By implication, the passage conflates the conversion of Saint Paul on the road to Damascus and the alleged change of heart of Nazi war criminals who were integrated into postwar society. Oskar's suspicion of both also acts as an indictment of the Church's protection of Nazis after the war. In fact, Protestant and Catholic religious leaders actively attempted to prevent war crime trials at the beginning of the Adenauer era (Herf 294).

Early West German discourse often referred to 1945 as *Stunde Null* ("zero hour"), implying a clean break with the past at the end of World War II. When Oskar discusses the function of the Pauline concept of hope in postwar Germany, it has been reduced to the desire for such a new beginning, requiring no understanding of what happened, as though the Nazi era were a historic interruption that could be likened to a few hours spent at the cinema. It is a hope, "daß bald Schluß sei, damit sie neu anfangen konnten oder fortfahren, nach der Schlußmusik oder schon während der Schlußmusik hoffend, daß bald Schluß sei mit dem Schluß. Und wußten immer noch nicht, womit Schluß" (263) ("that it would soon be over, so they might begin afresh or continue, hoping after or even during the finale that the end would soon be over. The end of what? They still did not know" [204]). Earlier in book 1, the narrative also refers ironically to *innere Emigration* ("inner emigration" or, in Manheim's translation, "psychic emigration"), an exonerating term for the silence and withdrawal from politics of some intellectuals who remained in Germany during the Nazi era (157; 124).

As students read about the postwar era in book 3, it will be important to explain that the discursive construct of *Vergangenheitsbewältigung* ("mastery of the past") "constituted a, and in many distinguished cases *the*, central preoccupation of postwar German intellectual, journalistic, literary, cinematic, theological, legal, and scholarly engagement" (Herf 8). Grass, however, has always dismissed the idea that the Nazi past could somehow be retroactively overcome. This position is evident in his comments from an interview in the late 1990s: "Mittlerweile hat sich herausgestellt, daß die Vergangenheit nicht zu bewältigen ist" (Grass and Zimmermann 46) ("In the meantime, it has turned out that the past cannot be mastered" [trans. mine]). In a satirical passage in book 3, Protestants and Catholics discuss their collective guilt after the war in the hopes of banishing it once and for all: "Machen wir es jetzt ab, dann haben wir es hinter uns und brauchen später, wenn es wieder aufwärtsgeht, kein schlechtes Gewissen mehr zu haben" (570) ("Let's do our stint now; when things begin to look up we'll have it over with and our consciences will be all right" [436]). Further satirical references to mastery of the past, which students might compare, are the postwar discussion of whether the war era is now "passé" between the guilty former soldiers Lankes and Herzog (718; 544) and Oskar's postwar encounter with two men attempting to carry out a defunct execution order stemming from the Nazi era (757; 573).

But such moments in the narrative are overshadowed by Oskar's references to his personal memories and traumas. The narrative appears generally to draw attention away from abstract and reductive discourse about the past, perhaps prompting postwar German readers to remember the Nazi era as they experienced it personally. Oskar provides no alternative interpretations of recent history and its implications. Rather, his viewpoint resists attempts at historical closure and presents memory as recurrent and uncontainable. While political and historical discourses restrain memory, Oskar's perspective emphasizes the excesses of memory and points toward an unresolved trauma underlying the lives of people in postwar West Germany. His voice, that of an outsider locked away in a mental institution, focuses on aspects of memory that his society has chosen to repress.

Once students have finished reading the novel, they might discuss and finally write about whether they see any connection between the satirical passages, in which the implied author appears to mock West German public discourse about the Nazi era, and the moments in which Oskar is unable to repress his own past or remember it selectively. It will be useful to remind students both of Grass's rejection of Adenauer-era rhetoric and of his conviction that objects can convey more than words. Students might be encouraged to explore questions such as, What does Oskar's perspective imply about the connections between language and memory? Does the narrative appear to valorize a certain way of remembering the past? What does this valorization suggest to German readers who lived through the war about how to remember their pasts? Here students might consider how Oskar's narrative alludes vicariously to the specific, unmediated, and repressed memories of the novel's original readers.

One could also draw students' attention to the problems involved in writing about the Nazi past in this object-centered way. If representing memory in language is so fraught with peril, how can a novel convey what is essential about the past? Does *The Tin Drum* add something to our understanding of Nazism that historical or political writing could not? What does the narrative itself imply about this possibility? In the novel, Oskar's drumming appears to be a fantastic artistic medium that magically solves all the problems surrounding the representation of the past; it is "eine mimetische Kunst und vergegenwärtigt Vergangenes in seiner Totalität" (Neuhaus, *Günter Grass* [1993] 37) ("a mimetic artform and makes what is past present in its totality" [trans. mine]). This power is most evident in Oskar's drumming performance in the Onion Cellar, through which he transforms his postwar audience into the bawling infants they once were (703–06; 533–35). If drumming is read as an allegory for postwar artworks in general, including novels, this passage appears hopeful about art's ability to conjure a repressed past. But does the novel not also imply that where such drumming succeeds, language must fail? Through Oskar's corporeal memories, the novel ultimately points to a sensory realm outside language as the terrain for resistance to the dominant political discourses of the Adenauer era, but by implication it questions the very ability of the medium of literature, with its reliance on language, to evoke this realm. Students should be encouraged to formulate their own ideas about how the narrative explores this problem and whether the problem is resolved.

Finally, it would be a useful exercise to compare the representation of memory in *The Tin Drum* with its manifestation in Grass's novella *Im Krebsgang* (2002; *Crabwalk* [2003]), which appeared forty-three years later. In *Crabwalk*, Grass weighs in on the debate surrounding the literary representation of specifically German suffering during World War II. This debate was sparked in part by the 1999 publication of W. G. Sebald's *Luftkrieg und Literatur* ("Air War and Literature") essays, which appear in English translation in the volume *On the Natural History of Destruction*. Without mentioning Grass by name, Sebald, born in 1944, chastises his generation of authors, as those entrusted with maintaining the nation's collective memory, for failing to represent adequately the horror experienced by German victims of the Allied bombings in World War II.

Crabwalk focuses on the memory of the 1945 Soviet attack on the *Wilhelm Gustloff*, a German ship bearing thousands of civilians, and thus shares Sebald's thematic concern with the representation of German war victims' experiences. An autobiographically based character pressures the middle-aged narrator to write about the maritime atrocity. The narrator resists, however, feeling that such horror cannot be put into language: "Was aber im Schiffsinneren geschah, ist mit Worten nicht zu fassen" (144) ("But what took place inside the ship cannot be captured in words" [136]). Much of the narrative refers to extant representations of the events surrounding the sinking of the ship, and this proliferation of discourse is involved when the narrator's estranged son murders another young man. A helpful discussion of the relation between Adenauer-era discourse and *Crabwalk* appears in Robert Moeller's "Sinking Ships, the Lost Heimat, and Broken Taboos." Far from fulfilling Sebald's call for a literary representation of German wartime suffering, *Crabwalk* emphasizes that discourse on the past and the meanings that are brought to it are unavoidably implicated in contemporary acts of violence.

Grass's later text lacks both *The Tin Drum*'s playfully satirical overtones and its appeal to an extradiscursive, personal memory. Of course, most of the original German readers of *The Tin Drum* had personal memories of the Nazi era. By contrast, most readers of *Crabwalk* can encounter this past only in a mediated way, through texts in the broadest sense or, as Marianne Hirsch has put it, through "postmemory." Nonetheless, as students explore the two texts' varied treatments of personal and public memory, Grass's sustained concern with both the inevitability and the insufficiency of representing memory in language will be evident. Despite the books' differences, the narrator in each is unable to formulate definitive conclusions about a wartime past that haunts him, and he portrays a contemporary social reality in which others use facile narrative versions of that past for their own troubling ends.

NOTES

Funding for some of the research informing this study was provided through a doctoral dissertation fellowship from the Graduate School of the University of Minnesota (2001–02).

[1] Although "schreckt mich gelb" means literally "scares me yellow," Manheim chose to translate the color as "green" here. Whereas *yellow* in English connotes cowardice, *gelb* in German does not. Manheim's choice of "green" avoids this idiomatic sense and conveys that Oskar actually turns pale from fear.

"Five Hundred Sheets of Writing Paper":
Getting Your Students Ready for the Big Book
Irene Kacandes

> This is what Grass's great novel said to me in its
> drumbeats: Go for broke. Always try and do too much.
> Dispense with safety nets. Take a deep breath before
> you begin talking. Aim for the stars. Keep grinning. Be
> bloody-minded. Argue with the world. And never forget
> that writing is as close as we get to keeping a hold on the
> thousand and one things—childhood, certainties, cities,
> doubts, dreams, instants, phrases, parents, loves—that go
> on slipping, like sand, through our fingers. I have tried to
> learn the lessons of the midget drummer. And one more,
> which I got from that other, immense work, *Dog Years*:
> When you've done it once, start all over again and do it
> better.
>
> —Salman Rushdie

Günter Grass's *The Tin Drum* is a very long book: just under six hundred pages
in the current Vintage paperback edition of the Ralph Manheim English translation and just under eight hundred pages in its current German dtv paperback
edition. The novel's heft at least measures up to some other major German
twentieth-century novels, like Thomas Mann's *The Magic Mountain* (777 pages
in its original 1924 edition) and Alfred Döblin's *Berlin Alexanderplatz* (about
600 pages, 1929). Grass's narrator himself, Oskar Matzerath, makes an issue of

size in the opening chapter, reporting to his readers that Bruno Münsterberg, his "Pfleger" (9) ("keeper" [15]) in the mental hospital, has brought him

> fünfhundert Blatt Schreibpapier. Bruno . . . wird, sollte der Vorrat nicht reichen, die kleine Schreibwarenhandlung, in der auch Kinderspielzeug verkauft wird, noch einmal aufsuchen und mir den notwendigen unlinier-ten Platz für mein hoffentlich genaues Erinnerungsvermögen beschaffen. (10–11)

> five hundred sheets of writing paper. . . . Should this supply prove insuf-ficient, Bruno . . . will go to the little stationery store that also sells toys, and get me some more of the unlined space I need for the recording of my memories. (16)

The resulting "too much" of *The Tin Drum* is something that is likely to impress our students, as it impressed and inspired Salman Rushdie, among others.

The potential problem is that my students, whether enrolled in the courses I teach in English for the comparative literature program or in the courses I teach in German for the Department of German Studies, are less and less likely to have read many serious, long novels. They often have read and loved fat books like Tolkien's *Lord of the Rings* trilogy (1956) or Rowling's Harry Potter series. But when I conduct surveys of what titles we all have read, I discover that among the books that everyone knows there is almost never a long novel. So one of the many missions I set myself is not only to nudge the students along in reading by assigning many works of literature in most of my classes but also to make sure that students read at least one very long, excellent novel.

To best ensure they have a good experience with that lengthy novel, I find that I must be particularly attentive to what point in the academic term they will read the book, so that they do not feel overburdened by the sheer number of pages they have to get through (i.e., the reading should not be too close to midterms or finals). I find, too, that I must get them excited about the prospect of reading the novel in question by making sure that they have certain themes, narrative strategies, and possible plot developments in mind from the outset. I do this primarily through what I call the title exercise but what could more accurately be described as a study of the novel's paratext, in Gérard Genette's sense of those parts of the book that surround the main text: the title, other in-formation and graphics on the cover and title page, the dedication, the table of contents, blurbs that may precede or follow the text, and so on (*Paratexts*). In this warm-up exercise, we also read the first sentence and the first paragraph. In this essay, I outline how I would do this exercise for Grass's *The Tin Drum* in one of my comparative literature classes—that is to say, were I to teach it in English translation for a general class in twentieth-century prose fiction. (I have not had the privilege of teaching *The Tin Drum* in English or German, though I do teach many long novels in English translation, and I have taught the second part of *The Danzig Trilogy*, Grass's novella *Katz und Maus* [1961; *Cat and Mouse*] numerous times in English and German. I use this exercise in almost all the courses I teach.) The professor can easily influence how the exercise unfolds, emphasizing points that may be relevant to a specific course context different from the general one I am presuming here.

The main idea of this exercise is to engender confidence and curiosity, by getting the students to make associations between the book and things they already know. I move the exercise forward by drawing students' attention sequentially to specific cues in the paratext and the book's opening. Occasionally, I offer important connections that they may have missed. I sometimes need to introduce certain literary or narratological terms to make my point. (For instance, the first time in the term we do this exercise, I need to introduce the term *paratext*.) I try to keep my interventions to a minimum, because again, this exercise is to help students realize that they already possess resources for decoding the text.

Since having enough time for all students to contribute is a key element for success, I try to schedule an entire class period for the title exercise. Typically, I conduct it on the first day, before I lecture on the novel or give introductory remarks. Students should have already begun the novel but are not likely to have finished it. I assign the first hundred pages or the entire first book, depending on how much time we have. We sit in a circle. I am near the blackboard to note the overall structure of the exercise, the ideas the students come up with, and the few selected terms I add to the discussion. For a work in translation, I usually come prepared with an edition of the original, and depending on possible helpful variations in the cover graphics, I may come with more than one edition of the translation as well. All students should have a copy of the text to consult during the discussion. My readers, too, may find it useful to have a copy of *The Tin Drum* next to them while perusing this essay.

We first consider the novel as a physical object. For *The Tin Drum*, this exercise is particularly helpful. I would have the students pick up the book in their hands and tell me what they notice. Size (length) is of course something they will mention right away, so I would ask them what they associate with long books. Many different things might come out here, depending on your students, but I would expect an answer like, Well, if it's long, it must relate a lot of things. I continue this line of thinking by asking what kinds of things can easily multiply in the telling of a story. I expect answers like "events," "characters," "places." The teacher might then make a few short comments about the epic form, the picaresque, German modernism and the *anti-Roman* (antinovel), and so on. Because my students would have already started to read the book, the word "generations" might come out in addition to events, and someone might mention that Oskar starts with his grandmother. At this point I might perhaps mention other novels that treat several generations from the perspective of one, and I might tell them that the story is even bigger than they think, as *The Tin Drum* is actually part of a trilogy.

We would then move to the visual aspects of the book, where I would again try to get the students to state the obvious: that there is an image on the front; writing on the front, spine, and back; no illustrations inside, just text—and a lot of it—divided into sections. I would then ask the students about the image and what they see: colors, shapes, design, and of course subject. The Vintage edition that teachers are likely to work with at present has a cover illustration by Angela Arnet rather than the original cover art by Grass, so I would hold up the German edition and ask students to compare it with the edition they are reading. The starting point may or may not be that both cover images depict a child with a drum. A student might add that this must be Oskar, the protagonist. Hopefully, something as obvious (and yet significant) as the child's blue eyes in the Grass image will be mentioned. We might discuss the crazed look on the child's face on the English translation or the child's open mouth in the Grass drawing. Someone may blurt out that Oskar is emitting the sound that will shatter glass. The red color of the drum and the inclusion of drumsticks are common to both. Again, depending on your overall course goals, you might pose a question or make a short statement about Grass's career, his interest in the visual arts, and the fact that he often created cover art for his literary works; or you might go in the very different direction of Nazism and racial stereotyping. While most students already know that the Aryan ideal included blue eyes, you might go so far as to explain the NSDAP's particular strategic choice of the color red to compete with the Communist Party during the Weimar period. In a more general and literary course, I would probably not add this specific a detail unless a student brought it up. I would ask about the four legs that are pictured on the cover of our American edition and about the effect of the overall design of each edition, drawing my students' attention to the font and layout; to how much or little other information is presented (e.g., the current American edition includes a gold circle informing the reader that Grass is the winner of the Nobel Prize in Literature); and to the fact that the background of the American edition is black, whereas for the German edition it is white. (One could use this last point as a springboard for raising the issue of the differences between reading this novel as an American in an American university versus reading it as a German in a German school or university. The black background of the American edition certainly sets a more ominous tone than does the neutral white of the German one.)

Especially when we are doing this exercise for the first time in the term, I emphasize that there are no correct answers. As readers, we respond to what we see, even if we do not always pause over things as we do here. At least once during the term, we have a brief discussion about blurbs or plot summaries on the back cover: some students read them, some skip them so as to form their own impressions. Again, I try to indicate that there is no right or wrong way to read but that it is worth noticing what habits we have acquired over the years and what their consequences might be. Thus you might ask your students, If you read on the back cover of the Vintage edition that this is "acclaimed as the greatest German novel written since the end of World War II," are you personally more likely to become motivated or skeptical?

Finally—as much as ten minutes may already have transpired—I would let the students move on to the text per se. I explain the concept of a semantic field, suggesting as an example that the words we associate with *child* are quite different from those we might group around *brat*. I might also throw out the words *dwarf* and *midget*, suggesting that these words, though related, may be considered part of different semantic fields. The students catch on quickly, and I now ask them to think about each word in the novel's title. For Grass's English translation, we would develop a semantic field for *tin*, *drum*, and *tin drum* separately. When I ask them to think only about *tin*, they may come up with *metal*, *steel*, *roof*, *ceiling*, *ear*, *poor*, *gray*; and for *drum*, perhaps *music*, *band*, *military band*, *drum set*, *drumstick*, *chicken*. It is important to the success of this exercise that you truly invite the students to spit out any association that comes to them, with no subtle messages that you are looking for certain kinds of words. We teachers can be overly eager to get to the point. But one purpose of this exercise is to help students develop confidence in reading in general and in reading serious literature in particular, by seeing that they already possess mental tools for that task.

When I ask what associations they make to *tin drum*, they might now volunteer things like *child*, *toy*, *fun*, *cheap*, *pathetic sound*, *irritating*, *tin soldier*, and so on. Not much explicit comment from me is needed for them to realize that different associations result when they think about two words separately or together. I do not need to tell them that an author chooses a title to put certain ideas out for the readers, though I might underscore this point by asking what difference it would have made to them if Grass had used the phrase "toy drum" instead of "tin drum." This question might lead to the story itself, if a student voices the idea that the associations we make with *toy drum* are usually less negative than those evoked by *tin drum*. Another student might suggest that *toy drum* ties us more closely to the world of childhood and innocence, whereas the unpleasant sound of a *tin drum* puts us more in mind of a child who might not be normal. I would also ask about the implications of using the definite instead of indefinite article. With an advanced class or in a course foregrounding narrative theory, I might use this question as a bridge to a short discussion on narrative perspective. For whom is this drum *the* tin drum?

In a discussion about titles in general, one could elicit comments about Grass's choice to name the book after an object rather than the protagonist. In a course on the German novel, I might offer a connection myself to Alfred Döblin's provocative naming of his great novel after a subway stop. I could tell students about Grass's admiration for Döblin (see Kontje's essay in this volume). Someone should notice too that the title foregrounds the sense of sound, for a novel in which all the senses are emphasized. I might prompt students in the class with knowledge of German to comment on the German title: *Die Blechtrommel*. They might observe that German nouns have gender and that this particular noun is feminine, even though culturally, in both Germany and the United States, drums are associated with men and tin drums with boys. Some members of the class might protest this generalization, and I would invite students to keep issues of gender and gender roles in mind as we work through the book. I might mention that compound nouns are more abundant in German than in English and that even though the components of such a noun could be considered separately, a German reader would not usually think about *Blech* ("tin") and *Trommel* ("drum") when spotting *Blechtrommel*. Before leaving the topic of the novel's title, I would point out that the German original contains as a subtitle the generic designation *Roman* ("novel") whereas the English translation includes only the main title.

We are now ready to open the big book, and I would ask the students to pay attention to each side of each page—or, if we are short of time, at least to note how the title page looks and what information it contains (eliciting hopefully another reminder that we are reading a translation). When looking at the copyright page, students might note the lag between the original German publication and the appearance of the English translation. Another student (or I) might connect this lag to the length of the book or to the fact that this was Grass's first major publication and that in 1959 he was not the celebrity he is today. Someone might note the year that Grass was born (1927), and a clever student who has read enough of the novel may be able to identify 1927 as the year Oskar decides not to grow anymore. The novel's relation to the life of its author may also come up, if someone comments on the dedication page and asks whether Anna Grass is the model for Anna Bronski.

I am of two minds about treatment of the table of contents during this exercise. On the one hand, in the German original it appears at the back of the book, which I would be sure to point out, so that students know that traditions are different in German publishing. On the other hand, the table of contents is frontmatter in the English version we are reading, so it becomes another piece of prereading input, whether one glances superficially at it or studies it carefully. In any case one should get the students to notice that the book is divided into three parts. Do they know other novels or lengthy pieces of writing that are divided into books? The division into three books—together with chapter titles such as "Good Friday Fare," "Faith, Hope, Love," "Maria," "The Imitation of Christ," "The Christmas Play," "Madonna," and "Thirty"—prompts a brief introduction of the role of Christianity in the text, and specifically of Oskar's Christ complex. (I find that I cannot take for granted that my students are familiar with the most basic elements of Christianity. Even symbols that have entered our secular culture, like the number 3, may need to be explicated.)

One could use the table of contents to go in a different direction. For instance, one might elicit observation of the predominance of chapter titles that mention physical locations, personal names, and place-names and ask if the students detect any shift from beginning to end, thus alerting them to the novel's move from the German-Polish prewar east to the war front to the German postwar west. A member of the class or I might also note the cryptic, terse nature of the chapter titles to comment that Grass is communicating the idiosyncratic, tunnel vision of the narrator-protagonist. With an advanced group one could introduce the term *synecdoche* and ask students to find chapter titles that function synecdochically.

One should pause briefly over the page that says, "Book 1," and ask students what kind of information usually comes at the beginning of a novel. With this prompt, a student might volunteer that Oskar himself pauses over the idea of beginnings (11–12; 17–18). One could briefly jump to those pages with the students or merely ask them to take note and reread that passage.

The exercise's next step is to pause over the title of the first chapter ("The Wide Skirt") in the way the group paused over the novel's title. Here are some of the points I would hope my students catch on to. This chapter title is structured like the title of the novel (though in German it consists of article, adjective, and noun rather than article and compound noun) and thus a few of the remarks we made about the book's title could be tested for relevance. Largeness (through use of the word "wide") is foregrounded, as it was foregrounded by the size of the book and number of chapters. I would definitely want the students to pick up on the introduction of gender, through the naming of an article of women's clothing, an article moreover that covers the lower part of a woman's body.[1]

Approaching the end of the exercise, we analyze the first sentence, which is also, being long, the entire first paragraph. Someone should read it aloud:

> Zugegeben: ich bin Insasse einer Heil- und Pflegeanstalt, mein Pfleger beobachtet mich, läßt mich kaum aus dem Auge; denn in der Tür ist ein Guckloch, und meines Pflegers Auge ist von jenem Braun, welches mich, den Blauäugigen, nicht durchschauen kann.   (9)

> Granted: I am an inmate of a mental hospital; my keeper is watching me, he never lets me out of his sight; there's a peephole in the door, and my keeper's eye is the shade of brown that can never see through a blue-eyed type like me.   (15)

Some ideas are so apparently connected to what we have just been discussing, that students are likely to blurt them out: the blue eyes, the importance of sight. Other ideas won't have surfaced yet; these might be expressed as well: insanity, incarceration. Because the group has been working on a word-by-word basis, it should be easy to get the students to consider the words one by one. Starting with "Granted," they may notice that the word foregrounds a theme (truth vs. appearance), sets the tone for what follows (skepticism and persuasion), and reveals something about the narrative situation (an exchange of ideas—whether between narrator and reader or between parts of the self, we cannot immediately decide—is already under way).

The next word, "I," and the next clause, "I am an inmate of a mental hospital," bring us to a likely place to introduce the narrative situation. As a class we can name novels we know that are narrated in the first person, and working from the students' examples, I can introduce two key concepts for *The Tin Drum*: that of the "narrating I" versus the "experiencing I" (Stanzel 33) and that of the unreliable narrator (Beyersdorf). The continuation of the sentence, chapter, and novel will provide many additional chances to bring up these concepts. One issue I would raise through comparison with the German original is the idea of possible healing. In contrast to the English phrase "mental hospital," a rather general but pessimistic term, Grass has Oskar use the term "Heil- und Pflegeanstalt," emphasizing healing or at least care. Similarly, the term Manheim translates with "keeper" is "Pfleger" in the German original—again a word that emphasizes care rather than incarceration. This observation is important to make at the start, because these terms help set the ambivalent tone. If readers think Oskar is completely crazy or paranoid, as the rest of the sentence in the German or English might lead us to believe, it is harder to grant him at least some credibility—the symbolic other half of the "granted" that he extends to us, by admitting that he is in a mental institution. Before ending the exercise, I would raise the issue of size once again. The setting of the act of narration in a mental institution can reinforce the idea of excess with which the class began the exercise and with which I began this essay.

There are obviously myriad themes, plot elements, and narrative structures highly relevant to *The Tin Drum* that my title exercise would not address. There are also clarifications that must be made. One that fascinates me as a narratologist is the fact that Oskar actually does turn over the act of narration twice (to Bruno and to Gottfried von Vittlar; see Hall's essay in this volume). My readers have surely thought of numerous valuable points to raise with the paratextual material that I did not have the space or the insight to make here. Still, I believe that this exercise is a good way to begin the study of a lengthy novel like *The Tin Drum*, precisely because it gives students a few concrete ideas to guide them, ideas that they have generated mainly themselves by paying close attention to the text. They continue their reading in the belief that they are capable of noticing other elements worthy of discussion. Besides, as Rushdie reminds us and as my students have informed me after other incarnations of this exercise, dispensing with safety nets and aiming wildly for the stars, as I am suggesting we do through the title exercise, can be a lot of fun!

NOTE

[1] Note that *Rock*, the word for "skirt," has masculine gender in German. Oskar himself discusses it: "Like its brothers—for skirts are masculine by nature—[the fifth skirt] was subject to change, . . ." (19).

Narration in *The Tin Drum*:
A Quirky Narrator in Search of the Truth

Sabine Gross

Oskar Matzerath, one of the most memorable characters in the history of literature, is made even more so by virtue of providing the narrative voice and focus
for the novel in which he stars. Oskar is agent and observer, victim and historical
chronicler, voyeur and blasphemer, Jesus figure and satanic tempter, artist and
maverick, breaker of taboos and innocent child. He combines deliberate regression to the state of infancy with precocious awareness and insight. And he does
not make life easy for readers—beginning with the first sentence, indeed the
opening word of the novel: "Zugegeben: ich bin Insasse einer Heil- und Pflegeanstalt" (9) ("Granted: I am an inmate of a mental hospital" [15]). How on earth
are we supposed to trust a main narrator who presumably is crazy or mentally
deranged? And to whom does he "grant" this admission, which thanks to that
first word acquires a tone of conversational contrariness that, we will find, is one
of the signature traits of our guide through the world of this novel?

With a single word, Grass takes us into an imagined conversation that Oskar
is having with us, as readers. The very first sentence sets the tone, assigns us a
role, and deliberately shapes and encourages a certain stance in the reader willing to take up its invitation: a stance of active engagement, of communication, of
confidences imparted, but also of suspicious alertness to whatever this narrator
may have in store for us. Indeed, there is a hint of danger: why does the keeper
not let his ward out of his sight? What has his ward done? Why has he been
committed? Clearly, he is capable of coherent statements. Despite his state of
captive helplessness, the narrator conveys a sense of sneaky defiance in the last
clause of the first paragraph: he cannot be "seen through" easily, and perhaps
this statement applies to us as well as to his keeper. "Seen through" introduces
us to the oscillation between the literal (as borne out by the actual color of the
eyes) and the metaphoric in a manner of punning that will recur throughout
Oskar's narrative.

Looked at closely, the opening paragraph is thus packed with information
even while it raises more questions than it answers, and in this respect it is representative of the novel as a whole. Surprising information or unexpected turns
are a constant feature of Oskar's story as well as his storytelling, as is his utter
lack of narrative economy. The plot advances with sometimes excruciating slow-
ness along several intertwined threads, with a wealth of sometimes unsettling
jumps and extended, layered digressions, reflections on the past, flashbacks as
well as inserts or commentaries on minor details, thunderhead-like syntactic
constructions, and constant changes in linguistic and stylistic registers. All these
features serve to alert us to the fact that this novel, beyond being narrated in
intriguing ways, is very much *about* the act of narrating.

Oskar explores the full range of narrative possibilities and stances. Among them are impersonal—"omniscient"—passages and explicit addresses to his readers; vivid and lovingly detailed scenes and extreme narrative compression of time; puns and metaphors; drastically concrete descriptions next to heavily symbolic language; dialogue, inner monologue, stream-of-consciousness-like passages.[1] He liberally pays homage to—or cannibalizes—a range of literary, cultural, and religious texts in allusions, quotes, or parodies, at times virtually speaking in tongues. Add to this the wildly fluctuating attitudes of the narrator toward his subject matter, from psychologically plausible ones to completely off-the-wall reactions and renderings of events. It is clear that readers have their work cut out for them. Oskar can be wrenchingly honest (as in his helpless love-hate reaction to Maria at the end of "Special Communiqués"), supremely manipulative (e.g., in the carefully modulated and staged plea for mercy he offers Bebra [731; 553]), and patently insincere in ways that allow us to form our own opinion and realize his biases while at the same time correcting for them. He moves from sensitive sympathy and pleas for our understanding to cold, even cruel detachment, from dramatic to laconic, from lyrical to drastically obscene, from understated or veiled descriptions to the blatant violation of taboos. And just like his constantly shifting language registers, his stance toward the events he narrates keeps us off balance.

Thus the text presents a distinct challenge to students, especially undergraduates, who are generally interested in and used to reading for the plot. They prefer to focus on the what rather than the how of a story, considering the form and linguistic shaping of a narrative as neutral and any attention demanded by these features as an imposition in novels that, after all, are supposed to tell a story. In addition, students generally expect a narration in the first person, and that is the dominant mode in *The Tin Drum*, to establish a psychologically convincing and believable narrative voice whose purpose it is to convey events and reactions and who draws us into an identificatory mode of reading. Students will expect a third-person narrator to follow the nineteenth-century model: reliably informative, largely neutral, and omniscient. Oskar's fractured, many-leveled narrative with its continuous stylistic shifts flies in the face of such assumptions and expectations.

Drawing students' attention to this fact from the outset is desirable for two reasons. First, it allows students to realize that the standard mode of textual realism or transparent language, which allows effortless access to the plot events, is only one possible mode of storytelling and by no means inevitable. Second, it encourages them to view the eccentricities of Oskar's narrative voice not as an obstacle but as a challenge, and such focused attention is repaid with additional dimensions of pleasure and insight into reading this text. The very demands that Grass's novel and Oskar's mode of narration place on us also train us to cope, to meet the textual strategies with flexible and insightfully analytic reading strategies. Thus we become better, more consciously responsive readers. Accordingly, urge your students not to discount their reading impressions and responses to the text but to monitor and respect them! These responses, even if they are critical, dismissive, or disparaging, help pinpoint important ways in which *The Tin Drum* and its main narrative voice deviate from more conventional novels. In other words, these responses are exactly what the author was aiming for, and they bring into focus a crucial dimension of this novel.

Our advice to students should be to read the text in a relaxed analytic mode that, in addition to teasing out events and developments, draws attention to the richness and ingenuity of how the story is told and the range of variation it offers. In particular, it is important to register, be it with disapproval or appreciation, how Oskar plays with our desire to get on with the story by interspersing events with commentaries, asides, flashbacks and flash-forwards, and extended detours and how cleverly he often starts a new episode with a slant that appears to be utterly unrelated and yet will turn out to be relevant, bringing us back to crucial characters and events. For instance, "Die Ameisenstraße" ("The Ant Trail") starts with an apparent non sequitur, a swimming pool scene, which turns out to be an extended simile of Oskar's first trial. The chapter ends—Matzerath has just died a horrible death—with a detailed observation of a trail of ants on their quest for sugar.

Another remarkable example of this strategy is the closing chapter of the first book, "Glaube Hoffnung Liebe" ("Faith, Hope, Love") with its fairy-tale innocuousness of "Es war einmal," the German equivalent of "Once upon a time" (rendered in the translation as "There was once"); it moves in recursive, overlapping miniature tales from a recap of information about Oskar's upstairs neighbor Meyn through Meyn's cats and their smell into a harrowing account of Kristallnacht and the Nazi extermination of Jews, progressing, with a persistent and highly misleading focus on minor details, from everyday normality to allegory and quasi-musical composition ("'Glaube–Hoffnung–Liebe' konnte Oskar lesen und mit den drei Wörtchen umgehen wie ein Jongleur mit Flaschen" [261]) ("'Faith . . . hope . . . love,' Oskar read and played with the three words as a juggler plays with bottles" [203]). When the chapter returns at the end to the featured biblical phrase in a combination of fairy-tale and biblical diction, all hope and faith have been purged from it: "Es war einmal ein Spielzeughändler, der hieß Markus und nahm mit sich alles Spielzeug aus dieser Welt" (264) ("There once was a toy merchant, his name was Markus, and he took all the toys in the world away with him out of this world" [206]).

Oskar's mode(s) of storytelling can be infuriating. Time and again Oskar acts as a highly inconsiderate narrator, one who seems to disregard our needs and wishes and who leads us astray and shocks us. If there is an implicit contract between narrator and reader that holds the narrator to the same rules that govern regular discourse and communication (give your listeners the information they need, tell them what is important and significant, distinguish new from shared and familiar information, move the story along), Oskar continually violates it. His language distorts and hampers our understanding of what happens; he digresses; he jumps backward and forward unpredictably to give us brief, tantalizing glimpses of as-yet-unexplained developments; he mentions new characters as if we should already be familiar with them and in general seems to take pleasure in slipping significant information past us rather than properly introducing or highlighting it. His visitors "clowned around, parodied scenes from my trial . . ." (38)—what trial is he involved in? How did he acquire the son, Kurt, who is mentioned without preamble on page 268 (210)? One of his favorite pastimes seems to be to spring information on us in ways that take us aback and generate questions. And we do want to know: Why is Herbert Truczinski brought home "in an ambulance once or twice a month, involuntarily but free of charge" (176)? After an artful delay, the answer is supplied on the following page. What has Oskar's rented dog Lux dragged up (740; 551–52)? After several digressing paragraphs, in which Oskar ignores or screens out the information, then withholds the actual word from us (never mind that it is the chapter title: we do not know that yet!) and inserts a one-sentence minilecture, we finally find out that the object is a severed finger. Are there two people in Münzer's room? Two pages later the Münzer-Klepp switch is explained in a way that additionally is made to tie in with one of Oskar's core family traumas. Oskar's predilection for this kind of apparently unconcerned scrambling of the felicitous informational sequence keeps attentive readers on their toes. (We may have ambivalent feelings about this kind of reward for close reading, of course!)

One of the main features—and strengths—of conventionally realist texts is to provide information unobtrusively, to assuage our curiosity as they awaken it, to provide answers to questions we might have before we become conscious of and formulate these questions. Clearly, Oskar's narrative does the opposite: it is designed to make us wonder, pause, ask questions. Thus, we read in a more active mode, keeping our questions—and the purposeful narrative indiscretions or infelicities that gave rise to them—in mind. The explanatory scenarios that we may come up with almost invariably end up getting trumped, to our astonishment, frustration, or delight, by the information Oskar finally divulges, dozens or even hundreds of pages later.

Oskar plays with our preconceptions of a "natural," plausible, convincing narration, sometimes ridiculing them explicitly in parodic assertions of narrative conscientiousness. After a brief flash-forward that includes Matzerath's worried face, he continues, in a metanarrative aside that also asserts the control of the storyteller over characters and narrative: "Oskar hat vorgegriffen, muß wieder Matzeraths Gesicht glätten . . ." (456) ("Oskar has been getting ahead of himself; now he must smooth the creases out of Matzerath's brow, for on the night of my arrival he beamed" [347]). Or he offers a tongue-in-cheek endorsement of strict adherence to the orderly temporal progression of his narrative when he states that he and his fellow jazz musicians "begannen etwa um zehn Uhr mit der Musik. Da es jetzt jedoch erst fünfzehn Minuten nach neun ist, kann von uns erst später die Rede sein" (689) ("We arrived at nine, unpacked our instruments, and began to play at about ten. But for the present it is only a quarter past nine and I won't be able to speak about us until later" [522]).

As readers will note relatively quickly, the text has two dominant time lines, representing a double progression of time throughout: Oskar's time in the mental hospital represents the time of narration and in this case of the actual writing of Oskar's account; the narrated time begins with his grandmother's skirts and his mother's conception in 1899, and its historical (if somewhat less than orderly) progression leads up to a narrative present where it finally merges with the second—later—time line. Telling from hindsight is a popular narrative convention, like other framing devices, frequently introduced to set up the narrative and then conveniently relegated to the background for the bulk of the narrative. *The Tin Drum* brings the later time of narration to life and turns it from a static vantage point into a source of dynamic interference. Oskar will rarely allow the framing time line to fade into the background. In virtually every chapter, he keeps alerting us to the doubleness of time. His references to his "today" in the mental asylum, inserted in sometimes jarring fashion (including references to events and characters we have not yet encountered) remind us of the gap between the two, a gap that gradually narrows and that, in addition, we are slowly able to bridge with the information that he supplies about events and characters (such as when we finally meet first Klepp and then Vittlar in the narrated time line, hundreds of pages after they were first mentioned as visitors to the asylum). The effect is by now familiar: we are prevented from the comfort of mentally settling into either of the two environments; and thus we are forced to keep jumping back and forth, instead of becoming immersed in the kind of flow that allows us to forget the mediating step of narration.

Oskar does take the pace of narration (the ratio of time narrated to words expended) to either extreme, offering drastic compression that approximates a fast-forward effect (the *Madonna 49* painting [619; 472], the first three years of his life [740; 559–60]) on one hand and extreme expansion and delay on the other. He may delve into a plausibility-breaking depth of detail in the middle of scenes or events that effectively brings things to a standstill for readers.

Both the temporal and spatial focus is extraordinarily changeable. Vividly fine-grained detail is often interspersed with broadly summarizing sweeps. The narrative employs quasi-cinematic techniques, creating a kind of split-screen or cross-cutting effect (e.g., the opening of "Bebra's Theatre at the Front" or the historical panorama inserted into the trial or moment of the diving-board jump in "The Ant Trail" [505–06; 384–85]) between different levels and locales or using the equivalent of a rack focus, sudden and jarring changes in depth and range, to move back and forth from close range and specific detail to a much broader temporal or spatial perspective (e.g., in Oskar's encounter with the gang in "The Dusters" [484; 369]). In "The Polish Post Office," the story of the outbreak of World War II is refracted through Oskar's focus on the need to repair, guard, or replace his precious drum. The two levels are yanked together repeatedly and made to converge in Oskar's mind: "Eine sterbende Kindertrommel hat bei uns Zuflucht gesucht. Wir sind Polen, wir müssen sie schützen, zumal England und Frankreich einen Garantievertrag mit uns abgeschlossen haben" (291) ("A dying toy drum has sought refuge with us. We are Poles, we must protect it, especially since England and France are bound by treaty to defend us" [226]).

As the complexity of his use of narrative time demonstrates, Oskar is an accomplished narrator who is well versed in the narrative techniques that he pushes to the limit, simultaneously honoring and defying them. Grass calls extensively on pre-nineteenth-century novel traditions, including the picaresque genre,[2] in which Oskar's strategies of foregrounding and highlighting the act of narrating have a legitimate place. Prominent among these is the involvement of the reader as addressee, which Oskar engages in from the very beginning of his narrative. We enter the novel as partners in a dialogue, it seems—even though it will turn out to be a one-sided dialogue, with Oskar offering praise and flattery, inferring and filling in our responses while pretending to defer to them: "Sie werden sagen: . . . Ich spreche, wie die Aufmerksamsten unter Ihnen gemerkt haben werden, . . ." (401) ("You will say: . . . I am referring, as the most attentive among you will have noted, to . . ." [307]).

But Oskar reminds us that this is a narrative in numerous other ways. Throughout, he keeps communicating to us his own evaluating, assessing, commenting presence in and behind all statements we read, in many variations of framing comments along the lines of, "But I have to admit," "Have I already mentioned," and so on, continuing his one-sided dialogue with readers and drawing them into his metanarrative deliberations about what to tell and how to share information. Other autoreferential passages and inserts keep foregrounding the act of telling and writing, starting with the ream of "unschuldiges Papier" (11) (the translation "virgin paper" [16] shifts the emphasis from guilt to sexuality) and continuing with regular references to the act of writing.

Many of these references involve the object that supplies the title and is of supreme significance in the novel. Oskar frequently reminds us that drumming equals narrating and its concomitant acts: writing, remembering, witnessing, creating, making present, and speaking out.[3] The drum emphasizes the performance character of narration. Much more than a prop, it is so indispensable for him that the search for a continuing supply gets him in dangerous situations, narrows and skews his focus, and leads to such crucial events as Jan Bronski's death (since Jan returns to the post office only to get Kobyella to repair Oskar's drum). The drum has an insistent materiality throughout the novel. Georg Just suggests considering the drum an "objective correlative" along the lines of T. S. Eliot's definition rather than a symbol (110–27, 142). It serves simultaneously as badge of infantility (allowing Oskar to pass as a three-year-old), call to arms, audible means of protest, and an instrument of witnessing and recording. As the narrator's most essential tool, it helps him access memory as he uses it to signal his interventions, and it (or, rather, the archive of drums that Maria is storing for him) is the material manifestation of his search for the past with its traumatic and pleasurable memories. More than any other object in *Tin Drum*, the drum is described repeatedly in anthropomorphic terms (e.g., in "Scrap Metal," as "sick" [214], "tired" [221], "mortally wounded" [222]).

A general point: a focus on detailed analysis should not obscure the fact that Oskar is a consummate storyteller who presents us with original and perceptively detailed character descriptions such as Greff waxing lyrical on the topic of potatoes and chopping swimming holes into the frozen Baltic, Gretchen Scheffler and her teaching, Klepp/Münzer and his ingeniously organized spaghetti-fed reclining existence, and Oskar's son Kurt as an accomplished six-year-old black marketeer. These scenes are fantastic yet vividly rendered. Other examples are the famous skirts passage (which brought Grass the Group 47 prize in 1958), the game of skat and sexuality between his mother and Jan that Oskar witnesses from underneath the table and later the game Jan and Oskar play with Kobyella to keep him from dying ("House of Cards"), Oskar's drumming intervention in the Nazi parade (in "The Rostrum"), the notorious eel scene ("Good Friday Fare"), Oskar's reading of Herbert Truczinski's back, Greff's suicide, Oskar's sleeping in the postal letter bins, the famous "fizz powder" episodes, Maria's impregnation, and the Onion night club. The list could go on and on.

On a more general level, Oskar's narrative is painstakingly shaped and constructed on the levels of language, motifs, individual phrases, characters, and plot developments. Underneath its gestures of rambling, jerky, undisciplined storytelling, this text is tightly structured and has an extensive system of cross-references, in which numerous elements and details are progressively woven into a complex coherence. Toward the end, the pattern culminates in passages whose density approximates that of a musical fugue (e.g., in several of the chapter-concluding passages of the novel). The cast of characters is surprisingly continuous; witness for instance the extraordinary Bebra's repeated appearances. Insistently formulaic repetitions that recur throughout the text—such as "meine arme Mama" ("my poor Mama"), "mein mutmaßlicher Vater" ("my presumptive father")—contribute to this effect, as do the occasional inventorying of characters and the recaps of previous developments, whose frequency increases toward the end of the novel.

On a local level, Oskar's narrative offers throughout a steady supply of word-level delights and pleasures to readers willing to pay attention to them,[4] as a very small selection can demonstrate: Klepp's face displays "speckglänzende Pietät" (367) (is "coated with unctuous piety" [282]); Bebra "lächelte . . . spinnwebendünn" (452) (wears "a smile as thin as a spiderweb" [345]); when Oskar is outraged, he states, "Wut gab mir die Haut eines Suppenhuhnes" (470) ("I had gooseflesh with rage" [358]); and October's leaf fall means "der Welt fallen die Haare und Zähne aus" (584) ("the world losing its hair and teeth" [446]). The Onion Cellar owner welcomes his guests with "äußerst beweglichen Augenbrauen" (687) ("mobile, expressive eyebrows" [521]), and his smile resembles "dem Lächeln auf einer Kopie, die man nach der Kopie der vermutlich echten Mona Lisa gemalt hatte" (691) ("the smile on a copy of a copy of the supposedly authentic Mona Lisa" [524]). Another small gem is Oskar's characterization of God and cemeteries:

> Gegenüber pinselte unser aller Sonntagsmaler von Tag zu Tag mehr tu-
> benfrisch Saftgrün in die Bäume des Werstener Friedhofes. Friedhöfe
> haben mich immer schon verlocken können. Sie sind gepflegt, eindeutig,
> logisch, männlich, lebendig.   (573–74)

> Across the way, our Sunday painter who art in heaven, was each day add-
> ing a little more green fresh from the tube to the trees of Wersten Cem-
> etery. Cemeteries have always had a lure for me. They are well kept, free
> from ambiguity, logical, virile, and alive.   (438)

Richly detailed accounts bring scenes and characters to life—such as Oskar's description of Maria (339; 262) or the fiber carpet and its successful laying (674; 511–13), after which "broad-headed tacks ran from end to end, up to their necks in the floorboards, holding just their heads above the surging, swirling coconut fibers" (512). Oskar repeatedly details the specific landmarks he passes on excursions throughout the city in ways that make them present and concrete for us (172–73; 137) (464; 353–54).

On the other hand, an excess of detail that relates to a situation but is by no means necessary or even helpful to the reader is employed to break narrative verisimilitude and to provide a level of information that is neither called for nor plausible. A deliberate oversupply of this kind interferes with the reader's immersion in a scene. Oskar's glass-shattering prowess includes lists of houses and a primer on stylistic authenticity (288; 439); a mention of Hindenburgallee prompts a dip into tree history (154; 122); and a verbal detour on crosses oc-curs while Oskar is in the church (178–79; 139–40), culminating in one of his rhythmic-associative riffs.

The use of detail in the novel thus contributes to a fundamental tension be-tween realism (in the sense of vivid concreteness) and antirealism that makes Grass's novel such a provocatively hybrid text. In its plot, its descriptions, and its use of language, Oskar's narrative provides a wealth of realistic detail along with flagrant instances of antirealism. That this contradiction opens the text up to different readings is significant for teaching, since it allows for divergent, even opposing assessments and interpretations. For instance, Oskar's narrative outrageousness can also be seen as defining Oskar psychologically and bringing him to life for us perhaps more sharply than a conventional narrative stance might. Oskar's narrative style and language use are conspicuous, in-your-face, irritating, sometimes shocking. In short, they are just like Oskar the character and entirely in keeping with his thoughts and actions. Besides acknowledging his clever inventiveness on the linguistic-narrative level, we may also read that inventiveness as evidence of his profound psychological conflictedness. In that sense, Oskar is not as fantastic a character as some commentators have made him out to be. Several instances of his narrative quirkiness clearly represent psychological states—such as Oskar's eliding the information that he plans to stab the pregnant Maria in her belly in a masterful linguistic approximation of repression, and his ingenious perceptual-mental block at the end of the infamous scene of Alfred Matzerath's death.

Oskar can also be seen as a verbal chameleon, a linguistic con artist who changes his style for other than psychological reasons. The inventiveness, storytelling talent, and virtuosity in using language that make Grass such a remarkable author are not merely channeled through Oskar, the narrator, as a matter of necessity or convenience. Oskar is a drummer and a musician (a famous and celebrated one, by the end), and so his ability to play the instrument of language masterfully, with sophisticated control of timbre, volume, mood, and pace, should come as no surprise. He is highly attuned to rhythms and adept at beguiling audiences. There are a number of stylistically prominent passages in the text where Oskar jumps the bounds of narrative propriety—and frees language from its subjugation to representation and description—by going into extended quasi-musical riffs; improvising on select words or ideas; taking them through different keys and undermining the sequentiality of language by establishing echoes, mirrorings, and overlays of tonal or rhythmic structures. Some passages stand out: the improvisation on colors (200–01; 156); the verbal variations on the Polish national anthem (a preview [135; 107–08] leads to a more extended version [324; 251], which segues into a vividly visual rhythmic "poem," a flight of fancy for which Oskar then apologizes facetiously); the spoon riff (395; 303); Mrs. Greff's screams (408; 312), which are echoed by the foregrounding-by-repetition of Oskar's laughter on the final pages of the novel; and the virtuoso linguistic interweaving of stones and happiness that in the original includes the untranslatable "Sandsteinglück, Elbsandstein, Mainsandstein, Deinsandstein, Unsersandstein, Glück Kirchheimer" (581).[5]

Oskar's mastery of rhythms infuses the narration everywhere—in ways that may draw our attention to the form rather than the content of what is told but also underscore the impact of statements. Oskar moves easily from the staccato rhythm of brief, simple clauses such as the initial approach to the fizz powder (353; 272), the whole aftermath of the Dorothea encounter (682–83; 517–18), the accelerated drummings of the past, and the description of his mother (209; 163) to elaborate multipart paratactic and hypotactic sentences that force us to slow down and grope our way through the wealth of detail and the labyrinthine construction. The longest sentence in the novel fills one and a half pages; Oskar's detail-studded summary account of his life for Klepp (one of the most extended of several such "recapitulations by drumming" [686–88; 520–22]) develops from a dramatic verb-driven paratactic opening to increasing hypotaxis. In addition, the German original has a number of passages insistently punctuated by anaphora for dramatic effect, many of which are not replicated by the translation, such as Oskar's scathing indictment of the Nazis (316) ("they" slightly weaker in English [245] than the German "die"; also "während" [212] and "da" [165]) and his feverish carousel fantasy in the German original (541; 411). The longest *da*-passage marks his panoramic vision during the trial (504–05; 384–85).

Other features of the text contribute to the effect of hybridity, as presented through a similarly hybrid narrator. One of the more irritating ones is the alternation between first-person and third-person narrator, found in every chapter of the novel. It seems random but is so frequent and blatant that it is clearly intentional: hundreds of times, "Oskar" and "I" are used in the same sentence or in adjacent clauses, occasionally supplemented by the self-addressing *du* or other third-person references to Oskar. Some instances of this technique, liberally dispersed throughout the narrative, can be found in the first paragraphs of the chapters "Special Communiqués" and "The Dusters."

We may be tempted to impose order on this feature and look for a systematic distinction. Might "Oskar" designate the "experiencing self" of the earlier time, while "I" is the narrating self with its hindsight and additional experience that is at a remove from the earlier events? But in general students will find that although the text invites such explanatory speculation and may bear it out locally, greater scrutiny will disprove this attempt at a logical explanation for the grammatical split and collision between the two.[6] *The Tin Drum* may serve as a counterexample to Christa Wolf's *Kindheitsmuster* (1967; *Patterns of Childhood*), another major postwar German novel on growing up in Nazi Germany, which is in many ways a complement and counterpart. Wolf's narrator explains her reasons for her distinction between the use of the third person for the experiencing self and the second person for the chronicling, remembering, narrating self. The distinction represents the divide between one's memories and the present and the ultimate inaccessibility of one's former self, especially if that self lived, experienced, thought in ways that after the end of the Nazi period had to be revised, censored, and reshaped. Oskar, fractured in less predictable or reassuring ways, cannot be neatly separated into two partial characters. The insistent clash of the first and third persons serves to alienate the reader from the narrator, to undercut the intimacy frequently established by the confidences imparted by the first-person narrator to the reader, just as the narrative as a whole simultaneously draws us in and distances us, engages and repels us, frustrating our attempts at homogeneous coherence with its insistent contrasts and contradictions.

Another verbal technique that combines coherence and contradiction is the punning use of idiomatic phrases that are carefully chosen to reliteralize the underlying metaphor and liberate it from the conventional and automatic use that defines idioms, encouraging—or forcing—readers to read the description on two levels simultaneously. These puns are frequently almost impossible to translate, but Manheim does a fine job on Oskar's idiom-studded reminiscence of his mother (209; 163) and in many other places.

One of the most delightful—and extended—examples of this verbal technique is found in the sections dealing with Oskar's becoming "angeschwärzt" ("blackened," "accused," in another allusion to the subject of guilt that permeates the narrative) during his tenure as model for art students' charcoal sketches. The passage describing Professor Kuchen combines the flavor of the kind of verbal riffing described above with this shading of description into idiom into pun into metaphor, in the process turning the artist into a satanic figure:

> Längere Zeit umschritt er mich, ließ seine Kohleaugen kreisen, schnaubte, daß schwarzer Staub seinen Nasenlöchern entfuhr, und sprach, mit schwarzen Fingernägeln einen unsichtbaren Feind erwürgend: "Kunst ist Anklage, Ausdruck, Leidenschaft! Kunst, das ist schwarze Zeichenkohle, die sich auf weißem Papier zermürbt!" . . . [S]echzehnmal knirschte hinter den Staffeleien Kohle, schrie mürb werdend auf, zerrieb sich an meinem Ausdruck—gemeint war mein Buckel—, machte den schwarz, schwärzte den an, verzeichnete ihn; denn alle Schüler des Professors Kuchen waren mit solch dicker Schwärze meinem Ausdruck hinterher, daß sie unweigerlich ins Übertreiben gerieten, die Ausmaße meines Buckels überschätzten. . . .
> (606–07)

> For a time he walked around me, darting coal-black looks, breathing black dust from his nostrils. Throttling an invisible enemy with his black fingers, he declared: "Art is accusation, expression, passion. Art is a fight to the finish between black charcoal and white paper." . . . Sixteen sticks of charcoal rasped behind sixteen easels; charcoal came to grips with my expression, that is, my hump, blackened it, and put it on paper. Professor Kuchen's students took so black a view of my expression that inevitably they exaggerated the dimensions of my hump. . . .   (462–63)

Probably the most remarkable passage of this kind reports the fiery devastation of Danzig's bombing at the end of the war street by street, in phrases that represent destruction through metaphors inspired by the actual street names:

> In der Kleinen Hosennähergasse ließ sich das Feuer für mehrere auffallend grelle Hosen Maß nehmen. . . . Die restlichen, noch nicht evakuierten Glocken . . . schmolzen . . . sang- und klanglos. In der Großen Mühle wurde roter Weizen gemahlen. In der Fleischergasse roch es nach verbranntem Sonntagsbraten. Im Stadttheater wurden Brandstifters Träume, ein doppelsinniger Einakter, uraufgeführt.   (512–13)

> In Breechesmaker Street, the fire had itself measured for several pairs of extra-loud breeches. . . . What bells had not been evacuated . . . melted in their belfries and dripped away without pomp or ceremony. In the Big Mill red wheat was milled. Butcher Street smelled of burnt Sunday roast. The Municipal Theater was giving a première, a one-act play entitled The Firebug's Dream.   (390)

The complete passage—excerpted here—is typical of Oskar's narration in com-
bining several of the features outlined above and below. It fuses the punning
use of idioms with excess of detail and specificity of locale and levels the distinction between tragedy and farce through the dissonance between playful
tone and the catastrophic event. Overall, as already illustrated in passing by
examples, there is an almost consistent playfulness in Oskar's use of language
that might well be taken as inappropriate for the serious subject matter of the
novel and that contributes to blurring the line dividing comic and tragic, serious
and farcical.

Some of the ambivalent and illusion-destroying qualities of the narration can
of course be attributed to Oskar's general quirkiness as a narrator-character.
But more seriously, Oskar misleads us by downplaying dramatic events or expressing them in less than straightforward terms—be they euphemistic, metaphoric, or affectively off key. This inclination to misrepresent by a mismatch of
focus or emphasis to subject matter is especially noticeable in cases of death and
violence. Oskar recounts his mother's death: "Wir atmeten alle auf, als sich in
meiner Mama keine Anlässe mehr für die ihre Schönheit so entstellenden Brech-
reize fanden" (207) ("We all sighed with relief when there was nothing more
within her to provoke that retching which so marred her beauty" [161]). Mother
Truczinski's death is described with misleading ambiguity (509; 387), grenade
devastation is rendered in a jarringly amusing way (301; 233–34), and a shooting
death is purged of the shooter (535; 407). Instances of rape are phrased with ap-
palling coldness and the same tendency to pun that Oskar displays throughout.
The reason for Greff's elaborately staged and described suicide (the chapter
topic hidden in plain sight behind the title "Fünfundsiebenzig Kilo" ["165 Lbs."]),
"a summons to appear in court on a morals charge," is coyly shared with readers
as an afterthought (414; 317).

Oskar seems to revel in staging discrepancies between language and content
and exploiting them to the fullest degree possible. He assembles for us a most
impressive array of unsuitability; stylistic lack of fit; inappropriateness; contrast;
and ludicrous deviation from the norms of expression, literary genre and tone,
and civilized discourse. Indeed, he seems to use his prodigious verbal agility
specifically to build dissonances between subject matter and events narrated
and the style in which they are told. Dramatic events are relayed with detachment; the bizarre acquires matter-of-factness; minor impulses are given the status of high drama; the excavation of a corpse becomes a succession of bad puns
(599–600; 458–59); the suffering of the Polish people is told like a pleasantly
entertaining tale (521; 396–97); a spooky, erotic encounter at night is deflated
by Oskar's rendering the dramatic dialogue in reported speech and summary
report (681; 516–17); and the traditionally innocuous form of the fairy tale is
chosen for a Kristallnacht episode that starts deceptively with a secondary character and marginal detail.

In other words, engaging with *The Tin Drum* and its narrator amounts to
a sustained challenge to read against the grain, and we need to keep caution-

ing our students how Oskar's presentation of events (in his exaggerations, his trivializing understatements, the naïveté with which Grass endows him, and his self-centeredness) frequently and drastically deviates from and misrepresents their actual significance and historical impact. A continuous awareness of the significant provocation Oskar's narrative represents compared with more straightforward (or factual) accounts of the Nazi period should be part of the reading process, of assignments and classroom discussions. Oskar offers us deliberate, often blatant, distortions of dramatic, tragic, traumatic, and devastating elements of historical reality: distortions that characterize him but simultaneously call for us and our students to undo them and reframe the narrative with factual knowledge of the political and historical gravity of events and developments.

This work amounts to an extended encounter with a narrator who does not merit our trust. Oskar's infuriating trait of making contradictory statements, wavering in his convictions, and blatantly reversing himself also belongs in this general context of programmatic dissonance and underscores his general lack of reliability tempered ambiguously with pretensions of conscientious detail-mindedness.[7] A prominent example is the thread of "my presumptive father" (223) that is insistently kept at the surface of the text but undergoes repeated and sometimes abrupt revisions as Oskar changes his mind about the roles of Matzerath and Jan Bronski (and by extension, about his own role vis-à-vis Kurt). A minor but captivating motif is the fate of his grandfather Joseph Koljaiczek, who is variously—and with varying degrees of tentativeness and probability—reported to have drowned, to have made his escape to a fishing boat or tanker, or escaped to Buffalo in the USA and made millions in lumber. The amount of detail—and the very fact that Oskar can authoritatively report his grandfather's earlier thoughts and actions in "Unterm Floß" ("Under the Raft")—is strongly at odds with his insistence that such versions are unconfirmed, indeed "unsinnige Fabel[n]" (38) ("preposterous fable[s]" [37]). Although Koljaiczek's death is initially stated with firmness (37; 36),[8] a little later Koljaiczek is reported both dead and alive with certainty (40; 37). The Buffalo millionaire version is brought up again with definitiveness (84; 70) (458; 349), yet later (668; 507) it has again become miraculous but improbable.

Oskar himself comments on the topic of certainty and definition, in particular as presented in convenient story form. In a statement that we would do well to read programmatically, he addresses the insufficiency of monocausal explanations along with the human desire for precisely such explanations (538–39; 409–10). Frequently, Oskar offers us a fractured, dialogic perspective marked by conflict or dissonance. While his acts of drumming are intensely individual (witness, once again, the "Rostrum" scene) and may be read as anchoring his narration in the realm of artistic creativity, the drum, at the same time, keeps getting inserted in the larger historical and political picture, just as in Oskar's narration the political resonates with the personal, childish grudges play off the historical ramifications of actions taken or omitted.

Oskar combines an obsession about detail with manipulation and unreliability. He acknowledges the horrors that mark the years of, leading up to, and following the Second World War but refuses to be implicated in them. He wavers between omniscience and an insistence on the limits imposed by his individual consciousness and perceptions. The reader's perspective is not limited to Oskar's; while we may partially share Oskar's perspective despite the many distancing effects, we are also asked to supplement and critically reflect on it. It is our task, not least, to construct a story of twentieth-century German tragedy and guilt from his ingeniously skewed and self-centered engagement with history and ideology. In reading the text attentively, we need to be engaged in a continuous effort to rebalance the significance of what Oskar imparts to us. The narrative form of *The Tin Drum* cannot be reduced to an ultimately autoreferential or narcissistic exercise in eccentric storytelling and artistic originality. In his sustained exploration of the possibilities of narrating, Oskar's dissonances and breaks in tone, narrative quirks and stylistic idiosyncrasies, the conflicting accounts and uncertainties he imposes on us all contribute to a central question: how to access and adequately represent the truth of what happened.

Oskar is the wise fool who mediates for us between the personal and the political, between fiction and historical reality. Our job is to help our students realize that the combination of narrative strategies with which Grass endows his narrator-hero ultimately amounts to a comment on the basic unreliability of human memory and judgment, on the limits of our ability to grasp reality and the degree to which our models of it are simplistically reductive. Ideally, students will come to view their experience of reading *The Tin Drum* as an exercise in complexity. The world Oskar observes and with which he engages poses more questions than it answers and defies our attempt to understand it as a coherent totality.

NOTES

[1] A brief note on narratological terms: the concepts of omniscience and point of view continue to be used in describing narratives. But the problematic epistemological assumption underlying the first and a degree of imprecision in the second have given rise in recent decades to a set of different, arguably more precise terms. *Omniscience* ignores the constructedness of any and all knowledge in a narrative and the fact that there is no objective body of information but only the effect of a narrator having limited or extensive knowledge. In its place, the influential structural narratologist Gérard Genette suggests "nonfocalized narrative" or "zero focalization" (*Narrative Discourse* 189; but see also Herman and Vervaeck 189 n65; Bal). *Point of view* or *narrative perspective* conflates the distinction between expression-opinion and witnessing, between who speaks and who perceives, and seems to limit perception to the visual. Following Genette once again, we can split the concept of point of view into two terms – both currently in usage – that allow a differentiation: *voice* and *focalization* (see, e.g., Abbott on both terms; Bal on *focalization*; Genette on *voice*).

[2] For discussions of Oskar as picaresque hero, see Krumme 52–65; Neuhaus, *Günter Grass* [1992] 28–33; and as a dissenting voice, Fischer.

[3] Such passages, too numerous to list (Fischer counts a total of 54 [117]), are prominent in virtually every chapter of the novel.

[4] The language does not necessarily run parallel in the German and English versions: some of Oskar's verbal fireworks and sparklers translate better than others. When they do not translate well, Manheim ingeniously compensates in other places.

[5] Manheim wisely refrains from attempting an English version of these words in his generally very impressive translation (444). In "Mainsandstein, Deinsandstein, Unsersandstein," Grass uses the homonymy of "sandstone from the river Main" with "my sandstone" to move to "Yoursandstone, Oursandstone" before continuing with more actual stones.

[6] In his analysis of what he terms Oskar's "schizophrenic self-reference," Botheroyd offers the most sophisticated attempt to impose order on the shifts by assigning them multiple identities (1). See also Fischer 114–15.

[7] This differentiation seems to me more appropriate than O'Neill's position, who argues that *The Tin Drum* "relentlessly urg[es] the reader throughout to recognize the total unreliability of its narrator," even though I fully agree with his conclusion that the novel "invites the reader to confront the question of narrative unreliablity itself, the question as to how reliable any discourse can even be" ("Implications" 438).

[8] The German text has "fest . . . glaube" and "glaubwürdig," wording that blurs the reliability of the information by undercutting the distinction. Manheim translates the first as "have no doubt" and the second as "devotion to the truth."

Triumph of the Creative Dwarf:
How Grass Uses Oskar to Defy the Power of Evil

Alfred D. White

In this essay four themes are used to elucidate Grass's implicit but considerable claims for the significance of his work. In four ways Grass departs from the conventions of the realist novel, and the result is directly or indirectly to set up Oskar Matzerath (and Oskar's creator) as an equivalent and opposite to the historical evils of the years depicted in the novel. These ways are the stylistic devices that make the novel such a tour de force, the construction of Oskar's empirically impossible character and way of being, the importance attached to his chosen artistic expression by drumming, and the relation between his magical powers and the claims of Christian religion.

The text must be enjoyed first, even if this enjoyment means allowing students to spend time in lubricious discussions of how a dwarf has sex and the arousing (or otherwise) effects of coconut matting. Before trying to understand the claims of the novel to essential significance, students should also study narrative technique and reproduction of reality, issues that are a preoccupation of modern criticism. Grass presents elements of everyday experience, but one needs to guide students' attention progressively from realistic, logical passages to metaphoric and symbolic elements and, finally, to frank unrealism. In addition, Grass often narrates parts chronologically from a simple viewpoint, but students need to engage with passages that conflate different times.

To deal with National Socialism in literary terms, Grass—despite his assertion, "*Die Blechtrommel* ist zu allererst ein realistischer Roman" (qtd. in Brode, *Zeitgeschichte* 9) ("The Tin Drum is firstly a realistic novel" [my trans.])—transcends realism. The project of writing an account of such a catastrophic age cannot work if it surrenders to realism: the means the realistic writer has are not sufficient to stand against six million dead Jews and all the other victims of hatred. Large-scale, concentrated, unrealistic transposition of events, attitudes, and fates is needed to help establish a counterweight to the horrible reality. That much knowledge about reality can be gained from Grass's novel has often been stressed (Brode, *Zeitgeschichte* 105–16, 58, 78); many of its pages are devoted to the reconstruction of scenes familiar to the young Grass and characteristic of mid-twentieth-century central European history. But that the realistic elements are only the first layer of a complex structure shows itself in the sequence of Oskar's birth (52; 46–47) if not before, with the monstrous claim that newborn Oskar already saw and understood his surroundings. Grass does not join those authors who believe that describing reality is sufficient, not even those who want through their work to influence people and thus change reality. He believes that a literary work must be autonomous. It does not recapitulate facts; it has a different, imaginary, but significant mode of being.

The real world of Grass's time presents monstrous facts that a creative writer cannot (though many have tried) deal with by bloodless symbols or clever transpositions. Grass's first works, poems, and slight absurd dramas cannot confront Hitler and the evil he embodied. Realistic writers, on the other hand, could not capture the imagination as Grass's novel did—there is too great a disproportion between the monstrosities of National Socialism and any individual experience. Grass's novel, straddling realism and fantasy, goes beyond anything that can be achieved by purely realistic techniques. To understand this is bound to expand the horizons of any student (and teacher).

While it is possible to envisage a great number of contexts in which this novel could be taught, my particular concerns here would be most relevant in a literature-oriented course—say, one on the modernist novel (perhaps alongside texts by Joyce, Woolf, Döblin, Robbe-Grillet) or a course entitled Literary Reactions to the Holocaust (with contemporaries Hochhuth and Böll, and more-recent German and non-German authors). Such a course would be at a fairly high level, for students who have experience in the critical reading of literature. I imagine a small group in which, whatever the theoretical approach of the teaching, informal discussions will play a major role.

Less opportunity to pursue the literary techniques but a chance to consider Grass's claims for the significance of art would be afforded by a cultural studies course on the Bonn Republic, in which clashes between a liberal literary world and a conservative political atmosphere could be thematized. In such a context, the novel's differences from a straight account of historical reality show how the novel form in general has value as a cultural artifact: artistic products, neither bound to the reproduction and interpretation of empirical facts nor confined to noncommittal fantasy, can alter public opinion by their special approach.

To define Grass's peculiarity, comparison is useful. Each class will have its own canon of texts, literary and filmic, but I mention some of my own points of reference as examples. First, there are realistic works with subject matter similar to that of *The Tin Drum*: perhaps Heinrich Böll's *Billard um halbzehn* (1959) or an equally detailed depiction of social circumstances and personal catastrophes, John Steinbeck's *The Grapes of Wrath* (1939). Apart from the huge scale of Grass's novel, is there a difference in intention and impact? One could consider also the *Blechtrommel* film by Volker Schlöndorff and ask what elements of the novel are lost in it and why? Is there a filmic equivalent to make up for them, or is the film stuck in the realist convention despite the obvious unreality of the données?

The novel needs to be distinguished from other kinds of nonrealistic literature as well, for instance works that use symbolism, myth, or fairy-tale components (Joyce's *Ulysses* [1922], Irving's *Rip van Winkle* [1820], Melville's *Moby–Dick* [1851]). Do these works have a realistic level that one could appreciate without taking notice of the mythical or symbolic, or are reality and unreality merged? Is myth used only to add an external structure to a narrative? Is fairy tale only a technique to allow a moral statement about unchanging human nature? In what way are such works different from *The Tin Drum*? One could also compare the novel's techniques of concentration and unrealism with those of other genres, canonical or not. In painting, the works of Otto Dix and of Pablo Picasso (esp. *Guernica*) come to mind. In theater, one might think of *Oh! What a Lovely War*, produced by Joan Littlewood. Art Spiegelman's comic *Maus* presents another unreal and entertaining reaction to Nazism. Other types of work with which students may be familiar are video clips—these often combine apparent realism and utter fantasy—and, more esoterically, vinyl record sleeve art. Even modern television advertising relies on the viewer's application of complex codes of reference and the ability to recognize the breaking of conventional modes of seeing.

Once aware of the realism-fantasy nexus and how many cultural products of today employ it, most classes can provide examples from their own experience. Inevitably a wide-ranging, formless discussion develops. In order to keep it focused, it may be useful to return to basic distinctions such as alternation of real and fantastic versus interpenetration or visual versus verbal expression. One could also historicize this debate by asking what medium might Grass have chosen if he were born in 1977 rather than in 1927? Could he have produced similar effects in the different medium?

Grass's brilliant use of figures of speech is the next area to explore with students. Grass implicitly tells us that words are greater than facts. The sheer extent of the virtuoso passages is important because it allows him to dwell on the magic of words. An example is the repetition of the fairy-tale opening "Es war einmal . . ." (253–61, and 264) ("There was once . . ." and variations [196–201, 205–06]). The quasi-musical structure parallels Oskar's drum solos.

Grass shows baroque love of excess, long lists, conscious juggling with language: "'Glaube – Hoffnung – Liebe' konnte Oskar lesen und mit den drei Wörtchen umgehen wie ein Jongleur mit Flaschen: Leichtgläubig, Hoffmannstropfen, Liebesperlen, Gutehoffnungshütte, Liebfrauenmilch, Gläubigerversammlung . . ." (261) ("'Faith . . . hope . . . love,' Oskar read and played with the three words as a juggler plays with bottles: faith healer, Old Faithful, faithless hope, hope chest, Cape of Good Hope, hopeless love, Love's Labour's Lost . . ." [203]). Words beget words—also as in the visionary paragraph (apropos of the eighteen days' war of 1939) on the Polish cavalry (324–25; 251) or in the fragments of description of the ship launched as Oskar's grandfather Koljaiczek disappears (36; 34–35). Grass likes shocking contrasts, as when in World War I every man who can stand up straight is sent to the front to be made to lie down permanently (46; 42). Bringing together incommensurate things is a mannerist trick: "Die Ameisenstraße" ("The Ant Trail") ends with the assurance that the Russian occupation of Danzig has not made the spilled sugar in Matzerath's shop less attractive to the ants (519; 394–95). Then we find the absurd idyll of the Russian occupiers' building obstacle courses out of looted objects to test their cycling skills (526; 399).

Particularly prevalent is the grotesque, which strictly speaking involves the fusion of incompatible elements: animal and vegetable, human and animal, dead and living. The very dustcover of *Die Blechtrommel* suggests that a thing is more important than the person using it: Grass's illustration envelops the drum in an inexplicable bulge of Oskar's clothing, as if it were a part of Oskar. Conversely, when Koljaiczek takes on the identity of the dead Wranka, he slips "zuerst in dessen Joppe, sodann in dessen amtlich papierene, nicht vorbestrafte Haut" (27) ("first into his jacket, then into his irreproachable official skin" [28]— reference to a paper skin is lost): documents enclose the man. The wooden figure of Niobe, bringer of bad luck and sudden death to men who come too close, is described as a living woman (240; 187) and murderer: "Dat macht de griehne Marjell mit de aijene Hände" (243) ("The Green Kitten does it with her own hands" [189]). Conversely, the young lady whom Oskar, by breaking the glass of a shopwindow, tempts into the theft of a pair of shoes seems to him for a moment "eine Modepuppe des Kaufhauses Sternfeld, wunderbarerweise unterwegs" (163) ("a model at Sternfeld's" [128]—which misses the point: she is inanimate, a window dummy, and yet walking). When in the Düsseldorf art academy Maruhn's sculpture class pupils fail to make their constructions hang together, the collapse is described as if Oskar himself were disintegrating: "da fiel mir der Kopf zwischen die Füße, . . . da rutschte mir der Buckel in die Kniekehlen" (612) ("My head fell between my feet, . . . my hump drooped nearly to my knees" [467]).

More generally, extreme disproportionality and paradox are grotesque. An instance is Oskar's physique: his head is too large even for a full-sized person, his arms too strong (563; 438). Oskar as narrator recognizes "die groteske Note" (594) ("the grotesque note" [453]) of his dancing—during his short-lived period of respectability before the currency reform of 1948—with the nurse Gertrud, his cheek to her bosom, and even accentuates that note with his virtuoso leading. An everyday game of skat turns grotesque with the doggedly continued play of Jan, Oskar, and the dying Kobyella in the Polish Post Office (Brode, *Zeitgeschichte* 30). Legs become the main parts of the body as Oskar observes the grown-ups from under the table (273–74; 213). Kobyella's Adam's apple is given permission to show that Kobyella is still alive (310; 240 [lost in translation]). The concentration camp survivor Fajngold treats his murdered family as living people to whom he must explain events and his actions. These reversals of the expected order of things combine with paradoxes of characters' behavior and fates. Thus Klepp (the cause of Oskar's postwar return to drumming), whom we meet in voluntary squalor among tinned olive oil, moist salt on newspaper, and lukewarm beer (660; 502), gets married merely to recover the photograph of himself he gave to a cigarette girl (60; 53).

The construction of Oskar involves a set of phallic symbols, a cumulative grotesquerie in which the *Schwanz* as "tail" or "penis," eels, fish, drumsticks, the horn attached to a horse's head in paintings, and the ring finger of a corpse become interchangeable (Thomas, *Grass* 60–61). Early sexual stirrings make

Oskar forget the drumsticks "um des einen, mir neu gewachsenen Stockes willen" (349) ("for the sake of the new stick I had developed" [269]); later he regards himself as having been promised the ring finger from birth, though enciphered as a drumstick (750; 567).

From the grotesque it is a short step to the carnival, with its anarchic freedoms and satirical exaggerations. Much has been written in Bakhtinian spirit about the carnivalesque in the novel. I agree with Peter Arnds that Grass uses grotesque, pornographic, blasphemous elements to portray National Socialist persecution and essays "a defense of the grotesque aspects of popular culture, which the Nazis had suppressed as degenerate" (Representation 30). But we must go further. Oskar is not just the archetype of the trickster, harlequin, dwarf, or picaro (3–4). The grotesque is here more than a technique of subversion, more than a way of finding a fresh approach to the business of representing Nazism, more than a "carnivalization of Nazi atrocities . . . a representation of German fascism through carnival motifs" (7). For the carnivalesque may embody artistic creativity, but it is a short-lived contrast in an otherwise supposedly ordered world. Oskar, contrariwise, uses his drumming as an autonomous, constant, and creative act of memory and self-assertion against the so-called adult world. Grass is not only representing in Oskar aspects of the Jews, Gypsies, and other groups "excluded by Nazi racist thinking" (152); he is also giving them a voice. Oskar is not only a victim of but also a rival to authorities.

The figure of Oskar is largely defined in the first half of book 1 (9–135; 15–108). Three characteristics stand out: his capacity, from birth, to perceive and describe his environment and to act autonomously in it, notably deciding to stop growing on his third birthday; his obsessive devotion to the art of percussion; and his uncanny ability to break glass, even at a long distance, by high-pitched screaming. These things, with his infantilism, opportunism, prurience, and manipulativeness, render him morbidly fascinating. His possible madness, propensity to lie, and explicit admission that he has exaggerated and simplified part of his narrative (318; 246) make it hard to discern, except where Grass uses other narrators, a layer of immanent reality in the novel—though there may be a deeper truth in fictions and lies. "Wenn Oskar, der Erzähler, lügt, dann im Dienste einer Kunst, die der glatten Oberfläche mißtraut, das Verborgene für aussagekräftiger hält als das nach außen Gekehrte" (Moser 35) ("If Oskar, the narrator, lies, then in the service of an art that mistrusts the smooth surface, an art that thinks what is hidden tells us more than what is on the outside" [trans. mine]).

The voice that can break glass, a by-product of the need to scream to stop anyone from taking his drum away, then used, on the Danzig Stockturm, without such an occasion, becomes an autonomous power, destructive, tempting Oskar to alter the outer world—a miraculous capability reminiscent of märchen. Sometimes the voice seems evil, as when described as a "Wunderwaffe" (489) ("secret weapon" [372]) and thus parallel to the V1 and V2 rockets unleashed against England; but precisely at this point the voice is used on behalf of an anarchic group, potentially part of the resistance to Nazism. It allows him to make holes in shopwindows and so favors theft, which may be a good thing, exposing the hidden character of the respectable citizens who are tempted: "du hast den Leuten vor den Schaufensterscheiben auch geholfen, sich selbst zu erkennen" (166) ("those silent walkers in the snow . . . you helped them to know themselves" [130]).

Himself a fairy-tale or nursery-rhyme figure, a Tom Thumb, he obsessively evokes characters of infantile fantasy such as the Schwarze Köchin (Black Witch). After his growth in 1945 he develops the hump in his back, also a märchen reminiscence, which becomes the symbol of his artistic side: after attempts to be ordinary, keep away from the drum, hold down a paying job, and propose marriage to Maria, "Da besann Oskar sich seines Buckels und fiel der Kunst anheim!" (604) ("It was then that Oskar remembered his hump and fell a victim to art" [461])—and joins the art academy as a model, a passive member of the world of creativity, fascinating the students with his abnormality. An artist offers him a new drum; soon his active, musical art is reawakened. Also reminiscent of märchen is the inexplicable, arbitrary fate that befalls the Onion Cellar landlord, Schmuh, when he shoots thirteen sparrows in a day instead of twelve. However real Danzig and Düsseldorf might appear, they are still in a make-believe world.

Beyond such unreal elements, Grass introduces into Oskar's person and the narration centered on him a couple of specifically modernistic effects. In the first masterstroke, a dissociation of perspective, events of many years are shown from the physical viewpoint of a three-year-old. Before about 1943, Oskar can crawl in everywhere, taken for a child with no understanding, and yet he registers things critically. As a narrator about the age of thirty, he sometimes reports how he saw things as a naive child, sometimes affects still to be naive. The possibility that the narrator is mad adds imponderables. Finally, there are times when as an older child he claims the privilege of a three-year-old. When Herbert Truczinski threatens to leave before explaining all his scars (suffered in international brawls in the bar where he is a waiter) to the early teenage Oskar, Oskar "strampelte, machte auf dreijährig; das half immer" (232) ("began to fuss and play the three-year-old, that always helped" [181]).

In an inward parallel to such tricks, the thirty-year-old is blasé but still infantile. Grass mixes childish and childlike: if the child need not recognize what is going on around him and wishes only to fit in with his environment, the adolescent ought to question it, the adult to shape it for himself—or at least come to a settled individual view of it. By clinging to a child's perspective, Oskar gains freedom to observe the horrors of the Nazi period sharply and yet not analyze them, still less resist them systematically. He is, at least at one level of his being (and of his function in the novel), the childlike hero who does not want to understand what goes on around and merely adapts, rather amorally, to the mood of the age (Brode, *Zeitgeschichte* 85).

The second masterstroke is making Oskar combine apparently incompatible characteristics of the age. Like a figure in some cubist painting viewed from the front and the side simultaneously, he displays contradictions: good and bad, rebel and conformist, principled and opportunistic, isolated and engaged. This incompatibility is a key to his role as mediator of historical experience. "Oskar is to be regarded rather as a narrative device or ironical viewpoint than as a person whose character can be understood in psychological terms and whose statements give us insight into his personality" (Thomas, *Grass* 24). Interpretations of Oskar as schizophrenic fail to account for much of his thinking and actions. Only superficially (and largely because of his predominantly subjective narrative—though that alternates between first and third person!) are we invited to understand him psychologically. Noel Thomas, after attempting analysis, has to conclude, "So fragmented is Oskar's personality that he does not emerge as a character. . . . He is a persona and not a personality" (*Grass* 19). Oskar seems to show conscience when, very belatedly, he takes responsibility for the deaths of Matzerath and of Bronski (731; 553)—but no development of personality follows. Like the postwar West German citizen, he divests himself of his guilt by superficial contrition. He confesses his crimes, real or imaginary, to Bebra and asks for mercy, but what he gets in reply is no Faustian pact, no signing away of his conscience, only a contract for concert tours (732; 554).

Thus Oskar is schematically seen in chiaroscuro, as lacking a center but continually moving between poles—for instance, between Satan and Jesus. His very early occupation with two contrasting figures, Rasputin and Goethe, shows how Grass uses the combination of incompatible elements. A settled personality is not to be expected: the warped malfeasance of Rasputin can coexist with a desire for good. Oskar admits to a suspicion that Goethe would have seen only "Unnatur" (112) ("anti-nature" [91]) in him.

As a construct, an artificial person, Oskar can have no development, no *Bildung*. Yet he can encapsulate the flawed innocence of the era in his oppositional deeds, its mass guilt in those personal guilts that he fails to exorcise. The paradoxical multiple persona, impossible to pin down, can also represent all sorts of outsiders. Thus Arnds correctly draws parallels between Oskar and various "characters grounded in popular culture and mythology – the clown, fool, trickster, harlequin/Erlking, and their literary relative, the picaro"—and sees these parallel characters as marginal figures of society, such as "criminals, psychopaths, and transients, groups that the Nazis labeled as asocial" (*Representation* 98). They are also typically "Proteus-like characters, shape-shifters" (129). Bebra does, indeed, accuse Oskar of daring to appear "in neuer Gestalt" (731), of having "the audacity to change your shape" (553).

We can now introduce further comparisons and invite another sprawling discussion. Many students will be familiar with science fiction, space opera, and the like; some will know the work of J. R. R. Tolkien. One could thus focus class discussion on the basic element of unreality in such novels and films and ask, Do such works offer disguised answers to questions of human life as we know it? Are radically different types of mentality explored in them, or are basic human drives replicated among strange creatures? In what ways can the imagined world, the galaxy, space and time travel be brought into contact with the world of our experience? Is Oskar like a cyborg or mixed organic and artificial being?

To explore the use of magical or inexplicable powers in a setting of reality, one could also consider the figure of Superman: what rules exist for the use of superhuman powers, and what effects do those powers have in life? With prompting, such a discussion might ask whether the exploits of Superman are not predictable do-goodery when compared with Oskar's malevolent, anarchic interventionism, which lays bare some unwelcome truths about human life and society.

One could refer to J. K. Rowling's hero, Harry Potter, who offers greater depth and complexity in the use and occurrence of magical capabilities and therefore presents more parallels with Oskar. Harry, like Oskar, grows up in an ordinary world. But the magical world can affect reality in ways that baffle the normal people or Muggles. Possession of special powers places responsibilities on the bearer; increasingly complex moral choices are demanded. Magic is revealed as a manifestation of a mystery, not just a set of tricks. Harry enters a complicated wizard society, whereas Oskar (more like Superman?) remains isolated in his glass breaking. A detailed comparison of a volume in the Harry Potter series with *Die Blechtrommel* would be a rewarding major project for any group with the stamina for it.

The protean Oskar is also an artist who reacts to his experience in a creative way by drumming, then by writing (40; 37). The music of young Oskar is "in die Aprilluft getrommeltes Tempelchen" (121) ("the little temple that Oskar's drumming had erected in the April air" [97]). He playfully likens himself, as he rises on the Métro escalator to face the police investigating the murder of the nurse Dorothea, to Dante returning from hell or to Goethe (does he not mean Faust?) returning from the mothers (771; 583). Only "über den Umweg, den meine Trommel vorschreibt" (229) ("indirectly, by way of my drum" [179]—in the original, the drum determines the path to the past) can Oskar remember past scars. The drum alone, when properly handled (23; 25), can divulge details of the conception of his mother. The verbs used are evocative: "heute einen langen Vormittag zertrommelt, habe meiner Trommel Frage gestellt" (51) ("drummed away a long morning, asking my drum all sorts of questions" [46]). His self-awareness is mediated through the drum: he knows he is in love with Maria when he notices that his improvisations are imparting this passion to the tin (343; 265). Personal experience is for him as important as history, perhaps even more so. "Es geht gar nicht um Polen, es geht um mein verbogenes Blech" (291) ("it's not Poland they're worried about, it's my drum" [226]), Oskar thinks in the chapter "Die Polnische Post" ("The Polish Post Office"). Such egocentricity can be seen as characteristic of the creative artist for whom everything external is just subject matter.

Asserting himself as drummer, Oskar maintains superiority over contemporary events, at the price of existence on the fringe and amorality. In the

much-quoted chapter "Die Tribüne" ("The Rostrum"), where the most concentrated statements about art and society are found, Bebra warns the young
Oskar, "Unsereins darf nie zu den Zuschauern gehören. . . . Unsereins muß
vorspielen und die Handlung bestimmen, sonst wird unsereins von jenen da be-
handelt. Und jene da spielen uns allzu gerne übel mit!" (144) ("Our kind has no
place in the audience. We must perform, we must run the show. If we don't, it's
the others that run us. And they don't do it with kid gloves" [114]). Oskar must
try, he says, always to be on the stand at great events, not among the crowd. To
some extent the novel thematizes the Nazis' campaign against the physically
abnormal, which obviously includes Bebra and Oskar. But more important is
that Bebra and Oskar are artists; the phrase "die Handlung bestimmen" ("run
the show") is meant seriously. Grass would like to wrest control from the politicians. Oskar goes beyond Bebra, finding an alternative to being on the stand
or in the crowd: he crouches under the stand and controls events secretly. As
the Nazi marchers approach, he takes up his drumsticks with the words, "Jetzt
mein Volk, paß auf, mein Volk!" (152) ("Now, my people. . . . Now, my people.
Hearken unto me!" [120]), and disrupts the demonstration with his rhythms
and makes the participants dance the Charleston instead of marching.

Oskar also breaks up the mass meetings of other parties, groupings, and
sects: "Was sie auch zu singen, zu blasen, zu beten und zu verkünden hatten:
Meine Trommel wußte es besser. Mein Werk war also ein zerstörerisches" (158)
("Whatever they might have to sing, trumpet, or proclaim, my drum knew better. Yes, my work was destructive" [124]). The artist's controlling work, here, is
a form of satire that exposes the ridiculous side of all convictions. In the surreal episode of the attempted arrest of Viktor Weluhn on the strength of a still
valid 1939 warrant calling for his execution as an insurgent (because he helped
defend the Polish Post Office), it is Oskar's drummed rhythm and Viktor's voice
intoning the Polish national anthem that call forth the ghostly Polish cavalry,
"ohne Laut, dennoch donnernd, fleischlos, blutlos und dennoch polnisch und
zügellos" (760) ("soundless yet thundering, fleshless, bloodless, and yet Polish,
down upon us they thundered" [575]), forcing Vittlar to the ground to avoid
them and removing Viktor and his persecutors. When Vittlar congratulates Oskar on this success, Oskar expresses the wish once in life to have no success
(761; 575)—that is, I suppose, to have a life in which art would not be needed
to right the injustices of reality.

Oskar's observation and particularly his disturbing memory of Nazism are
unwelcome in the Federal Republic of Germany, where people want only to
forget; that he is prosecuted or declared mad (or both) is a reversal of the
natural order of things. The world is topsy-turvy. West German society, having refused to reflect on its historical guilt, should be in the dock, accused by
Oskar. Instead, that society has neutralized its uncomfortable outsider because
he threatened its collective taboos: a sick society claims to deal with its illness
by declaring the diagnostician to be mad and continuing as normal (Brode,
Zeitgeschichte 105–07).

Oskar's memories are drum solos, already art, as seen in the chapter "Im Zwiebelkeller" ("Onion Cellar"). Here, between artists and ordinary citizens, he makes his living as a member of a jazz trio, providing musical background to the nightly ceremony of the cutting of onions to enable the bruised survivors of the epoch to weep. But on the one occasion when Schmuh's double dose of onions produces not a liberating outburst but an orgiastic frenzy, Oskar's art is called on:

> Als Schmuh mich um den Einsatz meiner Blechtrommel bat, spielte ich nicht, was ich konnte, sondern was ich vom Herzen her wußte. Es gelang Oskar, einem einst dreijährigen Oskar die Knüppel in die Fäuste zu drükken. Alte Wege trommelte ich hin und zurück, machte die Welt aus dem Blickwinkel der Dreijährigen deutlich. . . .   (704)

> When Schmuh asked me to step in with my drum, I didn't play anything I had ever learned, I played with my heart. It was a three-year-old Oskar who picked up those drumsticks. I drummed my way back, I drummed up the world as a three-year-old sees it.   (533)

Oskar's music has the effect of a kind of regression therapy, structuring the frenzy, returning the participants to early childhood until they wet themselves, freeing them to return gradually to adult normality. The drummed memories are transposed into language in a conscious process during the narration. Through Oskar's double formulation of his memories, Grass transforms his raw material. Similarly the string with which Bruno, the male nurse in charge of the putatively deranged Oskar, makes his sculptures is transformed: set in plaster, pierced with needles, and set on a stand. Though lightly satirized, Bruno is a creative person, who not only transposes themes of Oskar's narration into abstract visual form but also gives that form permanence and twists it into an enigma by giving his works allusive, humorous titles (552; 419).

The act of drumming also makes Oskar happy; when after 1945 he refrains from music and attempts to build up an ordinary life, substitute happiness comes from other aesthetic activity. Instead of drumming, he contents himself "mit dem kleinen Glück der Schriftklopferei in Korneffs Steinmetzbude" (597) ("with the modest happiness of cutting inscriptions at Korneff's" [455]). At the return to drumming, occasioned by Klepp's doubt of his musical expertise, something shoots from his head to his hump, the symbol of difference and artistry. He is almost passive: "ich . . . drehte mich oder wurde gedreht, . . . betrat wie ein Überlebender, der von langer Irrfahrt zurückkehrt, Klepps Spaghettiküche . . ." (666–67) ("I . . . turned or was turned . . . entered Klepp's spaghetti kitchen as a traveler returns from long wanderings" [506]).

Oskar's music as response to the reality of his age is comparable with that of Thomas Mann's Leverkühn in *Doktor Faustus* (1947), which portrays a composer in the German, mystic, demonic tradition. Oskar with his American rhythms, only dabbling in the Faustian pact, seems to parody Leverkühn. Yet his drummed world is Grass's answer to reality—even if Oskar, like Leverkühn, sometimes indulges in the very "irrationalism and inhumanity" (Thomas, *Grass* 90) that Mann and Grass oppose. With the drum, he can bring about desired results. If this is art, it is operative art. The drum does not represent "einen bewußten Rückzug aus der Welt in die Kunst" (Moser 42) ("a conscious retreat from the world into art" [trans. mine]); precisely this art, however egocentrically practiced, alters the world. Oskar's insistence on memory, reminding others of past wrongs, parallels Grass's concern that Nazi crimes not be swept under the carpet and thus undermines the easy consensus of the early Federal Republic in which former Nazis have recovered positions of power.

Religious aspects of the novel (esp. in the chapters "Kein Wunder" and "Die Nachfolge Christi" ["No Wonder" and "The Imitation of Christ"]) show again Oskar's duality. Baptism attaches him to Jesus, but insecurely, since the promise to renounce Satan is made only on his behalf, against his wish, by Jan.

> Bevor ich den Kopf schütteln konnte—denn ich dachte nicht daran, zu verzichten—, sagte Jan dreimal, stellvertretend für mich: "Ich widersage."
> Ohne daß ich es mir mit Satan verdorben hatte, salbte Hochwürden Wiehnke mich auf der Brust und zwischen den Schultern.   (174)

> Before I could shake my head—for I had no intention whatsoever of renouncing—Jan, acting as my proxy, said three times: "I do renounce."
> Without my having said anything to spoil my relations with Satan, Father Wiehnke anointed me on the breast and between the shoulder blades.
> (136)

Inspection of the baby Jesus figure in the Herz-Jesu-Kirche ("Church of the Sacred Heart") shows Oskar that he and Jesus are identical twins, with the same Bronski blue eyes and the same arm posture, as if Jesus were drumming (180; 141). Oskar demands a small miracle from Jesus: if Jesus starts drumming, Jesus can assert primacy; otherwise, Oskar will arrogate the name of Jesus (183; 144). As the miracle is not forthcoming, Oskar continues to produce his glass-shattering wonders. But he fails to break the church windows: perhaps Jesus protects them, thus performing the miracle he did not produce at Oskar's demand (185; 145). When, years later, Jesus does start drumming, even playing Oskar's favorite pieces, Oskar resents the competition, ordering Jesus, "Sofort gibst du mir meine Trommel wieder. Du hast dein Kreuz, das sollte dir reichen!" (469) ("Give me back my drum this minute. You've got your cross, that should do you" [358]). Jesus relinquishes the drum but addresses Oskar in the words once used to Peter: "Liebst du mich, Oskar?" and "Du bist Oskar, der Fels, und auf diesem Fels will ich meine Kirche bauen. Folge mir nach!" (469–70) ("Dost thou love me, Oskar? . . . Thou art Oskar, the rock, and on this rock I will build my Church.

Follow thou me!" [558]). Oskar's reaction to the first words is a spirited denial; to the second, to break off one of the statue's toes.

What are we to conclude (leaving aside theological points) from such scenes? I believe that Oskar can no longer accept the primacy of Jesus even when underscored by a miracle; he posits a strict division of drum and cross, art and religion. Jesus, on the other hand, who originally had no rock to build his church on but the flaky Peter, now has no rock but the dismissive Oskar. A church will therefore not be built; an alternative edifice based on the gospel of art may instead be erected. The creative work, however ironically viewed, represents a modern religion, asserting the superiority of its insights over the rational, materialistic stances that dominate the visible world and offering these insights as a guide to life in that world—a world it rejects. Oskar claims holiness for the printed word: "Auch schlechte Bücher sind Bücher und deshalb heilig" (111) ("Even bad books are books and therefore sacred" [90]).

The theme of Oskar's imitation or parody of Jesus, or his belief that he is Jesus, is bound up with the question of whether he is really mad or merely adopting eccentricity out of bravado or to escape imprisonment for murdering the nurse Dorothea (one murder, ironically, that he certainly did not commit). At any rate, obsession with Jesus brings us the claim that he can reach or leap over all the persons of the Trinity (459; 349–50); the whole *Stäuber* ("Duster") episode, ending with the (inexact) parallel of the trial of Oskar with that of Jesus (501; 381); the gospel reminiscences: "Auf die Fliesen ließ ich mich fallen und weinte bitterlich" (185) ("I sank down on the flagstones and wept bitterly" [145]); and embarkation, like Jesus, on a radically changed life at the age of thirty. In the chapter "Madonna 49," Oskar temporarily becomes the object of artistic endeavor rather than the creative subject. His passivity corresponds to the stripping and killing of Jesus in the Passion. Professor Kuchen invites the students of his drawing class to crucify Oskar in their sketches: "schlachtet ihn, kreuzigt ihn, nagelt ihn mit Kohle aufs Papier!" (607) ("I want you to slaughter him, crucify him, to nail him to your paper with charcoal!" [463]). But Oskar resists a full-blown reenactment of Jesus. To form a sect would be a concession to public expectations, against the vocation of drummer:

> Oder aber, ich gebe nach, lasse mich festnageln, gehe hinaus, nur weil ich dreißig bin, und mime ihnen den Messias, den sie in mir sehen, mache, gegen besseres Wissen, aus meiner Trommel mehr, als die darzustellen vermag, laß die Trommel zum Symbol werden, gründe eine Sekte, Partei oder auch nur eine Loge.   (774–75)

> Or I could give in and let them nail me to the Cross. Just because I happen to be thirty, I go out and play the Messiah they see in me; against my better judgment I make my drum stand for more than it can, I make a symbol out of it, found a sect, a party, or maybe only a lodge.
>   (585; sounds more definite in English, a mere possibility in German)

Whereas drumming is a creative act that allows Oskar to feel equal to the Deity and assert his autonomy, shattering glass is a destructive, secondary capability; here Oskar is still subordinate. He cannot shatter church windows with his voice, cannot destabilize the edifice of religion (Delaney 120). This failure makes him retain "jenen Rest katholischen Glaubens, der ihm noch viele verzweifelte Lästerungen eingeben sollte" (187) ("the vestige of Catholic faith which was yet to inspire any number of desperate blasphemies" [146]) and continually reminds him that he is split, "weder im Sakralen noch im Profanen beheimatet" (187) ("at home neither in the sacred nor the profane" [146]).

Oskar's glass-breaking voice, like Harry Potter's magic powers, becomes apparent without exercise of his will. His drumming, however, is connected with the use of full faculties of senses, intelligence, and willpower from the moment of birth: it is voluntary and active. Because Oskar is creative, he can have an effect on the world around him, and Grass certainly prefers such an effect to political influence: dancing, not marching! But since Oskar also unites light and dark, Goethe and Rasputin, contrary ethical directions, that creative effect is not predictably good. The different methods used by Grass to suggest or portray possible reactions to the complex moral world of his day coexist uneasily. Oskar the construct cannot be a realistic figure, but he has to bear the author's conviction that the artist's attitude to reality—also demonstrated by Grass in the whole course of the novel—is the modern version of religion, the better alternative to politics and war.

"But Even Herr Matzerath Is Unable to Keep His Story Running in a Straight Line": The Role of the Secondary Narrators in Günter Grass's *The Tin Drum*

Katharina Hall

The Tin Drum's Oskar Matzerath remains one of the most arresting figures of twentieth-century literature: even almost fifty years after the novel's publication in 1959, the originality of his characterization and the energy of his narrative voice secure the reader's attention from the very first page. The power of Oskar's literary presence derives largely from the number of key positions he occupies in the text. His role as implied author (*implizierter Autor*)[1] and first-person narrator (*Ich-Erzähler*) stamps the narrative with the dual authority of an authorial and autobiographical voice, which is in turn reinforced by his claim to the all-seeing perspective of the omniscient narrator (*allwissender Erzähler*).[2] At the same time, Oskar gives himself a starring role in the narrative, relating the story of his life and personal development in a quirky imitation of the nineteenth-century bildungsroman. He thus dominates the narration and the content of the text to an unusually high degree: he is simply impossible for the reader to ignore.

Given Oskar's dominant position in the text as author, narrator, and chief protagonist, it is perhaps not surprising that critics and readers have tended to overlook *The Tin Drum*'s two other first-person narrators, Bruno Münsterberg and Gottfried Vittlar. Their joint contribution totals only thirty-one pages, an amount that pales into insignificance when placed against the remaining 739 of Oskar's narrative.[3] While many critics give these "secondary narrators" a passing mention (Romberg 64), few have explored the significance of their role at any length (see Beyersdorf). This essay aims to make good the lack of critical attention given to Bruno and Vittlar and to show the value of including an examination of their narratives when teaching *The Tin Drum*. It argues that the presence of the secondary narrators constitutes an important textual strategy on Grass's part, allowing readers the opportunity of viewing Oskar from an alternative narrative perspective (*alternative Erzählperspektive*) and of gaining insights into his character that his own narration is unable to supply. The secondary narratives also invite the reader to reflect critically on Oskar's role as a first-person narrator and, most important, on the question of his reliability. In highlighting the contradictory nature of Oskar's recollections, Bruno's narrative in particular illustrates Oskar's problematic relation to his own and the larger German past. An analysis of Bruno's and Vittlar's narratives in the classroom can thus significantly deepen the student's understanding of the complexity of Oskar's role in *The Tin Drum* and the way he is used by Grass to explore the legacy of National Socialism in the postwar era.

Bruno is mentioned in the opening sentence of the novel and at the beginning or end of a number of chapters in his capacity as Oskar's *Pfleger* ("male nurse") at the psychiatric hospital.[4] His initial function is thus to draw the readers' attention to the novel's narrative framework (*Rahmenhandlung*), making them aware of the reality of Oskar's circumstances as a mental patient in the 1950s and raising the possibility that his words are nothing more than an outpouring of madness. This framework also highlights the constructed nature of Oskar's memoirs. Oskar's long drumming sessions in the hospital represent the mediation of the past by memory and language. While "die Kunst des Zurücktrommelns" (623) ("the art of drumming back the past" [474]) enables Oskar to remember, it is also made clear that his subsequent representation of past events is shaped, and at times distorted, by the guilt that permeates postwar German society following the cataclysm of the Holocaust (K. Hall).

As the beginning of Oskar's narrative emphasizes, Bruno keeps Oskar under constant surveillance through the peephole in Oskar's door: "mein Pfleger beobachtet mich, läßt mich kaum aus dem Auge" (9), ("my keeper is watching me, he never lets me out of his sight" [15]). At times Oskar finds this continuous observation oppressive:

> Es ist gar nicht so einfach, hier, im abgeseiften Metallbett einer Heil- und Pflegeanstalt, im Blickfeld eines verglasten und mit Brunos Auge bewaffneten Guckloches liegend, die Rauchschwaden . . . nachzuzeichnen.
>
> (23)

> It is not so easy, lying here in this scrubbed hospital bed in full view of a glass peephole armed with Bruno's eye, to give a picture of the smoke clouds that rose. . . .[5]

At other times Oskar seems to relish the attention he receives: "Wie gerne möchte ich . . . das verglaste Guckloch . . . der Zimmertür entglasen, damit mich Bruno, mein Pfleger, direkter beobachten kann" (171) ("How happy I should be . . . to unglass the peephole in my door so that Bruno my keeper might observe me more directly" [134]). While Bruno is to some extent figured as a jailer (Oskar is confined to the institution for a murder he supposedly committed), he also plays an important role as Oskar's caretaker and is protective of his patient, displaying "sein besorgtes Braunauge" (772) ("a concerned brown eye" [trans. mine; cf. 584]) at the peephole when Oskar remembers harrowing events.

However, the relationship between Oskar and Bruno extends beyond the conventional bounds of jailer-prisoner and caretaker-patient. Oskar comments on the opening page of the narrative:

> Liebgewonnen habe ich ihn, erzähle dem Gucker hinter der Tür, sobald er mein Zimmer betritt, Begebenheiten aus meinem Leben, damit er mich trotz des ihn hindernden Guckloches kennenlernt.   (9)

I've come to be very fond of him; as soon as the watcher-behind-the-door enters the room I tell him incidents from my life, so he can get to know me in spite of the peephole between us. (15; I have revised the trans.)

Bruno often leaves his position as "Gucker" ("watcher"), with its echoes of the anonymous, authoritarian eye of Jeremy Bentham's panopticon, to cross the threshold of Oskar's room. Here, in Oskar's personal space, the power dynamics appear to be inverted, with Oskar's natural authority setting new terms of engagement: Bruno addresses Oskar respectfully as Herr Matzerath and takes on the role of personal secretary, running errands for him when asked. Most important, he becomes Oskar's primary listener, the audience of one to whom Oskar regularly drums-relates the stories of his life. Bruno also contributes to Oskar's literary project in a number of other ways. He supplies Oskar with paper at the beginning of the narrative, enabling him to write down his memoirs, and plays a vital part in Oskar's drum rituals (unwrapping each new drum and removing the price tag before presenting it to its owner). Finally, he complements Oskar's storytelling with his own artistic activity, creating sculptures of string dipped in plaster with titles that echo Oskar's tales—"Apfel in vier Schlafröcken," "Die schöne Fischesserin," "Die beiden Skatdrescher" (552) ("Potato in Four Skirts," "The Beautiful Fish Eater," "The Two Skat Players" [419]).

Oskar rarely seems to feel intimidated or threatened by Bruno. He depicts him as a big, ugly, amiable, simple man, but above all, as someone who is naive and suggestible. When Bruno agrees to supply Oskar with paper, Oskar comments that "Liebe hätte den Freunden sicher verboten, etwas so Gefährliches wie unbeschriebenes Papier mitzubringen" (11) ("solicitous affection . . . would surely have deterred my friends from bringing me anything so dangerous as blank paper" [16]). Unlike them, Bruno does not appear to recognize that allowing Oskar to write has dangerous implications. He is figured as an innocent, who is unaware that the stories Oskar tells him are full of lies ("vorgelogen" [9]). But the impression the reader gains of Bruno from Oskar's narrative is one that must later be revised, for once Bruno begins his narration, it becomes clear that Oskar has considerably underestimated the intelligence and perceptiveness of his caretaker. This disjunction can be usefully pointed up when teaching the text, as it plays an important role in undercutting the reader's perception of Oskar as an omniscient narrator.

Bruno's thirteen-page narrative, which details the flight of Oskar and his family from Danzig to the West in 1945, is placed in the last chapter of the second book, "Wachstum im Güterwagen" ("Growth in a Freight Car"). Previously, Oskar had described the delirium that accompanied the beginning of his growth spurt after Matzerath's funeral at the end of the war. As he finishes his narration, Oskar realizes that his memories have triggered another period of growth in the present. Unable to drum or write because of the growing pains, he asks Bruno to take over. The impact of this change in narration over two-thirds of the way through the novel is substantial: the reader is so accustomed to Oskar's first-person voice that the introduction of an alternative narrative perspective comes as an unexpected and intriguing surprise. Bruno's narrative gives the reader the rare opportunity to see Oskar the way others see him. The defamiliarizing effect of this "other" point of view can be illustrated in the classroom through an examination of Bruno's description of Oskar, which allows the reader to appreciate the distinctive nature of Oskar's physical appearance fully for the first time:

> Mein Patient mißt einen Meter und einundzwanzig Zentimeter. Er trägt seinen Kopf, der selbst für normal gewachsene Personen zu groß wäre, zwischen den Schultern auf nahezu verkümmertem Hals. . . . Er blickt aus starkleuchtenden, klug beweglichen, manchmal schwärmerisch geweiteten blauen Augen.   (563)

> My patient is four feet one inch tall. He carries his head, which would be too large even for a person of normal proportions, between his shoulders on an almost nonexistent neck. His eyes are blue, brilliant, alive with intelligence; occasionally they take on a dreamy, ecstatic, wide-eyed look.   (428)

Bruno's narrative is characterized by a precise, measured tone and in many respects reads like a statement given before a court of law. It begins by establishing the particulars of the writer's identity and his relationship to Oskar:

> Ich, Bruno Münsterberg, aus Altena im Sauerland, unverheiratet und kinderlos, bin Pfleger in der Privatabteilung der hiesigen Heil- und Pflegeanstalt. Herr Matzerath, der hier seit über einem Jahr stationiert ist, ist mein Patient.   (552)

> I, Bruno Münsterberg, of Altena in Sauerland, unmarried and childless, am a male nurse in the private pavilion of the local mental hospital. Mr. Matzerath, who has been here for over a year, is my patient.   (419)

The final two words of this quotation, "my patient," subtly reconfigure the power dynamic suggested between the two in Oskar's narrative. This shift can be highlighted in the classroom by asking students to count how often the phrase is used as Bruno's narrative unfolds (no fewer than twenty-three times in the German original). It is now Bruno who appears to be in control of the relationship and who is able to manage Oskar without difficulty: "Herr Matzerath ist mein harmlosester Patient. Nie gerät er so außer sich, daß ich andere Pfleger rufen müßte" (552) ("Mr. Matzerath is my most harmless patient. He never gets so wild that I have to call in other nurses" [419]). The categorization of Oskar as "harmless" alters the reader's view of him, because it counters Oskar's self-perception of being a complex and challenging patient who has the upper hand in any dealings with the medical establishment. The narrative strongly suggests that Oskar's portrayal of Bruno as an intellectually inferior and malleable individual is misguided: it is more likely that Bruno merely allows Oskar to think of him in this way because this constitutes the most effective way of cultivating a harmonious patient-nurse relationship. This possibility is already present in Oskar's assessment of Bruno at the beginning of the narrative: "meines Pflegers Auge ist von jenem Braun, welches mich, den Blauäugigen, nicht durchschauen kann. Mein Pfleger kann also gar nicht mein Feind sein" (9) ("my keeper's eye is the shade of brown that can never see through a blue-eyed type like me. So you see, my keeper can't be [my] enemy" [15]). It is thus precisely because Oskar feels that Bruno does not pose any kind of threat that he accepts him. In actual fact, Bruno's narrative indicates that he is able to "see through" and handle Oskar with relative ease. Oskar's perception of the amount of power he exerts over Bruno is therefore revealed to be faulty and raises the possibility that his judgment on other matters may also be flawed.

Group work and classroom discussion can be used to identify the different functions of Bruno's narrative. Most obviously, it acts as the conduit by which Oskar's firsthand memories are transmitted to the reader; as such, it constitutes a form of testimony. Bruno communicates the factual details of the trip to the reader on Oskar's behalf—for example, that the family left Danzig on 12 June 1945 by train at approximately eleven o'clock in the morning (553; 420). However, Bruno also communicates the horrors of the family's journey (the Social Democrat's loud and messy death, the pillaging of the travelers' property and clothes, the discomfort caused by the cold), thereby allowing Oskar to bear witness to the traumatic dimensions of his family's experiences.

While in many places the narrative captures the immediacy of a firsthand account, the reader is also repeatedly made aware that this narrative is the product of a continuous transfer of memories and information from Oskar to Bruno. Bruno refers to himself as the "Nacherzähler" (558)—a term that is difficult to translate and does not appear in the English version—whose root is the verb *nacherzählen*, "to retell." This status as a reteller of events is emphasized through phrases such as: "Weiterhin möchte mein Patient sagen" (556) ("He has also asked me expressly to say" [422]), "Wie ich hier höre" (556) ("I am told" [423]), "Wie mich Herr Matzerath gerade belehren will" (557) ("Mr. Matzerath has just seen fit to inform me" [423]), and "sagt mein Patient" (560) ("my patient says" [425]).

The care Bruno takes to continually point up the source of the account could be read either as a means of foregrounding Oskar's key role as a firsthand witness or as a way of signaling that Oskar bears ultimate responsibility for the narrative, a precautionary measure that allows Bruno to avoid censure should the account prove to be inaccurate. The latter interpretation is supported by Bruno's repeated use of subjunctive (indirect discourse) verb forms (e.g., "habe" and "sei" [556]), which are employed in German when people "wish to indicate that they are only reporting what someone else has said but do not take any responsibility for the validity of the other person's statement" (Wells 347).

Another set of comments strikes a greater note of caution, suggesting that Bruno is actively skeptical about some aspects of Oskar's story. For example, Maria and Kurt are introduced as "Maria Matzerath, die mein Patient als seine ehemahlige Geliebte bezeichnet, Kurt Matzerath, meines Patienten angeblicher Sohn" (553) ("Maria Matzerath, whom my patient refers to as his former mistress, and . . . Kurt Matzerath, my patient's alleged son" [420]). These qualified statements, with their use of the terms "refers to" and "alleged," throw doubt on the way Oskar figures his relationships to Maria and Kurt and, by extension, undermines the authority of an earlier section of Oskar's narrative, in which he categorically claims that "ich, Oskar, war der [Kurts] Vater" (371) ("I, Oskar, was the father" [285]). Bruno's narrative thus subtly questions fundamental aspects of Oskar's story and begins to unsettle the reader's confidence in the authority of Oskar's memory and his representation of past events. This questioning is underscored by Bruno's use of phrases such as "[s]oweit sich mein Patient erinnern kann" (554) ("As far as my patient can remember" [421]) and "mein Patient behauptet" (556, 561) ("my patient tells me" [422], "my patient claims" [426]), which insinuate doubt about some of Oskar's assertions. The verb *sollen*, used here to mean "is said to have . . . ," is also found repeatedly throughout Bruno's account. The cumulative effect of these different types of qualifiers encourages the reader to examine Oskar's account more critically, particularly the more fantastical elements of the narrative: "Mein Patient behauptet, er habe . . . neun, wenn nicht zehn Zentimeter Körperlänge gewonnen" (561) ("My patient claims that he grew three and a half to four inches between Danzig-Gdansk and Stettin" [426]).

A class exercise to identify and highlight the significance of these stylistic features might involve giving students a short section of Bruno's narrative—for example, from "Herr Matzerath" to "erkannt haben will" (553) ("On June 12" to "Lucy Rennwald" [420])—and asking them to underline all the qualifiers and words that indicate a transfer of information from Oskar to Bruno.[6] Bruno's awareness of the problematic dimensions of Oskar's narration can also be effectively illustrated through close analysis of the following passage:

> Doch auch Herr Matzerath kann seine Erzählung nicht gradlinig in Bewegung halten. Abgesehen von den vier Nonnen, die er einmal Franziskanerinnen, dann Vinzentinerinnen nennt, ist es besonders jenes junge Ding, das mit seinen zwei Namen und einem einzigen, angeblich dreieckigen Fuchsgesicht seinen Bericht immer wieder auflöst und mich, den Nacherzähler, eigentlich nötigen sollte, zwei oder noch mehr Versionen jener Reise aus dem Osten nach dem Westen zu notieren.   (558)

> But even Mr. Matzerath is unable to keep his story running in a straight line. Aside from those four nuns, whom he refers to alternately as Francis-

cans or Vincentians, it's that young lady with her two names and her one supposedly triangular, fox-like face who repeatedly throws his story into disarray. To be a truly conscientious narrator of these events, I would have to write two or more separate versions of this journey from East to West. (424; I have revised the trans.)

Here Bruno highlights Oskar's tendency to change details in his story (the two denominations of the nuns and the double incarnation of a girl traveling on the train as Regina Raeck and Luzie Rennwand), to such an extent that it sometimes seems as though two completely different stories are being related.

Teachers can link this passage back to other parts of the narrative where Oskar relates two contradictory versions of one event. His accounts of the end of the Polish Post Office siege, which results in the execution of his uncle-father Jan Bronski, provide a striking example of this. In the first, at the end of the chapter "Das Kartenhaus" ("The Card House"), Oskar presents himself as an innocent bystander who happens to witness Jan's arrest by the National Socialists. The following chapter contains Oskar's admission that he effectively denounced Jan to the Nazis, meaning that he must bear some responsibility for Jan's death. In the first account, by his own admission, Oskar had managed "zu übertreiben, wenn nicht zu lügen" (318) ("to exaggerate and mislead, if not to lie" [246]). The second, "corrected" account attempts to put the record straight. This kind of retelling of events is used in the text to alert the reader to Oskar's status as an unreliable narrator *(unzuverlässiger Erzähler)*, one who is often rooted in a sense of guilt and the desire to cover up his own less-than-savory role in past events. In this context, Bruno's narrative can be viewed by students as one of a set of key textual strategies that allows the author to make readers aware of the flawed nature of Oskar's narration. It both highlights Oskar's problematic relation to the past and invites the reader to approach the narrative questioningly instead of simply accepting everything that Oskar says.

Interestingly Volker Schlöndorff's 1979 film adaptation of *The Tin Drum* dispenses with the novel's narrative framework, thereby cutting all reference to Oskar's status as a mental patient. The character of Bruno, with his alternative narrative perspective, is also omitted, as are the second version of the post office siege and the whole of the last book. Those teachers who choose to show students the film can thematize these differences as a useful means of pointing up the narrative strategies the novel employs and the ways in which these effect the reader's relation to the text.

The student's understanding of the significance of Grass's narrative approach can also be deepened through an awareness of two key contexts. The first is the historical moment of the novel's production in 1959, fourteen years after the end of the Second World War. As many critics have noted, Grass's personal experiences of National Socialism between the ages of five and seventeen mark all his writing. In his famous essay of 1965, "Ich klage an" ("I Accuse"), Grass describes the moment at the end of the war in which he and his generation finally understood the hollowness of the National Socialist ideals that he had been taught to revere: "Wir waren skeptisch und fortan bereit, jedes Wort zu prüfen und nicht mehr blindlings zu glauben. Jede Ideologie prallte an uns ab" (145) ("We were skeptical, and ready from then on to test every word and not to believe blindly anymore. We found all ideologies repellent" [trans. mine]). In particular, his comprehension of the reality of the Holocaust through a visit to Bergen-Belsen and the evidence given at the Nuremberg Trials in 1945 constituted a biographical watershed "that cannot be underestimated in any assessment of his work or influence" (Preece, *Life* 4). The impact of this moment has been further heightened by Grass's revelation in 2006 that he was a member of the Waffen-SS.

The rejection of ideology by writers such as Grass, Uwe Johnson, and Heinrich Böll, all of whom published novels in 1959, led them to adopt narrative strategies that emphasized a multiple point of view. Judith Ryan terms this kind of literary approach "perspectivism." Rooted in the conviction that "truth [is] to be found through an exploration of many different opinions rather than from the statement of a single point of view," it reflects the shift from the ideological insistence on one worldview to the pluralistic outlook embraced by postwar democracy ("Post-occupation Literary Movements" 191–92). This position is summed up most clearly in Grass's works by the author figure in *Aus dem Tagebuch einer Schnecke* (1972; *From the Diary of a Snail*), who says "ich [bin] gegen die Ansprüche des 'einzig Wahren' und für Vielfalt" (401) ("I am against the claims of the 'single truth' and in favor of multiplicity" [trans. mine]). Of course, not only truths but falsehoods too are revealed by means of the perspectivist approach, as contradictions and inaccuracies are highlighted through the juxtaposition of different points of view. In both cases, the result is a foregrounding of memory and the representation of the past, themes that are to take on an increasingly important role in postwar German discussions about guilt and moral responsibility after the Auschwitz trials of 1963–65. Grass develops this notion of perspectivism even further in his 1963 novel *Hundejahre* (*Dog Years*), in which three primary narrators give overlapping and sometimes contradictory accounts of events that took place under National Socialism.

Teachers can also place Bruno's narrative in a more general literary context that draws the student's attention to the processes of reading and interpretation. The critical theorist Terry Eagleton writes:

> Reading is not a straight-forward linear movement, a merely cumulative affair: our initial speculations generate a frame of reference within which to interpret what comes next, but what comes next may retrospectively transform our original understanding, highlighting some features of it and backgrounding others. As we read on we shed assumptions, revise beliefs, make more and more complex inferences and anticipations; each sentence opens up a horizon which is confirmed, challenged or undermined by the next. We read backwards and forwards simultaneously, predicting

and recollecting, perhaps aware of other possible realizations of the text which our reading has negated. Moreover, all this complicated activity is carried out on many levels at once, for the text has "backgrounds" and "foregrounds," different narrative viewpoints, alternative layers of meaning between which we are constantly moving.   (78–79)

Bruno's "different narrative viewpoint" accents the nonlinear structure of *The Tin Drum*. By pointing up the inconsistencies in Oskar's narrative, it invites readers to reread previous sections of the text, moving "backwards and forwards simultaneously," "retrospectively transforming" their perceptions of Oskar by highlighting the unreliable features of his voice as narrator.

Students might also be asked to consider the notion that Bruno provides the reader with a role model in terms of the way he responds to Oskar's fantastic narrative, questioning rather than passively accepting what he is told. The following passage, in which Bruno challenges Oskar's narrative directly about the contradictions it contains, provides a useful focus for discussion of this issue:

Nach mehreren Anfragen meinerseits gibt mein Patient aber zu, daß jenes Mädchen Regina Raeck hieß, spricht aber weiterhin von einem namenlos dreieckigen Fuchsgesicht, das er dann doch immer wieder beim Namen nennt, Luzie ruft; was mich nicht hindert, jenes Mädchen hier als Fräulein Regina einzutragen.   (553)

In response to a number of questions on my part, however, my patient admits that this young lady's name was Regina Raeck, but continues to speak of a nameless triangular fox face that he then does call by name, namely Luzie, again and again; none of which prevents me from entering the young lady's name here as Miss Regina.
(420; I have revised the trans.)

By contesting the dual identity of the young girl in the freight car, Bruno moves out of the passive role of scribe, whose job it is simply to record what Oskar says, and into a more active role, in which he interrogates what Oskar tells him before writing it down. Through his questions, Bruno successfully forces Oskar to relinquish one version of events and to admit the true identity of the girl (Regina). Although Oskar immediately reverts to calling her Luzie, Bruno is satisfied that he has established the truth of the matter and records Regina's name in his narrative. His role takes on stronger contours at this point; no longer a simple recorder of events, he becomes a historian who sifts and evaluates the information he is given. His willingness to question suggests the usefulness of a similar approach for the reader and can be linked to the credo of "I Accuse": "to test every word and not to believe blindly anymore."

Bruno's account ends with the suggestion that Oskar is innocent of the crime for which he was placed in the asylum and with a surprise: Oskar has grown two centimeters during the three days that Bruno was his scribe, echoing his growth in 1945 as the train carried him west. This final revelation lessens the impact of Bruno's narrative to a certain degree, because it suggests that Oskar's account of his extraordinary growth immediately after the war could be true; as a result, Bruno's skepticism about Oskar's narrative is itself partly called into doubt. Readers—and students—are thus left to negotiate a difficult path in terms of how to perceive Oskar as narrator. While his reliability is justifiably questioned by Bruno's narrative, the possibility remains that some of his fantastical tales may be true. These issues are taken up again in Vittlar's narrative in the final section of the novel.

Oskar's relationship with Gottfried Vittlar, like that with Bruno, is a complex one, characterized by contradiction and ambivalence. Vittlar is referred to in the course of the narrative as friend, employee, visitor, listener, accomplice, and betrayer. Oskar's descriptions of Vittlar are often negative: Vittlar is a vain dandy whose "bizarren Hochmut" (41) ("eccentric hauteur" [39]) and "hochmütige, geschraubte Näseln" (743) ("arrogant, affected whine" [562]) constantly get on Oskar's nerves. Vittlar is also described as egotistical, melodramatic, and sly, qualities that make him sound remarkably similar to Oskar: in both cases their eccentricities occasionally tip over into something close to madness. Vittlar's portrayal is also distinguished by the use of religious imagery. Oskar refers to him as an angel (368; 282) (744; 563) or, conversely, as the devil, in the guise of the snake in the tree of the Garden of Eden (745; 563). Vittlar is also incorporated into Oskar's messianic fantasies, styled as one of Oskar-Jesus's disciples, albeit a highly dangerous one: "ich [weiß] immer noch nicht, ob ich ihn Judas oder Johannes nennen soll" (171) ("I . . . still do not know whether to call him John or Judas" [134]).

In a teaching context, attention can be drawn to the symmetry in the positioning of Bruno's narrative and Vittlar's narrative: while Bruno's first-person account is placed at the end of the second book, Vittlar's appears in "Die letzte Straßenbahn oder Anbetung eines Weckglases" ("The Last Streetcar, or Adoration of a Preserving Jar"), the penultimate chapter of the third book. Both, then, offer an alternative narrative perspective at or shortly before a climactic point in the novel. Vittlar's narrative, which relates the events leading up to Oskar's arrest, trial, and sectioning, is longer than Bruno's (eighteen pages, rather than thirteen). Oskar tells us that it is the transcript of the incriminating statement Vittlar made to the police regarding Oskar's possible role in the murder of Nurse Dorothea that led to Oskar's arrest. Vittlar refers to Oskar throughout as "der Angeklagte" ("the accused"), mirroring Bruno's earlier emphasis of Oskar's status as "the patient." However, certain passages suggest that Vittlar has added some commentary in the present. For example, he boasts about his role as star witness in the Ring Finger Trial, which at the time of the statement had not yet taken place. Equally, his inclusion of the fantastical drumming episode on the streetcar and the assertion that he and Oskar engineered Oskar's arrest together would almost certainly have led the police to discount him as a credible or useful witness.

Oskar and Vittlar first meet on 7 July 1951, when Oskar is walking a dog in the countryside on the outskirts of Düsseldorf, close to the Vittlar family home. Vittlar claims that, while reclining in an apple tree in his mother's garden, he saw the dog retrieve an object from a field, which turned out to be the unfortunate murder victim's ring finger. He then relates how he accompanied Oskar to have a plaster cast made of the finger and was subsequently taken to view it, nestled in a jar of preservative fluid, as part of a macabre shrine to the nurse. After a year, during which he accompanies Oskar on a drumming tour, Vittlar makes his statement about Oskar's incriminating behavior to the police. Oddly, he appears to have done so with Oskar's approval. As Vittlar puts it:

> Auch jene Anzeige, die mich als Zeugen, ihn als Angeklagten . . . zitiert, ist ein von uns erfundenes Spiel, ein Mittelchen mehr, unsere Langeweile und Einsamkeit zu zerstreuen und zu ernähren.   (748)

> Even this denunciation, the act that brings us here, myself as the witness, him as the accused, is a game we invented, a means of diverting and entertaining our boredom and our loneliness.
>
> (566; I have revised the trans.)

This "game" allows Oskar to effect his escape from the confusions of postwar society to the psychiatric hospital, while satisfying Vittlar's desire for public fame. Vittlar's apparent betrayal of Oskar is therefore figured as a curious but mutually beneficial act of friendship.

One of the primary functions of Vittlar's narrative is to suggest that Oskar chose to enter the psychiatric hospital by deliberately allowing the world to think he was guilty of a murder he did not commit. Class discussion of this issue can be used to point up the irony that the psychiatric hospital represents an escape for Oskar from the madness *beyond* its doors: his sanctuary is a white hospital bed, its sturdy bars keeping a welcome distance between him and the outside world. The whole of Vittlar's narrative thus allows a fuller understanding of the crisis Oskar experiences at the age of thirty, when he hears the news that Nurse Beate has been identified as the real murderer and that he is likely to be released. If forced to leave his beloved hospital bed, he will have to reenter postwar German society and confront the nightmare apparition of "die schwarze Köchin" ("the Black Witch"), who appears to embody the trauma and guilt of his own as well as the larger German past. This prospect tips him into a final despairing silence ("Er hat keine Worte mehr!" [779]) ("He has no more words!" [589; I have revised the trans.]); he is paralyzed by the specters of the past as well as by the uncertain future that awaits him.

Vittlar's account of Oskar's unorthodox behavior after the nurse's murder and the disturbing *Gebet* ("prayer") Oskar recites in front of the finger in the jar are clearly designed to show the instability of his mental state. At the same time, Vittlar's testimony about the extraordinary events that take place when Vittlar and Oskar meet Viktor Weluhn supports the fantastical claims that Oskar has made throughout his narrative in relation to the power of his drumming. Vittlar describes how, when he and Oskar commandeer a streetcar one evening for fun, two former Nazis jump on board with Viktor, a resistance fighter whom they have been chasing in a Kafkaesque fashion since the Polish Post Office siege twelve years earlier. In order to prevent Viktor's execution, Oskar drums up the Polish cavalry, whose multitudes of horses sweep Viktor and his persecutors away. Vittlar's testimony is highly significant, because it is the first time that there appears to be objective verification of the fantastical effects of Oskar's drumming. In contrast with Bruno, who relates Oskar's experiences second-hand, Vittlar is presented as an eyewitness of what he relates.

If readers accept Vittlar's account, then they may also be inclined to accept Oskar's earlier descriptions of incidents such as his anarchic, drummed disruption of the Nazi rally in the chapter "Die Tribüne" ("The Rostrum"). Teachers can show that Vittlar's narrative has the opposite effect to Bruno's in this respect, because it encourages readers to suspend their disbelief of the fantastical elements in the novel. However, the possibility that they will believe Vittlar's account also has to be weighed against the fact that he is prone to dramatizing and therefore may be viewed as a less than dependable narrator (certainly in comparison with the more solid Bruno). As at the end of Bruno's narrative, readers are left uncertain as to quite what they should believe. This refusal of the novel to yield full interpretive closure chimes with Grass's own celebration of questions as opposed to an unthinking acceptance of answers.

An examination of Bruno's narrative and Vittlar's narrative thus allows students to gain a number of insights into Oskar's roles as character and narrator. Each of the secondary narrators offers a rare and valuable alternative perspective that defamiliarizes Oskar's reality and encourages readers to question what they may previously have accepted due to the authority of Oskar's first-person voice. This perspective is arguably the most important function of the secondary narrators, as it repeatedly brings the issue of Oskar's narrative reliability and his flawed relation to the past to the attention of readers. While never offering a definitive evaluation of Oskar's status, the narratives, like Oskar's contradictory accounts of events, form part of a collection of textual strategies that Grass uses to create "alternative layers of meaning" in his work and to demand an active, critical engagement with the novel on the part of readers and students alike.

NOTES

[1] I use the term *implied author* here to indicate Oskar's position as the author of a written account of the past and his awareness of the power that writers can exert over their readers.

[2] Oskar describes himself as "hellhörig" (52) ("clair-audient" [47]).

[3] Bruno's pages are 552–64 (419–29); Vittlar's are 745–62 (563–76).

[4] See the beginning of chapters 1, 2, 7, and 11 in book 1 and chapters 1, 7, and 17 in book 2, as well as the end of chapter 15 in book 1 and chapter 9 in book 2.

[5] I have revised parts of Manheim's original translation (25).

[6] Teachers might also like to take this opportunity to review the use of the subjunctive in German.

From Sea to Soup:
Teaching the Image of the Eel

Richard E. Schade

There is surely no more revolting scene in Grass's *Die Blechtrommel* than that of the fisherman's extraction of writhing eels from various orifices in a horse-head cadaver pulled from the waters of the Baltic Sea. Alfred Matzerath; his wife, Agnes; her cousin and lover, Jan Bronski; and Oskar seek Good Friday recreation, only to experience this stomach-turning activity, each in his or her own way. On the day commemorating Christ's crucifixion, Agnes vomits at the sight of this spectacle. To calm her, Jan pets her, while Alfred assists the angler. Oskar observes the behavior of his elders. As the seaside scene concludes, Alfred purchases several eels, serving them up as soup on return home—from sea to soup.

The impact of the scene on the reader (and moviegoer) is unforgettable, even profound. Instinctual revulsion is coupled with morbid fascination. The teacher's challenge is to take advantage of this fascination by harnessing the students' gut response. My own experience of teaching the novel in both undergraduate and graduate courses suggests that the optimal approach to the seaside episode is first to offer a discussion-based close reading of the function of the eel image in the textual narrative. To augment the close reading, a teacher may require students, in a second step, to view and analyze the relatively brief segment from the film and then review and report on a selection of relevant scholarship interpreting both movie and text. In a third step, the analysis might conclude with a viewing and discussion of Grass's artistic representations of the slimy fish. An understanding of the artworks gained in the classroom enriches significantly the students' reading of the literary statement, their analysis of the film, and their appeciation of previous scholarship. They come to understand the details of Grass's text and graphic images as well as the usefulness and effectiveness of linking literature and artwork in the interpretive enterprise.

The narrative of the chapter "Karfreitagskost" ("Good Friday Fare") takes the reader from downtown Danzig to the seaside and back home. The year is 1937. That the family group has Good Friday (historically 26 March) off from work at Matzerath's shop at all is because Alfred, a Protestant from the Rhineland, follows religious tradition. Agnes, a Catholic and a Kashubian, that is, Slavic, honors her husband's wishes (just as he would hers on the festival of Corpus Christi). Their confessional accommodation mirrors the marital split, and that her lover is Polish and Catholic underlines the inherent tension in the interpersonal triangle. As the players wander the beach, Alfred blithely skips stones on the calm sea, even as Jan searches for amber, a chunk of which he presents to Agnes. Here again, Grass emphasizes the underlying marital divide just before all four mount the breakwater of jumbled boulders projecting into the Baltic Sea.

The completion of the passage from city to sea is indicated by the group's arrival at a beacon located at the confluence of the dark and brackish Mottlau River with the Baltic. The site is liminal space—beyond them the sea, behind them the land—and here at the border stands the angling longshoreman. The narrative focus on the man is obsessive, intensifying the reader's curiosity, particularly as he methodically reels in his line, finally heaving the cumbersome bait onto the rocks: "einen Pferdekopf, einen frischen, wie echten Pferdekopf, den Kopf eines schwarzen Pferdes, einen schwarzmähnigen Rappenkopf also, der gestern noch, vorgestern noch gewiehert haben mochte" (191) ("it was a horse's head, a fresh and genuine horse's head, the head of a black horse with a black mane, which only yesterday or the day before had no doubt been neighing" [149]). Classroom analysis of the language and syntax of this passage makes clear that repetition heightens the effect of the uncanny image, an effect to be trumped later by the highly visual description of the slithering eels extracted from the grinning cadaver. Examples could include "Das vollständige gelbe Pferdegebiß lacht" (192) ("the great yellow horse teeth seemed to be laughing" [150]) or the depiction of the fisherman, who "zum Abschluß dem Gaul einen mächtigen Aal aus dem Ohr zog, mit dem Aal die ganze weiße Grütze aus dem Hirn des Gaules sabbern ließ" (193) ("in conclusion he extracted an enormous eel from the horse's ear, followed by a mess of white porridge from the horse's brain" [151]). The disturbing intensity of the imagery is heightened by the angler's laconic commentary that Baltic eels were "mächtig fett" (194) ("mighty fat" [152]) from feeding on human corpses after the Skagerrak sea battle of 1916 and that a woman is said to have serviced herself with an eel, when it bit her and did not let go, rendering her barren.

While reading and discussing the passages closely, the students should become aware of the meaningful conflation of human bodies and the horse's head, of death, carnality, and the eel. In the course of this discussion, they should come to understand the significance of these main themes of the narrative. On their way to the shore, Oskar's elders argue about a deserted cemetery, one in which Agnes would like to be buried, a wish that obviously points to death. Oskar is dressed in nautical gear, topped off by a sailor hat adorned with a ribbon on which the name of a Skagerrak battleship appears, highlighting again the themes of death and carnality. Jan and Agnes titillate each other behind the back of Alfred, who is too involved with the purchase of eels from the angler to notice the hanky-panky. Finally, the students will come to view the retching and vomiting of Agnes as key to the scene. Just as the beast's "Pferde*gebiß*" (italics mine) yields its eels, so does she violently expectorate her breakfast at the sight of two especially large eels: "da riß es auch meiner Mama das *Gebiß* auseinander: Das ganze Frühstück warf sie . . ." (192) ("my mother's *jaws* were also torn asunder: she disgorged her whole breakfast . . ." [150]; italics mine). The students can see here that Grass's choice of words links Agnes to the black head. After all, the novelist might have chosen the more appropriate word *Mund* (or possibly even *Maul*) to describe the human mouth, instead of *Gebiß* ("toothy jaw")—a word he had used for the horse. Taking the equivalency a step further, the students may conclude that her vomit is to be associated with eels. It is surely no coincidence, when vomit equals eels, that the ravenous gulls circling above are as drawn to the eels as they are to the chunks of vomit splayed on the rocks. The close reading reveals that the outing to the Baltic shore links human and animal carnality to death and eels, especially to those purchased by Alfred for the planned repast in celebration of Good Friday.

No sooner do they arrive home than Agnes and Alfred launch into a marital spat, since Alfred insists on cooking the eels. No matter, eels it will be—he slams the door and proceeds to execute the fish: "Der tötete die Aale mit einem Kreuzschnitt hinter dem Kopf" (198) ("He killed the eels with a crosswise incision in the backs of their necks" [154]). Meanwhile, Jan and Agnes flirt, titter, and play. Oskar retreats to a bedroom wardrobe to fantasize about the starched clothing, the Red Cross pin, the person and body of his doctor's nurse. Even as eels die and are cooked, carnal passion is palpable. The scene is soon consummated as Alfred triumphantly serves up the meal: "Matzerath [hatte] die getöteten, ausgenommenen, gewässerten, gekochten, gewürzten und abgeschmeckten Aale als Aalsuppe mit Salzkartoffeln in der großen Suppenterrine fertig zum Servieren auf den Wohnzimmertisch gestellt . . ." (201) ("Matzerath, having slaughtered, cleaned, washed, cooked, seasoned, and tasted his eels, had put them down on the living room table in the form of eel soup with boiled potatoes . . ." [157]). A classroom discussion of the passage's descriptive catalog of the entire process of preparation in the kitchen reveals that Grass purposefully narrates the transformation of the repulsive sea creature to soup. Questions, then, now center on what the meaning of the ingestion of this metaphorically charged Good Friday soup might be: is Agnes to partake of a broth with such horrific implications?

Just as Agnes became ill at the sight of the writhing eels at the shore, she now retches and refuses to partake of the soup, screaming at Alfred in Kashubian. The altercation in a language incomprehensible to her husband, her strident banging on the piano, and finally her sobbing retreat to the bedroom show the intensity of the crisis. She prostrates herself on the bed beneath an image of Mary Magdalene. Her cousin's caresses, his soothing words in Kashubian, and his penetrating finger calm her there—their suggestive foreplay has been consummated beneath the image of a contrite sinner. The marriage of Agnes and Alfred has all but foundered on the eels of Good Friday.

The chapter concludes with the adults' playing rounds of skat, a card game replicating the strident rivalries. Then the adults partake of scrambled eggs and mushrooms instead of the eels, another marital accommodation. Meanwhile, Oskar fantasizes on the transfiguration of his nurse into the eel angler on the Baltic. Eels are imagined, the horse's head reappears, seagulls swoop, the nurse catches an eel—a surreal series of events replicating the chapter's narrative sequence and culminating in a Pentecostal vision. Then Oskar emerges from his refuge in the wardrobe with a final pronouncement: "Zwar war der Karfreitag für Oskar zu Ende, aber die Passionszeit sollte erst nach Ostern beginnen" (204) ("Good Friday was over for Oskar, but it was only after Easter that his Passion began" [159]).

The ominous statement points to the death of Agnes (the name being the Latin word for "lamb," as in the Agnes Dei (Lamb of God—i.e., Christ), a suicide brought about by her gluttonous gorging on fish. What started with revulsion concludes with uncontrollable desire, a suffering unto death by a woman who her husband guesses and her doctor knows is pregnant. At her burial, the image of eel has been internalized, at least as Oskar sees it:

> . . . Aal von deinem Aal, denn Aal wird zu Aal . . . Aber es kam kein Brechreiz auf. Sie behielt bei sich, nahm mit sich, hatte vor, den Aal unter die Erde zu bringen, damit endlich Ruhe war. (210)

> . . . eel of thine eel, for eel thou art, to eel returnest . . . But my mama didn't retch. She kept it down and it was evidently her intention to take it with her into the ground, that at last there might be peace. (164)

The biblical phrase "for dust thou art, and unto dust shalt thou return" (Genesis 3.19 [King James Vers.]) is echoed in Oskar's graveside observations. The close reading of the chapter in a classroom setting, the focus on the eel image from sea to soup, is validated by the heightened significance gained by even this loose association with the Bible. Grass, as the students should come to realize, has created an intricate episode that far transcends the animal's revolting presence; it points to Christian religious images and traditions of suffering, carnality, and death.

The next step in the process of interpretation calls for a review and discussion of secondary literature on the novel's chapter. At this juncture, the instructor might introduce the class to the Cannes Film Festival and Academy Award–winning film by Volker Schlöndorff (1979). Already prepared by a close reading, students can become critical viewers of the film, noting how Schlöndorff interpreted the Good Friday episode. Why, for example, is Agnes dressed in red, right down to her shoes, in the ten-minute segment, whereas the men appear in drab attire? How does the cinematographer's sequence of tight shots establish an equivalency between her vomiting and the emergence of the writhing eels from the horse's head? What significance might be ascribed to the brutal decapitation of the three eels by Alfred in the kitchen? Does the display of the three bloody and twitching heads, which fascinate Oskar so greatly, comment on the unholy triangle in the room? Does it refer figuratively to the husband's emasculation? Do the three heads point to the eventual death of all three players? Finally, the students could conjecture, why, in contrast to the novel, does Schlöndorff have Agnes eat the eels? With both novel and film in mind, the students might be assigned class presentations on the significance of the transformation from one art form to the other. Reports that could be based, for example, on David Coury's article. Students might then move on to a reading and discussion of the previous scholarship on this intriguing chapter.

Edward Diller's scholarly analysis of the chapter "Good Friday Fare," for one, focuses on the mythic elements of the episode on the Baltic Sea. Agnes is linked to Aphrodite, the goddess of love. The eel angler is likened to an "oceanic god" (21), and Agnes sees in him "an oracle of her destiny" (22). More important, however, the black horse's head is held to partake of the imagination of Greek mythology, specifically of Demeter, who transformed herself into a black mare to escape the advances of the sea god, Poseidon. The grinning maw may be understood as an orifice of the Underground, its teeth like those of the fierce hound Cerberus. The ravenous seagulls are reminiscent of the Harpies, daughters of Poseidon. These and other analogues to myth expand the imaginative scope of the novel's scene, contributing to an explanation of the powerful effect of the imagery.

Volker Neuhaus, the dean of Grass scholarship, comments in passing that the eel signifies the lethal conflation of sexuality and death (*Günter Grass* [1992] 91, 117). Furthermore, he notes that only Agnes recognizes that her apparently senseless situation is not exclusively hers; it is a manifestation of a universal principle, a *Weltgesetz* (67) ("universal law"). Neuhaus's study neatly glosses the text, closing with six very brief suggestions on teaching approaches (118–19), a reticence not shared by Rainer Könecke. Cognizant of the difficulty of dealing with the complexities of *Die Blechtrommel* in German secondary schools, Könecke first establishes a theoretical basis for his approach (17–23) and then offers twenty-eight "Stundenblätter" ("lesson plans") keyed to specific chapters of the novel. The fifteenth teaching unit focuses on "Good Friday Fare," predictably informing the teacher of details of plot and emphasizing that the didactic goal is to achieve an appreciation of the complexity of this literary text. The seven deadly sins, specifically lust and gluttony, are held to be the conceptual paradigm informing the image of the eel (62).

Each reading of the image of the eel—myth, sexuality and death, the seven deadly sins—is useful to the instructor in explicating the chapter. Oskar's explicit reference to the Christian calendar (145; 185–86), the chapter's title, the repeated focus on the activities of the Catholic neighbors as they busily beat rugs clean, his mother's death as a passion, rituals from confession to burial, each and all are components framing a consciously Christian narrative. The eel-angling scene, on the other hand, is linked to folklore (Bächthold-Stäubli; Leach), to heathen belief traditions: "Eine Hexe bannt in Wiegendorf einer Ehefrau einen lebendingen Aal ins Herz. Als die Frau mit einem Kinde niederkommt, geht der Aal, der eine halbe Spanne lang ist und 40 Füße hat, durch den Mund ab" (Brückner 490) ("A witch in the town of Wiegendorf conjures a live eel into the heart of a married woman. When she gives birth, the forty-footed and lengthy eel emerges from her mouth" [trans. mine]). Here the eel is connected with black magic, sexuality—the witch's act of conjuring akin to impregnation—and grotesque birthing. Furthermore, textual interpretation requires specialization in Baltic folklore where tales of carnivorous eels abound (Eckhardt), and such stories are central to a complete understanding of Grass's complex use of the image.

The instruction is abetted, then, by numerous options from scholarship, approaches that may be supplemented by a brief examination of the eel image in Grass's later novel *Der Butt* (1977; *The Flounder*). In the chapter titled "Wie der Butt gefangen wurde" ("How the Flounder Was Caught"), the action is set in the Neolithic period, and the narrator explains: "An einem zeitlosen Tag . . . fing ich den Butt. Dort, wo sich der Fluß Wistulle . . . mit der offenen See mischte, hatte ich meine Korbreusen ausgelegt, in Hoffnung auf Aale" (24–25) ("On a timeless, partly cloudy day, I caught the Flounder. In the place where the river Vistula mingles in a constantly shifting bed with the open sea, I had set out my basket traps in hope of eels" [21]). As Grass's later novel has it, the eel traps are an invention of Aua/Awa, the three-breasted primordial mother, and the devices are constructed of bones discarded from prehistoric cult practices. Had there been caves on the Baltic coast, the narrator theorizes, there would have been cave-art representations of a Stone Age eel cult (27; 22). Given the seaside topography, it was not to be, yet the chance trapping of the flounder of the novel at the confluence of river and sea in just such an eel trap (28; 23) inextricably links the image of the eel to the talking fish, the novel's folkloristic protagonist.

As instructors embark on an interpretation of the image of the eel, they would do well to recall that Grass is a trained artist. He has routinely provided the dust-jacket images for his novels, and he has repeatedly said that the linkage of literary and representational arts (painting, printmaking, sculpture) is central to his creativity (Wertheimer and Allmendinger 17–62). Scholars have analyzed these connections (Hille-Sandvoss; Wertheimer and Allmendinger 63–129; Schade, "Günter Grass's *Mein Jahrhundert*," "Layers," and "Poet"), and the Grass-Haus, a museum in the city of Lübeck, bills itself as a venue for literature and representational art. The museum's richly illustrated guide lists the writer's many art exhibitions (Artinger and Wißkirchen 151–60), thus updating the record of exhibits documented in Grass's catalog *Werkverzeichnis der Radierungen* ("Listing of Etchings"; the volume is unpaginated, so the references here are made by item number). The author's explicit linkage of text to art legitimizes a cross-disciplinary interpretive methodology keyed to the image of the eel.

The catalog reprints sixteen graphics featuring eels (items 17–19, 24, 25, 29, 30, 41, 43, 45, 49, 54, 86, 99, 134, 146). Angelika Hille-Sandvoss comments on each of these, reproducing an additional image, a charcoal drawing (187–200). The task of the instructor, then, is to link selected graphic representations of eels to the Good Friday episode.

The startling image of a plump and determined eel slithering from Grass's mouth, an uncanny self-portrait (item 99), instantly catalyzes spirited discussion in class, which an instructor might channel by asking, Does the print reference the horse's head of the novel's episode, establishing an equivalency between the author and the animal cadaver? Does this eel signify the conflation of (oral) sex and death, or is the eel a surrogate tongue, the organ of literary speech? One could point out here that the author's spoken words are comparable to a cartoon's word-filled balloon. Answers to the first complex of questions might reside in a cross-reference to other sexually suggestive eel prints (items 17, 41, 49, 86) and especially to the startlingly explicit etching entitled "Kein Traum" ("No Dream"), which depicts an eel emerging from a vagina (item 43; see also Artinger and Wißkirchen 120–22). This illustration to a poem reinforces the notion of creative sexuality, even if the print may also be read as an uncanny birth.

The interpretation of an eel as an organ of literary speech might be enriched by reference to Grass's portrait of David Bennent, the child actor who plays Oskar in the Schlöndorff film (item 134; see Schlöndorff and Grass 183). The actor is shown holding the drum even as an eel curiously explores the instrument's head. As with the image of Grass and the eel, students should be encouraged to reflect on questions such as, Is the fish as depicted in the print meant to be a companion of the drummer Oskar? Is the eel invested with the satirical potential of the boy's drumstick? Why does the graphic artist link the eel to the protagonist and his instrument of strident satire, a connection not made explicit in the novel itself? In sum, why does Grass valorize the eel in the print, thereby enhancing the animal's significance?

Another set of images lending itself to a discussion of the cross-references in Grass's fictional and graphic oeuvre are "Kleine Auferstehung" ("Small Resurrection") and "Große Auferstehung" ("Large Resurrection"). They depict three and seven eel heads, respectively, breaching the sea vertically (items 29 and 30). Hille-Sandvoss interprets the images as a component of Grass's ecological conscience, as cryptic monuments (197–98). By now, however, students might be encouraged to discuss whether the titles of the prints explicitly reference the Christian context central to the chapter "Good Friday Fare" and the celebration of resurrection, Easter. As idiosyncratic as the connection may be, the prints underline the fact that the Good Friday meal of fish participates in the culinary ritual of the Christian holy days. The pregnant Agnes, the lamb, is hardly saved, let alone resurrected, by the meal. She is soon to die from her obsessive ingestion of fish, showing Grass's irreverently ironic take on her tragic condition of returning "unto dust."

Above all, the multiple renditions of eel images in his graphic art as well as in the form of his bronze sculpture (*Gebrannte Erde* 77–79) make apparent that the multitalented Grass created a highly personal iconography. While students may consider his literary and artistic imagination to be arcane, cryptic, or even weird, the instructor should remind them that the author has often privileged unusual creatures (snail, flounder, rat, toad, crab) on the dust jackets and as protagonists of his novels (Artinger and Wißkirchen 154–55). He has routinely linked his own person to the images—a snail-monocled Grass, a Grass embedded in a flounder (items 12, 15, 133)—thereby expressing his identity as an artist in terms of the various animals. When a snail is pictured as creeping over a fountain pen or when a flounder is shown speaking into a human ear (items 139, 106), it is clear that a meaningful if idiosyncratic iconography is in play.

Grass's pronouncement on the relation between literary and representational art, succinctly expressed in the title of his essay "Bin ich nun Schreiber oder Zeichner?" ("Am I Writer or Artist?") emphasizes that for him one art form is but an extension of the other:

> Und weil sich bei mir im Schreiben das Zeichnen fortsetzt, weil aus der zeichnerischen Struktur epische Perioden als Satzgefälle abzuleiten sind, hat mich die Frage . . . nie kümmern können. Wörtlich oder zeichnerisch genommen: Es sind die Grauwerte, die unsere Wirklichkeiten tönen, stufen, eintrüben, transparent machen. Weiß ist nur das Papier. Es muß befleckt, mit harter oder brüchiger Kontur belebt oder mit Wörtern besiedelt werden, die die Wahrheit immer neu und jedesmals anders erzählen. Ein schreibender Zeichner ist jemand, der die Tinte nicht wechselt.
>
> (qtd. in Wertheimer and Allmendinger 18)

> Because my writing is a continuation of my drawing, and syntax and narrative grow out of graphic structure, the question . . . never bothered me. It is not abstract black or white. It is the gray values that shape, grade, befuddle, or make transparent our reality. Paper itself is white; it must be covered, made alive with hard or broken contours, or covered with words, which tell the truth in a way that is always new and always different. A writing artist is someone who does not change from one ink to the other.
>
> (trans. mine)

In view of this statement (one worthy of classroom discussion) one could also add that Grass was fascinated by Albrecht Dürer's cryptic master engraving *Melencholia*. The complex image became the basis for a narrative excursus in his novel *Aus dem Tagebuch einer Schnecke* (1972; *From the Diary of a Snail*), which revealed his interest in and intimate knowledge of the academic scholarship on sixteenth-century iconography (esp. 341–45; 290–94). Grass's familiarity with seventeenth-century German literature, the novels of Hans Jakob Christoph von Grimmelshausen specifically, and with emblematic imagery and its interplay with texts is sophisticated and profound (Schade, "Poet"). The instructor's examination of earlier iconographic images of the eel is thus both warranted and legitimized.

While the novelist-artist Grass may not have known of the emblem featuring a writhing eel being controlled by a man and signifying the proper behavior toward fools, this image by Andreas Alciatus documents the Reformation era moralization of the fish (136–37). The seventeenth-century pundit Georg Philipp Harsdoerffer, a writer Grass knows well, as his narrative *Das Treffen in Telgte* (1979; *The Meeting in Telgte*) set during this time shows, equates eels with sly humans: "Der Aal bedeutet eine schlüpferige Listigkeit die sich nicht leichtlich ertappen lässet . . ." (114) ("The eel signifies a slippery cunning that does not allow itself to be easily caught" [trans. mine]). The influential *Iconologia* of Cesare Ripa links the eel to the human failing of enmity (*inimicitia*); as the dog hates the cat, as the eel is alleged to abhor other fish, so do some persons hate others (fig. 156). Finally, Guillaume de la Perrière devotes a decorative emblem to the supposedly devious traits of women: as fast as the eel slips from a man's grasp, so does a woman become unfaithful to him (fig. 88).

The instructor's review of the tradition of early modern eel imagery makes clear that the image of the eel alludes to human shortcomings, to foolishness, to cunning, to enmity, and to marital infidelity. Surely, the eel episode of the *The Tin Drum* is not conceived as a cautionary tale in the spirit of the past. Agnes is not some slippery eel metaphorically cannibalized by her husband for soup. The novel's chapter is hardly akin to an early modern moralization of human failings, yet an informed reading of the early emblematic images may deepen students' understanding of the text, since it reveals the eel's symbolism in preceding traditions. By supplementing the scholarship on the eel image with a broader evaluation of both Grass's idiosyncratic eel iconography and these emblems, the instructor explicates the function of the narrative from beginning to end, from sea to soup.

The Conflicting Claims of Fiction and History in *The Tin Drum*: Humor, Fairy Tale, and Myth

Jane Curran

Force of circumstances dictated that *The Tin Drum* would find its way onto the reading list of a first-year course, in which students are restricted to the English translation of the text. In that course we read texts by German authors whose fiction has found a wider audience through a significant transformation into film. The course has a high enrollment and caters principally to students not specializing in German or even in the humanities. The challenge, then, is to present texts in a way that will engage students who are moved more by the need to fulfill the university's essay-writing requirement than by a desire to learn about German culture. But *The Tin Drum* is also an obvious and frequent choice for the honors and graduate seminar History and Theory of the German Novel, a context in which motivation reaches much higher levels.

Some remarks in this essay arise from my experience teaching first-year students, who may not possess the sharpened tools of literary analysis and are reading the English version of the text only. Sometimes in the English translation of the novel difficulties arise where the tone is preserved at the expense of precise wording; sometimes, however, the translator brings the full potential of an opaque passage into the light. Other remarks present strategies adopted for working with senior undergraduate and graduate students reasonably or entirely fluent in German. In that context the students are better prepared to identify the literary traditions to which Grass makes oblique reference.

Naturally two such divergent groups learn in different ways and have different capacities and goals. The first-year class attends lectures and meets in small tutorials. A large proportion of the students enrolled in this course usually comes from a cultural tradition—Islamic or Asian—where twentieth-century European history is not a focal point. Thus an introductory thumbnail sketch of political tensions in Europe leading up to the period covered by Grass's novel and of the events described in it is indispensable.

In an honors and graduate seminar, by contrast, the reading experience permits more dialogue: students come prepared for discussion and debate. To make sure that everyone has the same background knowledge, I assign each graduate student a topic for an oral presentation. The topics are broad and require research: for example, one of the first would be the bildungsroman, to provoke a discussion situating this novel in that tradition.[1] This essay charts a course through other possible topics a graduate seminar might cover. In addition to the three areas I cover here—narrative and language, absurdity and humor, and fairy tale and myth—students need to be aware of more general questions about narratology, autobiography, and illusion.

Obviously introductory study and advanced study intersect to a certain extent, first and foremost on the question of reading strategies. It is useful to remind both groups of students that respect for the author demands that we develop the habit of paying attention to the signals provided in the title, genre designation, chapter headings, and opening words. Grass himself certainly thought carefully about how to begin, and students should devote equal care to the task of reading those first words (see the essay by Kacandes in this volume).

First, the title of the book should be considered.[2] Grass favors titles that highlight a totemic feature of his tale—an animal symbol, for example: *Katz und Maus* (1961; *Cat and Mouse*), *Hundejahre* (1963; *Dog Years*), *Der Butt* (1977; *The Flounder*), or *Die Rättin* (1986; *The Rat*). In *The Tin Drum*, an inanimate object is the central symbol. The drum, with its primitive percussive and sonorous qualities, its function of sounding the alarm, and its association with military ceremony—notwithstanding its limitations as a mouthpiece—is the protagonist's essential means of self-expression. Since protagonist and narrator are one, the drum offers a running commentary on the narration itself, taking on a paradoxical significance in tandem with Oskar's own.

To complicate matters further, the observant reader of the original will notice the work's designation as "Ein Roman" ("a novel," unfortunately missing from the English translation). Other genres and subgenres suggest themselves. Some readers see Grass's work as a historical novel (see the essays by Preece and by Kontje in this volume). The newer category of magic realism opens up further opportunities for interpretation. Then there are definite autobiographical components to consider. All in all, the laconic categorization "Roman" provokes discussion by concealing as much as it reveals.[3] The apparent disclaimer, "Personen und Handlung des Buches sind frei erfunden. Jede Ähnlichkeit mit einer lebenden oder verstorbenen Person ist nur zufällig" (4) ("The persons and plot of the book are purely imaginary. All similarities with persons living or dead are coincidental" [trans. mine]), which is again missing from the translation, is the next feature in the order of analysis. This disclaimer undermines the case for autobiography, but readers doubtless respond to those two sentences in the same ambiguous spirit: the intention may be prudent, but the claim is far-fetched.

The dedication to Grass's first wife is next: "Für Anna Grass" (5) ("For Anna Grass" [9]). Her name adds weight to the suspicion that the disclaimer may be tongue-in-cheek: since the grandmother figure in the novel is also Anna, Grass is evidently inviting his readers to conclude that this and other parallels are not inadvertent.

The paradoxical tone in the disclaimer is a salient characteristic of the novel as a whole. The title of the first chapter, "Der weite Rock" ("The Wide Skirt"), gives unexpected prominence to a garment normally considered unassuming. That this skirt should have such strategic and pivotal importance is not what one normally anticipates; nor is it possible to deny the absurdity of the circumstances that give it its catalytic role.

In what follows, I subject *The Tin Drum* to three broad categories of interpretation: humor, fairy tale, and myth. Even though they remain separate to
some extent, it is important to point out their interconnections to students. In
classroom discussion, students should consider the following three points.

First is Oskar's assertion that the sounding of his drum is inseparable from his
narrative speech. Using the three categories, an undergraduate tutorial might
profitably discuss the comic absurdity of such a claim; the drum as magic object,
as encountered in fairy tales; and how the drum offers protection against the
threat of current events.

Second, the categorization of a work full of autobiography and matters of
historical fact presented as fiction needs to be addressed. Related questions
of genre identification lend themselves to an undergraduate research essay, or
they could be the basis for discussion in a graduate seminar.

The third point is the disconcerting way that the well-known historical setting
is either clouded or elevated into fantasy in magic realism. Magic realism is a
common way for post-1945 writers to come to terms with recent events through
the medium of fiction. Graduate students might compare the fictional solutions
by Wolfgang Borchert, Max Frisch, Anna Seghers, Heinrich Böll, and Hans-
Ulrich Treichel, to give a few examples.

An oral presentation on the topic of narrative theory and strategies can provide an essential frame of reference in the analysis of *The Tin Drum* for graduate students. As we have seen, the paratextual elements (title, dedication, genre
designation, disclaimer, etc.) suggested lines of inquiry and sent out cautionary
signals, but they leave the reader unprepared for the first word: "Zugegeben"
("Granted") or indeed for the first phrase, "Zugegeben: ich bin Insasse einer
Heil- und Pflegeanstalt" (9) ("Granted: I am an inmate of a mental hospital"
[15]). The surprise occasioned by this one participle stems partly from its isolation, its inability, contrary to expectation, to relate to what went before, and
partly from its failure either to defend or to provide mitigating circumstances
for Oskar's confession. Both context and mitigation customarily accompany any
admission introduced by this defensive term. What follows, in fact, is a radical
subversion of the confidence that usually adheres to the narrative voice. The
first-person narrator begins by informing us that he is an inmate of a mental
institution: one deduces that his statements and views are therefore unreliable,
and yet he does describe his situation from a distanced, even objective, perspective. As readers, we are not yet sure how to assess the situation. Students should
ask themselves why Grass wants to achieve this unsettling effect.

The rest of the opening paragraph is also the rest of the opening sentence
and equally bewildering. Instead of continuing the introduction, the narrator
changes the topic in midstream to describe his keeper's constant watchful-
ness. Still in the first sentence, he adds complexity by changing gear, stating
that the keeper cannot see through him, and by offering as a rather shaky
basis for his claim the accident of their respective eye colors. The thought
introduced by "zugegeben" has disappeared as this sentence mutates into a

discussion of appearance and reality. Students might also detect an ominous subcurrent in the emphasis on accidental physical phenomena.

There is something disconcerting about the non sequitur both present in that transition and caused by it. More detours follow. The first sentence of the next paragraph posits a causal instance, "Mein Pfleger kann also gar nicht mein Feind sein" (9) ("So you see, my keeper can't be an enemy" [15]), but one without any foundation. Nothing in the first paragraph suggests that the keeper might be hostile, so there is no need whatsoever to dismiss the idea. With a single skillful stroke, the narrator both introduces and eliminates the thought of the keeper's animosity. More worrying for the reader is the subsequent revelation that the narrator manipulates his keeper and ensures his goodwill by telling him a pack of lies about his own life. By now, the reader's skepticism is fully engaged, and the description of the keeper's bizarre works of art that follows only highlights the tension. On the surface, the roles are being reversed, so that it is now the keeper who seems mentally abnormal, even simpleminded and deluded, and the inmate who must indulge him by catering to his fantasies.

Undergraduates could be asked to identify instances of narrative subversion. The narrator immediately erodes any confidence readers might have in this narrative by placing himself in a potentially delusional setting. This impression is then instantly counteracted by Oskar's acute observation of the watcher and his sly suggestion that the watcher is overlooking the truth. We falter at Oskar's non sequitur, where the expected discussion of his mental state transforms into the topic of his keeper's hobby. The whole argument comes full circle with the delusional suggestion that a fundamental dynamic is determined by eye color.

We know by now not to trust the narrator, even though he tries to ingratiate himself by a show of honesty in admitting to his lies. Grass is borrowing the brainteaser in an age-old riddle about two villages: In one village, everyone always lies; in the other, everyone always tells the truth. How can you discover which of the two villages a passerby comes from? Is Oskar telling the truth when he says he tells lies, or is he lying and therefore, paradoxically, telling us that he tells the truth? Students should be encouraged to connect this puzzle to the competition between apparent historical fact and the art of narrative fiction. Recognizing that these two major arteries nourish the work confronts the problematic status of eyewitness accounts and also introduces the inexpressibility topos: that one cannot convey a large-scale calamity in comprehensible terms.

Postponing the story about the grandmother and her capacious skirts in the first chapter, the narrator again disarms the reader by running swiftly, in somewhat cynical and perfunctory tones, through narrative options, particularly emphasizing the difficulties with the concept of a hero: "Es gibt keine Romanhelden mehr, weil es keine Individualisten mehr gibt" (12) ("a novel can't have a hero any more because there are no more individualists" [17]). He immediately undermines this statement by asserting that he and his keeper are indeed true heroes. Either this assertion means that they can be heroes since they are not mere figures in a novel, or it contradicts the claim that there are no longer any heroes in novels. The contradictory readings provide a clear example of the tendency for fact and fiction, past and present to merge in Oskar's mind. Grass has no intention of rescuing the reader from this problem, and again, students should speculate about the author's aim. In practice, once he steps into narrative mode, he brings another feature of the storyteller's art into focus by using in the same sentence the first-person possessive and the name Oskar: first- and third-person narrators alternate throughout the novel while remaining identical.

The identity-difference conundrum is not confined to the narrative voice. Having decided on a starting point in the past, the narrator launches into an account of how his grandparents met. Throughout, he refers to "meine Großmutter" ("my grandmother"), even though the justification for this name lies many years in the future. Thus Grass raises the problem that vexes historical accounts: all testimony is constructed from a limited point of view. It is anachronistic to refer to her as a grandmother before she has even conceived, yet this linguistic paradox is paradigmatic for all communication. Oskar makes the same point by constantly referring to his "zwei mutmaßliche Väter" (172) ("two presumptive fathers" [213]), thus drawing attention to the difficulty in reliably establishing anything as factual that derives from an external point of view. What are the universal issues Grass has in mind when introducing the proverbial doubt about paternity? He reminds us that uncertainty and subjectivity are unavoidable in any transfer of information.

The second chapter opens with an even more radical perspective on this problem. Here Oskar refers for the first time to the importance of the drum. The instrument is often personified: it experiences fatigue and is endowed with the powers of thought and recollection:

> Hätte ich nicht meine Trommel, der bei geschicktem und geduldigem Gebrauch alles einfällt, was an Nebensächlichkeiten nötig ist, um die Hauptsache aufs Papier bringen zu können, und hätte ich nicht die Erlaubnis der Anstalt, drei bis vier Stunden täglich mein Blech sprechen zu lassen, wäre ich ein armer Mensch ohne nachweisliche Großeltern. (23)

> If I didn't have my drum, which, when handled adroitly and patiently, remembers all the incidentals that I need to get the essential down on paper, and if I didn't have the permission of the management to drum on it three or four hours a day, I'd be a poor bastard with nothing to say for my grandparents. (25)

The drum has the power of speech, a crucial faculty that the translator shifts to the end of this passage. This shift avoids awkwardness, but unfortunately it removes the sense of *nachweislich*. If Oskar could not make the drum speak, he would have no grandparents to point to, he says; there would be no testimony to their existence. The implication is that he would have no past, no ancestors, had he not in a sense bestowed existence on them and preserved them by linguistic means. Existence becomes actual only when it receives form through the power of narration and communication.

After this insight it requires only a small step to reach the topic of magic realism. The drum's speech gives life to the grandparents; only through having their tale told do they acquire true, demonstrable existence. But what of Oskar's voice? Oskar uses it to safeguard his drum. If anyone threatens to remove the drum, he emits a high-pitched scream that shatters glass objects, whether priceless or practical, within an extensive range. Just as Grass has his third-person and first-person narrators peacefully coexist, the everyday rubs shoulders with the fantastic. After describing this implausible talent, the narrator explains his strategy of preserving and training his voice and restricting its use to that of a defensive weapon. He then elaborates in the most matter-of-fact way on the limits of this peculiar power. To his disappointment, it cannot do any damage to cloth: "Wenn es mir möglich gewesen wäre, mit den gleichen Tönen und Mitteln etwa langweilige, kreuz und quer bestickte, Gretchen Schefflers Musterphantasie entsprungene Tischtücher zu zerschneiden . . ." (77) ("If with the same tones and techniques I had been able to cut up Gretchen Scheffler's beastly, intricately embroidered tablecloths . . ." [65]). This ludicrous flight of fancy underlines the absurdity that a human voice could have such glass-breaking power. Why does his voice both possess the power and suffer restrictions of it? Oskar cannot summon his power to settle a matter of taste in the ornamentation of table linen, and this means that his gift is firmly grounded in magic realism. Protection of the drum is the important task, but in juxtaposing his voice's actual and hypothetical uses in musing about tablecloths he again characterizes the narrative function of his voice. This narrator has the preternatural power of remembering his birth, but he also demonstrates his own restrictions: his lack of omniscience and omnipotence.

As narrative voice the drum also has its shortcomings. It participates in Oskar's failure to distinguish between importance and triviality. Unlike Oskar's world, the fairy-tale universe is relatively sober and predictable. The rules of logic and cause and effect continue to apply, even in an unfamiliar setting; all one needs to gain entry is the willing suspension of disbelief. By contrast, in Oskar's world, where magic realism has been let loose, there is constant slippage between one realm and the other. No sooner has the reader accepted the crucial importance of the drum and the magical vocal powers of its owner than the narrator sets out a list of instances that can only be described as comic, precisely because there is no discrimination between what is significant and what is not:

> Um nicht allzuviel Schaden anzurichten, . . . zermürbte ich, wenn man mir abends meine Blechtrommel nehmen wollte, die ja zu mir ins Bettchen gehörte, eine oder mehrere Glühbirnen unserer viermal sich Mühe gebenden Wohnzimmerhängelampe. (80–81)

> To limit the damage, . . . I concentrated, when they tried to take my drum away at night instead of letting me take it to bed with me, on shattering one or more of the four bulbs in our living room lamp.   (68)

The narrator fuses mundane disciplinary problems familiar to all parents with a reasoned remark about damage control, then adds an offhand reference to a supernatural ability that the child summons at will. The distinction between this catastrophic little scene and its comic content becomes further blurred by the tone, including the ironic personification of the lamp ("viermal sich Mühe gebend" ["quadruply painstaking"], unfortunately suppressed in the English version). Practitioners of magic realism can find here a deft and striking early instance of their craft: realism and magic join forces to bring a narrative issue to the fore. Does the narrator's comic tone trivialize the scene or help convey its dark message?

Glass shattered by the human voice is a strong image that sounds a warning about the destructive powers of the spoken word. Grass draws on the still-fresh memories of Hitler's haranguing oratory to alert us to the manipulation of language available to a strong and malevolent will. In Oskar's long-suffering mother, who pays for the damage and sweeps up the shards, he provokes the sobering thought that it is a feature of human nature to be compliant and thus complicit in such abuse.

Most of my remarks so far have been devoted to signals that should guide students toward a fuller understanding of Grass's narrative craft. But the infinitely regressive preoccupation with the status of the narrator also yields some ground to entertainment in the purer sense; no narrative is simply about itself. Humor in *The Tin Drum* constitutes an important step toward extricating the narrative from that potentially referential circle. Humor here does not attempt to obscure the serious nature of Grass's social and political criticism; on the contrary, it sharpens that criticism.

To open the discussion, a graduate student might trace the etymology of the term *humor* and summarize important theories of humor (e.g., by Jean Paul, Hegel, Schopenhauer). Humor in this novel has two principal functions. The first is to present the incongruous to our view as an integral component of the comic art. The second is to cast the normal as abnormal, and thus play havoc with our habits of moral, epistemological, and aesthetic judgment.

Borrowing from the traditional court jester's role, Grass injects a comic element that imparts the truth in an irresistibly entertaining disguise while hovering on the borderline of acceptability. In Oskar, he has a ready-made type of court jester or fool, and in this role the protagonist-narrator becomes the one who tells the bold truth about the lies, both his own and those that others tell or live by. By giving the floor to a character abnormal in every way imaginable, the author challenges conformism and exposes the deficiencies of characters who count as normal.[4] In an incongruous combination of words and sentiments

Oskar echoes the merciless juxtaposition of tragic and comic that earmarks the jester's art. He dispassionately quips about his mother's death "[m]it dem Zerfall der schlanken Seele, des üppigen Körpers" (272), calling it the dissolution of her "slender soul and ample body" (212). And in staging bizarre or horrifying occurrences with Oskar at the center, the author provides crucial commentary on the actual historical events that form the backdrop to these scenes (Stern 178). One example is the tense basement episode ("Die Ameisenstraße" ["The Ant Trail"]), when the soldiers' threatening presence places everyone at risk, but Oskar is ludicrously preoccupied with the progress of an ant column across the floor. What does his attitude tell us? Through him, Grass embodies the distraction and insouciance shown by a large portion of the German population during World War II, even in the face of escalating daily horrors.

Because Oskar pretends to be mute and because his stature is diminutive, people treat him as though his mental capacities were correspondingly small. In fact, the opposite is true, or so we are asked to believe. Oskar has memories well beyond the reach of normal human capabilities. He says he remembers his birth and baptism and the thoughts and reactions he had on those occasions. This sort of claim is calculated to strain the reader's credulity, and the events as recounted are nothing short of absurd. What is the reason behind such blatant lying? At the point in the baptismal ritual where the officiant requires the infant, through the godparents, to renounce Satan and all his works, Oskar was allegedly on the point of shaking his head to indicate that he had no intention of renouncing the evil one, with whom he was already in alliance. This is a typical example of Grass's use of comic extremes to drive home somber insights: control over the propagation of information and over its recipients, a cold-blooded attitude toward the demise even of a close family member, and an avowed satanic allegiance make a threatening combination. One way Grass uses comedy, then, is to lead the reader away from what is merely entertaining and light in tone toward darker truths.

Oskar's portrait is painted in the bold strokes of the expressionist style, with distorted proportions and unnatural shading. But for all his eccentricities and extreme intransigence, does he behave very differently from his mother, who, revolted by the sight of the eels in the horse's head, first refuses to eat, then goes on a bulimic fish-eating binge that eventually leads to her death? The madness of her excesses stays just within the bounds of the credible, whereas Oskar's excesses fall just outside these bounds. When measured against his comic and unexpected abnormalities, the deviance in what passes as normal behavior in other people seems less deviant. This rapprochement of the monstrous and the human, however, is not an attempt to diminish our critical faculties by making what is outrageous seem familiar (Minden).

Grass has Oskar make a chilling observation about a horrific event, Greff's suicide by hanging: that a hanged man is not much more peculiar a sight than that of a man walking on his hands or standing on his head (412; 315). This shocking observation, negating the distinction between a violent, self-inflicted death and a gymnastic feat, exemplifies the second step for comedy in *The Tin Drum*: it narrows the gap between normality and abnormality, bringing with it all the sinister implications that accompany such leveling. Torture is not so far removed from satire, or violence from slapstick (O'Neill, *Günter Grass* 24).

Precisely this want of a sense of proportion is at work in "The Polish Post Office." How does the comic effect work here? The momentous incident, with its cataclysmic consequences, is apparently easy to describe: "Das schreibt sich so leicht hin: Maschinengewehre, Doppeltürme" (285) ("All that is so easily written: machine guns, double turrets" [222]). Entirely out of keeping with the surrounding danger and pandemonium, Oskar curls up to sleep in a barrel of letters, and his first, preposterous, concern on awakening is his battered drum. "Langsam setzte sich in mir der Gedanke fest: Es geht gar nicht um Polen, es geht um mein verbogenes Blech" (291) ("Slowly the thought took root in me: it's not Poland they're worried about, it's my drum" [226]). The often clairvoyant Oskar, who habitually exposes adult ways and sees beyond the duplicitous, self-seeking, and self-deluding front portrayed here as characteristic of the adult world is abandoned, at this moment, by his sixth sense. He reverts to a typically childish, all-consuming concern about a broken toy. As tragic counterpart to Oskar, Bronski and the other severely wounded men doggedly play at skat while under siege, and remain absorbed in the fragile stability of an allegorical house of cards.

The comic contrast works just as well in reverse. Oskar's worries over his damaged possession bring into clear outline events that would change the world. That first skirmish and its enormous repercussions are offset by the grotesque but comic picture of a freakish dwarf on a quest to retrieve his damaged toy from underneath one of the mortally wounded. Without such a point of reference, the scale of violence and calamity is difficult to grasp. Oskar recounts what he witnesses with a neutrality more suited to noting an event incidental to the main story line. His single-minded, incongruous fixation on the drum allows him to write of the siege disinterestedly. His childlike gaze focuses on details, like the patterned wallpaper in the playroom of the living quarters above the post office, that are supremely irrelevant to a record of historical events. Moments of humor transect the flow of the narrative, and they can be bittersweet too, as when Oskar stoops, intent on retying Bronski's shoelace for him, while the shooting is at its most intense.

The preoccupation with the shoelace is poignant: for once, Oskar, albeit under infelicitous circumstances, shows a little fellow feeling. This sentiment is the other side of his self-centered preoccupation with the drum. Both the drum-retrieving and shoelace-tying episodes are satirical pointers toward the evil that results from a vision whose realization demands so great a sacrifice. In case the readers' antennae should fail to receive this message, Oskar spells it out:

> Ich kann es mir nie, selbst bei wehleidigster Stimme nicht verschweigen:
> Meine Trommel, nein, ich selbst, der Trommler Oskar, brachte zuerst

> meine arme Mama, dann den Jan Bronski, meinen Onkel und Vater, ins Grab.   (320)

> Even when I feel most sorry for myself, I cannot deny it: It was my drum, no, it was I myself, Oskar the drummer, who dispatched first my poor mama, then Jan Bronski, my uncle and father, to their graves.   (247)

Disproportion is an essential tool of comedy, and in Grass's art it confronts us in a beguiling way, illumining the manic and evil lack of proportion that lies alarmingly close by.

The comic and the grotesque are inherent components of this novel's narrative voice, and Grass shows the voice's capacity to speak alternately in the first and third persons. Indeed, he essentially argues that this alternation is the only adequate way to tell the story. Nevertheless, when Oskar speaks of himself in the third person, a childlike naïveté not normally associated with an omniscient narrator voice clings to his words. This naïveté spawns both absurd situations and ludicrous commentary. Yet the lurking comic spirit is neither ingenuous nor artless; it sheds its oblique light to display human nature as fatally prone to perversions and obsessions. Oskar's childlike outward form belies a far from innocent interior, but it misleads adults to sympathize and make excuses for him and to suffer voluntarily on his behalf. With a contradictory command of self-analysis, he reports, "Oskar besann sich seiner . . . alles entschuldigenden Dreijährigkeit" (317) ("Oskar . . . remembered that a three-year-old is not responsible for his comings and goings" [245]). To make the complex magnetism of his protagonist comprehensible, Grass transforms Oskar into a figure familiar from fairy tales. Dwarves, disfigured soothsayers, and characters inextricably identified with an extraordinary possession or garment are common in this world of fantasy. The malevolent Rumpelstiltskin and the hapless Tom Thumb come to mind (Arnds, *Representation* 427–28). Oskar has a sixth sense of cause and effect, and his glass-shattering escapades are nothing less than the sorcerer's ability to cast spells.

A seminar on the related genres of fairy tale and myth as found in *The Tin Drum* would benefit from a student's oral presentation on the characteristics of fairy tales, their distinction from and kinship with legends and sagas, and the terms *Volksmärchen* ("folk fairy tale") and *Kunstmärchen* ("literary fairy tale").

How is the fairy tale put to use? As remote as this idiom may seem from his goal, mobilizing fairy-tale elements is one more attempt to accomplish the task Grass sets himself, of weaving a narrative around the events of World War II. By employing dual narrative voices, he provides both a personal and an objective perspective; his use of comic distortion cunningly elucidates the tragically grotesque; and finally, by draping the fantastic cloak of the fairy tale about the shoulders of his fictional protagonist, he consorts with a genre that presents the essential artifice of storytelling in condensed form. The effect is twofold:

Initially, when Grass opens an anecdotal episode with the familiar phrase, "Es war einmal . . ." ("Once upon a time . . ."), the reader associates the account with a sphere that is part fantasy, part admonition, but certainly divorced from the factual sphere. The intention may be ironic—for example, when what is narrated is at a far remove from the stuff of fairy tales. The other effect has less to do with avoidance of reality and more to do with time. By placing events that happen in real time into a framework of timelessness, the author manipulates our view of them. They slough off the appearance of particularity and come to seem ominously symptomatic of the way things always turn out. Factual material does not fit in the fairy-tale idiom; it wrests itself free and constantly reasserts its place in the time continuum (Neuhaus, *Günter Grass* [1993] 42). This process incidentally invites the reader to remember that reality is fluid and that events, however horrific, do eventually pass and fade from memory. Paradoxically, then, fairy-tale terminology explores the inexpressible and then returns it to its proper temporal sphere (O'Neill, "Musical Form" 303).

Reinforcements are necessary, since the fairy-tale framework is too fragile to bear the whole weight of the narrative. Accordingly, Grass briefly evokes another fantasy world in the modern myth of Don Quixote and uses it to draw a parallel with the futile quest of the Polish cavalry (in the chapter "Er liegt auf Saspe") ("He Lies in Saspe"). Oskar inserts two heavily dactylic lines of verse into his account and then weighs up the advantages of this textual strategy. He apologizes for turning the account of a battle into a poem and then wonders whether providing the statistics of losses in the Polish campaign would be preferable. Ultimately, he proposes to do both, relegating the poem to a footnote, but this decision is also merely hypothetical: the poem stays in the main body of the text, and the statistics are not forthcoming (205; 251–52). Why does Grass repeatedly pose such questions about the task of narration? He suggests that there can never be too many channels of approach: fact and fiction, poems and statistics, comedy and tragedy, history and fantasy. Statistics without a context as foothold have no real means of exerting force.

What then is the special contribution of the fairy tale? Elements peculiar to fairy tales include both supernatural powers and particular limitations. A fairy-tale character may have superhuman endurance or strength and yet be condemned endlessly to repeat the same task without any sign of progress. Aid usually comes at a price, and punishment is levied on those who act out of thoughtlessness or greed, who fail to heed warnings, who try to thwart predictions. Stylistic and rhetorical features abound, including chants, reiterations (anaphora), and refrains, often in sets, with a climax at the third instance (ascending tricola). In *The Tin Drum*, when Mother Truczinski hears of her son's death on the battlefield, the reader learns of the loss as an ironic, triple experience, a parody of the fairy tale's predilection for the number 3: "Der Unteroffizier Fritz Truczinski war für drei Dinge gleichzeitig gefallen: für Führer, Volk und Vaterland" (463) ("Sergeant Truczinski had fallen for three things at once: Führer, Folk, and Fatherland" [352]). Here the translation skillfully enhances the tragic sense of falling in battle with two subsidiary senses of *to fall for*: "to be duped by" and "to become infatuated with." All three meanings are well within the complex net Grass weaves in the novel: having been duped into patriotic love, the officer fell in combat.

In fairy tales, inanimate objects obey commands and magic works only under the right conditions. Oskar's role is a combination of the prince disguised as a frog, who must endure humiliation from the princess before being united with her in love, and the hopeful and dedicated suitor who discovers a magic potion (fizz powder). On a subsequent occasion, after Oskar comes across Matzerath and Maria in flagrante delicto on the couch, the proffered powder has somehow lost its magic properties: Maria vehemently and scornfully rejects it. The reader may even briefly doubt the veracity of Oskar's earlier accounts of their erotic games. In the present-day narration, the fizz powder Oskar has gone to considerable lengths to procure again now has the opposite effect on Maria: the fizz has gone from the elixir, the idyll is lost, and the mundane trappings of the twentieth century are only too apparent. Maria distractedly fiddles with the radio during visiting hour at the sanatorium and speaks of Stalin's death. She babbles about young Kurt and seems to have forgotten the young Oskar. Worst of all, she is nothing short of embarrassed when he tries to reenact the intimate feelings brought about by this magic potion. He has reverted to his frog status, and the fairy-tale veneer has lost its purchase (Arnds, *Representation* 423).

In both instances of failed magic the radio is playing; current affairs interfere with the ideal sphere. Historic events encroach on the preserve of fantasy. Modern culture is at odds with the fairy tale, with its rules and conventions. The medium of myth and fairy tale offers a context for understanding some of Oskar's characteristics but cannot altogether contain him.

Other facets of Oskar recall isolated figures familiar from myths and legends (Diller). These punctuate the story without offering an interpretative key. Oskar's self-identification as a hero outside the realm of the novel constitutes an entry into an ironic world of ancient mythology. Interpreted in such a light, his superhuman skills make him half hero, half god. Patrimony, so important to ancient heroes, is a positive obsession with him. Myth defines his self-image. The fairy tale is a medium he sometimes seems to inhabit, but the mythical side of him is an association born of his own fancy. Like Zeus, he inflicts punishment (by breaking glass) on the just and the unjust when he is displeased. Like any ancient god, he is jealous, exercises power over individual fates, undergoes physical transformation of his own volition, becomes the object of veneration and ritual, and looks on human warfare as his entertainment. Yet he provides entertainment for those engaged in battle when, now in a less grandiose role, he realizes a commonplace dream and runs away to join the circus. Together with a band of dwarves—another grouping straight out of the pages of Grimms' fairy tales—he appears in vaudeville acts to entertain the troops. On returning home, he compares himself with Odysseus and, more positively, likens himself to the biblical prodigal son.

In a horrifying perversion of the Christian injunction *imitatio Christi*, Oskar challenges and scorns Jesus Christ in extensive disturbing and sacrilegious scenes. He has no conception of his limitations; he refers to himself as a demigod and effortlessly takes over as leader of a criminal gang of youths, whether as a result of their adulation or indulgence, it is unclear. Why does Grass deploy such shock effects? The ominous parallel and target of his satire is not hard to find in Hitler, who, driven by crazed delusions of grandeur, constructed a myth around himself and controlled others, inciting them to plan and carry out systematic acts of death and destruction.

As we have seen, Grass draws on history, biography, mythology, and fairy tales in the composition of this lengthy novel. He balances realism with fantasy, history with fiction, and adopts the perspective of a distorted individual to look at a physically and morally shattered nation. His aim is a comprehensive artistic totality, but, as with a symphony, its creation is dependent on parts that contribute to the total sound while preserving their identity. An analysis of Grass's strikingly suggestive images shows them to be fertile and multifaceted. The eel scene recalls the head of Medusa, the serpent in the Garden of Eden, the infinite circularity of the snake with its tail in its mouth, or simply a phallic symbol. But there is a temptation for students to leave the main road, become involved in detail and miss the grander view. In isolating single aspects, one does a disservice to the novel's complexity and the novelist's craft. The novel demonstrates, through artistic means, that communication is unreliable, that historical knowledge is not fixed, and that human beings offer a frustrating variety of perspectives that are partial in both senses of the word but nevertheless crucial to the essence of modern fiction.

NOTES

[1] Grass himself states in an interview about *The Tin Drum*, "Das Buch steht in einem ironisch-distanzierten Verhältnis zum deutschen Bildungsroman" ("The book maintains an ironic distance from the German bildungsroman") (Arnold, *Günter Grass* 6).

[2] The work of Gérard Genette has been pivotal in bringing such features of the text to the reader's attention (*Seuils*).

[3] Grass, when interviewed, is not especially illuminating on this point: "Sicher ist *Die Blechtrommel* kein autobiographischer Roman. Aber es ist kein Zufall, daß ich das Geburtsjahr von Oskar nicht auf das Jahr 1927, sondern auf das Jahr 1924 gesetzt habe" (qtd. in Vormweg 16) ("*The Tin Drum* is certainly not an autobiographical novel. But it is no coincidence that I took not 1927 but 1924 as the year of Oskar's birth" [trans. mine]).

[4] Frizen discusses similarities with absurdist theater, in which, for example, the normal behavior of Ionesco's rhinoceroses shows up human abnormality.

"Unsereins muß auf die Bühne": The Tin Drum and the Stage

Elizabeth C. Hamilton

From the rostrum to Bebra's theater at the front to the Onion Cellar, the stage is the setting for some of the most incisive cultural criticism to be found in Günter Grass's *The Tin Drum*. Oskar Matzerath's encounters with the theater as an audience member and later as a performer of music provide a coherence that is often hard to find in this complicated and unruly narrative. That Oskar is featured on a stage in all three books of the novel in significant passages reveals an underlying structure to the seemingly chaotic story as well as a way to grasp his notoriously slippery character.

Serious and intelligent debate about how to assess *The Tin Drum* persists almost five decades after the novel's appearance. A study of its theatrical and musical performances can offer today's students entry into the larger cultural conversations about the nature of art and the writing of history. The episodes onstage encourage students to examine content, audience, and setting as vital elements of Grass's social critique. They serve as concrete expressions of Oskar's constant repositioning from viewer to performer to narrator. Additionally, the seemingly divergent visual, acoustic, narrative, and dramatic qualities of the story coalesce on the various stages of the novel. Finally, Oskar's perpetual movement among various stages serves as a metaphoric basis from which Grass examines the ethics of German citizens in the years surrounding the two world wars: were they actors or merely audience members in this century of turmoil?

The present discussion combines these profound conceptual inquiries with concrete activities for university-level literature study. A list of suggested classroom activities and research projects accompanies this essay as an appendix. The activities, which correspond to key points of this discussion, are arranged sequentially to introduce, analyze, and evaluate the novel. Instructors may wish to modify these activities for their graduate or undergraduate audiences. Modifications are suggested for selected activities.

Regardless of the academic level of the students or the language of instruction, the novel's meaning and form should be studied together. Its elaborate, baroque-styled episodes mark the events of twentieth-century German history as well as the varied, often recursive paths of historical narrative itself. *The Tin Drum* departs from the linear development of the edifying bildungsroman, revealing Oskar's kinship with the mischievous rogues of the *Schwank*, or comical tale, and *Schelmenroman* ("picaresque novel"). The novel offers satirical and ribald humor linking the Reformation and Renaissance eras with the postwar German state in dire need of reform and rebirth. Like his literary ancestors, Till Eulenspiegel and Simplicius Simplicissimus, Oskar Matzerath is a picaresque antihero who satirizes his society from below, exposing the foibles and moral laxity of his social class, the petite bourgeoisie, with often startling insight.

Yet that which Oskar does not expose—or which Grass chooses not to name—also raises insightful, if troubling, questions. Despite the novel's often penetrating vision, it routinely confounds readers by circumventing what logically should have been postwar German literature's most explicit question: What permitted Adolf Hitler's hold on the German people, which enabled the Holocaust? Explanations of the causes of fascist genocide are hinted at, danced around, nervously approached, and evaded. That a novel of *The Tin Drum*'s size and scope fails to elucidate this horrific history in detail has been viewed as the primary shortcoming of the work (see Lorenz's essay in this volume). It is true that neither the institutionalized anti-Semitism of the Third Reich nor the genocidal murder of Jews and other perceived non-Aryans is examined explicitly in the novel. Despite their arguably central role in the events described in *The Tin Drum*, Ruth Angress highlights their absence, noting that "Grass falls short of taking a steady look at German Jewry under Hitler" ("Jewish Problem" 222). Ernestine Schlant's assessment of this questionable lack is even more critical. Schlant finds in *The Tin Drum* "an ingrained obtuseness and insensitivity to those who suffered and died, evident in a language where silence is veiled in verbal dexterity and a creative exuberance rooted in pre-Holocaust aesthetics" (71). Responding to the early critical reception of the novel in which the novel's allegedly antireligious character was decried, Jost Hermand's particularly illuminating discussion identifies the lack of political conviction as the novel's truly most scandalous quality. For Hermand, "[hier] fehlt das Engagement, das über die in diesem Buch dargestellte 'Unpositivität' der kleinen Leute in eine Welt des Anderen, Besseren hinausweisen würde, in der ein Mann wie Hitler nicht mehr möglich wäre" (17) ("missing here is the engagement that would point the way out of the 'unpositivity' of the little people represented in the book toward another, better realm, in which a man like Hitler would no longer be possible").

Without undermining these incontrovertible objections to the novel, it is still paradoxically possible to view *The Tin Drum*'s lack of conviction as precisely its point and to value it as such. The novel foregrounds its own, often contradictory, attempts to provide a comprehensive view of German history, evident not only in the "observer-protagonist" Oskar (Schlant 69) but also in the repeated efforts of various characters to offer descriptive names for the twentieth century. Moreover, *The Tin Drum* remains at its core a portrait of self-centeredness and evasion. Nowhere in the novel is this self-centeredness more evident than on Oskar's various stages. On them, with few exceptions, this most public artistic forum becomes little more than a medium for private gain.

As an audience member Oskar is touched emotionally, receiving a fundamental lesson in how people can be persuaded by events on the stage. He learns at the theater that there is often a distinction between what is meant to be seen and what is not, and he also learns about the mechanics of creating illusions. His developing relation with the stage becomes a twofold lesson for the reader: first, in the socializing function of public performances; second, in the microcosmic views of life that the stage affords.

Oskar's first encounter with the theater is a destructive one that takes place before he even enters the building: "Indem ich die Foyerfenster unseres Stadt-theaters zersang, suchte und fand ich zum erstenmal Kontakt mit der Bühnen-kunst" (136) ("It was in singing away the lobby windows of our Stadt-Theater that I sought and found my first contact with the Thespian art" [108]). It is the first and last time that Oskar uses his destructive, glass-shattering voice against the stage. From this point on he will alternately expose its mechanisms of per-suasion or exploit them for his own benefit. Thus the passage offers a clear basis from which to examine his opportunism and lack of attention to the plight of others. It will become clear that each time he uses his drum or voice to entertain an audience, he deflects attention from his brutality.

When Oskar is eventually taken inside the theater to see *Däumeling* (*Tom Thumb*), he is greatly moved by the play. Acknowledging his affinity for the diminutive title character, he applauds the clever staging that creates a tiny figure from an adult actor. His next encounter with the stage is, significantly, in 1933, at the Zoppot Opera-in-the-Woods, where Wagner's *The Flying Dutch-man* is being performed: "Erst im Sommer dreiunddreißig sollte ich wieder Theater geboten bekommen. . . . [E]s ereignete sich in der Waldoper Zoppot, wo unter freiem Nachthimmel Sommer für Sommer Wagnermusik der Natur anvertraut wurde" (137–38) ("It was not until the summer of '33 that I went to the theater again. . . . [T]his took place at the Zoppot Opera-in-the-Woods, where summer after summer Wagner was poured forth upon nature beneath the night sky [109]). Much of the description of this open-air opera concerns everything but the opera itself—namely, the preparations for the outing: bath-ing, dressing, and getting there. At the opera, Oskar's awareness extends to such distractions as mosquitoes and the talk and actions of others around him, which have nothing to do with the substance of the text or its score. Even dur-ing the performance, Oskar focuses on all the things that he is not supposed to notice. The sailors onstage are in a forest, which strikes him, and consequently the reader, as an odd displacement. The lack of realism is unacceptable to Oskar. The singer appears to him to be crying out in pain, and Oskar has not suspended his own reality sufficiently to see her as a character. He assumes that the actress is blinded by the spotlight and wishes to be rescued. Again, he places on the same level the artifice of the production and the reality that he knows, either unwilling or unable to focus simply on the content of the perfor-mance itself. He screams in order to break the spotlight, wreaking havoc on the stage and in the audience.

The ensuing pandemonium prompts Agnes to change her mind about opera and introduce Oskar to the circus instead. There the Lilliputian Bebra recog-nizes Oskar as a kindred spirit, allows himself to be flattered by Oskar, and gives him the advice that will guide him throughout his life. When Oskar tells Bebra that he positions himself "lieber zu den Zuschauern" (144) ("a member of the audience" [114]), he conveys the view that his drumming is purely for personal pleasure or comfort. Bebra, however, counsels him to adopt a view that is both politically savvy and engaged:

> Bester Oskar, glauben Sie einem erfahrenen Kollegen. Unsereins darf nie zu den Zuschauern gehören. Unsereins muß auf die Bühne, in die Arena. Unsereins muß vorspielen und die Handlung bestimmen, sonst wird unsereins von jenen da behandelt. Und jene da spielen uns allzu gerne übel mit! (144)

> My dear Oskar, believe an experienced colleague. Our kind has no place in the audience. We must perform, we must run the show. If we don't, it's the others that run us. And they don't do it with kid gloves. (114)

Bebra's stirring and foreboding words predict that people like Oskar and him will be at the mercy of nefarious powers if they do not take an active role in defining and presenting themselves. With this, Bebra articulates the importance the Nazis placed on spectacular performances as well as the explicit function of those performances in mobilizing public support for National Socialism. In hushed tones he warns Oskar never to be found in front of the rostrum, for he senses the dangers to him there:

> Sie kommen! Sie werden die Festplätze besetzen! Sie werden Fackelzüge veranstalten! Sie werden Tribünen bauen, Tribünen bevölkern und von Tribünen herunter unseren Untergang predigen. (144)

> "They are coming," he whispered. "They will take over the meadows where we pitch our tents. They will organize torchlight parades. They will build rostrums and fill them, and down from the rostrums they will preach our destruction." (114)

Bebra's advice thus posits the stage as the site of a vital contest and conceives of it as a forum for principled resistance to fascism. The stage here is clearly a metaphor for power and authority and understood concretely by the characters themselves as a very literal platform for that purpose. The contest will be about who will control whom and about who will have the ability to influence public opinion. Although Bebra's use of "unsereins" indicates an emerging group identity and the implicit hope that Oskar will fight for himself and others like him, it is right to consider Angress's charge that Grass attempts to "reduce the Holocaust to a manageable size" ("Jewish Problem" 222). The ironically exclusionary term "our kind" implies those who are visibly different from the Nazis' Aryan ideal, underscoring Angress's point that so many others, like Jews, are given short shrift in Grass's novel.

Nonetheless, the hope that Bebra's admonition stirs warrants reflection here. Significantly, for the reader it is a retrospective hope, expressing Grass's wistful thought that German history could have taken a different course and that the stage could have been a catalyst for progressive change.

When Oskar soon thereafter disrupts a Nazi rally on the Maiwiese, these hopes are stunningly, though fleetingly, fulfilled. Bebra was right: "they" have built rostrums, on which they now perform militaristic march music to mobilize the citizens. The inflexible order of the music is echoed in the very architecture of the rostrum: "So war auch die Tribüne auf unserer Maiwiese neben der Sporthalle eine betont symmetrisch angeordnete Tribüne" (148) ("And that rostrum on our Maiwiese was indeed striking in its symmetry" [117]). Oskar gains new understanding from these observations and addresses the reader directly, underscoring that stages even beyond this one are built to ensnare audiences:

> Haben Sie schon einmal eine Tribüne von hinten gesehen? . . . Wer jemals eine Tribüne von hinten anschaute, recht anschaute, wird von Stund an gezeichnet und somit gegen jegliche Zauberei, die in dieser oder jener Form auf Tribünen zelebriert wird, gefeit sein. Ähnliches kann man von den Hinteransichten kirchlicher Altäre sagen; doch das steht auf einem anderen Blatt.   (150–51)

> Have you ever seen a rostrum from behind? . . . Everyone who has ever taken a good look at a rostrum from behind will be immunized ipso facto against any magic practiced in any form whatsoever on rostrums. Pretty much the same applies to rear views of church altars; but that is another subject.   (119)

Oskar offers wry commentary and a potentially liberating insight when he notes that knowledge of the inner workings of the stage will prevent the viewer from being manipulated or seduced. In this telling aside that links the church and the stage, he voices doubt about the truth content of religion. The stinging implication is that the church itself requires theatrics in order to maintain a hold over its flock. Even more audacious is the provocative pairing of the institutions of religion and Nazi politics. Oskar's view exposes their common deployment of the stage as an instrument of their power and authority. His words moreover betray the tacit assumption that the church will yield to Hitler's rule. Here in this context of emerging fascism and impending war, Oskar raises doubt that the church as an institution will take the lead in resisting National Socialism. Only knowledge of the stage—that is, of the mechanisms of public persuasion—will allow certain individuals to escape the rising tyranny.

Oskar enacts his own theory by hiding under the rostrum on the Maiwiese and drumming counter to the militaristic rhythms he hears above him, confusing and interrupting the Nazi band. The formerly rigid audience begins to dance as the four-four time of militarism turns to the buoyant and elegant three-four time of a Viennese waltz. Students of the novel can observe, however, that, despite this exhilarating scene of resisting Nazis, Oskar manages to thwart their dominating presence only for one afternoon. His offstage performance cannot be counted as a victory for the principled intervention of art into politics, for he is not so dedicated as to be kept away from his dinner: "Nein nein, Oskar war kein Prophet, Hunger verspürte er!" (155) ("But Oskar was no prophet, he was beginning to feel hungry" [122]). Though his achievement was brilliant, it did not stem from any conviction and would therefore not likely be reproduced. Despite his obvious power to engage in effective political resistance, he is really concerned only with his immediate comfort. This passage, then, clearly supports Hermand's critical assessment of the lack of political conviction in *The Tin Drum*. But a different conclusion—that this is a credible artistic rendering of people who were not politically engaged—can also be drawn from studying the apolitical posture of the merchant class portrayed in the novel. Readers can justly conclude that Grass's novel does not attempt to rewrite history but instead provides an opportunity to reflect on those moments when both individuals and groups could have acted differently. Once more, then, *The Tin Drum* invigorates debate on the capacity and limitations of art.

Opportunistic politics is in ample supply in Oskar's next series of performances, giving readers the chance to examine the dubious relation between the Nazi military and the arts. On the one hand, Grass cynically acknowledges the union of art and war in a century animated by violence but lacking the moral fiber compunction to condemn it. On the other hand, through this same text in which cynicism is portrayed, Grass teases readers with the possibility that art can indeed bring about understanding and peace.

The overtly cynical portrait comes first. Oskar has joined Bebra's theater at the front in order to better his own circumstances and out of relative indifference to the repercussions of National Socialism for others. The troupe's bizarre performances entertain the Nazis. Artistic endeavor has become simply a job, as Oskar has evidently little moral or philosophical trouble aligning himself with Nazis and wearing their uniform. He also does not insist on impeccable artistic standards: "Das war zwar nicht Weltklasse, was wir boten, aber es unterhielt die Leute, ließ sie die Front und den Urlaub vergessen, das machte Gelächter frei, endloses Gelächter" (429) ("Our offering was hardly in the international class, but it entertained the men, it made them forget the front and the furlough that was ended, and it made them laugh and laugh" [327]).

The second portrayal of art and militarism is more nuanced. The narration, as though in support of the characters in the theatrical troupe, changes from prose to drama in this interlude. Readers now find the script of a play about art and the military, with Bebra's troupe cast in the role of the Greek chorus. The setting is Normandy, shortly before the Allied invasion. Bunkers have transmuted into stages, militarism and war into theater. The players' own inability to see the stage is telling: Oskar and the troupe are right in the middle of the fighting action but do not seem to know it. This stage also depicts the collapse of spiritual faith among the soldiers, which may well soon extend to the population at large. Lieutenant Herzog admits, "Wir glauben hier so ziemlich an nix mehr" (437) ("We haven't much faith in anything any more" [333]). Lance Corporal Lankes, a self-described artist, seems little troubled to replace this lost spiritual faith with a coldly material foundation when he proudly asserts that concrete is immortal. The troupe responds heartily on seeing Lankes's Oblique Formations, artworks that decorate the bunkers, which he has titled "Mystisch, Barbarisch, Gelangweilt" ("Mysterious, Barbaric, Bored"; my trans.). To this, Bebra remarks, "Damit dürften Sie unserem Jahrhundert den Namen gegeben haben" (442) ("You have given our century its name" [337]).

When five nuns go by on the beach, Lankes is ordered to shoot them. He does, and the troupe is momentarily horrified. They are frightened for their own lives when they hear the shots, but they accept uncritically their own uniformed presence there as easily as they absorb the absurd and barbaric actions that they witness. Set against these killings is the death of Roswitha by artillery fire the next morning just as she is reaching for her coffee. Sympathy stirred by the death of Oskar's companion reveals that the reader has been well conditioned to care only for the daily well-being of the single person, Oskar, and is, like Oskar, distracted from seeing the whole picture of National Socialist violence and Oskar's complicity in it. The novel here pricks the readers' conscience by asking what the value of one love can be in the face of mass murder, when that one love is clearly not sufficient—and cares not—to take a stand against mass murder. Cynicism and self-interest are rendered perhaps more understandable as Bebra sadly recants his formerly vigorous view of art: "Wir Zwerge und Narren sollten nicht auf einem Beton tanzen, der für Riesen gestampft und hart wurde! Wären wir nur unter den Tribünen geblieben, wo uns niemand vermutete" (452) ("We dwarfs and fools have no business dancing on concrete made for giants. If only we had stayed under the rostrums where no one suspected our presence!" [345]). This devastating change of heart conveys a profound loss of confidence in the role that "unsereins" ("our kind"), even narrowly defined, could play on the stage. The stage has lost its power as a platform for resistance and become only a place to hide. Whether this course was inevitable remains open to debate.

The stage of the Onion Cellar chapter is less a place to examine the role of performers than a vantage point from which to study the postwar West German audience. Whereas the war's casualties have drastically altered the typical family structure, German society's new consumer orientation has brought about sweeping changes in the pace, purpose, and quality of life. A study of this passage and its stage will yield insight into the complicated relations among art, capitalism, family, and the repercussions of war.

Oskar's extended family no longer surrounds him now that the war is over, for Agnes, Jan, and Alfred are dead, as are others very dear to Oskar, including the Jewish toy store owner Sigismund Markus. Oskar, Maria, and his presumed son, Kurt, have left Danzig for Düsseldorf, where they quickly make their way in the new market economy of the *Wirtschaftswunder* ("economic miracle"). Oskar has tried many jobs but has the most success performing jazz music with his friends as one of the Rhine River Three. They perform in the Onion Cellar for an audience that has newfound leisure time and extraordinary psychological needs.

Owned by Ferdinand Schmuh, the Onion Celler is stylish and chic, its patrons historically more likely to be found in the theater:

> Die Gäste: Geschäftsleute, Ärzte, Anwälte, Künstler, auch Bühnenkünstler, Journalisten, Leute vom Film, bekannte Sportler, auch höhere Beamte der Landesregierung und Stadtverwaltung, kurz, alle, die sich heutzutage Intellektuelle nennen. . . .   (689–90)

> The customers—businessmen, doctors, lawyers, artists, journalists, theater and movie people, well-known figures from the sporting world, officials in the provincial and municipal government, in short, a cross section of the world which nowadays calls itself intellectual—   (523)

The historian Ute Poiger confirms that many patrons of early postwar German jazz music clubs were held to be "bourgeois nonconformists" (57). The reemergence of jazz in Germany after 1945 not only reflected the rejection of Nazi-era aesthetics but also defied conservative efforts by occupying forces and German administrators to elevate only high culture and restore bourgeois respectability. *The Tin Drum* imagines an additional, alternative function of jazz clubs in postwar Germany: Schmuh does not serve food to eat but instead passes out knives for peeling onions, which his guests then do on his command. The peeling induces them to cry, something that has not yet been possible without such a catalyst. In this passage, Grass makes clear the need for healing in Germany, linking collective psychological suffering with a scathing indictment of hypocrisy, exploitation, opportunism, and selfishness. Schmuh charges for admission, earning a profit from the steady supply of people who are unable to cry without his help, offering a "Naturereignis für zwölf Mark achtzig" (693) ("cataclysm at twelve marks eighty" [525]). The Onion Cellar does not restore them to stability, for they have to return again and again. Nothing essential has changed in their workaday lives, so the need to cry is ever present. As long as grief and guilt remain in the abstract—or, alternately, at the mercy of a profit-oriented proprietor—little healing is possible. Oskar is also not above reproach, for he has once again found himself on a stage before people who fall prey to unscrupulous actions.

The patrons' pain is afforded expression but remains unexamined. Even the guests' maudlin release is shown to hold the grieving in an infantile state: there is no rigorous engagement with the causes of the suffering. Perhaps an unintended example of the depth of these wounds is found in the novel itself. We see from this passage that sympathy lies with those who grieve. Their pain is illustrated clearly and poignantly. Far less clear are the moral repercussions of unreflected guilt. But these are pondered in subsequent chapters of the novel. Although the magnitude of the Holocaust defies accurate representation in fiction, Grass's efforts to depict its root causes in pure human selfishness are still viable today.

Consider the values conveyed in the chapter in which a car accident kills Schmuh. Oskar counts himself fortunate to have put away a little of his earnings, "denn da kam der Tod, nahm den Wirt Ferdinand Schmuh, nahm uns Arbeit und Verdienst" (707) ("for then came Death and carried away our Ferdinand Schmuh, our job, and our earnings" [536]). It is telling that a person, a job, and earnings now appear to carry equal weight. This is the second time in the novel where Oskar reflects on the death of a significant friend in terms of the loss that he, Oskar, incurs, not in terms of the injustice or the gravity of the death itself. Recall as well that on the Night of the Broken Glass or (*Reichskristallnacht*) Sigismund Markus dies and Oskar laments that "Markus . . . nahm mit sich alles Spielzeug aus dieser Welt" (264) ("he took all the toys in the world away with him" [206]).

The plot of the chapter ("Am Atlantikwall oder es können die Bunker ihren Beton nicht loswerden" ["On the Atlantic Wall, or Concrete Eternal"]) extends to Oskar's subsequent return to the bunker in Normandy. There, though he might also confront his past and gain insight into his contribution to National Socialism, he, like the Onion Cellar patrons, refuses any sustained examination of his earlier actions. The chapter concludes without any resolution of past crimes but with full concentration on a more prosperous future. Oskar signs a contract for a concert tour, because, like Lankes, "auch [s]eine Kunst schrie nach Brot: Es galt, die Erfahrungen des dreijährigen Blechtrommlers Oskar während der Vorkriegs- und Kriegszeit mittels der Blechtrommel in das pure, klingende Gold der Nachkriegszeit zu verwandeln" (727) ("for Lankes' art was not alone in clamoring for bread. The time had come to transmute the prewar and wartime experience of Oskar, the three-year-old drummer, into the pure, resounding gold of the postwar period" [551]). Oskar has simply redefined who "unsereins" ("our kind") are and inserted a more personally lucrative rationale for why they must return to the stage.

These passages give insight into the role that the stage has played in the social life of Germany before, during, and after the war. They contain Grass's critique of a public arena that falls far short of its humanizing and democratizing potential. Its tremendous capacity unrealized, the stage has been misused and rendered complicit in wartime atrocities and peacetime economic exploitation. The stages in *The Tin Drum* offer the shelter and comfort of illusion, a forum for the outpouring of emotion without the necessary intellectual or political analysis that could effectively bring about change and social progress. These stages are not places where ideas are examined or improved but places where performers disavow responsibility and the audience is lulled into reckless complacency. Instead of excusing performers and audience, Grass lays bare the consequences of self-centeredness that will burden Germany for generations to come.

APPENDIX
Suggestions for Assignments

QUESTIONS TO INTRODUCE DISCUSSION

What do you expect to learn from a postwar German novel?

What is the difference between telling a narrative and performing a play?

In what ways does the form of a literary work shape its content? (Under-graduate students may wish to compare form and content in works they have already studied. Graduate students may consider literary-historical scholarship or theoretical essays on the topic of genre before beginning *The Tin Drum.*)

QUESTIONS FOR SPECIFIC PASSAGES

"The Rostrum"

What do Oskar's experiences in the Stadt-Theater, the Zoppot Opera-in-the-Woods, and the circus teach him?

How much of the chapter is dedicated to the performances and their meanings, how much to other things?

What stands out about the architecture of the rostrum on the Maiwiese? How do you interpret Oskar's remarks on its physical structure?

Why does Oskar disrupt the rally on the Maiwiese? How does he feel about it afterward?

"Bebra's Theater at the Front" and "Inspection of Concrete, or Barbaric, Mystical, Bored"

Why does Oskar join the Theater of the Front?

How does he feel about leaving his home?

To what extent does the concrete bunker constitute a stage?

How does Oskar regard his family during his time with Bebra's troupe?

"In the Onion Cellar"

Find quotations from this chapter that can be grouped under the following headings: weapons/war, profit/capitalism, music, remorse, family. Where do your quotations overlap? What does this chapter say about the interrelations among those topics? (This can be done as a group assignment, with two or three group members focusing on a specific theme.)

Analyze the audience of the Onion Cellar. Who attends? Why? Over what do they cry? How do they see themselves? Is the onion an appropriate catalyst for their tears? Why or why not?

Describe the interior of the Onion Cellar. What sort of aesthetic qualities does this space have?

Why does Oskar refer to this century as "das tränenlose Jahrhundert" (693) ("the tearless century" [525])?

In Conclusion

What do the stages where Oskar performs (including the Maiwiese rostrum, the concrete bunkers at Normandy, and the Onion Cellar) have in common? How are they different? What motivates Oskar to perform in each of these instances?

What is missing from Oskar's performances in these passages? What did you expect from them, and how do you interpret what is not there?

To what extent does Oskar use his drumming performances in these passages to separate himself from his social class? Under what circumstances does he distance himself, and for what reason(s)?

RESEARCH TOPICS

Discuss *The Tin Drum* as a satirical novel. Give examples from the text. Who or what is satirized, and to whom is the satire directed?

Compare the novel's passages on performance with the corresponding scenes from Volker Schlöndorff's film.

The Tin Drum draws from the literary tradition of the picaresque novel and the *Schwank*. Consider the novel in the light of works by Thomas Murner (*Von dem großen lutherischen Narren*), Sebastian Brant (*Das Narrenschiff*), Hans Sachs (*Fastnachtspiele*), Hans Jacob Christoffel von Grimmelshausen (*Der abentheuerliche Simplicissimus Teutsch*), or Jörg Wickram (*Von guten und bösen Nachbarn*). How are these like or unlike Grass's *The Tin Drum*? How is the postwar era like or unlike the Renaissance and Reformation eras, from which these works originated?

Compare Poiger's research on jazz-club audiences with the portrayal of the audience in the Onion Cellar. Why, according to Poiger, did audiences gather to listen to jazz? What role does Poiger claim jazz music played in West and East Germany? To what extent does Grass's novel also reflect these historical findings? To what extent does this portion of the novel address cold-war ideologies?

CREATIVE INDIVIDUAL OR GROUP ACTIVITIES

Draw one of the scenes of Oskar's performances. Illustrate the spatial relations and stature of the performer. Let your drawing illuminate the optical perspective of both the audience and the performer. How do these visual perspectives help interpret the novel as a whole?

You are a critic who has attended one of Oskar's performances. Write a review of his performance for a newspaper. Pay attention to the place and time (i.e., year) of the performance as well as to the political climate and the makeup of the audience. End with a recommendation to those who might like to attend a future performance: Who should see Oskar? Who should avoid him and why?

You are Oskar's agent and negotiating his contract and tour schedule. Write the dialogues that you have with the owner of the Onion Cellar both before and after Oskar's performance there.

Write a letter to Oskar Matzerath in which you convey your understanding of his life story. Tell him what has changed in Germany since he was last seen and let him know what influence he has had on German culture.

What kind of performance might Oskar have brought to the stage in later decades of West Germany, as attempts at *Vergangenheitsbewältigung* ("coming to terms with the past") replaced outright repression of the Holocaust and the Nazi past? What might Oskar have offered after the unification of East and West Germany?

Teaching *The Tin Drum* from the Perspective of Jewish Cultural Studies and Holocaust Studies

Dagmar C. G. Lorenz

Günter Grass's development as a writer is characteristic of the transformations Germans of his generation had to undergo. A draftee into Hitler's SS, Grass began his career after the defeat of Nazi Germany in the context of the Gruppe 47 (Group 47), an association of West German and Austrian writers seeking a new start for German literature and culture. In his social critical writing, he positioned himself as a late son of the Enlightenment and a humanist. He also became a player in the political arena as an outspoken Social Democrat. His fiction, especially his autobiographical narrative *Katz und Maus* (1961; *Cat and Mouse* [1963]) and the historic-fantastic novel *Die Blechtrommel* (1959; *The Tin Drum* [1961]), appeals to college students who enjoy his colorful imagination.

That Grass's popular works may well be the only sample of contemporary German literature American students encounter in the context of their liberal arts curriculum poses a problem, because *The Tin Drum* reflects attitudes toward the Nazi past and the postwar condition specific to people of a particular social stratum, the lower middle class, who considered themselves war victims. From this vantage point, problems that plagued West Germany and continued into the postunification Federal Republic are hard to recognize. For example, the novel lacks the critical edge of 1960s leftist criticism, such as that of Ulrike Meinhof, who decried the continued lack of opportunities for women and the economically disenfranchised. Like other radical intellectuals, she also denounced the presence of former Nazi officials in politics and the corporate world and the residues of Nazi ideology in the larger society. In comparison with her political essays, a literary text like *The Tin Drum* is full of ambivalences that cannot be resolved.

Because of its potential for controversy, I have regularly included *The Tin Drum* in Ralph Manheim's translation in courses on literature and film about the Holocaust, including a two-semester honors curriculum core course, The Holocaust in Law, Literature, Film, History, and Politics. The language of instruction in this course is English, and Grass's novel occupies a somewhat peripheral but important place. The course is team-taught by two instructors, one an expert in law and criminal justice, the other an expert in Germanic literature and cultural studies. Both the novel and Volker Schlöndorff's film are introduced in the second semester. Like Bernhard Schlink's *Der Vorleser* (1995; *The Reader* [1998]), *The Tin Drum* reveals responses of a German male author of the mainstream toward Nazi racism and genocide. In contrast, the viewpoint of Helma Sanders-Brahms's *Deutschland bleiche Mutter* (1979; *Germany Pale Mother*), screened at the end of the first semester, is decidedly feminist.

By the time *The Tin Drum* is discussed, the students are familiar with the situation after 1945 and Germany's difficulties in coming to terms with the war of aggression, the Holocaust, and the problems of responsibility, guilt, and restitution for the Nazi victims. Excursions into legal, social, and political history have provided insight into the strategies of the federal government to end the Allied occupation. Literature and films have revealed aspects of the mentality of the generations involved in constructing the postwar democracy. The popular publications in postwar Germany reflect the experience and aspirations of men, most of them veterans of the lost war, and provide a blueprint for the new national identity. The writing of women and minority authors, among them Jewish exiles and survivors, remained on the margins. In this honors course, the focus lies on the experience of the Nazi victims and highlights anti-Semitism, persecution, exile, genocide, and memory of the Shoah.

The groundwork for an informed evaluation of the representation of Jewish characters and the Jewish experience in a German mainstream text has been laid before Grass's novel is introduced. Also the presence and function of the somewhat unexpected elements of humor and the grotesque in literature about the Nazi era and the Shoah have been explored in the context of both Edgar Hilsenrath and Jurek Becker (Bashaw; Bjornstad; Klocke; Gilman, "Is Life Beautiful?"). A close reading of key passages provides the basis for a class discussion on the function of the grotesque in Grass's novel and Hilsenrath's *Der Nazi und der Friseur* (1977; *The Nazi and the Barber* [1971]), revealing that similar representational elements carry an entirely different message in the work of the Shoah survivor Hilsenrath and that of the war veteran Grass.

Discussion of *The Tin Drum* focuses on, but is not limited to, the chapters featuring Jewish characters, "Fernwirkender Gesang vom Stockturm aus gesungen" ("The Stockturm: Long-Distance Song Effects"), "Glaube Hoffnung Liebe" ("Faith, Hope, Love"), "Desinfektionsmittel" ("Disinfectant"). In other words, this honors course considers the problem of anti-Semitism and the trivialization of the Holocaust in *The Tin Drum* instead of aiming at a general interpretation of the novel. Student reports and Web-based homework assignments serve to provide background information on Grass and his novel.

Grass paints a broad panorama of pre- and postwar society in his native city of Danzig, emphasizing the stories of ordinary men and women. Realistic and surrealistic narratives and fairy-tale motifs are skillfully interwoven. On its publication in 1959, *The Tin Drum* gave rise to controversy because of its direct, often vulgar, colloquial style and its exploration of Nazi Germany and the role of the lower middle class, the Nazi power base. Probing into the lives of ordinary people under Nazi rule was risky business then. The German public by and large resented the concept of collective guilt and the call to take responsibility for war crimes. These issues were discussed in historical and philosophical publications by exiled authors and social analysts such as H. G. Adler and Hannah Arendt, but mainstream literature approached them gingerly or not at all.

Aware of the international Holocaust research and the debates of the 1950s, students in the honors course frequently conclude that Grass's ostentatiously critical stance stops short of an indictment of average Germans during the Nazi era. This stopping short becomes even more obvious in a parallel reading with Hilsenrath's *The Nazi and the Barber,* and it may be the reason why *The Tin Drum* struck a positive chord with most German readers, whereas *The Nazi and the Barber* remained a cult book. Germans, as Ernestine Schlant notes, were accustomed to having the "knowledge of the Nazi past channeled into denial and repression" (24). By introducing German protagonists with only partial insight and limited responsibility, Grass set his presumably ordinary German characters apart from the Nazi elite, evil incarnate. The Matzeraths, despite their many failings and weaknesses, appear as victims of a regime whose intentions they do not grasp. Even Maria's thoughts about delivering her lover and later step-son Oskar to the Nazi authorities are made to sound naive rather than malevolent: "Nu beruhje dir doch, Alfred. Du tust grad so, als würd mir das nuscht ausmachen. Aber wenn se sagen, das macht man heut so, denn weiß ich nich, was nu richtig is" (474) ("Take it easy, Alfred. You talk as if I didn't care. But when they say it's the modern way to do, I don't know what to think" [361–62]). It is important to note that Manheim's translation leaves out the moral perspective implied in Maria's use of "richtig," literally "right" or "appropriate." The German text suggests a moral confusion rather than mere conceptual uncertainty. In the novel, low-ranking male Nazi characters and their likewise indoctrinated female counterparts make up the German collective, the Aryan *Volksgemeinschaft*. Grass's portrayal of the Matzerath family and their circle seems to have drawn on Theodor Adorno's analysis of authoritarianism in *The Authoritarian Personality* (1950; Adorno, Frenkel-Brunswick, Levinson, and Sanford) and Wilhelm Reich's *The Mass Psychology of Fascism* (1946), notably the notion that the lower middle class was the source of fascism (Koopmann).

An important issue, the ambiguity of national identity has already been addressed in our course in conjunction with earlier readings and the film *Germany Pale Mother*. It is crucial to point out that according to Nazi ideology identity was a matter of genetics, appearance, and physical fitness, so ambiguity of identity is most evident in the novel's protagonist, Oskar Matzerath. Selected short readings from George Mosse's *Nazi Culture: Intellectual, Cultural, and Social Life in the Third Reich* ("The Jew Has No Culture" [7], "Racial Soul, Landscape, and World Domination" [65–74], and "To Preserve the Strength of the Race: Compulsory Sterilization" [90–92]) illuminate this point and elicit debate on the attitudes taken by characters in the novel. An acquired rather than a congenital disability is the reason Oskar is persecuted; his race, religion, or ethnicity is not involved; he is undeniably German. But a discussion of his rebellious mind will lead to the issues of normalcy and conformity that come into play when Nazi ideology associates physical appearance and mental and character qualities.

Grass casts Oskar as a victim and perpetrator who turns his stunted growth to advantage by joining a theater group of little people who provide entertainment for Nazi troops. As a collaborator with the Nazi regime, Oskar is in a relatively safe position. During the war he lives well and even conducts his most fulfilling love affair with a woman his own size, Roswitha Raguna. In his young life—Oskar just turns thirty when he writes his memoirs, *The Tin Drum* narrative—he already had a hand in the demise of several characters, including his presumed fathers. Yet his story is void of any sense of guilt or tragedy—he is obviously a literary artifact. His self-inflicted disability, which makes him a Nazi target, is an important ingredient in the carefully constructed, fantastic universe of the book but puts into question the innocence of other Nazi victims and the perpetrators' unilateral guilt.

With its sexual language and sexually explicit scenes, the novel struck the German public as audacious and outrageous. Grass's naughty and macabre humor assailed political, social, and sexual taboos and challenged the established mode of speaking about the Nazi past. Yet the novel provided a framework for a new sense of community based on the common shortcomings and failings of average Germans. It and Schlöndorff's film contributed to the fabrication of a collective memory that was unflattering but that most people could live with. So in our course, Grass's memory work is critically explored against the corrective of Jewish writing.

Speaking from her experience as a Shoah survivor, Ruth K. Angress argues that Grass sentimentalizes and distorts the Nazi genocide. The portrayal of the toy-store owner Sigismund Markus as a pathetic weakling and a born victim reduces the scope of the Shoah in the readers' minds and makes it tolerable ("Jewish Problem"). Our students examine the novel in the light of her analysis, which is introduced in a student presentation, to determine whether the representation of Jews and Nazis can be considered a serious critical attempt of coming terms with National Socialism and the Holocaust. Angress denies that it can. Indeed, that in *The Tin Drum* the dominant culture is portrayed in a sometimes humorous, sometimes grotesque way allows readers to distance themselves emotionally from the past. That the narrative is so ambiguous, the protagonists so eccentric, and the key episodes so preposterous takes the edge off the brutality and crudeness of events. Tragedy is trivialized; perpetrators and victims alike are made light of.

Choosing as the narrator a mental patient places the entire novel in the sanatorium and puts Oskar's narrative about everyday life under National Socialism outside the normal world. His nightmarish tales belong in a realm beyond right and wrong, so no one can be held accountable. Partly because they are preposterous and partly because they are excitingly wicked, the characters and episodes are made palatable. Any documentary presenting facts and figures about the Holocaust and the world war pales in comparison. Grass's novel and Schlöndorff's film convey selected bits of information about the Nazi genocide in the mode of entertainment, bits that titillate and play with the readers, with the audience. In contrast, Alain Resnais's concentration-camp documentary *Night and Fog* (1955) and reflective films such as Bernhard Wicki's *Die Brücke* (1959; *The Bridge*) confront the audience with evidence of the atrocities committed by the Nazis. Students usually notice that Resnais, a non-Jewish French concentration-camp survivor, refrains from identifying the Nazi victims as Jews but that the narrative voice in his film refers to the victims by Jewish-identified names and to sites of mass exterminations. The contrast between Resnais's empathetic, victim-oriented representation and Grass's crude othering of Jewish characters by way of his linguistic and physical typecasting reminiscent of Nazi propaganda is astounding. Grass's narrator implicitly validates the continued undercurrent of anti-Semitism by allowing the negative stereotypes of Markus and Fajngold to become paradigms of the Jewish fate under National Socialism.

In some ways, Oskar Matzerath calls to mind the traditional picaro. Grandfather Koljaiczek's escape under Grandmother Anna's skirts and his clandestine lovemaking, Oskar's hiding out under the selfsame skirts, his amorous adventures with women of different ages and backgrounds, Agnes's trysts with her cousin, the slow decline of the adulterous wife after eating eel soup served by her husband, and Matzerath's death as a result of swallowing his Nazi Party pin are the stuff of tall tales. Because they are both grotesque and psychologically convincing, Grass's figures provoke laughter and create a sense of complicity on the part of the readers. Episodes such as the impregnation of Oskar's earthy grandmother in the potato fields evoke the German fairy-tale tradition, with which most German children are familiar. They produce nostalgia for a simpler life before the disasters of the 1940s.

Comparing *The Tin Drum* with Hilsenrath's macabre *The Nazi and the Barber,* Peter Arnds observes:

> Grass uses the fairy-tale tradition in the context of the Holocaust in a much subtler and less cynical way than Hilsenrath. While Hilsenrath's

view of the German fairy tale is entirely negative because in Jungian fashion he associates it with the realization of myth during the Third Reich
and sees reflected in the fairy tale the spirit of Wotan, Grass' perception of
the German fairy tale changes from *Die Blechtrommel* to his later work.
("On the Awful German Fairy Tale" 425)

It may be true that for Grass, who grew up in Nazi Germany, the fairy tale represented a wholesome alternative to the dominant Nazi discourse. But a look
at German fairy tales in the light of Bruno Bettelheim's criticism (introduced
in a student report or by a guest speaker) reveals how this seemingly innocuous tradition fed into National Socialist mythmaking and was co-opted by the
regime. To the Jewish near-victim Hilsenrath, the gratuitous violence and cruelty in Grimms' fairy tales and their poetic justice that calls for the death of the
outsider and the elimination of the out-group were obviously problematic, as
the use of fairy-tale motifs in *The Nazi and the Barber* reveals.

Grass's representation of two Jewish characters, Markus and the Shoah survivor Mariusz Fajngold, is informed by the anti-Semitic narrative tradition and
its stereotypes. Angress observes that Grass perpetuates the concepts and images of the Nazi media to stereotype and denigrate Jews ("Jewish Problem").
For example, Markus is portrayed as sexually unappealing. His characterization,
in conjunction with the topos of Jewish men lusting after non-Jewish women,
takes up where nineteenth-century and Nazi anti-Semitism left off. Markus may
not be the villainous Jewish antihero of German fiction from Freytag to Dinter,
but our students, familiar with the anti-Semitic writing and Veit Harlan's Nazi
propaganda film *Jud Süß* (1940), will speculate what might have become of
Grass's Markus in the framework of a Nazi narrative. He would have realized
his full potential as a lecher, winning Agnes's affection and fleeing with her to
England. Grass's textual strategies ensure that Markus appears not only ridiculous and sleazy but also devious and vaguely threatening. He is likened to a dog
and seemingly leads a parasitic life all by himself without religion, family, and
community (Angress, "Jewish Problem" 223). With his cunning he acts as a
procurer for Agnes and Bronski and helps the pair undermine the Christian
family structure.

Grass blends familiar stereotypes to forge Jewish characters. For Markus he
emphasizes the stubbornness with which many Jews held on to their trust in
Germany and the Germans well into the 1930s. Markus apparently lacks the
imagination to envision what the Nazis have in store for him. Yet he does not
stir compassion; his attempts to cope with the situation after the Nazis' rise to
power are too inept, and his opportunism renders him repulsive. Although his
fate has already been determined because he is of Jewish descent, he converts,
mistakenly assuming that taking baptism will protect him from persecution.
Worse yet, his demise ultimately seems his own fault: unlike other people, he
has the opportunity to escape to England—he has the necessary funds and a
sponsor. The allusion to Markus's international connections evokes a favorite

theme of Nazi propaganda—namely, that Jews cannot be trusted, because they are not real Germans. Associating the toy-store owner with England, a nation hostile toward Nazi Germany, intensifies the impression that he is an untrustworthy foreigner. Thus, instead of vindicating him, his offer to take Agnes and, as an afterthought, her endangered son to England casts further doubt on him. Finally, Markus commits the ultimate transgression of which Nazi propaganda accused Jewish men: he tries to lure a non-Jewish woman away from her community, her family, and her country. And, he eludes his would-be assassins by committing suicide, an act that National Socialists would consider cowardly.

The Tin Drum also validates the association anti-Semites made between commerce and business and Jewishness. The names of the store owners in Markus's neighborhood are listed as "Leiser, Sternfeld, Machwitz." The first two are recognizably Jewish (Angress, "Jewish Problem" 224). Angress concludes that the suicide of Markus, an unheroic dealer in goods of inferior quality, a Jewish man without principles and a slave to inappropriate sexual desires, elicits no sense of loss in the novel (23). She further maintains that even though Markus is only one of many grotesque minor figures, he has a key role because he serves as an abstraction of the Jewish fate and characters (24). Thus his character defines the range of what and who is German in Grass's novel.

Angress's argument is borne out on the linguistic level. The idiom attributed to Markus marks the toy dealer as other. He speaks the Yiddish-accented German termed *mauscheln*, which non-Jews as early as the beginning of the nineteenth century regarded as inferior and comical (Gilman, *Jewish Self-Hatred* 155). This accent makes his careful and rather sensible appeal to Agnes sound appallingly slick and banal:

> Oder wenn Se mechten setzen gefälligst auffen Markus und kommen Se middem Markus, wo er getauft is seit neilich. Gehn wä nach London, Frau Agnes, wo ich Lait hab drieben und Papiere genug, wenn Se nur wollten kommen, oder wolln Se nich middem Markus, weil Se ihn verachten, nu denn verachten Se ihn. Aber er bittet Ihnen von Herzen, wenn Se doch nur nicht mehr setzen wollen auffen meschuggenen Bronski, dä bei de Polnische Post bleibt, . . . (133)

Manheim's translation tries to give a sense of Markus's jargon, but there is no equivalent anglophone idiom that carries the same ideological implications as the German-Jewish *mauscheln*:

> Or do me a favor, bet on Markus seeing he's just fresh baptized. We'll go to London, I got friends there and plenty stocks and bonds if you just decide to come, or all right if you won't come with Markus because you despise me, so despise me. But I beg you down on my knees, don't bet no more on Bronski that's meshugge enough to stick by the Polish Post Office . . . (106)

In this and similar instances it is important to point out to English-speaking students how the original text differs from the translation.

For most German readers in 1959, Markus's name, the way he talks, and his aspirations and circumstances immediately evoked the old prejudicial image of the Jew. Like the author himself, Germans who lived in the Third Reich were indoctrinated with anti-Semitic propaganda (Bering). There are passages in *The Tin Drum* that adopt Nazi speech, suggesting a consensus between the unrehabilitated narrator and the readers. For example, the sentence, "[M]an . . . holte das Söhnchen beim Juden ab" (172) deprives Markus of his individuality: it does not have to be this specific person, it could be any Jew. Through the contraction of *bei* and *dem (beim)* the term "der Jude" ("the Jew") becomes generic and makes Markus an emblem of Jewishness.[1] As such he is juxtaposed against the Germanness of Agnes and her son. Regardless how unsavory their circumstances, the Matzeraths and Bronskis exclude and reject "the Jew" for who he is while using him for their purposes.

Angress observes that even in death Markus is denied his individuality. In an elegiac prose poem marking the end of Oskar's, and presumably Nazi Germany's, childhood and their relative innocence before Kristallnacht, the nationwide pogrom of 1938, Oskar deplores the death of the toy dealer because of the tin drums the dealer sold him. He does not mourn the person (264; 206). On the contrary, the narrator describes the dead Jew's body as so repulsive that his death is unlikely to rouse sympathy: "Hinter seinem Schreibtisch saß der Spielzeughändler. Ärmelschoner trug er wie gewöhnlich über seinem dunkelgrauen Alltagstuch. Kopfschuppen auf den Schultern verrieten seine Haarkrankheit" (260) ("The toy merchant sat behind his desk. As usual he had on sleeve protectors over his dark-grey everyday jacket. Dandruff on his shoulders showed that his scalp was in bad shape" [202]).

Markus is associated with the pre-Holocaust era, but through a parallel plot he is also connected with the character of a survivor, Fajngold, in "Desinfektionsmittel" (536–50) ("Disinfectant" [407–18]). This Jewish character likewise engages in shady business practices. Worse yet, in the death camp, he used to perform services for the Nazis. As "disinfector" in Treblinka, he had

> jeden Mittag um zwei die Lagerstraßen, Baracken, die Duschräume, Verbrennungsöfen, die gebündelten Kleider, die Wartenden, die noch nicht geduscht hatten, die Liegenden, die schon geduscht hatten, alles was aus den Öfen herauskam, alles was in die Öfen hineinwollte, als Desinfektor Mariusz Fajngold tagtäglich mit Lysolwasser besprenkelt hatte. (543)

> Every day at 2 p.m., in his official capacity as Disinfector Mariusz Fajngold, he had sprinkled Lysol on the camp streets, over the barracks, the shower rooms, the cremating furnaces, the bundles of clothing, over those who were waiting to shower, over those who lay recumbent after

their showers, over all that came out of the ovens and all who were about to go in.   (413)

The macabre humor in this passage is produced by the use of euphemism of Nazi practice. Of course, Grass's readers know that taking a shower in Treblinka means to be gassed, that those lying on the ground after taking such a shower are corpses. The most problematic phrase, "was in die Öfen hineinwollte"—literally, "everything that wanted to get into the ovens"—suggests that not only Jews who committed suicide, like Markus, or Jews who did the Nazis' dirty work, like Fajngold, but even the dead Jews were collaborators. Note also Grass's reification of human beings as "alles" ("everything").

Fajngold shares Markus's proclivity for non-Jewish women. His rejection by Oskar's former lover and stepmother, Maria, calls to mind Markus's rebuff by Oskar's mother, Agnes. In neither case does the expected manly fight for the desired woman ensue. The Jewish men respond by pleading, attempting bribery, and finally yielding to the woman's wishes. None of this behavior is surprising after Markus has set the pattern. Moreover, Fajngold is described as unmanly (from a pseudo-heroic Nazi point of view) and as unattractive as Markus. Maria has the readers' complete sympathy when she chooses an uncertain future in West Germany to an alliance with a well-to-do but physically unappealing Jewish man. With their unpleasant physical features, Markus and Fajngold call to mind the generic Jewish figures played by Wolfgang Krauss in *Jud Süß*: there is a clear continuity of representational strategies from the literature and films of the 1930s to those of the 1950s.

Fajngold's hallucinations of his dead family members take up all his emotional energy. Yet one can never be sure just how much of the survivor's grief is play-acting and how much is real. The ease with which Fajngold gets over the death of his wife and his entire family once Maria wakens his interest suggests that his losses affected him only minimally. In fact, it is difficult to imagine Fajngold in a relationship or as the member of a community at all. Portrayed in complete isolation—he is the only Jewish survivor in the novel and remains excluded from Gentile society—he seems something like a wandering or eternal Jew, a motif from the anti-Semitic tradition that Fritz Hippler in his Nazi propaganda film *Der ewige Jude* (1940; *The Eternal Jew*) revived and filled with new content.

Foreignness is a key feature for both Jewish characters. Markus suggests that he has his best connections in England. Fajngold is associated with Eastern Europe. By assigning Fajngold and the murdered Jews Yiddish and Polish names, Grass relegates them to a separate, non-German sphere:

Seine ganze Familie, nicht nur die Frau Luba, rief er in den Keller, und sicherlich sah er alle kommen, denn er nannte sie beim Namen, sagte Luba, Lew, Jakub, Berek, Leon, Mendel und Zonja, erklärte den Genannten, wer da liege und tot sei, und erklärte gleich darauf uns, daß alle, die er so soeben gerufen habe, auch so dalagen, bevor sie in die Öfen von Treblinka kamen, dazu noch seine Schwägerin und der Schwägerin Schwestermann, der fünf Kinderchen hatte, und alle lagen, nur er, der Fajngold, lag nicht, weil er Chlor streuen mußte.   (524)

He called not only Luba his wife, but his whole family into the cellar, and there is no doubt that he saw them all coming, for he called them by name: Luba, Lev, Jakub, Berek, Leon, Mendel, and Sonya. He explained to them all who it was who was lying there dead and went on to tell us that all those he had just summoned as well as his sister-in-law and her other brother-in-law who had five children had lain in the same way, before being taken to the crematoria of Treblinka, and the whole lot of them had been lying there—except for him because he had had to strew lime on them.   (398)

Unlike Maria, Fajngold does not mind living in Danzig after its annexation by Poland. Maria's plan to move to her late husband's home in the Rhineland, close to the celebrated German river associated with the Nibelungen saga and nineteenth-century German mythmaking, defines her in national terms. A German woman, she wants to live among Germans in German lands. Fajngold's staying in Poland reenforces the impression that he is a non-German other. Yet the thought that after the Shoah a Jew would opt to live in Poland is out of keeping with historical fact. In the 1950s Polish anti-Semitism was well known and deterred many survivors from settling in that country. The Nazis had eradicated Poland's Jewish communities and cultural networks. The 1946 pogrom at Kielce, instigated by Poles against death-camp survivors, caused a mass exodus of the remaining Jews. Neither the general conditions for Jews in Poland nor the pogrom, which postdates the Matzeraths' departure from Gdańsk, are reflected in *The Tin Drum*.

The notion that Fajngold and, for that matter, all Jews belong in Eastern Europe is anti-Semitic. The geographic markers "east" and "west" in association with the postwar era draw attention to the cold war, which in 1959 was in full force. So was the mutual hate propaganda. The Western media painted Eastern Europe as an evil empire, the seat of Bolshevist oppression. It is not difficult to link postwar Western propaganda with the Nazi discourse that portrayed Bolshevism as the product of a Jewish conspiracy. On a subliminal level, Fajngold is associated with the anti-Communist rhetoric of the Nazi period and the postwar era and cast as a dangerous element. Leaving him outside Germany corresponds with the Federal Republic's strong pro-Israel policy and the simultaneous opposition to Jewish survivors' remaining in and exiles' returning to Germany (Kaufmann 191–193; Broder and Lang 170, 222–232, 304; Kacandes 209).

In Grass's novel, Fajngold's future seems secure. Fajngold is firmly installed in Matzerath's grocery store. The last impression the reader is left with is Fajngold's waving after the train "mit rötlich wehendem Haar" until he "nur noch aus Winken bestand, bis es ihn nicht mehr gab" (550) ("He stood there with his reddish hair blowing in the wind, becoming smaller and smaller, as is fitting and proper when trains leave, until nothing was left of him but a waving arm, and soon he had ceased to exist altogether" (418). This visual image of a Jew and one of the major emblems of the Holocaust, a train, suggests that the last Jew is being left behind. The image echoes the Germans' frequent call to move on and forget about the past. Moreover, the departure of Maria and Oskar separates the rightful owners of the Matzerath business from their property. In other words, Grass stages a macabre reversal of historical fact: the Aryanization of Jewish businesses by German Nazis in the 1930s and 1940s as well as the strategies of the *Ariseure* ("Aryanizers") to avoid returning the stolen property after the war are flagrantly ignored. Instead, *The Tin Drum* features a Jew taking advantage of non-Jews by usurping their business.

In a course that focuses on literature and films about the Holocaust, the presence of anti-Semitic stereotypes in *The Tin Drum* will be immediately apparent. Literary devices creating a German insider position while positioning Jewish characters on the periphery exist throughout the novel's extensive network of plots and characters. Classroom debates center on the factually and morally questionable allusions and strategies, used with impunity because Grass's narrator is configured as a mental patient. That Oskar is a mental patient makes it difficult to assess the stories about his collaboration with the Nazis, his Nazi expressions and ideological residue. How seriously are they to be taken? Possibly his socialization in a dysfunctional, less-than-respectable family during the Nazi era can also be considered a reason to exonerate him and small-time villains like him (Arnds, "On the Awful German Fairy Tale": Preece, "Danger").

The mental asylum further suggests that in West Germany Oskar's point of view is unacceptable. In other words, Grass constructs Oskar as the unreliable narrator par excellence. A mixture between fool and clown, he is at liberty to make statements for which other people would be held accountable. Grass's virtually impenetrable narrative told by a German who is neither child nor adult, neither victim nor perpetrator, seems to have entertained German readers after the Shoah as Oskar's antics entertained the fictional Nazis in wartime (Thomas, "Oskar"; O'Neill, "Implications").

Frequently students resort to the obvious parallels between Oskar's fictitious and Grass's actual background to resolve these issues. The author and his protagonist were children when the Nazis assumed power. Both became embroiled in the system. From a biographical point of view, Oskar exonerates the author on a personal level and the author's social class and generation on a historical level. The narrative suggests that Oskar lacked the insight and power to change anything, that a disabled child like him, and others living on the fringes of Nazi society, could not avoid indoctrination. This assumption is discussed in our class in the light of previous readings—for example, works by Daniel Goldhagen, Christoper Browning, Fania Fenelon, and Jerzy Kosinski. The debate leads to a conversation about the traumatic impact the collapse of Nazi Germany had on the Germans of Grass's generation and their need for reeducation in view of the new reality. A comparison of Grass's background with that of Hilsenrath helps students explore differences of point of view and positionality. Hilsenrath was born in 1926 in Leipzig and fled with his mother to Romania in 1938. Eventually he was deported to the ghetto Moghilev-Podolsk, where he barely survived starvation. After an odyssey that extended over several decades and took him to numerous countries, including Israel and the United States, he moved to Berlin.

Humor and the grotesque are among the stylistic and representational similarities in *The Tin Drum* and *The Nazi and the Barber*. But the two authors use these elements to fundamentally different ends, because the claim of each to German identity rests on different assumptions. As does the success of each as an author. Grass rose to a dominant position in the Federal Republic as a spokesman for a morally and socially responsible Germany. Hilsenrath fought an uphill battle to gain recognition against accusations of (Jewish) anti-Semitism and faced intrigues instigated by his own publisher (S. Moeller).

Comparing Hilsenrath's radically oppositional novel with Grass's text clearly shows how much Grass's text is part of the dominant culture. *The Tin Drum* avoids the issue of guilt—all the characters are somewhat guilty and somewhat innocent—and even accommodates Holocaust denial by suggesting both that the Jews participated in their own destruction and that they benefited in the end. Hilsenrath's adverse experience with German publishers and critics reveals how unwelcome were representations of Jews and the Holocaust that challenged the German consensus. Critics feared that unconciliatory texts by a Jewish author "would not create sympathy, but rather anti-Semitic reactions" (S. Moeller 230). His fortunes changed somewhat after the revelations made in the Eichmann Trial (1960) and after the Frankfurt Auschwitz Trial sparked relentless questioning of the Nazi generation by young Germans and precipitated the Holocaust debates of the 1970s and 1980s.

Historical, biographical, and literary materials are an integral part of our course and inform the discussion of *The Tin Drum* as well. Thus students question often-made assertions such as Arnds's, that "before the 1980s there was no significant discourse on the Holocaust in Germany" ("On the Awful German Fairy Tale" 424). Topical research shows that in the 1940s and 1950s writers and historians such as Eugen Kogon, Victor Klemperer, H. G. Adler, Paul Celan, Nelly Sachs, Ilse Aichinger, Peter Edel, and Rahel Behrend published documentaries, fiction, and poetry on the topic of the Nazi genocide (Lorenz). Such earlier publications show that the larger context of Grass's novel did not have to be unfamiliar to German readers.

Considering the centrality of the Jewish characters in *The Tin Drum*, the following observation by Arnds misses the implications of Grass's thematic choice:

> The persecution of Jews and their elimination in concentration camps is not a central theme in this novel, it is in its entirety a text about the

> persecution of another minority group that the Nazis considered *art-fremd*, the physically and mentally handicapped, exemplified by the dwarf Oskar Matzerath.   ("On the Awful German Fairy Tale" 422)

Oskar is precisely not portrayed as *artfremd*, as being of a different race or ethnicity, like Markus and Fajngold. Rather, he is positioned at the very center of Grass's novel, unquestionably German despite his disability. In fact, *The Tin Drum* casts non-Jews as the actual Nazi victims.

Grass uncovers plenty of malice among Germans of the Nazi era, which is why his novel is generally considered socially critical. But, drawing an extensive social portrait of Germans, he does not explore Jewish German history. There is not even an acknowledgment of the extent to which Jews were victimized already at the time when Sigismund Markus acts as babysitter and procurer for Agnes and Jan. To connote all Jewish society, Grass introduces only two male characters, one who survives the Nazi era and one who does not. Oskar, his friends, and his relatives, on the other hand, are overindividualized. An exuberant creation of Grass's imagination, Oskar plays the role of evil goblin as well as that of victim of history (Mouton)—he occupies, as it were, the position of both German and Jew. He showcases the disorientation and moral uncertainty of Grass's generation.

Henryk M. Broder explores the denial, confusion, and self-assertion that he observes in Holocaust discussions of the 1990s. Considering that as late as the turn of the millennium the Holocaust continued to present German-speaking societies with conceptual, moral, and legal problems, the ambivalence with which Grass inscribes Oskar Matzerath is hardly surprising. Despite his opportunistic and criminal behavior, Oskar assumes a tone of moral superiority when condemning Nazis and Nazi practices. A similar blind spot was shared by many Germans.

The central issues in *The Tin Drum* are German problems, which are thematized to the exclusion of the Jewish catastrophe. When Fajngold is relegated to Eastern Europe, the Jewish problem, as Angress calls it, is laid to rest. The absence of Jewish characters in the final part of the novel suggests a social homogeneity that makes rethinking of the relationship between majority and minority, Germans and Jews, a nonissue. In Grass's postwar scenario the element of the other, the uncanny, exists only symbolically, on the fairy-tale level as the "Schwarze Köchin" (779), translated by Manheim as "the black, wicked Witch" (589).

Comparing *The Tin Drum* with *The Nazi and the Barber* sheds light on Grass's uneasy relation to the past and the difficulty he has envisioning multicultural Weimar Germany with Jews of different levels of assimilation (Bjornstad). Hilsenrath's narrative lacks the ubiquitous nostalgic tenor of *The Tin Drum*. It leaves no room for ambivalence. The novel's protagonist, Max Schulz, no less a literary construct than Oskar, is squarely referred to as a mass murderer and a war criminal. Despite his Jewish looks, which facilitate his assimilation into

Israeli society, he epitomizes the German lower-middle-class Nazi, adaptable because he ultimately has no backbone.

In Hilsenrath's dual biography of Schulz and his neighbor and victim, Finkelstein, the Jewish victims are the true protagonist even though the perpetrators end up victorious. Hilsenrath's obscene and explicit language, far more abrasive than Grass's, drives home the point that obscenity is not in sexuality but in the destruction and extermination of body and mind committed during the Holocaust. There is nothing seductive about Hilsenrath's overtly sexual passages. Grass teases and occasionally criticizes, but he makes his readers complicit in lewd scenes. Yet he lets them shrug off the atrocities of the Shoah. Hilsenrath lambastes his German readers and exposes their appetite for sexual violence, murder, and money.

Grass's Jews, because they are surrounded by grotesque characters such as Oskar, Agnes, Matzerath, Bronski, and Grandmother Anna, become, among other things, objects of laughter. But they do not draw the indulgent mockery that is bestowed on non-Jewish figures. Their discursive otherness, stressed at every turn, keeps them apart from the German insider circle—a circle of Catholics and Nazis. Grass's narrative reconstructs the position assigned Jews in the anti-Semitic discourse whose legacy continued to shape the imagination in the postwar years.

NOTE

[1] My literal translation of the phrase would be, "one picked the boy up at the Jew's." Manheim's translation reads, "pick up the boy along with a few of Markus' compliments and a package of sewing silk" (135), thus avoiding altogether the offensive term of the original, "Jew" in the singular.

Teaching Race in Günter Grass's *The Tin Drum*

Peter Arnds

> The single genuine power standing against the principle
> of Auschwitz is autonomy . . . the power of reflection,
> of self-determination, of not cooperating.
> —Theodor Adorno, "Education after Auschwitz"

While Günter Grass's *The Tin Drum* may indeed use the language of silence with regard to the Holocaust (Schlant 69–71; Donahue), it is in part a literary reaction to the Nazi ideology of race and eugenics culminating in the persecution of asocials as "life unworthy of life" and in their extermination in psychiatric institutions in the Third Reich (Arnds, *Representation*). Grass's book aims for a union between Apollo and Dionysus, between rationalism in the tradition of Socrates and the Enlightenment and an irrationalism steeped in myth, in marked contrast to the monologous pseudo-scientific rationalism of the Third Reich and the continuity of rationalism as *Vernunft* ("reason") in the Adenauer period, which interpreted Nazism solely as irrational. The irrationalism of *The Tin Drum* arises from its rich intertextuality with myth and folk culture, which the text literally reclaims from their entanglement with Nazi ideology. Grass revives the grotesqueness of myth and folk culture, which under National Socialism were as closely intertwined with racist ideology as most other aspects of life and the arts (Broszat; Kamenetsky, "Folklore" and "Folktale"). The dense intertextual fabric of mythological material in this novel, the dwarf-fairy tales of the Brothers Grimm and Wilhelm Hauff, and various manifestations of the trickster archetype—the fool, the clown, the harlequin, and the picaro, who is the literary cousin of the mythological trickster—offer a fascinating approach to teaching the theme of race and racism.

In structure and content, Grass's novel connects the silencing of these grotesque (degenerate) cultural manifestations to the persecution and extermination of several minority groups: the physically and mentally handicapped, criminals, homosexuals, and vagabonds. Although the drummer Oskar Matzerath has traditionally been seen as an embodiment of fascism, a grotesque incarnation of Germans as perpetrators, I would argue that the persecuted dwarf also becomes a central metaphor and voice for these less discussed minorities that the Nazis targeted. In classes focusing on aspects of race in *The Tin Drum*, Oskar ought therefore to hold a prominent position, since unlike any other character in postwar German literature he embodies a racism that went so berserk that it had the potential to wipe out the entire German population. Oskar can indeed be discussed as an ambivalent figure embodying both perpetrator and victim, for it is in the image of the concentration camps, an ever-present shadow in Grass's novel, that the destitution of modernity is rendered visible and that the perpetrators mirror themselves in the victims and try to eradicate the stranger within.

Issues of race in *The Tin Drum* can be explored through a variety of texts, including the work of cultural thinkers like Mikhail Bakhtin, Michel Foucault, and Hannah Arendt;[1] some historical documents of Nazi racism; other novels; as well as some visual material, such as sculpture (Arno Breker) and film (Volker Schlöndorff). Students could be encouraged to compare race and racism in imperialism with that in totalitarianism by reading Joseph Conrad's *Heart of Darkness* and selected passages from Arendt's *The Origins of Totalitarianism*. The comparison would help them understand how these two systems differ. A reading of passages from Foucault's *Society Must Be Defended* and a discussion of his two functions of racism and how they can be applied to the distinction between nineteenth-century imperialism and Nazi racism could then lead to a definition of the central paradigms of race in *The Tin Drum*. These paradigms are the body, the mind, gender, art, sexuality, and genre. As I outline below, the discussion of them can be approached through a mix of theoretical texts and cultural representations.

A detailed analysis of *The Tin Drum* using these parameters will enable students to understand the connections between the fictional representation of aberrant people and the racist mechanisms of expulsion and marginalization based on their bodies, minds, and sexuality. One could teach an entire course on *The Tin Drum* along these lines, but it would make for an attractive comparative literature class at the graduate level if Grass's novel were discussed in connection with the texts of other works of magic realism, such as Michel Tournier's *The Ogre*, Mikhail Bulgakov's *Master and Margarita*, Salman Rushdie's *Midnight's Children*, Chinua Achebe's *Things Fall Apart*, Gabriel García Marquéz's *One Hundred Years of Solitude*, and Toni Morrison's *Beloved*. These fictional works could be supplemented by a selection of theoretical texts. The class could be taught in three phases. The first would explore the question of why myth lends itself to representations of racism. In the second, *The Tin Drum*'s paradigms of race would be analyzed in detail. The third would open the course to other works of magic realism and racism in the context of Nazism, Stalinism, and colonialism.

Why does myth lend itself to a literary representation of race? The unreality of a totalitarian regime, which Arendt has described as a "superior realism" (353), may be the reason why some artists in such a society respond with works of magic realism. The protagonist, Abel Tiffauges, in Tournier's *The Ogre*, for example, thinks that he is in some kind of horrific fairy tale when he arrives at Goering's hunting lodge. In *The Master and Margarita*, Bulgakov, for fear of retribution, never talks openly about Stalinism but refers to it as witchcraft:

> And it was two years ago that inexplicable things began happening . . . : people started disappearing without a trace. Once, on a day off, a policeman appeared, summoned the second lodger (whose name has been lost)

> into the front hall, and said that he had been asked to come down to the
> police station for a minute in order to sign something. The lodger told
> Anfisa . . . he would be back in ten minutes. . . . Not only did he not return
> in ten minutes, he never returned at all. . . . [I]t was witchcraft pure and
> simple, and . . . as everyone knows, once witchcraft gets started, there is
> no stopping it.   (63)

The famous line, "once witchcraft gets started, there is no stopping it," expresses
totalitarianism's self-consuming racism, the never-ending need to find enemies.
In such passages, the conflation of reality with sur- or unreality justifies magic
realism. Evidently, in times of extreme censorship, only metaphoric language
can save the artist from persecution; hence the magic realist novel becomes a
tool to express and attack the politics of a totalitarian regime.

It is easy to see why fairy tales, legends, and myths, with all their goriness and
uncanniness and rooted in some dark pre-Enlightenment age, lend themselves
to a literary depiction of the horrors of totalitarianism. While in the wake of
the Enlightenment, bourgeois society tried to displace the irrationalism and
violence displayed in myth and cover it up with a "universe of refined customs,"
totalitarianism's project of reenchanting the world through its own forms of
mythology goes hand in hand with a "return of barbaric, pre-civilized mythic
patterns" (Žižek 36–37). Although the universality of myth works against partic-
ularization—the mechanism of segregation inherent to racism—and supports
the artist who espouses liberalism, myth also provides models for the marginalization of people. Such marginalization is reflected, for example, in the liminal
status of the trickster archetype, in the physical and mental grotesqueness that
marks him as uncanny and hence unworthy to be included in normal society
(think of ogres, dwarfs, and werewolves). Moreover, myth and racism are related through the phenomena of homelessness and wandering, a part of the
rootless lives that outsiders are forced to lead. These concepts are central to any
discussion of racism. Although wandering can be a consequence of outlawry
(*Friedlosigkeit*) in the medieval sense, wandering per se does not trigger racism.
A brief look at Nazi euthanasia documents shows us that the Nazis distinguished
between good and bad wanderers.[2] The racism toward roaming Gypsies and
nonsedentary Jews derives from a deeply rooted cultural memory of their outlawry in earlier ages.

One way to enable students to understand that the connectedness of myth
and race has a long history is through the writings of Giorgio Agamben, particularly chapter 2 ("The Muselmann") from *Remnants of Auschwitz* and chapter
5 ("Feast, Mourning, Anomie") from *State of Exception*. According to the Italian philosopher, the suspension of law characterizing the state of exception, as
it does in the Nazi concentration camps, may have its roots in "some archaic
juridical institutions, such as the Germanic *Friedlosigkeit* or the persecution of
the *wargus* [the werewolf] in ancient English law" (*State* 71). Agamben argues
that carnivalesque rituals, medieval

charivari and other anomic phenomena precisely replicate the different phases of the cruel ritual in which the *Friedlos* [the outlaw] and the bandit were expelled from the community, their houses unroofed and destroyed, and their wells poisoned or made brackish. (72)

If racism has its roots in these ancient rituals of marginalization that then entered the realm of myth and the charivari-like phenomena of the Middle Ages and the Renaissance, the realm of myth, in turn, has inspired twentieth-century cultural representations of racism. Equating the state of exception as carnivalesque ritual with the Nazi camps may at first seem an affront, but it underlines the unreality, the hell-like character of the camps. After all, the charivari-like phenomena of which Agamben speaks are all steeped in the imagery of hell, from the Saturnalia through the commedia dell'arte to today's Halloween.[3] Besides lending their imagery of hell to such descriptions, these carnivalesque forms also have the function of disrupting all forms of rationalism.

Myth thus becomes a vehicle not only for a representation of racism but also for the tragicomic subversion of and resistance to the rationalism of modernity, which is responsible for the escalation of racism during the nineteenth and twentieth centuries. Because of its connection with laughter and tragicomic hope, myth has the power to deflate ideologies, to shatter the sacred through the profane. Myth is a counterdiscourse to the officialdom of imperialism, totalitarianism, and postwar rationalism. The quixotic, grotesque aspects of myth preserve the spirit of liberalism, as they do in Grass's novel. Students could be encouraged to explore the charivari-like phenomena of which Agamben speaks, by way of short presentations supplemented by the reading of passages from Agamben's *Homo Sacer* (part 2, chapter 6: "The Ban and The Wolf") and *State of Exception* (chapter 5: "Feast, Mourning, Anomie") as well as the introduction of Cornel West's *Democracy Matters*, in which West explores the tragicomic hope in the face of racism experienced by African Americans. While Agamben's work is important for the discussion of wandering, homelessness, and the camps, the introduction to West's book prepares students for a discussion of the functions of Oskar's carnivalesque musical performances.

Discussion of racism in *The Tin Drum* could open with an analysis of Arendt's *The Origins of Totalitarianism* (specifically, chapters 6 and 7). With reference to imperialism's "scramble for Africa," Arendt defines race as "the emergency explanation of human beings whom no European or civilized man could understand and whose humanity so frightened and humiliated the immigrants that they no longer cared to belong to the same human species" (185). She describes how imperialism reduces human beings to the level of animals or even less than animals, to inanimate nature:

[R]aces in this sense were found only in regions where nature was particularly hostile. What made them different from other human beings was not at all the color of their skin but the fact that they behaved like a part of nature, that . . . nature had remained in all its majesty the only overwhelming reality—compared to which they appeared to be phantoms, unreal and ghostlike. They were, as it were, "natural" human beings who lacked the specifically human character, . . . so that when European men massacred them they somehow were not aware that they had committed murder.   (192)

Imperialism's reduction of the indigenous to beings outside humanity foreshadows the indeterminacy of human existence in the camps and under the euthanasia apparatus. A close reading of some historical documents preceding the Nazi euthanasia program and certain passages in *The Tin Drum* support this argument. The indeterminacy in the gap between life and death is reflected, for example, in the words of Oskar's stepmother. Searching for an argument for his institutionalization, Maria claims, "das macht man heut so" (474) "(the modern way to do" [362]), and she supports her arguments by pointing to Oskar's lack of normality: "Aber siehst ja: is nich jeworden, wird überall nur rumjestoßen *und weiß nich zu leben und weiß nich zu sterben!*" (474; my emphasis) "(But you see how it is: nothing has happened, he's always being pushed around, *he don't know how to live and he don't know how to die*" [362]; my emphasis). This quote also reflects Alfred Binding and Karl Hoche's argument in their pamphlet *Die Freigabe der Vernichtung lebensunwerten Lebens: Ihr Maß und ihre Form* (1920):

> They [the euthanasia victims] *have the will neither to live nor to die.* Therefore they do not agree to their own killing, nor does their killing conflict with their will to live, which would have to be broken. Their life is absolutely useless, but they do not find it unbearable. For their relatives as well as society they are an awfully heavy burden. Their death does not cause anyone grief—except perhaps to the feelings of the mother. I cannot think of any legal, social, moral, or religious reason to stop the killing of these humans, who are the terrible counter-image of real humans and who cause feelings of horror in almost everyone who encounters them. (qtd. in Klee 22; my emphasis)

To understand the intensification of racism from the nineteenth to the twentieth century, students could take a closer look at the concept of the usefulness versus superfluousness of a human being. A key word in the Binding and Hoche passage is "useless," which evokes Arendt's discussion of "utilitarianism" and "superfluousness" in totalitarian regimes: the superfluousness of the dregs of European societies populating the colonies, the superfluousness of capital with which the enterprise of colonialism is undertaken, the superfluousness of the raw material the imperialist went after (gold, diamonds, ivory), and the ultimate superfluousness of all those whom the totalitarian regimes condemned to "not belonging to this world at all" (475). Since self-hatred arising from an understanding of one's own superfluousness leads to disrespect for human life in general, racism is directed at the other as it is at the self, a process to which Arendt keeps referring by applying the term *superfluousness* to both perpetrators and victims, both in imperialism and totalitarianism. Her discussion of the "anti-utilitarian character of the totalitarian state structure" (411) stands in obvious contrast to the utilitarianism governing Nazi race ideology, which judged each person as fit or unfit, worthy or unworthy according to the person's usefulness for the state. Could it then be argued that Nazism sensed its own lack of purpose and consequently tried to fill the void resulting from this intimation of its own uselessness by demanding that every individual be useful? This contradictory process can also be observed with the phenomena of homelessness and rootlessness, "having no place in the world" (475), in relation to race. *The Tin Drum* demonstrates that these ideas are essential in understanding the racism at work under National Socialism.

The Tin Drum reflects the extent to which Nazi Germany became a race society at its worst. It demonstrates the all-consuming power of racism, the constant radicalization of a racial selection that ultimately chooses its victims at random: the Jews (Sigismund Markus, Fajngold), the physically and mentally disabled (Oskar), criminals (Oskar), rootless drifters (Oskar), women (Agnes), and homosexuals (Greff). These are the groups that Grass's book addresses and that his characters represent. The work of Foucault, specifically his lectures at the Collège de France in 1975–76 (*Society*), can be useful in this context. Foucault discusses two functions of racism that complement each other. Racism, he argues, establishes a break between what must live and what must die. It creates caesuras in the biological continuum. While in imperialism this caesura was created once, between the colonizers as the good race and the colonized as the bad race, in totalitarianism Foucault's second function of racism is at work, racism as perpetual war.

Arendt calls this process the notion of the "objective enemy." As soon as one group of people is exterminated, a new enemy has to be found, for totalitarianism cannot return "to the rules of normal life and government" (424). Hence the multiplication of targeted groups and constantly new groups of people who fall victim to totalitarian terror—a phenomenon that Bulgakov recognized for Stalinism as Grass did for Nazism. In Grass's novel, racism as the official rational discourse is pitted against the principle of the grotesque or degenerate in the eyes of the Nazis. Racist paradigms connect, as *The Tin Drum* demonstrates, the metaphoric level with the historical, the outsiders of myth with those marginalized through racism: fairy-tale dwarfs with the physically disabled, the fools with the insane, and picaros with vagabonds. In Grass's representation of racism, the body, insanity, and genre are interconnected and closely allied.

For the Nazis' persecution of the physically disabled, Oskar's body is a central metaphor, a body that in its refusal to grow is the ultimate antithesis to the ambition of perpetual movement of National Socialism. If because of their dwarfism Oskar and his friend, the circus clown Bebra, did not prove their usefulness as entertainers, they would no doubt be considered superfluous by the Nazis.

When Oskar finally does grow, ironically in one of those freight cars that only a few years earlier may have transported undesirables to the camps, he becomes completely deformed. A metaphor for the ugliness of Germany, he is also a literary image for what Bakhtin discussed as the grotesque body in the novels of Rabelais, which inspired Grass in Paris as he worked on *The Tin Drum*. In body shape Oskar's opposite is the greengrocer Greff, who likes to jump into the Baltic Sea at subzero temperatures in order to toughen his body. Greff is an incarnation of National Socialist body politics, their dislike of the grotesque body, and their idea of hardening the male body into a likeness of the statuesque classical body. He has what Bakhtin calls the classical, closed body, which presents a perfect assimilation to the Nazi body cult that joined the Hellenic with the Nordic ideal of beauty:

> Greff liebte das Straffe, das Muskulöse, das Abgehärtete. Wenn er Natur sagte, meinte er gleichzeitig Askese. Wenn er Askese sagte, meinte er eine besondere Art von Körperpflege. Greff verstand sich auf seinen Körper. (382)

> Greff liked everything that was hard, taut, muscular. When he said "nature," he meant asceticism. When he said "asceticism," he meant a particular kind of physical culture. Greff was an expert on the subject of the body. (293)

Greff's body culture, through which he chastises himself for his desire for teenage boys, highlights the relation between race and sexuality in the Third Reich and follows a strange logic expressed in Hitler's *Mein Kampf*: "The youth who achieves the hardness of iron by sports and gymnastics succumbs to the need of sexual satisfaction less than the stay-at-home fed exclusively on intellectual fare" (253). Greff's exaggerated subscription to the Nazis' body ideal and body culture reveals his fear of discovery and persecution at a time that sees manliness in crisis and aspires to reassert its heterosexuality not only by eliminating all homosexuals but also by rooting out any effeminacy in the male body, whether in real life or artistic representation. The most prominent quotidian manifestation of this social pressure on all people to pull themselves together (as cold water pulls Greff together) was the "Heil Hitler" salute, whose rigidity and angle evoke an ersatz phallic exercise.

A discussion of the body as a racial paradigm in *The Tin Drum* ought to involve a close reading of passages in which Oskar's and Greff's bodies and body cults are described, particularly the chapters "Die Ohnmacht zu Frau Greff tragen" ("How Oskar Took His Helplessness to Mrs. Greff"), "Wachstum im Güterwagen" ("Growth in a Freight Car"), and "Madonna 49." It could also involve a variety of materials that highlight the Nazi body cult as well as the marginalization of the physically disabled. Students' cross-reading might include the dwarf-fairy tales by Wilhelm Hauff, "Der Zwerg Nase" ("Dwarf Longnose") and "Die Geschichte von dem kleinen Muck" ("The Story of Little Muck"), and the Grimm Brothers' "Daumesdick" ("Tom Thumb") and "Däumerling's Wanderschaft" ("Tom Thumb's Travels"). These mythological subtexts will help students understand how metaphoric language can become a vehicle for historical representation.

It would be useful also to discuss how, because of their obviously degenerate heroes, these fairy tales were unpopular among Nazi educators; others were better suited to represent the heroism of the Germans (Franke; Führer). For teaching the racial politics associated with these diverging body types, I would suggest a blend of historical texts (Haug; Kaltenecker; and Wildmann) and the chapters on the grotesque/classical body in Bakhtin's *Rabelais and His World*, which students could present to one another to demonstrate how representations of the body in the arts can either support or resist the official political discourse. Particularly rich with regard to the theme of the body is Grass's chapter "Madonna 49," in which the distinction between the degenerate body and the classical body is carried into the realm of art: degenerate art versus classical art. The discussion of these materials would be substantially enhanced by visual aids, such as images of the classical beautiful body in Arno Breker's statues or Leni Riefenstahl's photographs of the Nuba tribe in Sudan.

The segregation of the mentally insane since the Enlightenment and their extermination in the Nazi euthanasia apparatus is a theme that accompanies the reader throughout Grass's novel. Oskar only narrowly escapes Nazi persecution, and he narrates his story from inside a psychiatric institution. The mythological subtexts of insanity encompass the trickster, the harlequin of the commedia dell'arte, the clown, as well as the historical court fool, who was typically a dwarf. Teaching racism from the perspective of insanity demonstrates the increasing suppression of these figures from the Middle Ages all the way up to the Nazis' ideological appropriation of the carnival (Foucault, *Madness*; Hamelmann; and Welsford).

In typical carnival fashion Oskar's insanity is directed against the church and the state. The chapters "No Wonder" and "The Rostrum" demonstrate in particular this function of civil disobedience and should be central to this segment of the course. By letting Oskar beat his drum in church and stick it into the hands of a muted Jesus, from whom he can expect no miracles, Grass denounces the church for its silence during the Holocaust and attacks the religious conservatism of the Adenauer period. What makes *The Tin Drum* truly Rabelaisian is that Grass carries what may at best be *pro-fanum*, outside the temple—that is, in the marketplace (see Bakhtin on the marketplace as the traditional location for the grotesque [109])—into the sacred realm of the church. His blasphemies reach their climax in "No Wonder," in which Oskar feels Jesus's penis, his watering can, as he calls it, which he keeps stroking until he has a pleasant but strangely new and disturbing sensation in his own watering can, whereupon he decides to leave Jesus's penis alone in the hope that Jesus will leave his alone. This passage allows students to realize that blasphemy and sacrilege in the arts are necessary in resisting the powers that be. A discussion of *The Tin Drum*'s reception from the Allgäu to Oklahoma could complement this phase of the course (see Brockmann's essay in this volume).

With regard to Oskar's comical subversion of the state apparatus, Schlöndorff's film also offers a good teaching aid, showing how Oskar disperses a Nazi party rally from inside the rostrum, where his drumming to a different rhythm has the power to dissolve the uniformity of the saluting *Volkskörper* ("folk body"). How does the text differ from the film? The jazz music in the film conveys more vividly the voice of freedom, to which, in the novel, Oskar resorts as he drums to the beat of the Charleston "Jimmy the Tiger." What are the functions of jazz music in Grass's novel, and how can this dimension be aligned with Bakhtin's carnival? In accordance with West's thoughts on the potential of jazz to give tragicomic hope to African Americans experiencing racism, Oskar's music dissolves the rigidity of the *Sieg Heil* salute, thus providing a temporary line of flight from fascist ideology. But Oskar also plays jazz after the war in the Onion Cellar, where Germans are weeping over onions. How does the function of Oskar's music differ here from his earlier, subversive use of it? A look both at music and architecture in Grass's novel adds a stimulating interdisciplinary dimension to the discussion of clashing ideologies, and it can be theoretically underpinned by Gilles Deleuze and Felix Guattari's concept of the rhizome (vs. arborescence, as discussed in *Thousand Plateaus*).

The theme of insanity is closely connected to gender. Nazi racism was also a gender issue, since German women were expected to produce healthy Aryan offspring. With her own form of insanity, which climaxes in her suicide through fish overconsumption, Oskar's pregnant mother, Agnes, resists this Nazi gender expectation—as she does through her incestuous sexual adventures. Ultimately, Oskar's own incestuous desire to return to the uterus, indicated explicitly in his own words and implicitly through his Tom Thumb–like escape into womb-like spaces (the skirts of his grandmother, the rostrum, a closet), is a gesture of resistance against conservative expectations regarding the family. In Bakhtinian terms, the Oedipus myth as part of the grotesque (Freudian, Jewish, degenerate) family model is held against the classical (healthy) family model (see R. Moeller, *Protecting* and "Reconstructing"; Höhn).

Race is also closely linked to the question of genre in *The Tin Drum*, which plays with the two principal novelistic genres, reflecting the clash between myth and reason in modernity—namely, the picaresque novel and the bildungsroman. One way to approach this genre discussion is to encourage students to read segments from Rabelais's *Gargantua and Pantagruel* (published from 1532 on) and Grimmelshausen's *Simplicius Simplicissimus* (1668) in connection with anti-Semitic sections from select nineteenth-century bildungsromans, such as Wilhelm Raabe's *Der Hungerpastor* (1864) and Gustav Freytag's *Soll und Haben* (1855).

While the picaresque tradition is steeped in myth and folk culture, the bildungsroman is a product of Enlightenment reason. Decidedly picaresque,

Grass's book is a parody of *Bildung* ("formation" or "acculturation") and the bildungsroman. It attacks concepts such as Goethe's famous dictum to his secretary, Johann Peter Eckermann from 2 April 1829, that the classical be healthy while the Romantic be diseased (Eckermann 300). Oskar, for example, surmises that had he lived and drummed in Goethe's time, this "man of the Enlightenment" would have thought him unnatural, would have condemned him as against nature, and would have hit him over the head with *Faust* or a big heavy volume of his *Theory of Colors* (112; 91). Arguably, the bildungsroman can be interpreted as carrying that totalitarian impulse of which Slavoj Žižek thinks when he says, "Throughout its entire career, 'totalitarianism' was an ideological notion that sustained the complex operation of 'taming free radicals'" (3). This impulse is inherent to the teleology of the bildungsroman of social integration in the interest of the nation-state.

The transnational picaresque genre, with its homeless protagonist, does not reflect the totalitarian impulse. The picaresque novel is the first literary genre to centralize the theme of rootlessness and homelessness associated with modernity. The bildungsroman appears on the literary stage in order to regain a primordial sense of totality. With its concept of bringing the hero home and having him cared for in David Copperfield fashion, it tries to fix the dilemma of the loss of dwelling. It surprises little that the Nazis preferred bildungsromans like those of Raabe and of Freytag, in which the cosmopolitan Jew is punished by life while the German hero finds roots. The bildungsroman best reflected the kind of Faustian quest to which Nazism as a project, the project of the master race, had subscribed. In the light of this history of the bildungsroman, it becomes understandable why this genre and the concept of *Bildung* receive a major blow when Oskar experiences his *Missbildung* ("deformation") in the train car.

Such a discussion of *The Tin Drum* in view of genre and race helps students understand Oskar as a personification of homelessness. The Tom Thumb fairy-tale subtext corroborates this idea through its theme of abandonment. Oskar's homelessness—in part due to his dysfunctional family, in part to his wish not to grow up and become part of the adult world—is closely linked to his madness and criminal instincts. These are the very tendencies that make him a victim of racism.

This discussion of homelessness and wandering as targets for racism could be facilitated by a closer look at Georg Lukács's *Theory of the Novel* (1920). According to Lukács, "crime and madness are objectifications of transcendental homelessness" (61), a homelessness that sparks the totalitarian impulse (the loss of self) and in turn becomes a target of racism. As with the notions of superfluousness and uselessness, the homelessness associated with modernity is the uncanny felt within oneself, which becomes a race issue once it is projected outward on others. The Nazis tried to stamp out their own rootlessness through a ruthless persecution of those they perceived as pernicious wanderers: Jews, Gypsies, and others who because of their nonsedentary lifestyle were traditionally associated with crime and the spreading of bacilli—"wandernde Bazillenherde" (Klee 63) ("wandering germ carriers"). Racism toward wanderers was a form of hypercorrection for what the Nazis could not accept in themselves, Germany's loss of roots as part of the destitution of modernity.

Students may gain additional insight into the complex notion of homelessness by way of a brief introduction of etymology to Martin Heidegger's notion of being (*sein* or *dasein*), which is central to his understanding of homelessness. The German *ich bin* is derived from the Old High German *buan* ("to dwell"), and for Heidegger to dwell is

> to be at peace, to be brought to peace, to remain in peace. The word for peace, *Friede*, means the free, *das Frye* [in old German], and *fry* means: preserved from harm and danger, preserved from something, that is, taken-care-of [*geschont*]. . . . The fundamental character of dwelling is this caring-for.   (Young 63–64)

With their loss of all freedom, in their extreme peacelessness[4] of racially marginalized people, who are completely uncared for unless they can renew their usefulness, the camps, unlike any other location, stand for the loss of dwelling typical to modernity.

Consequently, thinking about the paradigms of race in *The Tin Drum* can teach us that the Nazi project attempts to render visible the ailments of modernity that led to this project. The camps are an image for the Nazis' fear of homelessness, rootlessness, and the degeneration of the body, for their insecurity about their masculinity, sexuality, and sanity. In the camps, source and target merge completely; the perpetrators make the utmost effort to eradicate through their victims that which torments them, to the point where perpetrator and victim become identical. The Nazis of the camps see in the *Muselmann*, that figure between life and death, the reflection of their own loss of humanity. The perpetrators reduce the victims to the state of nonhumanity so they can mirror themselves in the *Muselmann* and recognize themselves. The camps can therefore be seen as the ultimate expression of the German desire to render the crisis of modernity visible and thereby defeat it, because an abstraction cannot be defeated. Oskar, in his infinite complexity, his ambiguity of perpetrator and victim, and his reflection of the many paradigms of race that this essay has discussed, can be read as an embodiment of this crisis.

NOTES

[1] I want to thank the National Endowment for the Humanities, as well as Russell Berman and Julia Hell for their support, because this essay was substantially inspired by the NEH seminar Terror and Culture: Revisiting Hannah Arendt's *Origins of Totalitarianism* at Stanford University in the summer of 2005.

²See Ernst Klee: "Unsere Wanderfürsorgeanstalten leiden unter der Masse der wander- und arbeitsunfähigen sowie der arbeitsscheuen vagabondierenden Wanderer. Diese Masse lastet wie ein Ballast auf unseren Wanderfürsorgeanstalten. Erst wenn wir diese Masse los sind, werden wir die arbeitsfähigen und ordentlichen Wanderer mit wirklicher Hilfe erfassen können" (31) (Our institutions that assist wanderers are suffering from the multitude of wanderers who are unable or unwilling to work. This multitude is a major burden for these institutions. Not until we have got rid of these people can we really assist those proper wanderers who are able to work [trans. mine]).

³Hell, as Arendt has pointed out, may indeed be the most suitable cultural icon for a literary description of the camp. Indeed the literature about the camps keeps taking recourse to such imagery. See, for example, Peter Weiss's *The Investigation* or Primo Levi's use, in *Se questo è un uomo*, of the Tantalus myth and the "Canto di Ulysse" from Dante's *Inferno.*

⁴The concept of peacelessness has its roots in the medieval *Friedlosigkeit* and is discussed by Agamben in *Homo Sacer* and *State of Exception* and by Arendt in *Origins of Totalitarianism* (302).

"The Black Witch": Gender, Sexuality, and Violence in *The Tin Drum*

Barbara Becker-Cantarino

My teaching approach addresses gender discourse and gender relations in *The Tin Drum*, and it allows for an analysis of sociocultural content and narrative form. The search for the ideological underpinnings of patriarchy (Bornemann; Walby) and for the construction of male domination (Bourdieu) and male fantasies (Theweleit) receives high priority. I have taught the novel in an undergraduate German culture class (in English), a literature class for majors (in German), and in a graduate class (in German) and have always encountered students' need and desire to receive some historical and literary background material for the classroom discussion of this complex text. The novel's sheer length, irony, and grotesqueness; its intertextuality with the literary-cultural tradition; its sophisticated language play and puns; and its shifting narrative voice present a challenge to the students, especially if read in German. Thus I encourage non-native readers of German to read the (very fine but at times interpretative) English translation along with the German. I assign guide questions and specific chapters or pages for a close reading, especially in German classes.

We begin class discussion by turning to the surface-level narrative, the story of a seemingly picaresque hero in a wide panorama of twentieth-century political events in Germany (and Poland and France), events that center on Germany's Nazi period and role in World War II and the reconstruction years of the Federal Republic of Germany in the 1950s. Some history (and geography) needs to be reviewed here; our present student generation was not yet in kindergarten when the two Germanys were unified, and they often lack an understanding of the very different contours of postwar Europe. We also look at the poetological level, the (unreliable) narrator-author Oskar who wrestles with the labor and act of writing, with creativity, and with the meaning of literature and life. Only then do we turn to a third level, the violent, sexual gender relations that are embedded in the plot, run parallel to the historical and poetological levels, and intertwine with them. The narrative frame, Oskar's confinement to a mental institution and his being accused of the murder of the nurse Dorothea, serves as an overarching concept for the representation of gender, violence, and sexuality. From here we turn to a closer reading of selected chapters that center on women figures and male-female interactions. Finally, we connect Grass's treatment of gender discourse and gender relations to the literary tradition and gender ideology in 1950s Germany. Proceeding from *The Tin Drum*, we add a class discussion on violence and gender, on pornography and literature, and—depending on class interest—on blasphemy.

I begin by asking my students to assemble the details of the narrative frame that gradually reveal a plot of sexual violence: Oskar is confined to a mental hospital for what we learn only much later to be the accusation of having raped and killed Dorothea. A close reading of the opening pages reveals Oskar's preoccupation with women and guilt. Oskar is confined to a "weißlackiertes metallenes Anstaltsbett" (9) ("white-enameled, metal hospital bed" [15]) resembling a cage or prison bars, which he terms "das endlich erreichte Ziel" (9–10) ("a goal attained at last" [15]), his "Trost" ("consolation"), and possibly his "Glaube" (10) ("faith" [15]). He easily persuades his keeper, Bruno Münsterberg, to provide him with a ream of "unschuldiges Papier" (11) ("virgin paper" [16]) in order to begin telling his story. Using "unschuldig," Grass may also be playing with the common phrase "Papier ist geduldig" ("paper is patient"), which a German reader would expect when the subject is paper and writing. But Grass chose instead a wordplay with "unschuldig"—corrected by Bruno as "white," reinforced by Oskar's insistence on "virgin" and extended to the salesgirl's blushing at the word—thus encapsulating a gender discourse: Oskar's relationship vis-à-vis women—his guilt or innocence—will be a theme in his story. The trajectory, as in the innocent paper-purchase scene, will move from an active, covertly aggressive Oskar, the male and his buddy, to a naive yet emotionally responsive, receptive female.

As the first section of book 1 concludes, the three-year-old Oskar refuses to grow, although "something" in him "gewann schließlich messianische Größe" (71) ("did grow . . . taking on Messianic proportions" [61]). What is that something? He gradually reveals his story of self-inflicted, intentional deformation and of his quaint, irrational, and disturbingly destructive powers, his relentless drumbeat and his high-pitched scream. Oskar was "in der Lage, Glas zu zersingen" (75) ("had the gift of shattering glass" [64]). While the visible deformity of his body provides a shield of seeming innocence and serves to excuse him from taking responsibility for his actions, his ability to use his high-pitched voice at will gives him an irrational power over others, especially women who have to deal with the shards his tantrum has caused: his kindergarten teacher, his first-grade teacher, his mother, the Virgin Mary. Students are quick to point to the paradox of little Oskar and his power of domination.

Class discussion then turns to the mysterious figure of the Black Witch, whom Oskar (the unreliable narrator) instinctively fears from childhood on. He hears other children playing the game of "Ist die Schwarze Köchin da" (76) ("Where's the Witch, black as pitch?" [64]).[1] He joins in, and the other children make him eat a brew of beastly concoctions resembling a witch's brew. Fear of the Black Witch haunts Oskar to the very end and appears to be the evil demon lurking behind his outrageous fantasies, especially his lurid oral and anal sexual fantasies, and behind his entire world. In the very last section, "Thirty," a caricature of the messianic thirty-year-old Jesus ("I am Jesus" is doubly on his mind, in German and in English 777 [587]), he is still afraid of the "Black Witch" and imagines her as ever present in all his actions and thoughts.

That the novel closes with a ditty using the word "black" prominently should not be read as a racial slur or even comment. Grass plays with several symbolic—

all derogative, if not politically problematic—meanings of "black" in German: "schwarze Währung" referred to the unofficial exchange rate between the West German D-Mark and the East German R-Mark (as much as one to seven) in the 1950s, also to counterfeit money or illicit currency; the "black market" was the (illegal) trade of goods after World War II; "black" is a reference to the Catholic Church and to the Christian Democratic Party (CDU, then the ruling party), and of course to the devil. The ditty reads:

> Schwarz war die Köchin hinter mir immer schon.
> Daß sie mir nun auch entgegenkommt, schwarz.
> Wort, Mantel wenden ließ, schwarz.
> Mit schwarzer Währung zahlt, schwarz.
> Während die Kinder, wenn singen, nicht mehr singen:
> Ist die Schwarze Köchin da? Ja–Ja–Ja!   (779)

> Always somewhere behind me, the Black Witch.
> Now ahead of me, too, facing me, Black.
> Black words, black coat, black money.
> But if children sing, they sing no longer:
> Where's the Witch, black as pitch?
> Here's the black, wicked Witch.
> Ha! ha! ha!"   (589)

Grass's novel ends ambivalently: if the children sing no longer, are they dead? Or do they no longer sing this song? The German syntax allows both readings. But the translator rendered the affirmative "yes" ("Ja–Ja–Ja!") to the existence of the Black Cook as what appears to be laughter, a sign of madness and a liberating comic relief.

As a literary image, the Black Witch or Cook—always referred to as "she"—encapsulates the distrust of women. Here some cultural commentary is called for: Grass's reference to the witch's domesticity and cooking is also reminiscent of ancient wise women and their herbal cures before the rising university medicine in early modern Europe devalued and displaced them. With the Black Cook figure, Grass conjures up the fear of witches and a faint memory of the witchhunts in the sixteenth and seventeenth centuries, when people (mostly women) were fingered as evil-bringing witches and publicly executed. One might expect that Oskar, victimized by society and a chaotic world, would feel sympathy for other victims, but there is no compassion in him for those victims of the past. Rather, in his creation of the Black Cook or Witch as a leitmotif, Grass revives the age-old fear, a gendered fear, of the evil-bearing female. Even if we consider that his narrative technique is estrangement, distancing, and ambiguity mixed with satire and irony, the female is still coded, the disturbing and disruptive figure of the Black Cook or Witch is still an objectification of woman in the form of an existential fear.

I ask my students to look at another mythic figure: Niobe, in the chapter titled after her in book 1. In classical mythology, Niobe, a daughter of Tantalus, is the mother who prides herself on her seven daughters and seven sons and is punished for this hubris (of her female fertility): all her offspring are killed by Apollo, and she is turned into a weeping rock. Grass's Niobe is the figure-head from a large Florentine galleon, a prize exhibit in the Danzig Maritime Museum:

> Ein üppig hölzernes, grün nacktes Weib, das unter erhobenen Armen, die sich lässig und alle Finger zeigend verschränkten, über zielstrebigen Brüsten hinweg aus eingelassenen Bernsteinaugen geradeaussah. Dieses Weib, die Galionsfigur, brachte Unglück. (240)

> A luxuriant wooden woman, green and naked, arms upraised and hands indolently clasped in such a way as to reveal every single one of her fin-gers; sunken amber eyes gazing out over resolute, forward-looking breasts. This woman, this figurehead, was the bringer of disaster. (187)

Marked by stark sexual features, this woman as figurehead has, as the narrator explains in great detail, destroyed every person—all of them male—who ever owned or tried to possess her. The "Green Kitten," as she is popularly called (189), has killed every man who came close to her. Grass exchanges Niobe's fertility and motherhood for a destructive sexuality with the power to destroy the male world, a harbinger of evil. Niobe is thus yet another coded female, a mythic figure personifying the evil principle.

Grass then links Niobe symbolically to the historical disasters of Danzig and German-Polish strife and the events of World War II yet to unfold, as a close reading of the Niobe encounter reveals. Oskar's friend and newly employed mu-seum guard, Herbert Truczinski (Maria's brother), and Oskar play with the fig-ure, taunt, caress, and beat her. Truczinski gets so fixated by the figure's "golden" eyes set on fire by the afternoon sun that he, "der Brünstige" (251) ("[i]n a frenzy of lust" [195]), jumps her and gets killed. Grass's graphic description of this sexual assault on a wooden female figure underlines the vexed, uncanny place of the feminine, here a bloodless femme fatale, in the novel's gendered discourse. Niobe, like other mythic females, is a bearer of evil, a variation of the Black Cook or Witch. The grotesque scene also highlights male sexual aggres-sion. If Oskar is "a pathological personification of his time" (Keele, *Understand-ing* 13), he is driven by his instincts, seeking sexual gratification in his relentless pursuit of Maria and other women.

In classroom discussions, I dwell on the irony of Oskar's story, beginning with a realistic description of his grandmother, Anna Bronski, in her wide skirts next to a fire on a potato field chewing roasted potatoes. This is a vivid yet styl-ized portrayal of the great earth mother: earthlike in the color of her dress, she eats products of the earth and is close to nature and fertility. Anna accepts a fleeing soldier under her skirts to hide him from his pursuers and thus fulfills her motherhood function, giving birth to Agnes, Oskar's mother. Students have repeatedly pointed out to me that this scene reminds them of a rape in which the woman is falsely believed to be a willing participant. The mother figure instinctively protects the fleeing young man, and, as grotesque as the scene may appear, the fugitive takes advantage of the situation under the cover of the wide skirts. Had Anna refused, she would have betrayed him, my students argued. They also wondered whether she had the choice of saying no. Reading this scene as rape shows, I suggest, our changed sensitivity with regard to sexual encounters and perhaps a different point of view. Grass presents intercourse as the most natural interaction between a woman and a man and believes that a man has the prerogative to initiate it. He wished to create, I would argue, a natural parentage for his hero along very traditional lines: a mother representing nature and sexuality, a father representing civilization and society.

The challenge for students lies in reading Grass's symbolic gender discourse as steeped in tradition. Oskar's maternal grandfather is a political activist, a subversive laborer championing the revolution, who presumably dies while trying to escape the authorities. Mother and revolutionary make up, according to traditional gender norms, Oskar's maternal heritage. His paternal side is left undetermined: his father is either the German Matzerath, whom his mother marries, or the Pole Bronski, who is his mother's lover and relative. Both men turn out to be weak, gullible, and are eventually killed off by Oscar. While the male rivalry of the two fathers over Agnes and then Maria and Oskar's undetermined paternity become a symbol for the growing binational tensions between Poland and Germany as played out in Danzig, Oskar, the son, can make his mark by displacing his German father (he gets Maria, Matzerath's second wife, pregnant). He causes Bronski's death when his whining makes German soldiers believe that Bronski abused an innocent child ("Das Kartenhaus" ["The Card House"]). Later Oskar is involved in Matzerath's death, when he intentionally hands Matzerath his Nazi Party pin—needle first—during a control by Russian soldiers and Matzerath swallows and chokes on it. Having killed off his father(s) and married his mother (getting Maria pregnant), Oskar completes an oedipal plot of familial relations (see Ludden's essay in this volume). Grass portrays only dysfunctional families throughout his novel, as a sign of the turbulent, violent times from the end of the Weimar Republic through the Nazi years, World War II, and the war's aftermath. The political level of the text and Grass's attempt at coming to terms with the past (*Vergangenheitsbewältigung*) have received most of the critical attention.

By contrast, the violence in gender relations has not been commented on, with the exception of Claudia Mayer-Iswandy's work ("Danach ging das Leben weiter," *Günter Grass*, and "*Vom Glück der Zwitter*"). Grass endowed his protagonist with a naive, self-centered, and disturbingly militant and animalistic concept of masculinity in his predatory, sexual approach to women. Oskar develops a sharp eye for and a keen interest in sexual encounters. When Maria, the young sister of Herbert Truczinski, joins Matzerath's grocery store, Oskar pursues her relentlessly, trying to arouse her sexually, as in the scene at the beach where he places fizz powder in her hand and wets it with his saliva. He watches her having sex with Matzerath (his father or stepfather) and prides himself on being the father of her son, Kurt. His interest in and description of Maria ("War Maria schön?" [339]) ("Was Maria beautiful?" [262]) are purely physical, though Maria is—as the name also indicates—a mother figure, who indeed takes the place of Oskar's mother. His relations with Maria "[waren] ständigem Wechsel unterworfen . . . selbst heute noch nicht geklärt" (339) ("were in constant flux and have not been fully stabilized to this day" [262]). After the war, he buys her a grocery store in the best part of Düsseldorf.

When discussing the figure of Maria, I ask my students to consider Grass's use of biblical references. Maria shows, of course, little resemblance to the Virgin Mary; in her sexual promiscuity she is rather a perversion of the Christian Mary. Throughout the novel Oskar stylizes himself as Jesus, as the Messiah, as on the cross, especially in the chapter "The Imitation of Christ." Here he lends Jesus his drum and responds to his three-time question: "Liebst du mich, Oskar?" (469) ("Dost thou love me, Oskar?" [358]) with an indignant: "Ich hasse dich, Bürschchen, dich und deinen ganzen Klimbim" (470) ("You bastard, I hate you, you and all your hocus-pocus" [358]). Is that blasphemy? Is it obscene? Some readers thought so when the novel was first published. Along with the numerous biblical and messianic references, some critics and readers also objected to the explicit sexual scenes and went to court against the novel in the early 1960s, charging blasphemy and pornography but without much success (Preece, *Life* 47–50; Arnold and Görz).

We next turn to Grass's insistence and apparent delight in portraying in detail Oskar's (and most other male characters') sexual appetite and prowess, though the realism is conflated with fantasy and the imaginary. Oskar's graphic description of the rape of the widow Greff is a minor incident compared with his pathological fixation on the nurse Dorothea. The Greff episode is a precursor to his sexual fantasies and aggression involving the nurse, who is the reason for his confinement to the mental institution. Oskar schemes and fantasizes about Dorothea, even hides in her closet rummaging through her underwear ("In the Clothes Cupboard"). Reading this behavior as Freudian (his desire for his mother, the nurse as an extension or substitution of the mother) totally ignores the invasion of Dorothea's privacy, her right to be acknowledged as a human being and not be used merely as the object of a sexual fantasy. Oskar is stalking her instead of communicating with her. His chance to play out his sexual aggression comes when he, holding only a coconut-fiber runner in front of his naked body, corners Dorothea in the bathroom and makes her believe he is Satan or makes her play along with his satanic sexual act. Grass has Dorothea become an apparently willing participant and utter repeatedly, "Komm Satan, o komm doch!" (680) ("'Come Satan,' she sighed, 'oh, please come'" [516])—another veiled reference to woman as the Black Cook or Witch, who wishes for intercourse with the devil.

For centuries, the association of woman with the imaginary figure of the witch was a popular superstition and fear in western and central Europe (Roper; Brauner). In the witch-hunt trials in Germany during the sixteenth and seventeenth centuries, the major point of accusation and of "evidence" presented was precisely the act of intercourse with the devil. This satanic ritual was abhorred and punished by burning at the stake. Torture was used to make the accused, mostly women, confess to the crime. Grass reenacts the heinous act of satanic intercourse in this scene (albeit in Oskar's erotic fantasy): Dorothea pines for an orgasm with Satan as Oskar rapes her (and makes her an accomplice) in the disguise of Satan. The misogynist undercurrent of this scene is uncritically presented and remains unmitigated in the narrative. "Isn't there a bit of a witch in every woman?" one of my student readers asked slyly and added, "Even if only in a man's imagination?" Certainly in Grass's imagination.

Grass has his protagonist remain in control of the woman who buys into his satanic game, though his impotence prevents her gratification and she leaves. The irony in this grotesque episode may be directed against the sexually frustrated Oskar, but it supports yet another cultural cliché about women: they want to be raped.

I ask my students to consider carefully Oskar's role and guilt in the murder of Dorothea. What do we learn about the murder? By strange coincidence, his dog finds her ring finger—an obvious phallic symbol—which Oskar keeps like a fetish. What are we to make of this pathological fixation on women? By the end of the novel, the nurse Dorothea and, with her, all women seem to have vanished into a phallic symbol in a male-authored and male-controlled text. Throughout, they are described with male eyes, from a male perspective. The author has little interest in treating his female characters as individuals; rather, they are conceptualized as objects of male desire, be it for sexual gratification or the lust of destruction. They are assigned significance only on the basis of their usefulness to the male characters. They are objectified into a critique of the socioeconomic and political order, which in Grass's narrative is an entirely male-dominated world.

The proliferation of gender stereotypes for women remains unquestioned while the narrative presents and satirically scrutinizes Oskar in a broad spectrum of individualized male characters. The woman is symbolized by a triangle, the sign for female sexuality. For all the male figures and especially for Oskar, the female body holds everything terrible of this world, and thus the female must be conquered. The male characters develop and enact their grotesque, violent fantasies while yearning for the impossible return to the mother's womb. Psychological and social clichés from the early twentieth century—such as the Freudian concepts of sex drive and death wish—inform Grass's portrayal of violent gender relations, which are mostly seen as a battle between the sexes, ranging from sly fight to brutal war.

Historicizing *The Tin Drum* leads to a better understanding of the novel's sexual violence. Written half a century ago and reflecting a society quite different from our own, Grass's narrative employs the dichotomy of Eve and Mary, traditional in much of Western literature before the twentieth century, with its demonic, threatening female and the angelic, motherly counterimage. Grass sexualizes all his characters; his women elicit, represent, enjoy, and demand sexual gratification (forgetting mostly about motherhood). Emotion is played down; the focus is on sexual aggression. Oskar's drumbeat and glass-shattering voice are also a sign of the author's potency in society as narrator.

The Tin Drum's central plot revolving around a sexual murder recalls Alfred Döblin's novel of 1929, *Berlin Alexanderplatz: The Story of Franz Biberkopf.* Grass admired Döblin (1879–1957), a writer and physician (for the poor in Berlin) who portrayed a wide panorama of lower-middle-class people (*Kleinbürger*) not unlike Grass's characters. Franz Biberkopf has served prison time for the murder of his girlfriend. His best friend, Reinhold, who exercises a powerful homoerotic hold over Franz, killed Franz's girlfriend, Mieze, in a sexual encounter. Rape, the brutalization of women, and sexual murder were prominent narrative features in Weimar Germany and its cultural legacy (Tatar). Grass called Döblin his teacher in an early essay (*Über meinen Lehrer*). Sexual violence against women serves, so critics tell us, to mirror and critique society's ills. Do we content ourselves with such an explanation? I ask my students.

I consider it important, especially in a graduate course, to discuss how Grass's gender discourse and his treatment of women characters also reflect the 1950s, the period in which he wrote his novel. His women are close to nature (beginning with Anna Bronski's potato-colored skirts) and motherhood (the nurses), while intellectual women are flat, manly, unattractive (e.g., Dr. Hornstetter, the female physician treating Oskar). His few working women are uninteresting, not fulfilling their female reproductive role. Oskar's first-grade teacher, Fräulein Spollenhauer, is described as masculine in her suit, in flat-soled shoes, with a "mannish look"—though she has a profession held mostly by women (96; 79). Grass reflects the traditional, gender view dominant in the 1950s, which relegated women to "Kirche, Kinder, Küche" ("church, children, kitchen"). This view was a caricature; a product of wishful thinking and outright propaganda in conservative circles; a mixture of inherited religious beliefs, remnants of Nazi propaganda, and patriarchal complacency.

In the social and cultural sphere, German women actually played a major role in Germany's reconstruction after the war. Some vocal politicians, survivors from the first women's movement of the early twentieth century in Germany, were able to introduce the concept of *Gleichberechtigung* ("equal rights") into the constitution when the Federal Republic of German was founded in 1949. A woman, Annemarie Renger, was the first president of the Federal Republic's parliament. *Gleichberechtigung* was much discussed in the 1950s, and it aroused fear and anger not only in the dominant Christian Democratic Party but also in many men who feared for their privileges. Grass's novel, an astute, critical assessment of the *Wirtschaftswunder* ("economic miracle") years of the 1950s, reflects nothing of these debates and beginnings. The much-acclaimed social critic had a blind eye as far as the women's movement was concerned, even when the impetus of this early feminism was taken up again in the late 1960s and 1970s. Journalists and women writers fighting for feminist causes were often ridiculed by their male colleagues or anxiously shoved into the niche of women's literature. Grass, too, was criticized by feminist readers. In later works, notably in his novel *Der Butt* (1977; *The Flounder*), he attempted to revise his ideology of gender and to address feminist concerns, albeit with mixed success. But in *The Tin Drum*, he had continued the German modernist narrative tradition of the male gaze at and fear of the female body and sexuality (Angress, "Der Butt").

In teaching this novel, I have found that students are eager to discuss gender concepts, the issue of violence, as well as aspects of the novel's controversial reception—the charge of pornography and blasphemy. The issues of pornography and the ubiquitous display of sexuality in our culture lend themselves to a classroom discussion, beginning with *The Tin Drum*, on the role of literature in our society.

NOTE

[1] The translation of "Köchin" ("female cook") as "witch" makes explicit Grass's veiled reference. "Schwarze Köchin" ("black female cook") was a circumlocution for *witch* during the witch hunts of the sixteenth to eighteenth century, to avoid being hexed by the real witch.

"Getting Back to the Umbilical Cord": Feminist and Psychoanalytic Theory and *The Tin Drum*

Teresa Ludden

Sie werden es erraten haben: Oskars Ziel ist die Rückkehr zur Nabel-schnur; alleine deshalb der ganze Aufwand und das Verweilen bei Her-bert Truczinskis Narben.   (229)

You've guessed it no doubt: Oskar's aim is to get back to the umbilical cord; that is the sole purpose behind this whole vast verbal effort and my only reason for dwelling on Herbert Truczinski's scars.   (179)

Some of the most engaging aspects of *The Tin Drum* are the character of Oskar and his unusual mode of representing the world and thus what is communicated about contemporary identity and reality through this protagonist and narrator. Students encounter the novel in the context of Misfits and Miscreants in Post-1945 German and Austrian Fiction, a BA (honors) final-year advanced literary studies module designed for students with advanced German-language skills, who are typically studying single-honors German or German in combination with another language or arts subject. Students in these modern language pro-grams are encouraged to create pathways to their degrees by choosing modules in the light of their interests and grades previously achieved. So they can spe-cialize in history, politics and society, linguistics, film, or literature (or combina-tions of these) of the country or countries whose languages they are studying. This advanced literature module thus builds on skills that students gained in introductory and intermediate literary studies modules.

The module is taught and assessed in English, but primary texts are read in the original German. All these works feature protagonists who are misfits or miscreants, such as Thomas Bernhard's *Ja* (1978), Monika Maron's *Animal Triste* (1998), and W. G. Sebald's *Austerlitz* (2001). The study of the texts gives students a sense of trends in contemporary German and Austrian fiction and enables comparison of themes and styles across the decades. Representations of crises of identity are considered with reference to wider cultural and historical events, modernity and postmodernity, and discussions focus on major topics: literary modes of representing consciousness, modes of being, the crisis of iden-tity, alienation, trauma, memory, embodiment. Grass's novel ties in thematically with the other texts through topics such as the relation between personal and cultural history, the unreliable narrator, guilt, trauma, the activity of memory as unsettling narration, and the narrating self.

Students generally respond well to *The Tin Drum*, although many find the length daunting. Hence the pedagogical strategy of close reading of specific chapters and extracts, as explained below. Students are often interested in Oskar as a character and enjoy his peculiarities; they note his stunted growth, his rejection (and betrayal) of the father figures and his alignment with the mother and grandmother; his desire to return to the womb and his obsession with womblike spaces, such as his grandmother's skirts, Maria's nightdress, and enclosed spaces; the recurring motifs of sexuality, bodily functions and secretions, and (often fragmented) bits of fleshy bodies. But the status of some images remains unclear, making Grass's intention difficult to grasp. Is Grass parodying or twisting the Freudian notion of sublimation, for instance, when he has Oskar say that getting back to the umbilical cord is the sole purpose of the narrative?[1]

Using the students' initial responses, I ask students to reflect on the following: Is the whole text really a substitute for the lost mother? How do we interpret the ambiguous mother-son relationship and the mother's death? Students often note that there are elements of homage to the mother as well as depictions of her body as monstrous. There are suggestions of her power, but the son also controls our access to her in his narrative. After reading and hearing lectures on some theories, we formulate questions like, "Does Oskar's privileging of the mother question the classic Freudian Oedipus complex because he does not transfer allegiance to the father?" Paternity, moreover, is uncertain in the novel. Or does his narration of his implication in the deaths of the fathers act out oedipal fantasies that in psychoanalytic terms should be repressed? I get students to think of the different levels of interpretation and ask them to pay attention to the negotiation between the personal and political meanings in the novel. The motif of getting back to the umbilical cord appears both as a personal desire to undo the trauma of separation through a return to the wholeness of the womb and as an indirect political comment alluding to the urge to escape German history and responsibility for National Socialism. Simultaneously this urge to escape history is criticized in the text.

The discussion in interactive lectures and seminars concentrates on origins, which appear so fraught with difficulty. In the sections for close textual analysis below, which are used for group interpretation exercises, thinking origins appears to undermine the notion of originality, because it requires us to think interrelationality, change, and history. Furthermore, anxiety surrounds Oskar's imagining of his origins in a female body, and crises surrounding the early stages in the formation of his identity are alluded to. Finally, these crises can be linked on a historical level to a complex relation with the parents' generation. Oskar's narrative suggests a hatred of this generation—particularly of the father figure, Matzerath, who is tainted with participation in National Socialism. Yet an acknowledgment of Oskar's provenance and beginnings can also be discerned in his narrative.

A variety of perspectives from theory and philosophy are used as critical tools to study the texts in the module. In The Tin Drum, psychoanalytic and feminist theories provide interesting ways of thinking about crucial aspects of the novel. I deliver the theoretical background material in the form of interactive lectures.

I explain the key terms and concepts in psychoanalysis, approaching the topic historically, starting with Freud; including some carefully chosen contemporary commentators;[2] and then addressing more recent theories, criticisms, and perspectives from philosophers whose work fundamentally questions some of the basic premises of psychoanalysis, such as Luce Irigaray and Adriana Cavarero. I solicit students' questions and comments at every stage. A week before the lectures, I set them specific passages for reading in pairs or groups from the theorists: for example, Freud's "On Narcissism," Freud on ego formation, Irigaray on the self-other and self-mother relations (see *Le corps-à-corps* and *Speculum*). I set assignments that ask for descriptions and summaries of the theories and also ask analytic questions. Students are encouraged to share their answers and ideas with the whole class, and I integrate their contributions and summaries of the theories into the interactive lecture by managing the discussion, restating students' points, clarifying their contributions, and using their ideas and questions to get my points across.

One of Freud's most basic and most important insights was that the ego is not immediately unified and stable but formed through time and through a series of interactions with others, objects, and the world. The parents are, of course, central in this early development, and the relationship with the mother is especially important. According to psychoanalytic theory, during the first few months of life a baby does not experience itself as a whole but as a mass of fragmentary body parts and sensations. This stage precedes the development of the ego and is associated (especially in post-Freudian psychoanalysis) with an asocial fluidity and the lack of boundaries between self and others. The infant has no corporeal or psychical unity or stability at this stage and no sense of itself as separate from the mother. This state cannot be experienced or remembered: there is no direct access to it; it can only be reconstructed at a later stage after the oedipal realignments.

In psychoanalysis, ego formation is always based on a disruption to an original, pre-oedipal sense of fluid boundaries with the mother. A cut from the mother must occur in order for the child to start to perceive itself as separate, as an object and eventually subject. By looking at whole objects and other people—for instance, the mother as object—the infant starts to perceive itself as whole. The original split in the human psyche then is linked to the alienation that comes from the development of subject-object relations with the mother. In narcissism, though, there is "infantile megalomania" (Mitchell 2), as the child's undeveloped ego takes itself as its own love object and the ego becomes both subject and object. Freud suggests that the infant does this to compensate for the loss of the mother, because at this stage there is also a growing realization that it does not have absolute control over her.

Psychoanalytic theory states that at around the age of five a series of crises arises when the father intervenes in the mother-child relationship and the male child realizes that he cannot have the mother entirely to himself and starts to perceive the father as a rival for the mother's affection. The Oedipus complex can be understood as the child's real but repressed fear that the father will castrate him in retaliation for the desire for exclusive possession of the mother (Stafford-Clark 94). The child internalizes the prohibitions and rules of his father, identifies with him, and renounces his desire of the mother. As one of the extracts, which the students have read, states:

> This renunciation is only temporary; he gives up the mother in exchange for the promise (a "pact" between father and son) of deferred satisfaction with a woman of his own. This pact, in other words, founds patriarchy anew for each generation, guaranteeing the son a position as heir to the father's position in so far as he takes on the father's attributes. In exchange for sacrificing his relation to the mother, whom he now recognizes as "castrated," the boy identifies with the authority invested in the father.
>
> (Grosz 68)

In Freudian terms, there has been an overall transition from the pleasure principle to the reality principle, in other words, a movement away from unity with the mother's body or the pleasures of narcissism toward an acceptance of laws and social reality, which is the prerequisite for forming adult relations with the world.

Reading the first chapters of *The Tin Drum*, students are asked to consider Oskar in the light of these theories. To guide their reading of key chapters, I provide worksheets with questions, asking them for instance to pay particular attention to the narrative style (Where in this passage does Oskar start referring to himself in the third person?), or to how female characters are presented, or to how humor works in the selected passages. Many immediately note that Oskar's relations with his mother are an important aspect of the novel. She appears in his narrative as the only character capable of understanding him, in an at times uncanny symbiosis, yet she dies early in the book, which suggests the loss of the mother as something unsettling that haunts the rest of the novel.

Many also see Oskar (in books 1 and 2) as developing abnormally, because he remains a three-year-old, and students can apply their knowledge of Freudian concepts such as narcissism and the pre-oedipal to articulate arguments about his development. In psychoanalytic terms, he resides in a realm that under normal circumstances is replaced after the drama of shifting allegiances during the oedipal crisis. They then reflect on what Grass suggests through this character: something seems to have gone wrong with Oskar's subjectivity, as normal progression and growth have been stunted. Might this be a comment on contemporary subjectivity per se? Is it merely about the individual character of Oskar, or do his peculiarities point to something amiss on the cultural and social level?

Students are also asked to think about Oskar's relations with his mother and apply their knowledge of Irigaray's theories gained through reading extracts and listening to lectures. For Irigaray, thinking the mother and birth is fraught with difficulty in Western culture because normal ego formation always occurs through a cut from the mother. She argues that the mother is silenced and that Western culture is even founded on matricide (*Corps-à-corps*). This statement should be understood symbolically as the prevalent marginalization of women and the forgetfulness of the body, especially the mother's body as the origin of an embodied self. In the philosophical tradition, for instance, imagination and spirit are privileged over the (maternal) body and matter. Creation and birth become linked not to the mother but to abstract, nonbodily spirit or mind, often associated with the mind of a male genius who gives birth to ideas, art, and so on. In addition, there is a prevalence of myths of male autogenesis in the Western tradition, which also occasions a forgetfulness of the corporeal and maternal. Irigaray emphasizes that in the discourse of psychoanalysis the umbilical cord and the sojourn in the womb must always be repressed: a fetal situation or regression might occur if the male child does not sever this overintimate bond with the primal womb. She rewrites psychoanalytic ideas when she alludes to a conscious type of forgetting, suggesting that the mother has not really been properly repressed—we carry constant reminders of intimate relations with the mother and the placenta: navels, for instance. The work of culture is to suppress this knowledge. Given the lack of appropriate ways of representing the maternal body, it often takes on elements of horror and absence in the male imaginary. The castration complex itself might be an example. Irigaray describes other types of inversion at work: the mother is frequently represented as a devouring monster in our imaginary, which detracts attention from the prevalent consumption of the mother. In this context, Irigaray suggests the economic, material, and emotional debt owed to the mother. A reversal occurs whereby the infant's utter dependence on the mother becomes fantasized as the mother's dependence on the child, a fantasy that is needed to cover over the sense of extreme helplessness and dependence of the child in the pre-oedipal stage, an idea that can be extremely debilitating to some (male) egos.

Forgetting birth also comes to mean that death replaces birth as that which confers meaning on life. Rather than narratives that privilege birth as crucial in the understanding of the self, notions of teleology and death become the measure of life. Again, the tables are turned: the womb is often linked with death, not life, and remains fundamentally unthought because the ways we have available to think it are again post-oedipal projections that keep it at a distance as a threatening abyss or locus of death.

These theories can help us unpack some of the layers of meaning in *The Tin Drum*, for they are applied not to reduce the text to a singular meaning but to articulate ambiguities and difficulties. In seminars, my basic pedagogical strategy is close reading of key chapters and passages. Students are assigned select readings and questions and are obliged to meet in study groups for at least two hours in the week preceding the seminar. They report their findings and conclusions to the seminar class in the form of presentations, which I expand, develop, and integrate into the discussion. This way of working with the text particularly helps those students who struggle with the length of the novel, because they can concentrate on smaller sections. It also enables me to teach such aspects of the novel as linguistic and stylistic matters, narration and characterization, because I can contextualize these features instead of lecturing about them in the abstract. Several chapters are chosen in order to concentrate on the problem with origins: the scene of writing ("The Wide Skirt"), the birth scene ("Moth and Light Bulb"), and the mother's illness and death ("Good Friday Fare"). They form the basis of seminar thematic discussions.

The text's own origins are narrated and reflected on in "The Wide Skirt":

> Man kann auch ganz zu Anfang behaupten, es sei heutzutage unmöglich, einen Roman zu schreiben, dann aber, sozusagen hinter dem eigenen Rücken, einen kräftigen Knüller hinlegen, um schließlich als letztmöglicher Romanschreiber dazustehn. Auch habe ich mir sagen lassen, daß es sich gut und bescheiden ausnimmt, wenn man anfangs beteuert: Es gibt keine Romanhelden mehr, weil es keine Individualisten mehr gibt, weil die Individualität verlorengegangen, weil der Mensch einsam, jeder Mensch gleich einsam, ohne Recht auf individuelle Einsamkeit ist und eine namen- und heldenlose einsame Masse bildet.   (12)

> Or you can declare at the very start that it's impossible to write a novel nowadays, but then, behind your own back so to speak, give birth to a whopper, a novel to end all novels. I have also been told that it makes a good impression, an impression of modesty so to speak, if you begin by saying that a novel can't have a hero any more because there are no more individualists, because individuality is a thing of the past, because man— each man and all men together—is alone in his loneliness and no one is entitled to individual loneliness, and all men lumped together make up a "lonely mass" without names and without heroes.   (17)

Notions of writing, originality, and individuality are closely linked in this passage. Just as Oskar will later narrate his beginnings, the text's origins are addressed here. They are not taken for granted but directly addressed. I ask students to describe and reflect on the narrative situation, which is complicated because of the levels of time. Oskar is narrating from the present moment in 1953 of his incarceration in a mental asylum and is represented on this level as writing down his memories. That means that the narrator is himself a character on the level of time from which the narration is told. So we are presented not just with a narrator as a remembering and reflecting consciousness but also with a physical figure who interacts with other characters, visitors, his male nurse. We are constantly returned to the scene of writing in the novel, which reminds us of the origin of the words—*narration* is *narrated*.

The first chapter reveals anxiety about origins of words. Students first describe the basic details of the plot and then analyze passages, such as the one quoted above. On the one hand, Oskar contests the claim that there are no individuals in the contemporary world and asserts his belief that he is an individual and singular hero. On the other hand, the text, through levels of meaning and registers of words, alludes to a crisis of individuality. This passage illustrates how narrative style and linguistic registers play a crucial role in creating meaning. Students can start to read on multiple levels—there's the immediate meaning of the sentences, and then there are meanings hidden in between the lines, which can be discerned through the humor and from the work of clashing registers. Students struggle with some of the words and have to work with dictionaries to unravel linguistic connotations, for instance, the colloquial phrase "einen Knüller hinlegen" ("give birth to a whopper"). While claiming to be an individual and creative genius, Oskar is, at the same time, using clichéd and colloquial expressions that point to the shared, inherited, and used nature of the language he employs. Thus, students gain an awareness of how the text can convey double meanings: even as Oskar claims that there are still heroes, the text manages to hint at a crisis of individuality.

In this first chapter, Oskar also asks Bruno to buy "unschuldiges Papier" (11) ("virgin paper" [16]) on which to write his story and memories, "meinem unablässig Silben ausscheidenden Geist zum Gebrauch freizugeben" (11) ("making it [blank paper] available to this mind of mine which persists in excreting syllables" [16]). The levels of meaning in the words again undermine the ideals of originality and individuality. The use of the word *Geist* recalls the concept in the German philosophical tradition and here, as Oskar talks of excreting syllables, also the division between the abstract (mind or spirit) and the material (corporeal). Oskar mixes the two when he assigns a bodily function to his *Geist* (excretion). "Unschuldig" means "not guilty" or "innocent," but also "virgin," and students are asked to reflect on why a sexual connotation is given here. It seems to conjure up Oskar's image of himself as a powerful creator, who is also sexually powerful, able to project his creations onto the previously blank world—as if spilling his seed onto the blank virgin paper and creating something sensational.

Lots of ideas thus come together: the notion of creation ex nihilo is both raised and debunked. This term refers to God's creating everything from nothing and could allude here to the narrator and the author behind him as kinds of gods creating the universe of the novel. It is also an idea often associated with the lone Romantic genius writing his unique visions. But the idea of a unique creator is simultaneously debunked through the connotations of the language. The syllables (and the novel's words) are linked to excrement, which parodies the inherited idea of genius and undermines the status of the work of art as the expression of unique individuality. It also implies that Oskar is not the originator or creator of these words but rather that they come from a preexistent outside and have been ingested and passed through his body and consciousness. Thus this passage is not a straightforward example of the male myth of isolated creativity or autogenesis: despite Oskar's assertions of greatness, the text intimates that he is not in full control of the production of the novel. The clash of images about writing also underlines the many ambiguities. The language associates the novel's creation with birthing but at the same time evokes defecation, an action to which Oskar accords great value but that puts into question the authenticity of his authorship.

This worry about originality also appears in the narration of Oskar's birth in 1924, when Oskar describes an event that logically he cannot remember:

> Ich erblickte das Licht dieser Welt in Gestalt zweier Sechzig-Watt-Glühbirnen. Noch heute kommt mir deshalb der Bibeltext "Es werde Licht und es ward Licht" wie der gelungenste Werbeslogan der Firma Osram vor. Bis auf den obligaten Dammriß verlief meine Geburt glatt. Mühelos befreite ich mich aus der von Müttern, Embryonen und Hebammen gleichviel geschätzten Kopflage. . . . Ich gehörte zu den hellhörigen Säuglingen, deren geistige Entwicklung schon bei der Geburt abgeschlossen ist. . . . So unbeeinflußbar ich als Embryo nur auf mich gehört und mich im Fruchtwasser spiegelnd geachtet hatte, so kritisch lauschte ich den ersten spontanen Äußerungen der Eltern unter den Glühbirnen.   (52)

> Well, then, it was in the form of two sixty-watt bulbs that I first saw the light of this world. That is why the words of the Bible, "Let there be light and there was light," still strike me as an excellent publicity slogan for Osram light bulbs. My birth ran off smoothly except for the usual rupture of the perineum. I had no difficulty freeing myself from the upside-down position so favored by mothers, embryos, and midwives.
>
> I may as well come right out with it: I was one of those clairaudient infants whose mental development is completed at birth. . . . The moment I was born I took a very critical attitude toward the first utterances to slip from my parents beneath the light bulbs.   (47)

This scene is shot through with the cynicism and distance characteristic of the narrative style of the novel as a whole, but it strikes us as particularly odd at this point, when we are faced with the paradox of the newborn child narrating his own birth. Students often complain that the narrative is "odd," that there is something "not right" about the presentation of birth. I encourage them to spend time reflecting on that strangeness and use their initial responses to analyze further the nature of Oskar's existential crisis and his relations with his origins. I use their comments about the text's strangeness to highlight that this strangeness is in fact a constitutive element of the text. Thus I get them to think about what work the strangeness is doing in the text. We can then consider the peculiarity of having just one dominant perspective, which gives Oskar control over the facts and over what we know and do not know.

The conventions of magic realism, which encourage suspension of disbelief, are obviously employed in this passage. We can also interpret it as Oskar's fantasy, as retrospective imaginative construction of an episode in which he was present but not fully conscious. We see the birth from his angle of vision; he tells the story in a way in which he is the active interpretative presence while his parents appear relatively passive. We hear their voices but always through his consciousness, which of course could not possibly have assessed what he heard. The representation of birth is odd: that the child is self-sufficient and detached humorously jars with our experience and knowledge of the capabilities of new-born babies. Oskar appears incapable of thinking of himself as not being able to think, and the passage indicates his fantasy that his mental faculties and critical judgment are complete at birth. From our knowledge of psychoanalytic theory, however, we know that at birth the infant is totally helpless and has not yet developed a sense of separate, homogeneous selfhood.

The text thus again makes ridiculous the assertion of originality and individuality. The event of birth is the paradigmatic illustration of how we cannot think a person without another—we cannot think the newborn without the mother. It is also an example of the need for the other: we are reliant on another and on a perspective from another for representations of our beginnings, because we literally cannot remember them. A focus on our beginnings illustrates the incompleteness of the human being and our lack of autonomy. We have no choice but to engage in a shared relationality, which might not necessarily lead to completion. It is a state we are born into and a situation we cannot undo. It is this relationality that Oskar wants to escape. But through the strangeness and irony of these passages, criticism of Oskar and his delusions is also implied.

The motif of return to the womb is first introduced at the end of this chapter ("Moth and Light Bulb"), as birth becomes linked in Oskar's mind not with life but with tragic isolation and the death drive:

Äußerlich schreiend und einen Säugling blaurot vortäuschend, kam ich zu dem Entschluß, meines Vaters Vorschlag, also alles, was das Kolonialwarengeschäft betraf, schlankweg abzulehnen, den Wunsch meiner Mama jedoch . . . wohlwollend zu prüfen.

Neben all diesen Spekulationen, meine Zukunft betreffend, bestätigte ich mir: Mama und jener Vater Matzerath hatten nicht das Organ, meine Einwände und Entschlüsse zu verstehen und gegebenenfalls zu respektieren. Einsam und unverstanden lag Oskar unter den Glühbirnen, folgerte, daß das so bleibe, bis sechzig, siebenzig Jahre später ein endgültiger Kurzschluß aller Lichtquellen Strom unterbrechen werde, verlor deshalb die Lust, bevor dieses Leben unter den Glühbirnen anfing; und nur die in Aussicht gestellte Blechtrommel hinderte mich damals, dem Wunsch nach Rückkehr in meine embryonale Kopflage stärkeren Ausdruck zu geben.

Zudem hatte die Hebamme mich schon abgenabelt; es war nichts mehr zu machen. (54–55)

Outwardly wailing and impersonating a meat-colored baby, I made up my mind to reject my father's projects, in short everything connected with the grocery store, out of hand, but to give my mother's plan favorable consideration. . . .

Aside from all this speculation about my future, I quickly realized that Mama and this Mr. Matzerath were not equipped to understand or respect my decisions whether positive or negative. Lonely and misunderstood, Oskar lay beneath the light bulbs, and figuring that things would go on like this for some sixty or seventy years, until a final short circuit should cut off all sources of light, he lost his enthusiasm even before this life beneath the light bulbs had begun. It was only the prospect of the drum that prevented me then from expressing more forcefully my desire to return to the womb.

Besides, the midwife had already cut my umbilical cord. There was nothing more to be done.   (48–49)

In this passage, we can see the split that occurs in the narrative as Oskar starts referring to himself in the third person. Oskar, the I narrator and subject, starts speaking about himself, Oskar, the object of narration, as if seeing himself from the outside. This mixture of first- and third-person pronouns suggests the development of self-consciousness, which is linked to a primal alienation and detachment and expressed both in the subject matter and through the narrative style. Subjectivity is revealed to be fundamentally split, because it consists of a self that acts and experiences and a self that reflects on this self. This self does not coincide with itself, because it exists in a world with others who observe it from the outside. Oskar concludes that he is doomed to a life of loneliness and incompletion, because he cannot fashion unity out of these different views of him.

In these passages, fragmentation and alienation are fundamentally linked to the moment of birth and the loss of the amniotic sac, which is represented as the only place where the self reflects a perfect image of itself so there is unity, no disparity between subject and object. We can also see the reversal and forgetfulness Irigaray perceives at work in patriarchal culture. In the very moment of the arrival of a newborn child, the text introduces the idea of decay and death. Separation and alienation appear immediately and as synonymous with birth, which points to a forgetting of the phase of dependence, connection, and intimacy with the mother.

It seems impossible for Oskar to think himself as egoless, helpless, and dependent. Instead of reflecting on connections with and dependence on others, he thinks about death. But because of the work that the text's strangeness does, we can deconstruct his thoughts to glimpse that his crisis stems less from the thought of death than from the inability to represent and remember birth and from his defenselessness and total reliance on the mother. We can see that Oskar denies relations with the world and represses an underlying awareness of interrelationality.

At the same time that the womb/mother is represented as a lost wholeness, the text elsewhere evokes the maternal body as disgusting. I ask students to read the chapters concerning Agnes Matzerath's demise, which begins with the infamous eel episode in "Good Friday Fare," when the family encounters a man on the beach fishing for eels by using a dead horse's head as bait. The eels have also likely become fat through eating human flesh (see Schade's essay in this volume). I draw students' attention to the other times the episode is narrated in the text and ask students to suggest meanings. They often say that the horse's head is an omen, signaling the rise of the Nazis and war, and that it is often associated with female sexuality.

I also prompt them to think about the implications of Agnes's pregnancy. The knowledge of her pregnancy seeps into the narrative, as Agnes, more sensitive than usual, vomits at the sight of the horse's head. The subtle association of pregnancy with a proliferation of disgusting bodily secretions, which other animals feed on (seagulls gobble up the fisherman's spit), and the animal carcass sustaining other life suggest a sense of revulsion surrounding the female pregnant body. The thought of the mother's fleshy body and of new life taking root in that body appears to be extremely unsettling. The result is that the maternal body turns into an image of death. That Oskar and the text obsessively return to this image indicates its importance in understanding the nature of his existential crisis. But we could read such images not as a straightforward fear of death but as evidence of anxiety surrounding thinking the flesh that preceded and sustained him—his ancestors and specifically the mother.

Students have prepared oral presentations on how the mother's death is represented and Oskar's reactions to it in "Tapered at the Foot End" and "Herbert Truczinski's Back." They state that the images are revolting and horrific. The novel thus presents a dual image of the mother: she is aligned with images of lost wholeness as well as with the monstrous. It is this dialectic that propels Oskar's narrative about his mother: she is a source of both fascination and horror, an object of longing but also something terrifying. This presentation is analogous to Freudian-Lacanian psychoanalysis, where the mother is both castrated (the sight of the female genitals horrifies the male observer because she lacks male genitals) and phallic (she possesses a mysterious power). But in Grass's novel something has gone wrong with the normal formation of masculinity. Oskar wants not to be separated from the mother but to be reunited with her in death: "Mit Mama und dem Embryo wollte Oskar in die Grube. . . . [N]icht hochkommen wollte Oskar, auf dem verjüngten Fußende wollte er sitzen" (212) ("He wished to go down into the pit with Mama and the fetus. . . . [N]o, Oskar didn't wish to come up, he wished to sit on the tapering foot end of the coffin" [165]).

Rather than an idea that has to be completely repressed, burial in the mother's womb is something Oskar longs for. Even as his articulated desire questions the psychoanalytic idea of repression, the womb becomes associated with death rather than life. The mother dies with her unborn fetus, rejecting life, an impulse echoed by her son. The text evokes Oskar's trauma surrounding his mother's death and hints at his feelings of complicity and guilt, even alluding to a self-hatred linked to the loss of the mother. But these crises are simultaneously a source of creativity. As the opening quotation of this essay suggests, Oskar associates the whole novel's coming into being with the desire to get back to the umbilical cord. This desire appears productive for the male imagination undergoing a crisis: Oskar does not return to the womb and does not die with the mother, who can no longer give birth, but he is inspired to remember and write. Remembering the mother and remembering history thus become crucially linked, and this link is reiterated in "Herbert Truczinski's Back." The motifs of drumming, getting back to the umbilical cord, and remembering-writing become joined as Oskar suggests that his fascination with body parts and with drumming are replacements for the womb and represent attempts to get back to the mother/womb. Because remembering and drumming are both ways to evoke the smallest detail of the past, German history itself is brought into connection with the attempt to remember the womb/mother.

Guilt and trauma surrounding the loss of the mother are linked, then, with a sense of loss and guilt in relation to German history. Students often argue that the anxiety surrounding origins can be understood on a historical level as Oskar's rejection of his parents' generation—his rejection especially of his German father—because of its connections with National Socialism. It is also possible to interpret the longing for the womb as an indirect comment on the times, as a rejection of specific societies and historical realities (e.g., Nazi Germany, the *kleinbürgerliche* ["petit-bourgeois"] quarters of Danzig). But criticism of Oskar's attitude of withdrawal from society and reality is also implied. The complex character of Oskar points to the dangers of both engaging and not engaging with the world and society. In both writing birth and avoiding thinking it fully, the text suggests Oskar's reluctance to think origins, change, and relationality, which is symptomatic of his desire to escape from history. But the text simultaneously emphasizes that such escape is impossible.

I teach students the complex way that imagery works in Grass's text. In *The Tin Drum*, images do not correspond to just one idea (as students often expect) but resonate with multiple meanings, and often a motif can mean two opposing things at the same time. The motif of returning to the umbilical cord at first appears to signify escapism but is then associated with an intense remembering. "Getting back to the umbilical cord" thus means both escape from history (not facing reality) *and* getting back to history (remembering the details of the past that we have repressed or forgotten). The motif of escaping/remembering history resonates on other levels of time—such as West Germany in 1959—and can highlight complexities of specific historical moments: the general reluctance to engage with German history during the 1950s, together with the growing realization of the impossibility of avoiding this activity and articulations from some quarters of the critical need to think through the German past. Of course, the dialectic of escaping/remembering the past was also reflected in the controversy surrounding the publication in 2006 of Grass's autobiography *Beim Häuten der Zwiebel*, in which Grass reveals his long-repressed memories of his participation in the Waffen-SS.

NOTES

[1] To my knowledge Grass himself has not commented on the use or parody of Freudian ideas and motifs in *The Tin Drum*.

[2] On Freud, see Stafford-Clark; Mitchell. On Lacan, see Grosz. On the role of the mother and birth in the Western philosophical tradition, see Oliver; Cavarero; and Battersby.

Can Nazi Childhood Be Innocent?
Teaching Volker Schlöndorff's *Die Blechtrommel*

Stephen Brockmann

Every few years I teach a course called History of German Film, in which Volker Schlöndorff's *Die Blechtrommel* (1979; *The Tin Drum*) plays a major role. In this fifteen-week course, which has a lecture-discussion format, I generally spend a week on each film. This means that Schlöndorff's film gets two to three hours of class time, excluding the film screening. Sometimes students are so riled up about *Die Blechtrommel* that classroom discussion of it spills over into an additional week, meaning that it can get up to four hours of class time if students are sufficiently disturbed about it. In this essay I discuss some of the issues that have come up in my teaching of this film, particularly Schlöndorff's depiction of a sexualized childhood, which I find that many students object to. I show the ways in which I respond to their concerns by addressing *Die Blechtrommel* pedagogically as a response to Nazi images of childhood superiority on the one hand and to postwar conceptions of a guilt-free German zero hour on the other.

Schlöndorff's *Die Blechtrommel*, based on Günter Grass's 1959 novel, is one of the key works of the New German Cinema, which flourished from the late 1960s to the early 1980s. This renaissance of the German cinema challenged traditional German and American filmmaking by introducing political problems into film and by confronting audiences with disturbing and difficult material. In addition to Schlöndorff, the main contributors to the New German Cinema were Rainer Werner Fassbinder, Werner Herzog, Wim Wenders, Alexander Kluge, Hans Jürgen Syberberg, Edgar Reitz, and Margarethe von Trotta. *Die Blechtrommel* cemented Schlöndorff's reputation as one of the most important

German directors of his time. As an adaptation of Grass's novel, it is typical of Schlöndorff's films: his general procedure, unlike that of many of his colleagues, who tend to create movies from scratch, has been to transform novels into movies. Another basic difference between Schlöndorff's film and most of the other works of the New German Cinema is that *Die Blechtrommel* was not only a critical but also a popular and financial success. In 1979 it shared the Palme d'Or at the Cannes film festival with Francis Ford Coppola's *Apocalypse Now*, and it was the first German film to win an Oscar for best foreign film (in 1980; the only others were Caroline Link's 2001 *Nirgendwo in Afrika* ["Nowhere in Africa"], which won an Oscar in 2003, and Florian Henckel von Donnersmarck's 2006 *Das Leben der Anderen* [*The Lives of Others*], which won an Oscar in 2007). Schlöndorff has consistently tried to combine popular appeal with an artistically high level of filmmaking; he seeks in part to overcome the divide between high art and the conventional, artistically uninteresting pandering to popular tastes that is so widespread in Hollywood filmmaking. Paradoxically, however, the popular success of *Die Blechtrommel* and other Schlöndorff films has caused a negative critical reaction: because of his films' appeal to wider audiences, Schlöndorff has occasionally been criticized for "conventional narratives" (Hake 160) and lack of daring (Pflaum and Prinzler 55).

As accessible as it is, *Die Blechtrommel* is also controversial and disturbing. That Schlöndorff is sometimes seen as conventional but has caused major controversies is a testament to the distance that divides high art and criticism from certain kinds of popular sentiment. In June 1997, after *Die Blechtrommel* was released on video and became available in many public libraries, a procensorship group in Oklahoma City named Oklahomans for Children and Families succeeded in convincing a local judge to rule informally that parts of the film constituted child pornography ("Rights Group"). Police in Oklahoma City then removed every known copy of the movie from video stores and at least one private home. Six months later, in December 1997, a federal judge ruled that such seizures were unconstitutional (Weisberg 161).

Although *Die Blechtrommel* is far less sexually explicit than many ordinary Hollywood movies, the uproar arose because Oskar Matzerath, the film's main character and narrator, is played by a child actor, David Bennent, who was only eleven years old when the film was made. Even if the film does not explicitly depict its main character engaged in sexual intercourse, it strongly suggests that he is sexually active; in one scene his face appears to come into direct contact with the genitalia of an adult woman. *Die Blechtrommel*, reported an article in the *Los Angeles Times* that appeared after Oklahoma City police had seized the video, "includes one scene where a boy about 6 or 7 has oral sex in a bathhouse with a teen-age girl" ("OK City Police"). Of course neither the actor playing Oskar nor Oskar himself is in fact "six or seven" in the relevant scene, which, moreover, cannot easily or definitively be described as depicting "oral sex," since the woman's genitalia are never shown and since it is not clear exactly what Oskar, whose face also cannot be seen, is doing with his mouth and tongue.

Nevertheless, Schlöndorff's film does suggest that Oskar ultimately has regular sex with the woman, his own stepmother, Maria, and that he therefore might be the biological father of his stepbrother, Kurt. For some public officials in Oklahoma, these facts alone seem to have sufficed to condemn Schlöndorff's film as child pornography. Bob Anderson, a member of Oklahomans for Children and Families, declared when he heard that Grass had won the 1999 Nobel Prize for literature, "I guess congratulations to him, but I also know that the people that are making these awards are the same liberal people that are pushing our children to have sex anytime, anywhere, with animals, etc." (Vognar). Anderson's claim is of course baseless and in no way reflects Schlöndorff's or Grass's views on sexuality or childhood, let alone the views of the Swedish Academy. But Anderson's statement does succinctly demonstrate one reason why *Die Blechtrommel* is so controversial: its perceived association with child sexuality and even pornography. My experience teaching *Die Blechtrommel* regularly to American undergraduates suggests that police officials, judges, and advocates of censorship in Oklahoma are not alone in being disturbed by the film. Inevitably, many of my students volunteer that they find Schlöndorff's sexualized depiction of Oskar to be deeply disturbing and, indeed, offensive. They do not necessarily want the film banned, but they do not understand why Schlöndorff (and by extension also Grass) seems to go out of his way to depict childhood as anything but innocent and cute.

Of course, as any reader of Grass's novel or any careful viewer of Schlöndorff's film knows, Oskar Matzerath is not simply a child. He is born in 1924 and decides to stop growing at the age of three because his mother promised him a tin drum at that age. Over the next decade and a half he continues to look like a small child physically, but mentally, emotionally, and sexually he develops into adolescence and adulthood. Therefore if he is having sex with Maria in 1940, he is not a three-year-old having sex or even a six- or seven-year-old. Rather, he is a sixteen-year-old who looks like a small boy having sex. This does not seem to have been a major problem in the reception of the novel—as controversial as Grass's *Tin Drum* was—since the novel's readers have a good deal of freedom in how they wish to imagine Oskar physically and since Oskar, the narrator, is in his thirties when he tells the story. But Schlöndorff eliminates the last third of Grass's novel, the part that deals with Oskar's experiences in West Germany as an adult, so the director can hardly have an adult Oskar as his narrator; his narrator is Oskar the child. In Schlöndorff's film, Bennent does indeed look like a small child—the actor had a physiological disorder that made him look younger than he really was—and his childishness is reinforced by the clothes he wears and the tin drum he constantly carries with him. Hence the film's viewers are forced to see Oskar as a small child, not as an adult or even an adolescent.

It is no wonder that when that small child begins to behave sexually and even perversely, many viewers are upset. This sexualized depiction of childhood contravenes deeply held and probably well-meaning notions of what childhood is or ought to be. As Gary Cross has pointed out in a perceptive study of Americans' notions of childhood, faith in "the innocence of childhood is one of the few beliefs that all share" (6). Moreover, Cross notes, "we resent and fear the young when they threaten our illusions about the purity of childhood" (10). Oskar certainly threatens such illusions. Schlöndorff himself calls Bennent and his performance "shocking." According to him, Bennent "is the opposite of a child actor who everyone thinks is touching. He has no pity, no tact at all, no sentimentality" (Rentschler, *West German Filmmakers* 177). He is, in other words, not a cute little boy. Richard Weisberg argues that in at least one sense the Oklahoma censors are right: neither Grass's novel nor Schlöndorff's film can be seen as "family friendly" (168).

Far from impeding an understanding of Schlöndorff's film, viewers' shock at this sexualized depiction of childhood can be an aid in understanding it. The two key sets of questions in approaching the film from this direction involve, first, the depiction of Oskar Matzerath and, second, the reasons that Schlöndorff or Grass may have had for choosing such a depiction. In the first set: What kind of a person is Oskar? How does he differ from prominent child heroes in other movies? Is he a hero at all? Are viewers invited to sympathize with him or dislike him? Is Oskar a victim or a perpetrator? In the second set: If Schlöndorff's or Grass's depiction of childhood is unconventional, why might the director or the author have chosen it? Are there aspects of German tradition that their depiction criticizes or takes issue with? Does their depiction of childhood have political implications, either now or in the past?

The first set of questions is intended to get students thinking about other depictions of childhood in other movies they have seen. Clearly, in most movies that have a child as the protagonist, the child is portrayed as innocent, even if the adults around him or her are not. Students will of course have watched a great many movies with child protagonists. Prominent examples are *Heidi* (1937), *The Wizard of Oz* (1939), *National Velvet* (1945), the classic western *Shane* (1953), *The Yearling* (1946), as well as more recent movies like *E.T.* (1982), *Annie* (1982), *Home Alone* (1990), or *Spy Kids* (2001). Students can come up with their own lists of movies with child heroes, and they can also be invited to think about how, even beyond American movie culture, conceptions of an innocent childhood are deeply ingrained in Western society and why.

The most prominent story of an innocent child in Western culture is that of the Christ child, with whom Oskar spars in both the movie and the book. Unlike the children in most films and unlike the Christ child, Oskar is never innocent, even at the moment of his birth, when viewers are invited to see the world from his already jaded perspective from inside his mother's womb. In fact the narrator Oskar tells the film's viewers that he does not really want to be born at all, that the only reason he bothers coming out of the womb in the first place is the promise of a tin drum on his third birthday.

Students can be asked to analyze this scene and think about how it contravenes conventional notions of the value of life and the joy associated with giving birth and being born. In this scene, Oskar depicts himself as having been victimized by being born. Although he is the film's narrator and hence could, if he wanted to, depict himself in an entirely positive light here and elsewhere, he does not choose to do so. He may look like a small child, but he constantly resists other people's (and viewers') inclination to treat him as innocent and cute. Part of this resistance comes in the form of a high-pitched scream that is capable of breaking glass at key moments: cracking the eyeglasses of an overbearing schoolteacher who wants to treat him like a baby, for instance, or breaking the containers in which an octopus, a fetus, and other biological oddities are preserved in formaldehyde in a doctor's office.

It is instructive to ask students to come up with a list of the ways in which Oskar inhibits viewers' sympathy for him and, by extension, the ways in which he resists being placed in Western culture's assigned role for fictional—and real—children. Above and beyond his high-pitched scream and his sexual exploits, the list might include the fact that on his third birthday he intentionally falls down a flight of stairs in order to present his parents with a plausible reason for his refusal to grow; that he tyrannizes his brother/son, Kurt, as well as other family members; that he is indirectly responsible for the deaths of the two most important male authority figures in his life; that he attacks his stepmother and lover Maria while she is pregnant, evidently trying to induce a miscarriage; and that he desecrates a statue of the Virgin Mary and the Christ child in a Danzig church. In many ways he is selfish and despotic, concerned only with his own welfare and gratification. As Weisberg notes, "Oskar instantly eschews all claims to heroic status, urging his listener instead to accept him as sick, distorted, grotesque" (163). This is hardly the picture of children we like to imagine. After all, as Cross notes, "we love children for all the things we are no longer and often wish we were" (3). Oskar short-circuits such idolization from the very beginning, suggesting that our sentimentalized images of childhood are a fantasy, not a reality, and that they are based more on our narcissism than on genuine concern for children's welfare. In conventional, sentimental images of childhood, we live a fantasy; Oskar, in contrast, peskily insists on showing us who and what we are.

But Oskar is not just a perpetrator. His jaded view of the world is all too often accurate. None of the adults around him—with the possible exceptions of his Kashubian grandmother and the Jewish toy store owner Sigismund Markus—is a paragon of virtue. Because of the conspicuous lack of virtue of the adults around him, so many of whom are Nazis, Oskar is not even sure who his biological father is. Two men come into question, and Oskar thinks of both as his father. Oskar's German father, Alfred Matzerath, becomes a Nazi, while his Polish father, Jan Bronski, is a coward and an adulterer. His mother, meanwhile, is an adulteress who ultimately dies of an eating disorder that is at least partially self-induced. Oskar may be a freak, but the world in which he lives is freakish. In other words, he represents an entire society that has become freakish. As Weisberg notes, the audience of *The Tin Drum* "gradually begins to understand the universality—rather than the peculiarity—of the protagonist's life" (164).

When Oskar disrupts a Nazi Party rally in Danzig with his drumming, turning a solemn fascist ritual into a folk festival complete with waltzes, viewers sympathize with him. And when he joins other midgets to entertain German troops at the French front, viewers can empathize with these physical misfits trying to survive in a Nazi world of self-proclaimed supermen. Students can easily come up with these and other factors that encourage viewers to sympathize with Oskar. But ultimately Oskar does not seek to disrupt the Nazi world in any profound way—after all, how could he? He simply tries to survive.

Clearly, Oskar is not a black-and-white figure. Again and again viewers are drawn to sympathize with him because of his childish looks, but again and again that sympathy is blocked because of his actions. In his moral ambiguity, he is in fact very much like an ordinary human being, and like many ordinary children. That he is not at all like the children we imagine in movies and literature makes him disturbing.

Two other postwar film depictions of a not-so-innocent German childhood resonate with Schlöndorff's *Blechtrommel*. The first is Roberto Rossellini's *Germania anno zero* (1948; *Germany, Year Zero*), which tells the story of a fanatical Nazi boy who winds up killing his father in the final days of World War II. The second is Bernhard Wicki's *Die Brücke* (*The Bridge*, released in 1958, just one year before Grass published *Die Blechtrommel*), which tells the story of doomed Hitler Youth boys desperately trying to keep American invaders from taking a German bridge in 1945. In addition to these two filmic tales of youthful fanaticism, Walter Kolbenhoff's 1946 novel *Von unserem Fleisch und Blut* ("From Our Flesh and Blood"), one of the first works of postwar German literature by a younger generation of German writers—a generation that ultimately formed the Gruppe 47, of which Grass himself became one of the most prominent members—tells the story of a Nazi boy who hates the entire adult world because of its cowardice in giving up to the Allied invaders. Grass's and Schlöndorff's depiction of childhood as not so innocent is different from these works in that Oskar never simply becomes either a victim or a proponent of Nazi ideology; he remains skeptical about it, and he survives into the postwar era. It is entirely appropriate that in one of the film's most painful scenes, Oskar causes his German father literally to swallow, in the form of a swastika lapel pin, the Nazi ideology that he has espoused and thus die at the hands of the invading Red Army soldiers, who shoot the elder Matzerath when his body begins to shake uncontrollably after he has swallowed the pin.

Once students have established that Oskar is not a black-or-white but rather a gray figure and that Schlöndorff's depiction of him contravenes conventional depictions of a sentimentalized childhood, they can address the second set of questions, the ones that ask why Schlöndorff and Grass chose such a dark portrayal of childhood. If so many stories about children, particularly in films, portray them as innocent victims or cute and cuddly tots, why do Schlöndorff and Grass portray a child who is neither cuddly nor innocent nor a victim? Since this is a story about a Nazi childhood, it is important to understand, in answering the question, how child heroes were portrayed in Nazi film and literature and how the Nazis conceived of childhood in general.

Fortunately there is a wealth of documentation about how the Nazis treated childhood in film, in literature, and in ideology. One of the very first Nazi films was a movie entitled *Hitlerjunge Quex* (1933; "Hitler Youth Quex"), which tells the story of a brave, chaste Aryan Nazi boy in Berlin who does battle with and is ultimately murdered by sexualized, dissolute Communists. This film is in fact referred to by Oskar in Grass's novel (for a good analysis of the film, see Rentschler, *Ministry* 53–69). It is likely that both the fictional Oskar and the real Grass saw this film. I have occasionally taught *Hitlerjunge Quex* to my students, and each time it has been successful; but to my surprise, I often find that my students sympathize with the upright Nazi boy hero. Their sympathy shows how powerful Nazi ideologies of heroic childhood can be even now, even in the United States; it also suggests how closely our own myths of childhood parallel those prevalent in German culture from 1933 to 1945.

A typical Nazi children's book by Wilfrid Bade entitled *Trommlerbub unterm Hakenkreuz* (1934; "Drummer Boy under the Swastika"), which can be read easily by undergraduates with some understanding of German, tells a similar story about a Nazi child martyr. I have also occasionally asked my students to read this book, and here too I have enjoyed positive results. Because its ideology is so close to the surface, I find that students see through it more easily than through the film *Hitlerjunge Quex*. It is also possible that students have simply learned to read books more critically than they view films. At any rate, I find that it is helpful to discuss with students the ways that the Nazis instrumentalized notions of a heroic, innocent childhood for their own purposes.

The Hitler Youth was a massive organization involving the overwhelming majority of German boys, and it was intended to educate them to fanatical devotion to their führer, Adolf Hitler. The anthem of the Hitler Youth, sung at all major rallies, including the annual Nazi Party rallies in Nuremberg, urged boys to defend the Nazi flag even at the cost of death. Children bombarded by such propaganda may in some sense still have been innocent, but they were not harmless. The extent to which the Nazis identified themselves with youth rather than with old age is hard to overestimate. Hitler himself was presented as a youthful, strong leader radically different from his elderly predecessors. Only forty-four years old when he came to power in 1933, he was unmarried and had the air of a still youthful Bohemian, never having settled into a traditional bourgeois, adult life. "Youth is always right in any conflict with old age," declared the eponymous young hero of Joseph Goebbels's 1929 novel *Michael* (3); Goebbels went on to become Hitler's minister of propaganda. Baldur von Schirach, the head of the Hitler Youth, proclaimed that "in a higher sense youth is always right because youth carries within itself the new life" (qtd. in Mosse, *Nazi Culture: A Documentary History* 300–01). In Nazi propaganda it was the system of the Weimar Republic that was old-fashioned and decadent; in contrast, the National Socialist Party and its charismatic führer were depicted as young and vigorous.

The Nazi Party created youth organizations, such as the Jungvolk and the Hitlerjugend for boys and the BDM (Bund deutscher Mädel ["Federation of German Maidens"]) for girls; such organizations represented not only a means for socializing children into National Socialist ideology but also a bulwark of influence independent from home and school. In his 1947 memoirs, the socialist school reformer Paul Oestreich wrote that during the years of the Third Reich "the great majority of . . . youth has grown up abandoned, betrayed, lonesome, and without true parents" (qtd. in Mosse 275). Two years earlier, Wilhelm Röpke, one of the architects of the postwar West German economic miracle, observed that, while twelve years of Nazi tyranny had infected the German people itself, damage had been especially horrific "in the souls of the particularly easily influenced German youth" (60). As the young writer Anna Ozana noted in 1946, the Nazis had not simply made the "theoretical claim . . . of extending their influence into people's personal affairs" (81), they had also implemented such policies in reality. Indeed, she argued, "if it had been possible they would have put even the very youngest children into barracks and thereby removed them completely from the dreaded reactionary and softening influence of their parents' homes" (77). One of Bertolt Brecht's most moving depictions of the Nazi period is a short sketch entitled "The Informer," which shows a mother and father desperate for fear that their son has betrayed them to the Nazis. Even five years after the end of the war and the defeat of the Nazis, Brecht expressed his belief that the Nazis had completely corrupted German youth: "In short, our youth is a Hitler youth" ("Von der Jugend" 131). Brecht and many others were suggesting that the Nazis had killed the possibility of an innocent childhood.

Understanding the Nazi obsession with youth goes a long way to explaining the choices Schlöndorff and Grass made in their depiction of childhood in *Die Blechtrommel,* which is intended precisely to counteract Nazi assertions about the superiority of youth and its necessary innocence. Had Schlöndorff and Grass portrayed Oskar as an innocent victim of despicable older people, they would have failed in at least three ways. First, they would have failed to do justice to Nazism's conception of itself as a righteous youth movement superior to old age. By depicting youth as necessarily innocent, they would have given a convenient alibi to the millions of young Germans who had supported Hitler. Second, and ironically, if Schlöndorff and Grass had constructed their story simply as a critique of older people and a defense of the young, they would have repeated Nazism's own critique of old age and celebration of the superiority of youth. Finally, they would have failed to comprehend how the very concept of a guilt-free youth had become deeply problematic in the aftermath of the Nazi dictatorship (Brockmann, *German Literary Culture* 170–207). The only way for Schlöndorff and Grass to avoid these mistakes was to depict a German childhood that is implicated in guilt but also not wholly dominated by Nazism. Unlike the child martyrs of Nazi ideology and unlike Rossellini's and Kolbenhoff's youthful Nazi fanatics, Oskar does not die; he has a future, and that future lies in postwar Germany, in the Federal Republic.

This survival leads to the final question: whether *Die Blechtrommel*, in addition to being an interpretation of the Nazi past, is also a political intervention in the German present. Here too, students can be asked their opinion. They should be encouraged to think about what implications the film's depiction of a Nazi childhood might have for postwar Germany. The answer is clearly yes, there is a political intervention. For the interpretation of the Federal Republic and its history, it matters greatly whether one sees it as being the creation of a largely guilt-free post-Nazi younger generation or whether one sees it and its creators, young and old, as wrapped up in a nexus of shame and guilt coming from the Nazi period.

Grass, born in 1927, is a prominent member of the first postwar West German generation, the generation sometimes referred to in German as *Flakhelfer* ("antiaircraft helpers"), because, although many of them were too young to be soldiers in World War II, they were old enough to be conscripted into home-front service as antiaircraft helpers. Another prominent member of this generation is Pope Benedict XVI (born in the same year as Grass, 1927), formerly Joseph Ratzinger and, controversially, a member of the Hitler Youth and of an antiaircraft battery in his childhood—like so many other German men his age (McAllester; Stanford; Bernstein and Landler). Another is former West German Chancellor Helmut Kohl (born in 1930), who once infamously spoke of his generation as enjoying a "grace of late birth" (Brockmann, *Literature* 140). The implication of Kohl's phrase was that youth alone was a guarantee of innocence and that hence any German collective guilt could not possibly touch his own and later generations. In turn this argument meant that the Federal Republic itself, in so many ways the product of Kohl, Grass, and Pope Benedict's generation, was fundamentally guilt-free. Kohl's concept resonates with widespread German notions of 1945 as a "Stunde Null," a zero hour in which history begins anew, unencumbered by the problems of the past and with a clean slate. Grass is devastatingly critical of such notions: "Und als dann Schluß war, machten sie schnell einen hoffnungsvollen Anfang daraus; denn hierzulande ist Schluß immer Anfang und Hoffnung in jedem, auch im endgültigsten Schluß" (263) ("And then when the end came, they quickly turned it into a hopeful beginning; for in our country the end is always the beginning and there is hope in every, even the most final, end" [204]). He is suggesting that Germany's new beginning was really nothing but an end: the end of Germany as innocent, and perhaps of any belief in the fundamental innocence and goodness of Western civilization itself.

If one contrasts zero-hour conceptions of youthful innocence with the figure of Oskar Matzerath in Grass's novel and Schlöndorff's film, then one can see how both are a statement not just about the Nazi past but also about the German present. If Oskar is the representative figure of the *Flakhelfer* generation in the film as well as the novel, the implication is that the Federal Republic, far from being built on a clean slate, is built on a questionable foundation. Both

Grass and Schlöndorff are suggesting that in the Nazi period an innocent childhood was impossible and, even more devastatingly, that in the wake of the Nazi
period, any notion of an innocent childhood has become untenable, at least in
Western culture. There is no such thing as a "grace of late birth"; everyone is
caught up in the nexus of guilt. Schlöndorff's film, coming precisely two decades
after the publication of Grass's novel, furthermore suggests that even after the
turn from the conservative Christian Democratic government of the 1950s and
1960s to a more liberal government dominated by the Social Democrats in the
1970s, Germany has no innocence. The film also appeared two years after a
major terrorist scare in West Germany called the German Autumn (*Deutscher
Herbst*), in which Red Army terrorists sought to destabilize the West German
government, which responded with overwhelming force. The German Autumn
of 1977 led to speculation that even the younger generation of Germans was
tainted by the specter of Nazism.

Schlöndorff's and Grass's depictions of a guilty, problematic childhood can
be contrasted with other, more optimistic—and therefore politically less critical—depictions of childhood in the Nazi period, such as Martin Walser's 1998
novel *Ein springender Brunnen* (A Gushing Fountain), in which the youthful
protagonist seems relatively untouched by Nazi indoctrination (Taberner 76–80;
Brockmann, "Martin Walser"). It can also be contrasted with an American filmic
epic that many students are probably familiar with: Robert Zemeckis's *Forrest
Gump*, which depicts a witless young American who, precisely because of his
witlessness, is able to go through some of the most controversial parts of American postwar history morally unscathed (Brockmann, "Virgin Father"). In fact,
since both Oskar Matzerath and Forrest Gump are misfits and since both in a
sense represent their respective nations allegorically, it might be useful to ask
students to compare the two figures and draw conclusions about how their creators portray their nations through them. Students familiar with *Forrest Gump*
should not find it difficult to see that it depicts an America that always remains
innocent, no matter what horrors the nation endures or perpetrates, whereas
Die Blechtrommel depicts a Germany that is always already guilty, no matter
what the nation does to atone for its crimes. Students could be asked to think
about the implications these differing views of national innocence or guilt might
have for politics and policy in the two nations. If they can grasp these differences and their implications, they will have deepened their understanding not
only of Germany but also of the United States. Grass's novel and Schlöndorff's
film tell us that Western culture has lost any claim to innocence in the wake
of Nazi crimes. It is no wonder that some object to this message. As Weisberg
cogently argues, *The Tin Drum*, as both movie and novel, "has to be either censored or fully grasped" (162).

A final pedagogical exercise might be to organize a debate among students
for or against the censorship of *Die Blechtrommel*. One can divide the class in
two, with perhaps two or three judges who rate the arguments on the basis of
their merits. Such a debate might bring out how much is at stake culturally and

politically in defending or attacking notions of childhood innocence in any nation. As Cross has pointed out, "today, as perhaps never before, we are obsessed
with kids" (4). Such a debate might help students understand the nature, and
power, of that obsession.

Critics have well understood Oskar Matzerath's status as an icon of his generation and of the Federal Republic. At the moment of German reunification
in 1990, Hans Jürgen Syberberg, the controversial film director whose most
famous work, *Hitler: A Film from Germany*, was completed in 1977, two years
before Schlöndorff's *Blechtrommel*, criticized what he saw as a static West German cultural scene, which, he believed, prevented any kind of normal growth or
development. For Syberberg, Oskar Matzerath was a metaphor for West German culture generally, representing the West German "preference for the small,
the low, for crippling, for the sick, for filth" (38). As Syberberg wrote, "The fact
that the central figure of the best-known postwar novel in Germany is a dwarf
illustrates my observations" (39). Only a few months later the critic Frank Schirrmacher, decrying what he saw as the stunted growth of West German culture,
declared, "Oskar Matzerath, the hero of *The Tin Drum*, is the representative of
[West German] consciousness . . . from a certain point on it refused to grow,
it has become old, but it still likes to play the child" (L2). Oskar represented
what Schirrmacher called the "frozenness, the timeless ageing of the Federal
Republic" (L1), and its failure to develop beyond the experience of a single
generation, that of Grass's and Kohl's *Flakhelfer*. Both Syberberg and Schirrmacher were suggesting that with German reunification, it was time for German culture to leave Oskar and everything he symbolized for them—stunted
growth, grotesqueness, and an excessively critical spirit—to the past, moving
forward to a new, more normal, and more innocent Germany.

It is notable that both these critics, although they refer to Grass's novel, actually
seem to be responding more to Schlöndorff's film. In Grass's novel Oskar does
indeed grow up to become an adult, albeit a highly problematic one, whereas
Schlöndorff's film ends just as Oskar is beginning his journey to the West and
toward adulthood. Syberberg's and Schirrmacher's attacks are testaments to the
power of Oskar as both a metaphor for and a criticism of Germany specifically
and of Western culture in general, something surely intended by both Grass and
Schlöndorff. Although the two critics attack Oskar primarily as a representative
of childishness, what seems to bother them most is Oskar's—and, by implication,
postwar Germany's and the postwar West's—lack of innocence. In this way they
are very much like Oklahomans for Children and Families, and perhaps also like
some of my students. For all of them, childhood innocence provides an alibi for
adults' desecration of innocence. As Cross observes, "in the final analysis, modern innocence has let adults evade the consequences of their own contradictory
lives" (206). If childhood is innocent and good, then the adults who made such a
childhood possible cannot have been all bad. It is that alibi that both Grass and
Schlöndorff successfully destroy in *The Tin Drum*. It is no wonder that censors
want to protect people from both the novel and the film.

Keeping Time: Sound and Image in Volker Schlöndorff's Film *Die Blechtrommel*

Margaret Setje-Eilers

One of the most intriguing aspects of Volker Schlöndorff's celebrated 1979 film adaptation of Günter Grass's novel *Die Blechtrommel* is that it maintains unity while keeping time with many different characters through a long period of history. Aurality and visuality, the very strategies that engage, focus, and keep our attention, also help in teaching this cinematic classic. In this essay, I present activities, both in and out of the classroom, that help students identify ways in which the film keeps time, not only by salvaging and representing time as memory but also by presenting characters who follow and keep time with the beat of the majority and who keep time from progressing by holding on to a state of prolonged childhood. In other words, students will consider how sound and image keep time by re-creating, referencing, and critiquing history.

Schlöndorff's film is included in German 270, German Film, an upper-level survey course that introduces students to cinematographic principles and the skills of reading films in the historical context of German cinema. Since the course also attracts students from disciplines outside the German department, the language of instruction is English, and films are viewed in German with English subtitles. The course covers five units: Weimar Cinema, Early Sound Cinema, Nazi and Post-war Rubble Cinema, New German Cinema, and Post-Wall Cinema.[1] Course requirements are nine response papers, a sequence analysis of a video clip of choice that should demonstrate interrelated cinematic techniques and themes in a film from the course, a paper based on this presentation, a midterm, and a final exam.

In tandem with the chronological structure, the course is also organized around three groups of cinematic devices: image, movement, and sound. In most cases, we spend three days on each film. Before the screenings on day 1, I distribute lists of cinematic terms I consider important for the specific film and ask each student to prepare definitions of certain terms. We discuss these concepts before viewing the films. In one-page response papers due on the second day, students show how a certain technique on the list—for instance, framing or editing—helps convey a particular theme. We follow this strategy for almost every film we view, since the writing exercise gives students practice in discussing important cinematic devices central to creating meaning in the film. Although focusing on individual techniques may be reductive, it demonstrates that certain filmic devices express particular concepts effectively or solve specific problems well, and the approach keeps students from being overwhelmed by having too much to discuss. In Schlöndorff's film, our focus is on image and sound, but, because the film is long, we review the terms the day before the screening.

In discussing *Die Blechtrommel*, it is essential to keep aural and visual techniques in mind, for this film multiplies meanings of keeping time by infusing images and tunes with ambiguity, such as Oskar Matzerath's drum, his scream, and the song about the ubiquitous Black Cook. The resulting climate of vacillation affects not only sound and image but also the film's triangular geometry. In repeated constellations of three characters, a woman darts between two men, taking the indecisive role of a sympathizer supporting two causes at once. Agnes Matzerath (Angela Winkler) moves between Jan Bronski (Daniel Olbrychski) and her husband, Alfred Matzerath (Mario Adorf); Maria (Katharina Thalbach) flits between Oskar (David Bennent) and Alfred; and Roswitha Ranguna (Mariella Oliveri) positions herself between Oskar and Bebra (Fritz Hakl). Triangulated relationships can result in uncertain parentage, and consequently the paternity of Oskar as well as of Kurt, who is possibly Oskar's son, remains unclear. Beginning with such observations of ambiguity, I ask students to identify similar instances in which a theme or an image invites an interpretation that is challenged in a subsequent sequence. The idea is to enable students to draw tentative conclusions from the film's own ongoing revision of visual and aural material, so that they learn to articulate ways in which this film uses sound and image to portray history and reconstruct memory.

The first class meeting on *Die Blechtrommel* is devoted to screening the film. On the second day, after students turn in response papers, we isolate several important metaphors based on image and view clips to inspire discussion. On the third day, I explore with students how select songs intersect with and critically reflect historic events—in other words, how music keeps time in the film. Our objective is to examine how the film uses cinematic techniques to present the possibility for change and protest, specifically in the case of Oskar, who ignores the call to action. The format on day three differs from the third day for other films in the course, since I do not show clips to inspire discussion. Instead, students or small groups hold five-minute presentations to show how music recreates both ahistorical and historical moments and interweaves them into the film's fictional background. Information is available on the Internet for topics ranging from the history of Danzig, for students who need to work in English, to individual songs, for students who can read German. Not every song needs to be assigned, since they all show in some way how music keeps time by recovering history, creating cultural identity through historic events, and thus arresting time in an ahistorical sense. The process of isolating and critically examining these musical segments from the film and its historical setting naturally involves extracting these moments from their historical continuum. In the final exam, students need to comment on topics such as the cinematic representation of history, memory, or childhood, or they can do a comparative film analysis. Frank Beyer's *Jacob the Liar*, which also uses the focus of childhood, lends itself particularly well to a comparison with *Die Blechtrommel*.

Since New German Cinema pays particular attention to the past, we explore the critical stance of Rainer Werner Fassbinder's *The Marriage of Maria*

Braun (1979) with regard to German postwar history. Before screening *Die Blechtrommel*, we review our discussion of how Fassbinder's film represents history, and I ask students to reread Anton Kaes's "The Presence of the Past: Rainer Werner Fassbinder's *The Marriage of Maria Braun*," for his observations on the nexus of fiction and history are also relevant to Schlöndorff's film: "The viewer senses, even if unconsciously, the unresolvable dual status of historical narratives, as document and fiction, authentically true and at the same time used within a freely invented story" (88). In addition, I assign Frederick W. Ott's short essay on the film, for despite some factual errors it provides a good plot summary. Students also receive handouts on the film with information from the *Internet Movie Database*.

To understand how history is organized through sound and image in *Die Blechtrommel*, students review select cinematic terms before the 142-minute film screening. We open our cinematic toolboxes and review terms concerning image, such as framing, camera distance, and camera angle as well as different types of sound, including dialogue, voice-over narration, ambient sound, sound bridges, sound flashback / flash forward, and the difference between diegetic and nondiegetic sound and space—that is, the difference between the environment inside and outside the story line. The diegetic-nondiegetic distinction is a crucial aspect of the architectural design of sound and space in *Die Blechtrommel*. Oskar lives and speaks in both worlds, in the events of the unfolding story and in a vague space outside these events, occupying an undefined position from which he narrates. Likewise, diegetic music originates in the narrative world and is heard by the characters; nondiegetic music plays outside the world of the characters. While Oskar's narration seems unconcerned with keeping time in nondiegetic space, timekeepers densely populate the diegetic world.

The diegetic space of the film overflows with ideas, events, and characters. There are so many that the sheer number was one of the daunting tasks facing Schlöndorff, who collaborated with Jean-Claude Carrière, Franz Seitz, and Grass in adapting Grass's novel of roughly eight hundred pages. The story line, or diegesis (including remembered or imagined events), proceeds from 1899, when Joseph Koljaiczek (Roland Teubner) hides in a potato field under Anna's (Tina Engel) four-layered skirt, to the end of the Second World War in 1945, when Oskar leaves Danzig.

I begin the discussion of the film's images by asking students to name what they consider to be the most powerful visual experiences. Students typically mention the child, the tin drum, and the horse's head, topics they have often selected for their response papers. In examining the metaphoric referents for these images, we discover that their associations are not fixed but shift across a range of historic events and areas of cultural identity. Thus we need to ask how the ambiguity of the metaphors comments on and critiques history.

The child as a cultural symbol initially creates an atmosphere of innocence and anticipation of the future in the story, since it refers to a (third) birthday with its promise of a tin drum (see Brockmann's essay in this volume). Yet the significance of Oskar's childlike, distorted viewpoint changes dramatically. Students remark that the perspective of the child seems to take a critical stance toward the older generation, first from his vantage point inside the womb and later in the upside-down perspective of the 1924 birth scene and the many low-angle shots. But they note that this point of view gradually takes on aspects of evil. For example, to establish a reason for not growing, Oskar allows public opinion to pronounce Mazerath guilty of leaving the cellar door open for him to plummet to the bottom of the stairs on his third birthday. Eleven years old while performing in the film, David Bennent as Oskar is a narrator whose reliability cannot always be trusted. As he takes on more sinister characteristics—for example, by luring Bronski into the Polish Post Office and thus leading to his assassination by German troops—his stunted growth acquires a negative aura.

Oskar's refusal to grow shifts from what first seems to be a means of maintaining critical distance from the questionable double standards of the parent generation to making time stand still. In other words, Oskar's three-year-old perspective initially signifies resistance to become like his elders, but later it is an attempt to keep time from progressing. When students recognize the multilayered metaphoric images of the child as potential critique of the older generation, they can view Oskar on a more abstract level, as the embodiment of a German nation of onlookers and sympathizers during the Third Reich, people who did not protest, who refused in a childlike stance to take responsibility. Seen from this perspective, Oskar reflects Grass's view of Nazism as "the infantilism of an epoch and a society" (qtd. in Ott 289). Our discussion of the Hitler Youth in conjunction with songs on the third day suggests further links between the child in Oskar and the vision of youth in the National Socialist agenda as the future of the nation.

The polysemy in the images of the child trying to stop time inspires students to join Oskar and unwrap the layers around the package containing his various tin drums. In a short brainstorming session, groups of students isolate some associations of holding and beating a drum. The first sound of beating for Oskar is of course his mother's heartbeat. Accordingly, his drumming is linked to Agnes. As the externalized heartbeat of Oskar and perhaps the German nation as well, the drum conjures up other images, such as warning, protest, war, marching, and soldiers. Most of these images are inspired by the sequence at the Nazi rally, when Oskar disrupts the military music by changing the rhythm of the event with his drumming. Here, he experiences firsthand that he can make everyone follow a new beat, his beat, and thereby discovers his drum's potential for changing as well as for keeping time. He turns the straight-lined 4/4 beat of district leader Löbsack's march into a chaotic jumble of people twirling to the 3/4 rhythm of the Blue Danube Waltz with much enjoyment and almost gracefully, until a thunderstorm disperses the rally. Students comment that high-angle shots of Oskar drumming from his hiding place under the platform imply his weak position, while low-angle shots of musicians in the Hitler Youth suggest their superior stance. Later, straight-on shots during the waltz indicate that musicians and rally attendees have relinquished their elevated position.

Although Oskar learns in the Nazi rally sequence that his power for change lies in his drumming, he never goes on to realize this important aspect of the drum, the potential for protest. Instead, he keeps the beat of the political environment around him. Students notice that Bronski and the Jewish toy merchant Sigismund Markus (Charles Aznavour) are also associated with and desperately need to use the drum's ability to warn or change the beat, but their vague insights lead to nothing more than providing Oskar with drums and encouraging his drumming. Alfred, who finds Oskar's drum annoying and wants to take it away, voices no criticism of the prewar social situation, and he becomes an ardent party member. Much later, Oskar joins Bebra's Nazi entertainment group and leads a march of little people on a bunker at the Normandy coast. As they sing a children's song about the much-feared black witch (a topic on day 3), his drumming keeps time with the music. At a Nazi event shortly thereafter, he beats his drum in time to the same song, but it is soon interrupted by air-raid sirens and the Allied invasion. In contrast to Kattrin in Brecht's play *Mutter Courage und ihre Kinder* (1941; *Mother Courage and Her Children*), whose successful drumming warns a whole town, Oskar sinks into complacency, and the power of his drum to dissent fizzles into failed protest.

We next turn to the perplexing and startling image of the eel-filled dead horse's head (see Schade's essay in this volume). Walking along the beach, Oskar, Agnes, Jan, and Alfred see a fisherman who pulls eels out of a horse's head used as bait. When the man enthusiastically recalls the size of the eels after the naval battle at the Skagerrak (1916), the image keeps time by salvaging the historic event in which thousands lost their lives when ships on the British and German sides were destroyed. Thus the image of the eels packed into the horse's head unites the incompatible drives of life and death. On another level, Agnes is pregnant again, the child's paternity is unsure, and she associates her intense feelings of guilt with the fish, the traditional sign of the church for Christ. Later, she dies by gorging on fish, literally embodying her guilt. By shifting from extremely long to medium shots to close-ups, the camera forces viewers to concentrate on Agnes's shock and nausea, while extremely long shots distance viewers from Oskar's drumming and his lack of emotional response. In this sequence, fiction and documented history are closely intertwined, and while the meeting with the fisherman causes Agnes to reflect on her life, we see how unmoved Oskar is. In the next class meeting, we examine more closely whether characters in the diegetic world of Danzig process and reflect on history—in other words, if and how they keep time.

To contextualize their presentations on sound and music, students need to know about the status of Danzig as a free city, Poland's right since the Versailles Treaty to maintain postal, telephone, and telegraph systems there, and the role of Danzig's Polish Post Office at the beginning of the Second World War. These research topics can be assigned as homework, or a summary can be distributed before the film screening. A short overview of Danzig in English should address the Kashubian minority and the triangulated, tricultural makeup of Danzig's Germans, Poles, and Kashubians. The film documents the German assault on the Polish Post Office, an act of aggression that initiated the Second World War, and re-creates the annexation of Danzig into the German Reich on 1 September 1939, from the German attack and flamethrowers to the Polish surrender and assassinations in October.

The film shows the battle in the Polish Post Office through Oskar's mostly silent observation, framed by two narrative statements from an undefined time after the events. Therefore, as a prelude to the short oral reports on sound, we analyze Oskar's narrative position inside and outside the story line and ask how the unifying strategy of his voice-over narration relates to his silence at the time. In other words, we search for a point at which language, history, and silence intersect. The role of silence merits attention, since Oskar's failure to use his noise-making skills effectively and his frequent silence in the diegesis collide with his almost incessant talking in the nondiegetic world, the technique of voice-over. Oskar discovers early that his strengths lie in the sounds he can make, yet his language vacuum and voyeuristic stance become emblems of his unwillingness to make sounds of protest. During long stretches of observation in the diegetic world, his silence replicates and implicates the virtual lack of critical language in the Third Reich. We conclude that at some point mute critical observation turns into failure of critique and unvoiced acceptance.

In the voice-over and in those instances when he does talk, Oskar refers to himself in both the first and third persons, using his name like a child that has not yet mastered the "I" form. For example, he announces at Greff's vegetable shop, "Oskar schreiben lernen" ("Oskar learn to write"). Linguistically, this practice indicates that he has not yet self-individuated; politically, viewers might implicate the German population in this critique.

In our discussion, I prompt students to consider that voice-over narration also links Oskar and postwar Germany in terms of conscience. Voice-over offers an opportunity for reflection and criticism of past actions, but neither the more objective flashback technique nor the omnipresent childlike voice with its tale of the past undertakes these tasks. The characters in the story line, as well as Oskar the storyteller, refrain from critical assessment. Students are reminded that Kaes makes a similar point about *The Marriage of Maria Braun*: "The characters in the film neither discuss nor reflect upon such major historic events as the founding of the Federal Republic, the final division of Germany in 1949, or the uprising in East Berlin in 1953" ("Presence" 87). Although the thirty-year-old narrator in Grass's novel explains that he is writing his story in a mental institution after the war, the narrative position and age of the narrator in the film remain ambiguous. Standing at Mazerath's grave at the end of the film, Oskar announces that he is in his twenty-first year of life. We can calculate that the year is 1944, yet we have no such temporal reference point for Oskar's voice-over that simply announces, "Ich beginne weit vor mir" ("I'll begin long before I ever existed . . ."). Floating in an undefined narrative present, Oskar the narrator has no time to keep, contrary to the sounds and music that do capture and represent history as memory in the space of the film.

After Oskar's voice-over introduces the post office attack sequence, the Polish employees hear fast-paced gunfire, while the audience hears slow, dreamy piano music as well. Therefore this sequence provides an opportunity to review the distinction between diegetic sound (gunfire) and nondiegetic sound (piano). Because the musical leitmotifs for various characters also fall into the category of nondiegetic sound, I ask why certain tunes are repeatedly associated with the same characters—for example, Anna, Sigismund, and Oskar. Oskar and the drumming motif are obvious, but many other leitmotifs in Maurice Jarre's sound track, including the sound track during the opening and closing credits, help manage a large group of characters in a protracted time frame. For instance, the reoccurrence of Anna's theme, with an added twang when Joseph appears, invites viewers to associate her with the Kashubians, who as Anna says are the underdogs for people to beat up on. In a small musical leap, the twang of minority abuse becomes associated with the Jewish chime theme, a leitmotif that evokes the magical fairy-tale world of the toy store, full of tin drums, silk stockings, plans for escape to London, and unrequited love for Agnes. Sigismund's shopwindows are broken on Kristallnacht, and the chime motif plays during a close-up of Oskar's silent observation of the suicide scene. Now it is apparent that the leitmotif of clattering broken glass has foreshadowed the historic occurrences of the night of 9–10 November 1938.

The most memorable diegetic sound for many students is Oskar's piercing scream. When Oskar screams to stop Mazerath from tugging at his drum to take it away, he is as surprised as everyone else when the glass of the clock shatters. This instant is one of many in which a very long lens foregrounds intensity and power in an extreme close-up of Oskar's face, while blurring the background. His act of protest seems to stop time by breaking the clock, but the ticking continues and the pendulum sways back and forth in a low-angle point-of-view close-up.

Oskar subsequently tests the power of his scream with extraordinarily grotesque results. He breaks his teacher's glasses, and he sends contents of the glass containers in his doctor's office plunging to the floor. From a position of superiority, a high-angle vantage point in the famous Marienkirche bell tower, he demolishes the windows in surrounding buildings, including a cheap hotel where his mother and her lover Jan have just spent a passionate moment. The camera comments in a long shot that distances Oskar from the destruction, as the sound of shattered glass admonishes his mother and foreshadows the Kristallnacht and Oskar's Nazi allegiance (sound flash-forward). Later, he shows off for Bebra by exploding several lightbulbs after visiting the circus. Finally, he allows the political system to appropriate him. What might have become a mighty *Urschrei* in the magnitude of Edvard Munch's *The Scream* ends trivially, simply etching a heart in Roswitha's champagne glass. Dressed in a diminutive German army uniform and introduced as "Oskar, der Trommler, Oskar, der

Glastöter" ("Oskar the drummer! Oskar the glass killer!") with Bebra's ironic good wishes ("Mazel tov"), Oskar uses his scream to break wine and champagne glasses while performing for Nazi troops in France.

Probing their visual memory, students find that the inherent protest of the scream remains as undeveloped as the potential of the tin drum, and they relate Oskar's failure to utilize the hidden power of his "Wunderwaffe" ("secret weapon") to the insufficient protest of the German population during the Third Reich. Although Oskar's strength lies in the sounds Oskar can make, drumming or screaming, he remains essentially silent and chooses the role of observer, admitting after the circus encounter with Bebra, "Wissen Sie, Herr Bebra, wissen Sie, ich rechne mich lieber zu den Zuschauern und lasse meine kleine Kunst im Verborgenen" (cf. 144 in the book) ("You know, Mr. Bebra, to tell the truth I prefer to be a member of the audience and let my little art flower in secret" [my trans.]). Students familiar with Tom Tykwer's *Run Lola Run* (1998) remember that in contrast to Oskar's impotent screams, Lola's two post-Wall glass-shattering screams of protest spur her on to achieve her goal, saving her partner, Manni (who ironically saves himself).

While Oskar vacillates among drumming, screaming, and silence, his mother, Agnes, sings a melodious, traditional love song: "Wer hat uns getraut?" ("Who Married Us?"). The student researcher will find that the song is an aria from Johann Strauss's operetta *Der Zigeunerbaron* (1885; *The Gypsy Baron*) (act 2, scene 3). Sung by Agnes and Jan on Oskar's third birthday in 1927, while Agnes plays the piano, the lyrics suggest that they are as deeply in love as Barinkay and Saffi, married by a bird:

> BARINKAY. Wer hat uns getraut? Ei sprich!
> SAFFI. Sag' Du's!
> BARINKAY. Der Dompfaff, der hat uns getraut!
>
> BARINKAY. Who married us? Go on, tell them!
> SAFFI. You tell them!
> BARINKAY. The cardinal bird married us.

Their relationship, like Agnes and Jan's, is already marked by sexual love, as Strauss hints at offspring. Here, the lack of historical context is revealing. Almost half a century old, the song by the Austrian composer has no German patriotic connections, and it is also ahistoric, far removed from history and time. Similarly, the lovers Agnes and Jan physically separate themselves from the mundane conversation of the other guests. Their music keeps time from encroaching into their lives by encapsulating them. It seals them in a vacuum of historical unconsciousness, as did the unwillingness of many people in pre-Hitler days to heed the danger signs of rightist politics and acknowledge the existence of a historical present.

In contrast to the love song by Strauss, the children's song "Ist die schwarze Köchin da?" ("Is the Black Witch Here?") awakens associations of childhood anxiety, abuse, and historic exclusion. Borrowed from the novel, the ambiguous lyrics give voice to underlying fears that allow many referents, including Hitler, Jews, the Allies, and even Oskar himself. The Black Cook or Witch with a pot conjures up images of Frau Holle, who, besides making snow in the Grimms' fairy tale of the same name, administers her own form of justice. In the Grimms' tale about two half sisters, the beautiful, hardworking sister is rewarded, while the lazy, ugly sister is punished when Frau Holle dumps a pot of pitch over her. Marked for life, this sister can never rid herself of her blackness, and thus the tale hints at anti-Semitism. The Nazi reading of this fairy tale would cast the daughter covered with pitch as Jew. To deconstruct this fairy tale, one should consider reversing cause and effect: the daughter covered with pitch is lazy and ugly. Along the lines of Jack Zipes's observation that fairy tales were interpreted differently during National Socialism, anti-Semitic sentiment in the tale might also explain the alternative title, "Goldmarie und Pechmarie" ("Gold Mary and Pitch Mary" [140]). We know which group was the target for Hitler's pot of pitch.

The song is a leitmotif with a shifting referent, so its meaning varies. When a group of children led by Oskar almost interrupt a Nazi march down the street, the song appears exclusionary, expressing protest and criticism of Hitler as the Black Cook with a pot of pitch. The singing children march behind the drumming Oskar. They stop and wait in eager anticipation for him to punctuate the song by breaking a streetlight. Seconds later, a Nazi parade comes around the corner, but although the children cut in front of the standard bearer, they fail to deter the Nazis. Instead, their small procession seems to mock the Nazis as members of another children's gang, as eternal children who keep time from progressing into adulthood and who fear an uncertain black entity. As both groups keep marching, each song continues in sync with its own beat, and each parade keeps time to its own music. Later, some of the same youngsters who stood behind Oskar in admiration when he broke the streetlight now exclude him and force him to drink soup they have concocted in a pot. Toward the end of the film, the song is integrated into Nazi ideology at a show given by "Bebras Fronttheater" ("Bebra's Front Line Theater") in France, while Oskar keeps time on his drum. Now, the Black Cook stands for the Jew. The song that first mocked the Nazis becomes a song of solidarity among Nazis and their sympathizers, and at the same time it is an exclusionary song about Jews: "Ist die schwarze Köchin da? Nein, nein, nein! Dreimal muß ich 'rum marschieren, 'vierte Mal den Topf verlieren, 's fünfte Mal komm mit!" The English subtitles cast the witch as a powerful, feared being: "Is the black witch here today? No, no, no. She will make an evil brew. She will put you in her stew and then she will devour you. Is the black witch here today? Yes, yes, yes. Look there she is."

Despite or rather as a result of its suggestive eroticism, Zarah Leander's song "Kann denn Liebe Sünde sein?" ("Can Love Be a Sin?") from her film *Der Blaufuchs* (1938; "The Blue Fox") established itself in the pop culture of Hitler's Germany. As Maria sings a few lines from it while she washes the stairs, she wags her behind in time to the music. These moments give Oskar great pleasure before their beach outing, and they also suggest to the viewer that Maria is susceptible to the beat of the majority. Leander (1907–81) is regarded as a cinematic femme fatale who subverted important gender aspects of Nazi culture. Her songs do not celebrate women in the roles of mother and homemaker but overflow instead with transgressive sexual allusion. Eric Rentschler writes that Leander's position "ran counter to Nazi notions of a contained and dutiful femininity" and that she "challenged Nazi prudery" with her unconcealed eroticism (*Ministry* 128). In the context of the film, the song "Kann denn Liebe Sünde sein" comments ironically on Maria's role as she performs a homemaker's task, washing the stairs. Maria, already established as a Catholic, sings only a sampling of the tune—later heard on the radio—but enough to show that the lyrics are about love without the context of marriage: "Liebe kann nicht Sünde sein, doch wenn sie es wär', dann wär's mir egal" ("Love can't be a sin, but if it were, then I wouldn't care").

Singing Leander's pop song, regardless of its sexual innuendos, places the sixteen-year-old Maria in the context of passive Nazi sympathizers. Leander's notoriously celebrated career won her the status of "one of the most popular female star figures of Nazi Germany, arguably even *the* most popular, male or female, within and beyond the borders of the Third Reich" (Ascheid 155). Later, when the song is played on the radio, one could interpret it as ironic commentary on Maria's own sexual adventures. Her sexual encounter with Matzerath, interrupted by Oskar, results in pregnancy, marriage to Matzerath, and bearing a child whose paternity is unknown. Leander's song happens to be playing on the radio when Oskar turns it on to console Maria after intruding on the lovers. His attempt to reconcile reveals his particular combination of innocence and malice.

Leander's radio voice resounds in the Matzerath household in defense of Maria's sexual encounter with her employer, for she still works as the family maid and marries Matzerath only much later. But no one excuses Maria, least of all Oskar, who is infatuated with her, who is jealous of her affair with Matzerath, and who has just intervened in her lovemaking at a crucial moment. Because Leander's voice enters the Matzerath household via radio, it is crucial to inquire why the film has radio play such a significant role. What role did it play in the Third Reich? Hitler's first radio address took place on 31 January 1933, the day after he became chancellor. Agnes is impatient to have Hitler's voice in the Matzerath home; Hitler can be heard on all her friends' radios, she tells her husband angrily after returning from her rendezvous with Jan. Soon Matzerath dramatically unveils a radio, and as he replaces Beethoven's image with a picture of Hitler, we hear jazz playing. When Mazerath leaves to attend a Nazi rally, Oskar switches the radio station from jazz, music the Nazis considered degenerate, to a speaker at the National Socialist gathering, and the speech becomes a sound bridge to the rally Oskar will disrupt by drumming to his own beat. In this context, I ask students to consider the role radio assumed in German mass culture beginning in the 1930s and how it helped create support for the Nazi regime.

The radio also plays several popular Nazi songs, and in this respect the film keeps time in songs that re-create the context and beliefs of National Socialism. In addition, the grocer Greff (played by David Bennent's father, Heinz Bennent) sings several tunes that invite research on the Hitler Youth and its connection to the scouts (*Pfadfinder*). Greff, both gay and vegetarian, is a former scout leader who is closely associated with the Hitler Youth. In the company of three of its members, he sings a few bars of "Wann wir schreiten Seit' an Seit'" (1939; "When We Walk Side by Side"). The text was written by Hermann Claudius, who signed the Oath of Loyalty of the German Poets in 1933 and became a strong supporter of Hitler. Gathering information from Web sites on the Hitler Youth and its appropriation of the scouts, students can discover the central Nazi conviction that the future of Germany lay in the hands of the younger genera-tion. Claudius's song, with its glorification of youth and the future of Germany, squarely supports this ideology. Discussion in class can thus focus on how the theme of the child relates to Nazi tenets. In his refusal to grow, Oskar appears to be a grotesque rendition of the Nazi cult of youth. The film editing unmistak-ably connects the Hitler Youth and childhood with the theme of stunted child-hood in Oskar and the Third Reich, for after Oskar's miniature parade crosses the Nazi march, the film cuts to Greff's vegetable store, where Greff and several Hitler Youths sing part of Claudius's song.

At a dinner celebrating Kurt's baptism, Greff also sings several bars of a popu-lar song by Werner Altendorf, a writer and member of the Reichstag, Hitler's puppet parliament: "Ein junges Volk steht auf, zum Sturm bereit! Reißt die Fahnen höher, Kameraden!" ("A young nation arises, ready for the attack! Hold the flags higher, comrades!" [trans. mine]). This choice tune of the Hitler Youth explains that the older generation expects unconditional devotion from young soldiers, promising in return God's support. Greff prefaces this song with a few bars from "Das Engellandlied" ("The England Song"), a song about the imag-ined conquest of England. At the same time, another Nazi song plays on the radio. No one appears to listen to this jumble of Nazi tunes, but everyone is confident that Germany will win the war soon. By singing the melody from the Hitler Youth, Greff gives the naval song the perspective of childhood, and little Kurt's loud gurgling in the background reminds viewers that National Socialism is cast as infantilism in its strategy of keeping Germany in a lasting state of child-hood and thus blocking the transition into adulthood. Because students have explored the prominent role of childhood, they can understand that the musical ambiguity of the Nazi songs emerges from the ironical relation between the historical context and the fictional story line, Oskar's refusal to grow. The Nazi music lures Oskar's family members away from wartime events and invites them to retreat into the safe realm of childhood.

During the two days we discuss the interacting images of the child, the drum, and the horse's head, as well as music, drumming, and voice-over narration, students become aware of the many ways that images and sound keep time. Because we have considered Fassbinder's re-creation of wartime and postwar

Germany in *The Marriage of Maria Braun*, students are receptive to the critique voiced in *Die Blechtrommel*. But they are hardly prepared for the magic realism that Schlöndorff's film adopts from Grass's novel. A short student presentation on the characteristics of magic realism, with examples from the film, usually clarifies their bewilderment. It also helps to have students identify aspects of National Socialism that appear to us today as unreal so that they can come to understand the function of magic realism in the film.

As a summary exercise, I assign students the songs discussed in this essay (texts and background information can be found through Internet searches) and ask them to analyze how these songs relate to time and history, either by keeping time from progressing or by re-creating moments of National Socialist history.[2] The songs they explore range from ahistorical tunes to those associated with Nazi Party members and sympathizers in the setting of Danzig before and during the war. As students discover, the music reveals that many characters are content to keep time with the pack and march to the same beat instead of trying to change the rhythm of history.

The images and songs investigated in discussions and presentations re-create to some extent the environment of citizens who appropriate National Socialism and are appropriated by it. By looking at and listening to the musical-cultural environment of Strauss, children's songs, Leander, Nazi tunes, family feasts, and the Mazerath dining decor, students become aware that National Socialism attracted not only destitute, unemployed people. The film presents members of a rather comfortable lower middle class who little understood the power of drums and screams and who were best at keeping time with the beat of the majority. Students also see that Oskar, who dimly recognizes a need for both drumming and screaming, keeps hold of his time, his childhood, and falls silent. Paradoxically, through its rich visual and acoustic signals, Schlöndorff's film sounds a warning against immaturity and silence.

NOTES

[1] The films viewed are Robert Wiene's *The Cabinet of Dr. Caligari*, F. W. Murnau's *Nosferatu*, Fritz Lang's *Metropolis* and *M*, Joseph von Sternberg's *The Blue Angel*, G. W. Pabst's *The Threepenny Opera*, Veit Harlan's *Jew Süss*, excerpts from Leni Riefenstahl's *The Triumph of the Will*, Wolfgang Staudte's *Murderers Are among Us*, Rainer Werner Fassbinder's *The Marriage of Maria Braun*, Volker Schlöndorff's *Die Blechtrommel*, Frank Beyer's *Jacob the Liar*, Sönke Wortmann's *Maybe, Maybe Not*, Tom Tykwer's *Run Lola Run* and *The Princess and the Warrior*, and Caroline Link's *Nowhere in Africa*.

[2] The songs are "Wer hat uns getraut?" ("Der Zigeunerbaron," by Johann Strauss), "Ist die schwarze Köchin da?" (children's song), "Kann denn Liebe Sünde sein?" (Zarah Leander, *The Blue Fox* [1938]), "Wann wir schreiten Seit' an Seit'" and "Ein junges Volk steht auf" (Hitler Youth songs).

Storytelling and Desire
in the Film *Die Blechtrommel*

Susan C. Anderson

Volker Schlöndorff's award-winning film *Die Blechtrommel* (1979; *The Tin Drum*) attracted worldwide attention for its criticism of the German petite bourgeoisie during the first half of the twentieth century and for David Bennent's riveting performance as Oskar Matzerath (Mayer-Iswandy, *Günter Grass* 149). The film presents the story of Oskar, his family, and acquaintances as an analogy to the history of Germany during this time. Yet this narrative also calls attention to its fictionality. It does so through the figure of Oskar as storyteller and through the ways the story unfolds. Oskar is a conflicted figure; he desires both to narrate his story and to evade it. These contradictory impulses parallel how the film both uses and calls into question conventional forms of storytelling, now affirming, now frustrating spectators' expectations. But students are at times so disoriented by the film's alienation effects that they have difficulty making sense of such processes.

An analysis of the formal elements in selected scenes from Schlöndorff's film can help sharpen their focus. Students scrutinize each scene or sequence for manifestations in the action and dialogue of desire to narrate or of fear to narrate. They analyze how these expressions relate to the use of perspective, sound, symbolic objects, and so on. The following approach uses theories about narrative desire to reveal the dynamics between the film's form and content. It shows how storytelling techniques and thematics oscillate along a continuum between the two poles of desire and fear in these selected scenes and sequences: Kashubian Potato Field, Oskar's Birth, Oskar's Third Birthday—Fall down Cellar Stairs, Greff's Vegetable Shop, Oskar and Anna Bronski by Fire, Kristallnacht—Toy Shop, Train Taking Oskar Away, Kashubian Potato Field (these scenes are listed in Schlöndorff's *Tagebuch* [142–47]; see also Reimer and Zachau 119–42). Once students understand how these dynamics function, they can explore links between the film and the ethics of memory in postwar Germany. Such an approach will also help connect the film to German culture and politics in the 1970s (when the film appeared) and to the present.

This essay gives examples of how to teach the film *Die Blechtrommel* in either an advanced undergraduate-graduate course on German narrative and film (taught in English) or in an advanced course on Günter Grass for German majors and graduate students (taught in German). My suggestions are based on my experiences teaching similar courses. The scene analyses and short reports on narrative theory (augmented with information on Grass, Schlöndorff, and postwar German culture from a course Web site and short lectures from the instructor) could be done in either course in three class hours. It is important for students to consider how the story is narrated cinematically in order to understand what is being narrated. They do not have to read the novel to see the film as a form of narrative, but the instructor may wish to refer to the novel to provide a broader context for discussion. In a course specifically on Grass, the film would be introduced only after discussing in detail his aesthetic concerns and the literary traditions in which he works. Students can make presentations of Grass's essays "Der Inhalt als Widerstand" (1957; "The Content as Resistance"), "Über meinen Lehrer Döblin" (1967; "On My Teacher Döblin"), "Rückblick auf *Die Blechtrommel* oder Der Autor als fragwürdiger Zeuge" (1973; "*The Tin Drum* in Retrospect; or, The Author as Dubious Witness"), and "Schreiben nach Auschwitz" (1990; "Writing after Auschwitz"). These texts explain his focus on the petite bourgeoisie, among whom Hitler's politics found broad support (Krumme 103–08; Thomas, *Grass* 13–14). They furthermore illustrate his choice of literary genres, his skepticism regarding art for art's sake, his view of politics and art, and his ideas about history and individual responsibility.

These issues are also linked to Grass's concerns about German accountability for fascism and for the part each person plays in shaping history. With his emphasis on the interface of politics and art, Grass expresses the hope that intellectuals may prompt their audiences to act responsibly. How then, one needs to ask, do Schlöndorff's storytelling techniques address Grass's goal in the medium of film? Oskar challenges viewers to figure out what kind of role he played during the Nazi period. Students should consider how Oskar differs from those around him who supported the Nazis. The novel is permeated with Oskar's feelings of guilt, but how does the film deal with guilt? Is Oskar's desire to tell his story a yearning to assuage his culpability? The scene analyses and suggestions for classroom discussion revolve around these questions.

As the film is an aesthetic rendering of complex ideas and emotions in the form of a visual narrative, students should first review some general characteristics of narratives. For instance, narratives respond to basic needs, as J. Hillis Miller contends. He argues that human beings need narratives to configure their experiences and lend meaning to their lives. Yet every narrated story leaves uncertainty; no narrative can give order to experiences in a completely satisfactory fashion. Thus there is an unquenchable thirst for more narratives (68–72). Although the term *story* can be synonymous with narrative, it is also used to denote a narrative's set of events, as opposed to the term *plot*, which refers to the ordering of events. Peter Brooks posits plot as the driving force of a narrative, and desire (for closure, for meaning) as the engine that propels the plot forward to its inevitable end. His interpretations of selected literary texts show how narrative desire can also permeate the different layers of a narrative, functioning as a central element of the plot. Thus desire helps structure the sequence of events.

Students can learn about Schlöndorff's efforts to render the novel into an engaging film by reading excerpts from his diary and from interviews with him and Grass about the filming process. The most important problem to solve, apparently, was that of the doubled narrative perspective, of the frame Oskar, in a mental institution in 1950s West Germany, and the experiencing Oskar. Instead of complicating the film with flashbacks, Schlöndorff decided to omit the frame narrative, centering on the child Oskar's perspective (23). He rejected the idea of having a small adult play Oskar, because, in his words, "sich dann jeder sagt, das sind Zwergprobleme, das ist das Problem eines Zwergs, das interessiert mich nicht" (24) ("then everyone says those are dwarf problems, that's the problem of a dwarf, that doesn't interest me" [trans. mine]). The director needed a child actor, but it had to be someone who could also appear mature and someone with whom the spectator could identify. Schlöndorff stated, "Meine Filme sind nur gut, wenn ich mich mit einer Person so identifizieren kann, dass sie mir den Einstieg möglich macht" (39) ("My films are good only when I can identify myself with a person in such a way that the person allows me an entry"). This desire for identification counters the function of the novel's narrator, who, deceptive and grotesque, prevents identification. Yet even in the film, as Schlöndorff recounts, "Es gelingt nicht immer, in Oskars Haut zu schlüpfen. So wie er von sich bald in der ersten, bald kindlich verfremdend in der dritten Person spricht, muß auch die Filmerzählung mal ganz subjektiv sein, mal ihn erschrocken von außen zeigen" (44) ("It's not always possible to slip into Oscar's skin. Just as he speaks of himself at times in the first person, at times in the third person, in a childlike and alienating manner, the film narrative must sometimes be entirely subjective, sometimes show him terrified from an outside perspective"). But the subjective element is very strong.

Before students deal with any one scene, they should have viewed the entire film, so they can draw connections between overall themes and techniques and those introduced in the first scene. One way to make it easier to compare scenes is to place copies of the DVD of the film on reserve and to digitize key scenes on a password-protected class Web site. Students can then view the scenes as many times as they wish and prepare study questions in advance. In class, these scenes can then be shown again, but students, given time to reflect beforehand, should have a more stimulating intellectual exchange. Issues for discussion are the use of sound, color, speech, perspective, space, and movement and how these cinematic devices help express different forms of desire and fear.

A careful analysis of the film's first scene provides the entry point for addressing which forms of desire are apparent in the film. *Die Blechtrommel* begins as a fictional family history, thus pointing to the genre of autobiography and its implicit desire to outline a public persona. The film's chronological order reworks the complex structure of the novel into a seemingly straightforward story about Oskar's coming of age. Oskar's first statement, "Ich beginne weit vor mir" ("I'll begin long before I existed"), introduces Oskar as the narrator and also sets the story into motion. By starting far before his birth, he makes clear that he is also telling someone else's story, for he did not experience the events he first narrates. He thus reveals the imaginary dimension of the unfolding scenes, as what Schlöndorff characterizes as "seine pränatalen Vorstellungen" (119) ("his prenatal imaginings"). Schlöndorff aimed to tell an uncomplicated story, but Grass insisted that he include "mehr harten Realismus einerseits, mehr Mut zum Irre-alen andererseits. Phantasie als Teil der Wirklichkeit, Oskars Wirklichkeit" (49) ("More hard realism on the one hand, more courage to show the unreal on the other hand. Fantasy as part of reality, Oskar's reality" [trans. mine]). The combi-nation of Oskar's disembodied voice and the twangy music further emphasizes the scene's fictionality.

The shifts in perspective mark how the narrative is set into motion. Students can observe the changes in camera position to create changes in perspective, which alternates among Oskar as narrator; the figure of his grandmother, Anna Bronski; and an all-encompassing perspective. Robert C. Reimer, Reinhard Zachau, and Margit Sinka describe this last perspective as a "neutral or directo-rial viewpoint" (152). After we hear Oskar's initial statement and see his grand-mother plant herself on the ground, resembling the potatoes she has dug up, the perspective shifts to her point of view as jerkily moving figures appear on the horizon and the Polish character Joseph Koljaiczek runs up, throws him-self before her, begs her to help him, and hides under her skirts. The camera pulls back as we watch the gendarmes search for Joseph. This wider perspective helps convince spectators to believe the tale, according to Reimer, Zachau, and Sinka (153). Yet the neutral viewpoint conflicts with the unrealistic features of the story—the way Joseph impregnates Anna with Agnes, Oskar's mother. Class discussion can focus on how such features help propel the narrative. For one thing, strange elements make us want to hear and see more in order to under-stand the story. In this respect the film resembles the novel, about which Patrick O'Neill asserts that it "gains much of its distinctive fascination precisely from the way in which the discourse pervasively hinders us in determining exactly what the story told really is" (Günter Grass 30).

The film situates Oskar's mother at the transition from a cyclical, generations-old family history to a linear, socially fragmented one, from mythic to modern times, represented by the choice of 1899 as the point of her conception—that is, near the end of the era preceding the "modern" twentieth century (Jahnke and Lindemann 18; Keele, Understanding 13). The tint and speed of the scene on the potato field, imitating the look of early cinema, suggest a distant and strange past, which gives it a timeless quality (Head 361–62; Kilborn 36). This quality links the scene to myth, suggesting that the narrator wishes to universalize his story to be more representative of greater forces than his individual origins.

What aspects of a desire for mythic origins, one might ask students, can be detected in this scene? Note the brown earth tones that predominate and em-phasize the earthiness of the main figure, Oscar's Kashubian grandmother. We see Anna sitting in the field in her four skirts, as if rising out of the earth. Ed-ward Diller interprets this scene as representing the four elements of earth, wind, fire, and water, thereby complementing Anna's evocation of the mythic figure of the Great Mother (8; see also Gockel 49–50; Jahnke and Lindemann 18). Walter Jahnke and Klaus Lindemann also interpret Anna in this way, as a figure of creation. Joseph, the alleged arsonist, is in their view a figure of destruction (19).

Students can then debate whether Anna and Joseph's begetting of Agnes is a merging of creative and destructive elements, elements that lie at the base of Oskar's conflicting drives of desire and fear. Throughout the film, however, Anna remains almost otherworldly, different from her offspring in appearance and character. She returns to the potato field at the end of the film, almost oblivious to the train riding away from her, as if she and the train existed in two different worlds. The two parts of the frame that Anna and the train inhabit contrast with the first scene, in which Joseph invades Anna's space. By comparing these first and last scenes, students can perceive that the loosening ties between Anna's harmonious world and Joseph's destructive one have been dissolved by the film's end. There is no way back for Oskar.

Another thread to explore is how the first scene plays with the Catholic belief of Mary's immaculate conception (Mary's mother was named Anna, according to Christian legend; *Agnes* means "lamb" [Jahnke and Lindemann 18]). The implication is that Oskar shares qualities with the Christ child, a sentiment to which the movie alludes when Oskar hangs his drum around the statue of the Christ child in the church where his mother is saying confession. Both the film and the novel link Oskar's violent tendencies, his longing for messianic power, and Hitler. One way Oskar tries to escape this horrible association is to return to his origins, to his grandmother.

Joseph's hiding under Anna's skirts, as students should note, is the first visual manifestation of desire in the film. Joseph wants to hide under them to save his life. Anna's long, multilayered skirts also point to the layers of the story to be traversed before closure can be achieved or regained, for this very first scene presents a metaphor of closure in the sexual union between Anna and Oskar's grandfather. Although it does not take Joseph long to get under and out from under Anna's skirts, the rest of the story generated by their congress resists closure: Joseph later leaves Anna; Oskar's paternity is unclear; Oskar and Anna part at the end.

Yet the skirts remain a symbol of the promise of fulfilled desire. Oskar attempts several times in the film to hide under them, in a metaphoric effort to return to the safety of the womb, to a time before his story began. But his efforts to merge with his grandmother by crawling under her skirts are repeatedly rebuffed. Instead, he must spin his story further. Thus the end of the film, where he cries out for Anna as the train pulls away, also signals the beginning of another story or phase of his life (recounted only in the third book of Grass's novel, which Schlöndorff also considered filming one day [44]). By analyzing in detail the episodes in which Oskar tries to hide under his grandmother's skirts, students can see how the film connects a desire for the grandmother both to storytelling and to the wish to stop narrating. Each time he tries to take refuge under Anna's skirts, the narrative comes to a halt or turning point and resumes in a different direction (including the final scene's implication that Oskar's journey will continue).

Scholars have interpreted Oskar's attempts to hide under his grandmother's skirts as a longing for death or nonexistence (Neuhaus, *Günter Grass* [2000] 89; Roller 101). His taking cover signals a yearning to escape the world. In the sequence about his third birthday, disconcerted by the sights of lust and drunkenness around him, he tries to go under Anna's skirts, but Anna prevents him. Students should remark on how the film connects Oskar's thwarted effort to his crawling under the table beside Anna, where he can witness, as he could not have under the skirts, the erotic play between his uncle and mother.

Class discussion can then revolve around whether his subsequent decision to halt his growth by throwing himself down the cellar stairs is but another attempt to find a refuge. Students might note how the cellar is represented, as a dark entry into a subterranean world, with an earthen floor, thus recalling Oskar's grandmother in the first scene (Lawson 33). Critics have also characterized the drum as another substitute womb (Moser 31). Thus by throwing himself down the cellar stairs, at the bottom of which he first carefully placed his drum, Oskar both enters and returns to sites of refuge. At the same time, these sites threaten his existence. He survives, but the fall kills him off as a regular figure of the story. From then on, he is an outsider.

The efforts to withdraw from the adult world also demonstrate a reluctance to continue the story, breaking the forward momentum, retarding the trajectory toward the rise and horrors of Nazism. Yet Oskar's return is impossible, and the story always continues. Students can debate why, in the sequence after Agnes's funeral, when his grandmother finally allows Oskar to hide under her skirts, it is too late for her to help him. They should consider why Schlöndorff follows this scene of apparent harmony by a fire with the sequence about Kristallnacht, which shows broken glass, fire, and Sigismund Markus's death. Oskar's return from the skirts to his storytelling implies that there is something about the story he narrates that also fascinates him, something about the fire that attracts him. What kind of storyteller, then, is Oskar? To help develop a response to this question, advanced students could be assigned to report on Walter Benjamin's essay "Der Erzähler" ("The Storyteller").

Benjamin writes about the storyteller as a figure who is connected to other people and whose stories sustain a sense of community. In his view, storytellers spin their tales either from personal experience or from hearing other stories. The storyteller's experience can be spatial, such as that of a roaming seafarer, or temporal, such as that of a farmer whose family has lived on the land for generations (440). A story has something useful to impart, such as a moral or piece of wisdom (442). It engages listeners in such a way that they absorb it and want to repeat it, thereby maintaining communal ties (446). The story can never be completely understood, which is part of its attraction. It is mythical, mysterious, and enduring (445–46). The rise of information since the printing press has endangered this type of storytelling, by focusing attention on what can be proved, on what is current, on what can be explained (444–45). The rise of the novel with its solitary reader has also helped eradicate the story and the storyteller. The novel for Benjamin attempts to give sense to a meaningless life, in contrast to the wisdom that a story used to convey in an ordered world (442–43, 454–57).

While Grass has long praised the tradition of storytelling and his narrators are often compared with storytellers, there is no ordered life in the film's fictional world, unlike the mythic world. By beginning the novel with Oskar's confession, "Zugegeben: ich bin Insasse einer Heil- und Pflegeanstalt" (9) ("Granted: I am an inmate of a mental hospital" [15]), Grass questions his narrator's reliability and thereby emphasizes the aesthetic basis of the story. He also introduces questions of guilt and innocence by starting with the word "zugegeben" ("granted"). In the film, however, the 1950s mental institution plays no role, and Oskar's present appears to be shortly after the end of World War II. At times Oskar stirs the sympathy of the spectators, connecting them to his story so that they see it as a protest against the corruption of the adult world in general and, specifically, against the history of German culpability and evasion of responsibility for the horrors of the Nazi regime. Grass's interest in the individual isolated in mass society also finds expression here, and this theme brings his narrative closer to Benjamin's concept of the novel. Both the film and the novel combine storytelling and novelistic elements, but the film stresses identification, albeit an incomplete one, between spectator and storyteller. Because of the lack of a frame narrator, the cinematic Oskar assumes more authority in spinning his tale, despite the fantastic details of his willed childlike body and his piercing scream. The partial identification between storyteller and spectator, as well as the story told, does not sustain a sense of community, however. Rather, it reveals a community degenerating into violence, a community of which the storyteller is a part.

By imaginatively re-creating the process of decay, the film seeks to provoke the spectator into making sense of it, a process that necessitates looking back into the past, just as Oskar begins the tale before his birth. Yet his birth also contributes to the themes of desire and fear. If we consider Oskar's fear of and fascination with the story he tells as constituting the tensions that sustain the rest of the narrative, how do his desire and fear manifest themselves during his birth? How does his birth scene fit into the movie's larger narrative?

The birth appears both from Oskar's perspective—that is, from within the womb—and from the perspective of the adults awaiting the birth. By portraying the child Oskar, as played by the eleven-year-old Bennent, looking skeptically out from the womb while Bennent's voice expresses Oskar's reluctance to be born, the scene encapsulates the backward-looking trajectory of the film, which at the same time propels it forward. It shows the narrator as already fully formed, although in the eyes of the figures he narrates he is a baby. They cannot recognize his role as narrator, but the viewer can. Oskar's will is pitted against the force of his mother's labor, and he holds his own as long as he can. He gives up his desire to remain in the womb only when his mother promises him a drum for his third birthday and when he sees a moth flapping against a lightbulb, a symbol of his conflicting desires to gain the light (to live) and to stay with his mother (to die). The drumming wings against the glass bulb characterize his later powers of drumming and breaking glass. The alienation effect produced by Oskar's child's body, unnoticed by the characters in the film, suggests his hyperawareness and the blindness of the others. His larger-than-life appearance also connects to his role as storyteller, for he emerges as the embodiment of the voice that has been narrating the film from the start, and he stays in the same body throughout the narration.

At this point, students could be assigned to read Goethe's poem "Selige Sehnsucht" (1814; "Blessed Longing"), which describes a butterfly's fatal attraction to candlelight and the need to strive constantly to reach the light in order to transcend earthly existence, despite the fact that attaining the light means death. Students could also be directed to the film scene in which the vegetable seller, Greff, praises a potato. They should note that he then discourages Oskar from trying to write, telling Oskar he will never learn the eternal truths of the German classics, such as the command, "Stirb und werde!" ("Die into life!") quoted from "Selige Sehnsucht." They can link these ideas to Oskar's move from the darkness of the womb to the artificial light in his mother's bedroom. This birth scene provides an ironic commentary on Goethe's celebration of striving to leave the shadows of darkness and rise "zu höherer Begattung" ("to a higher union" [71]). The brown moth, which calls to mind the earth tones of the first scene and also the brown of Nazi uniforms, is a pale imitation of Goethe's *Schmetterling* ("butterfly").

By comparing this scene with the one in which Oskar throws himself down the dark cellar stairs to prevent himself from growing into one of the decadent adults surrounding him, students can see a thread of resistance to overpowering forces (forces like birth, aging, decay, etc.). The narrator as creative artist wants to embody this resistance, but it is more like a flight from the film's reality. If Oskar cannot return to the womb, then he will stay a child, although he continues to mature otherwise. The stunted growth of his character corresponds to the film's episodic structure, reminiscent of picaresque adventures. By no longer growing, Oskar cannot achieve a successful integration into society. In his world, development is only an illusion, as Bruce Donahue asserts (118).

Yet students should consider whether Oskar's disgust with society is what prompts him to cast himself down the stairs. His regressive act also incorporates the desire for comfort that the drum represents to him. This desire explains the force of his response when adults later threaten to take away his drum. By removing the only thing that allows him to assuage his fears, the adults are threatening his existence. His destructively piercing scream is his way of expressing fear. Violence in this film thus implies both an inability to communicate and a fear of loss.

The sequence based on the novel's chapter "Glaube, Hoffnung, Liebe" ("Faith, Hope, Love") is the strongest representation of violence, fear, and non-communication, and students should examine the parallels drawn among Oskar, Markus, Hitler, and Santa Claus. Culminating in the scenes of Kristallnacht (the night of broken glass) and Oskar's discovery the next morning of Markus's suicide, this sequence needs a different type of narration to express its horror. The choice of fairy-tale discourse in the narrator's chilling voice-over "Es war einmal" ("Once upon a time") has a number of effects for students to discuss. For one thing, it appears to distance the narrator from the awful events he recounts. By juxtaposing the reenactment of Nazi violence against Jews with the aesthetic form of the fairy tale, Schlöndorff suggests that Oskar is using art to escape a reality that he cannot bear to confront. Perhaps Schlöndorff is also referring to his own time in the late 1970s, from which the Nazi past seemed so distant. Yet we, the spectators, perceive Oskar's evasion. Also, by having a fictional figure speak in such a fictional mode about things that are so terribly real, this episode emphasizes the failure of language to represent such horrors (Minden 150). By linking himself as drummer to Markus's death (he obtained his drums from the toy shop) and to Hitler (at times called "the drummer" [Thomas, *Grass* 58]), Oskar betrays his culpability and, by extension, that of the petite bourgeoisie of which he is a part, in these crimes (Neuhaus, *Günter Grass* [2000] 79–82). The fairy-tale mode also shows a need to believe in something that is not real and the violent consequences of that belief, by connecting Santa Claus to the "Gasman" (i.e., Hitler). This mode produces alienation and underscores the constructed nature of Oskar's story, prompting the spectator to probe beneath his version of events.

The drumming and screaming also embody Oskar's desire to be powerful, although at first Oskar prefers to keep his talents to himself, as he tells the dwarf Bebra after the circus scene. At Bebra's urging, he tests the power of his artistry at a Nazi demonstration, an episode that encapsulates individual resistance to overpowering forces. Hidden underneath the stands, Oskar beats his drum and disrupts the rhythm of the Nazi event. Yet when students contrast this evidence of his subversive drumming with the later episodes of his travels with Bebra and his company of Liliputians entertaining the German troops, they can discuss how his desire both to be different and to fit in converge to make him complicit in the Nazi war machine. Oskar shows his artistry through his drumming, but he is not a resistance fighter (Minden 158; Schilling 44). His illusion of power is just that, an illusion (McElroy 320). Oskar is powerless to change events and to change himself. His varied attempts to hide underneath things do not bring him strength, nor do they bring closure to the narrative.

Like Brooks, the film theorist Teresa De Lauretis regards desire as the driving force of narrative plot, but she claims this force is gendered as male. In her view, cinematic narratives seduce viewers into accepting socially constructed gender roles by having them identify with two narrative positions, that of movement and that of closure. She connects these positions to notions of male and female, respectively. For her, heroes, whether portrayed as women or men, are gendered as male positions in a narrative, and their goal is always toward fulfilling a desire for closure, which De Lauretis denotes in turn as a static, female position, as if returning to the womb. De Lauretis regards cinematic stories as media for modeling gender roles. She proposes that spectators learn to view the conventional gender identities they encounter in mainstream films "against the grain" so as to become aware of the ways that gender is constructed. How does *Die Blechtrommel* construct gender?

Anna Bronski is the archetypical mother figure, present at beginning and end, as if nothing has changed. She is the goal of Oskar's desire, which both connects the end to the beginning and drives him away. If he is the hero, then what notion of masculinity does the film proffer? Oskar does move throughout the film toward women figures and their promise of security—represented in the various scenes of him under the covers with Maria, Lina Greff, and Roswitha—yet the women all leave him in one way or another. Students might give examples of why movement as a male impulse culminating in satisfying closure does not work in this film. Figures such as Joseph Koljaiczek and Jan Bronski, for instance, are consumed by inextinguishable lust.

The most positive example of masculinity, Sigismund Markus, moves very little, occupying a static position. His shop is a refuge for Oskar and a convenient stop for Agnes on her way to see Jan. Donahue sees humanity and caring nature exemplified in Markus's very passivity (118). The character's warmth and association with drums link him to Anna and the utopian world Oskar imagines. But students should also consider how Schlöndorff's depiction of Markus employs stereotypes of the feminized Jewish man and what this reveals about how Oskar remembers. Although the cinematic Markus corresponds closely to Grass's depiction of him in the novel, students can debate Carol Hall's critique of Schlöndorff for sentimentalizing this figure to such an extent that the film "causes us to mourn the loss of Markus instead of looking into the ugly face of Nazism" (241). Hall faults the film for omitting Grass's "chilling satire" (240).

While the other main figures embody stereotypical gender roles, the narrative positions of movement and closure, which De Lauretis sees as the basic poles of any narrative plot, become confused and do not function as expected. The final scene shows motion away from the stable subject, Anna Bronski, both as the train disappears into the distance in the film and as the camera pans away from her. Students can observe that Anna begins in the center and is then pushed to the side of the frame as the train increasingly dominates our view, overpowering her position, just as the train's smoke blows over the smoke from her fire. The scene seems to end with Anna pushed out of sight and the train in the center. Yet as the credits roll, viewers notice that Anna's seated figure slowly reappears on the margin of the frame, with the fire flaming beside her. On the one hand, her image and all that it connotes survive. On the other hand, the stability she represents cannot sate the powerful impulses that drive Oskar from her.

As Oskar calls out for and moves away from his grandmother toward an uncertain future, he also enters more deeply into the fiction of the film and into the horrible past it embodies, swallowed up by his narration. Instead of becoming one with Anna and gaining oblivion, he is caught inside the train headed toward his present narrating position, but the narrative ends with him still in motion. This frustration of closure is not only a foreshadowing of Oskar's deformed growth spurt but also a challenge to the viewer to reflect on the meanings that such a narrative structure implies. The frame to the horrible story suggests that the cycle of violence and destruction has not ended and could begin again at any time.

Although critics fault Schlöndorff for sentimentalizing Oskar, they ignore his ironic use of identification (C. Hall). As students can learn from the above analyses, Oskar's mode of storytelling, his scratchy voice, the alienation effect of his words, the visual images, and the events he describes all work together to prevent his portrayal as a victim of circumstances. They expose instead his complicity in supporting the violent Nazi regime that is also his undoing; in fact, the memory of it terrifies him, and he narrates to deflect his fears.

Yet the insatiable desire to order his experiences into a soothing narrative of development can never be fulfilled. In Grass's view, according to Schlöndorff, Oskar never develops: "*Die Blechtrommel* ist das Gegenteil eines Entwicklungsromans: alles und alle um Oskar entwickeln sich—nur er nicht. Oskar verkörpert die Rachsucht des Kleinbürgers und seinen anarchischen Größenwahn" (39) ("*The Tin Drum* is the opposite of a novel of development: everything and everyone around Oskar develop, only he doesn't. Oskar embodies the vengeance of the petit bourgeois and his anarchic megalomania" [trans. mine]). Rainer Scherf asserts that Oskar develops negatively, as if in a "Mißbildungsroman" ("novel of miseducation") about *Vergangenheitsbewältigung* (99) ("coming to terms with the past" or "overcoming the past"). Discussion might center on whether and how the film supports such an interpretation.

The film and novel have long been connected to the continuing postwar German project of *Vergangenheitsbewältigung*, a term, however, that does not articulate the ongoing nature of collective remembering. More recently, scholars have begun to refer to this process as *Vergangenheitsbearbeitung* ("working through the past"), which captures the open-ended aspect of the process (Eigler 10). Students should deliberate on how these terms relate to West Germany in 1959, when Grass's novel appeared; in 1979, when the film appeared; and to Germany in the early twenty-first century, especially in light of debates in 2006 and 2007 over Grass's revelation of his membership in the Waffen-SS. They could look at how Grass addresses his long silence about his past in the cycle of poems and drawings in *Dummer August* (2007), including one poem, "Wohin fliehen," that refers to the impossibility of fleeing under a grandmother's skirts because they are already occupied (10). How does Oskar's story in *Die Blechtrommel*, indeed his very incarnation as an impotent three-year-old, reflect, as Scherf maintains, a desire for *Vergangenheitsbewältigung* (100)? Grass's novel challenged inclinations in 1950s West Germany to forget the Nazi past and to focus on consumer prosperity (Brode, *Günter Grass* 81). Schlöndorff's film appeared at a time when a new generation of West Germans was taking issue with what they perceived as the persistence of German authoritarianism and fascist tendencies (Hamilton 132–33). John Vinocur notes that the film's critical and popular reception also stimulated young West Germans to read the novel: "*The Tin Drum* as film is a kind of national participatory event: the book is on virtually every young German's bookshelf" (17).

Now, at the beginning of the twenty-first century, Germans are still questioning the residues of the Nazi past, ways of commemorating the victims of the Holocaust, the consequences of trauma, and the need to continue remembering the horrors of Nazism after the survivors are no longer alive. Thus the film's relevance persists.

Although this model analysis cannot encompass all facets of the film, hopefully it can provide a framework for further investigation of the dynamics of the film's content and form.

NOTES ON CONTRIBUTORS

Susan C. Anderson, professor of German at the University of Oregon, is the author of *Grass and Grimmelshausen: Günter Grass's* Das Treffen in Telgte *and Rezeptionstheorie* and the coeditor of *Water, Culture, and Politics in Germany and the American West* and *Water, Leisure, and Culture: European Historical Perspectives.* She is currently working on a book on ideas of difference and identity in contemporary German narrative and film.

Peter Arnds is professor of German and Italian at Kansas State University. He is the author of *Representation, Subversion, and Eugenics in Günter Grass's* The Tin Drum *and Wilhelm Raabe's* Der Hungerpastor *and Charles Dickens's* David Copperfield: *Intertexuality of Two "Bildungsromane."* He is currently at work on an interdisciplinary study titled "Modernity, Myth, and the Twentieth-Century Novel of Political Dissent."

Barabara Becker-Cantarino is research professor at Ohio State University. She is the author of numerous books on German women authors, especially Romantic women authors, and editor of *The Eighteenth Century: The Enlightenment and Sensibility* (vol. 5 of *The Camden House History of German Literature*) and coeditor of a volume on Ingeborg Drewitz. She is currently working on a book titled "Gender and Sexuality in German Romanticism."

Stephen Brockmann, professor of German at Carnegie Mellon University, is the author of *Nuremberg: The Imaginary Capital, German Literary Culture at the Zero Hour,* and *Literature and German Reunification.* He was managing editor of the *Brecht Yearbook* (2002–07).

Patricia Pollock Brodsky, professor of German and Russian at the University of Missouri, Kansas City, is the author of *Rainer Maria Rilke* (Twayne's World Authors Ser.) and *Russia in the Works of Rainer Maria Rilke.* Her current book project has the working title "Modes of Resistance: The Antifascist Tradition in German Letters."

Jane Curran, professor of German at Dalhousie University, is the author of *Goethe's* Wilhelm Meister's Apprenticeship: *A Reader's Commentary* and *Horace's* Epistles, *Wieland, and the Reader: A Three-Way Conversation.* She is coeditor of *Denken und Geschichte: Festschrift für Friedrich Gaede, Schiller's "On Grace and Dignity" in Its Cultural Context,* and a journal issue on Hans-Ulrich Treichel. Her current book project is on the topic of reading aloud in the eighteenth century.

Sabine Gross, professor of German and affiliate professor of theater at the University of Wisconsin, Madison, is the author of *Lese-Zeichen: Kognition, Medium und Materialität im Leseprozeß.* She is coeditor of *Early and Late Herder: Continuity and/or Correction* and *In Bildern schreiben / Writing in Images* (forthcoming). Her current research is on the intersection of narration, language, and perception in literature.

Katharina Hall, professor of German at Swansea University, Wales, is the author of *Günter Grass's* Danzig Quintet: *Explorations in the Memory and History of the Nazi Era from* Die Blechtrommel *to* Im Krebsgang *and the editor of* Esther Dischereit. *Her* current book project is titled "Detecting the Past: Representations of National Socialism in Crime Fiction of the Postwar Era."

Elizabeth C. Hamilton is associate professor of German at Oberlin College. Her publications include articles on German literature, film, and foreign language pedagogy. She is the coeditor of a forthcoming volume, *Worlds Apart? Disability and Foreign Language Learning* and is currently working on a book about the history of disability in German literature.

Irene Kacandes is associate professor of German studies and comparative literature at Dartmouth College. She is the author of *Talk Fiction: The Talk Explosion and Literature* and coeditor of *A User's Guide to German Cultural Studies* and of *Teaching the Representation of the Holocaust*. She is currently working on two manuscripts concerning the nature of generational transmission of trauma.

Todd Kontje is professor of German and comparative literature at the University of California, San Diego. His books include *Women, the Novel, and the German Nation, 1771–1871* and *German Orientalisms*; he also edited *A Companion to German Realism*. He is currently writing a book on Thomas Mann.

Dagmar C. G. Lorenz is professor of Germanic studies and director of Jewish studies at the University of Illinois, Chicago. She is the author of *Keepers of the Motherland: German Texts by Jewish Women Writers* (1997) and *Verfolgung bis zum Massenmord: Diskurse zum Holocaust in deutscher Sprache* (1992). She edited the *German Quarterly* and five books, including companion volumes to Canetti and Schnitzler.

Teresa Ludden is lecturer in German at the University of Newcastle upon Tyne, England. She is the author of *"Das Undarstellbare darstellen": Kulturkritk and the Representation of Difference in the Work of Anne Duden* and has published several articles on German philosophy, literature, and film.

Timothy B. Malchow is assistant professor of foreign languages and literatures at Valparaiso University. He has published articles on Thomas Bernhard and George Tabori and is currently working on a monograph on Grass and memory.

Julian Preece is professor of German at Swansea University. He is the author of *The Rediscovered Writings of Veza Canetti: Out of the Shadow of a Husband* (2007) and *The Life and Works of Günter Grass: Literature, History, Politics* (2001). He has been an editor of the Leeds (formerly Bradford) Series in Contemporary German Literature and also edited *The Cambridge Companion to Kafka* (2002). He is a member of the Wissenschaftlicher Beirat der Günter Grass Stiftung, Bremen.

Richard E. Schade is professor of German at the University of Cincinnati and serves as the managing editor of *The Lessing Yearbook*. He is the author of a monograph on German Renaissance comedy and is currently working on a book on Grass's art and literature.

Margaret Setje-Eilers is Mellon Assistant Professor of German at Vanderbilt University. She has published articles on German film, Bertolt Brecht, and foreign language pedagogy and created an online interactive German course. She is currently working on a book about Helene Weigel and the Berliner Ensemble.

Monika Shafi is Elias Ahuja Professor of German and director of women's studies at the University of Delaware. She is the author of *Gertrud Kolmar: Eine Einführung in das Werk* and *Balancing Acts: Intercultural Encounters in Contemporary German and Austrian Literature*.

Alfred D. White is professor in the German Department of Cardiff School of European Studies, Cardiff University, Wales. He is the author of six books, the most recent being *Choose Not These Vices: Social Reality in the German Novel, 1618–1848*. He is currently working on an edition of a pseudonymous novel by Paul Doma.

SURVEY PARTICIPANTS

The following scholars and teachers of Grass's *The Tin Drum* contributed essays for this volume or participated in the survey that preceded and provided materials for the preparation of this book:

Susan C. Anderson, *University of Oregon*
Peter Arnds, *Kansas State University*
Stephen Brockmann, *Carnegie Mellon University*
Patricia Pollock Brodsky, *University of Missouri, Kansas City*
Helen Chambers, *University of Saint Andrews, Scotland*
Jane Curran, *Dalhousie University*
Amir Eshel, *Stanford University*
Elizabeth C. Hamilton, *Oberlin College*
Alan Keele, *Brigham Young University*
Todd Kontje, *University of California, San Diego*
Dagmar C. G. Lorenz, *University of Illinois, Chicago*
Teresa Ludden, *University of Newcastle upon Tyne, England*
Ursula Mahlendorf, *University of California, Santa Barbara*
Timothy B. Malchow, *Valparaiso University*
Bill Philipps, *Dartmouth College*
Julian Preece, *Swansea University*
Richard E. Schade, *University of Cincinnati*
Margaret Setje-Eilers, *Vanderbilt University*
Patricia H. Stanley, *Florida State University*
Rita Terras, *Connecticut College*
Frank Trommler, *University of Pennsylvania*
Alfred D. White, *Cardiff University*

WORKS CITED AND RECOMMENDED

Books and Articles

Abbott, H. Porter. *The Cambridge Introduction to Narrative*. Cambridge: Cambridge UP, 2002.

Adler, Hans, and Jost Hermand, eds. *Günter Grass: Ästhetik des Engagements*. German Life and Civilization 18. New York: Lang, 1996.

Adorno, Theodor W., Else Frenkel-Brunswick, Daniel J. Levinson, and Newitt R. Sanford, eds. *The Authoritarian Personality*. New York: Harper, 1950.

Agamben, Giorgio. *Homo Sacer: Sovereign Power and Bare Life*. Trans. Daniel Heller-Roazen. Stanford: Stanford UP, 1998.

———. *Remnants of Auschwitz: The Witness and the Archive*. Trans. Daniel Heller-Roazen. New York: Zone, 2002.

———. *State of Exception*. Chicago: U of Chicago P, 2005.

Alciatus, Andreas. *Emblematum liber*. Paris, 1544.

Angress, Ruth K. "'Der Butt': A Feminist Perspective." *Adventures of a Flounder: Critical Essays on Günter Grass*. Ed. Gertrud Bauer-Pickar. Munich: Fink, 1982. 43–50.

———. "A 'Jewish Problem' in German Postwar Fiction." *Modern Judaism* 5.3 (1985): 215–33.

Arendt, Hannah. *The Origins of Totalitarianism*. New York: Harcourt, 1973.

Arnds, Peter. "On the Awful German Fairy Tale: Breaking Taboos in Representations of Nazi Euthanasia and the Holocaust in Günter Grass's *Die Blechtrommel*, Edgar Hilsenrath's *Der Nazi & der Friseur*, and Anselm Kiefer's Visual Art." *German Quarterly* 75 (2002): 422–39.

———. *Representation, Subversion, and Eugenics in Günter Grass's* The Tin Drum. Rochester: Camden, 2004.

Arnold, Heinz Ludwig. *Blech getrommelt: Günter Grass in der Kritik*. Göttingen: Steidl, 1997.

———, ed. *Günter Grass*. Text + Kritik 1. Munich: Text und Kritik, 1988.

Arnold, Heinz Ludwig, and Franz Josef Görz, eds. *Günter Grass: Dokumente zur politischen Wirkung*. Munich: Text und Kritik, 1971.

Artinger, Kai, and Hans Wißkirchen, eds. *Wortbilder und Wechselspiele: Das Günter Grass-Haus*. Göttingen: Steidl, 2002.

Ascheid, Antje. "Diva, Mother, Martyr: The Many Faces of Zarah Leander." *Hitler's Heroines: Stardom and Womanhood in Nazi Cinema*. Philadelphia: Temple UP, 2003. 155–212.

Bächthold-Stäubli, Hanns, ed. *Handwörterbuch des deutschen Aberglaubens*. Vol. 1. Berlin: de Gruyter, 1927.

Bade, Wilfrid. *Trommlerbub unterm Hakenkreuz*. Stuttgart: Loewes, 1934.

Bakhtin, Mikhail. *Rabelais and His World*. Trans. Hélène Iswolsky. Bloomington: Indiana UP, 1984.

Bal, Mieke. *Introduction to the Theory of Narrative*. Toronto: U of Toronto P, 1997.

Bashaw, Rita B. "Witz at Work: The Comic and the Grotesque in Edgar Hilsenrath, Jakov Lind, and George Tabori." Diss. U of Minnesota, 2001. *DAI* 62.11 (2002): 3800A.

Battersby, Christine. *The Phenomenal Woman*. Oxford: Polity, 1998.

Benjamin, Walter. "Der Erzähler." *Gesammelte Schriften*. Vol. 2.2. Ed. Rolf Tiedemann and Hermann Schweppenhäuser. Frankfurt am Main: Suhrkamp, 1977. 438–65. Trans. as "The Storyteller." *Illuminations*. Trans. Harry Zohn. New York: Schocken, 1969. 83–110.

Bering, Dietz. *Der Name als Stigma: Antisemitismus im deutschen Alltag, 1812–1933*. Stuttgart: Klett-Cotta, 1987.

Bernstein, Richard, and Mark Landler. "Few See Taint in Service by Pope in Hitler Youth." *New York Times* 21 Apr. 2005: A12.

Beyersdorf, H. E. "The Narrator as Artful Deceiver: Aspects of Narrative Perspective in *Die Blechtrommel*." *Germanic Review* 55 (1980): 129–38.

Bjornstad, Jennifer Irene. "Functions of Humor in German Holocaust Literature: Edgar Hilsenrath, Günter Grass, and Jurek Becker." Diss. U of Wisconsin, Madison, 2001. *DAI* 62.4 (2001): 1425A.

Die Blechtrommel. Dir. Volker Schlöndorff. 1979. 1 Oct. 2005 <http://www.imdb.com/title/tt0078875/>.

Die Blechtrommel Volker Schlöndorff. Sequenz: Film und Pädagogik 5. Nancy: Goethe-Institut, 1992.

Bornemann, Ernest. *Das Patriarchat: Ursprung und Zukunft unseres Gesellschaftssystems*. Frankfurt am Main: Fischer, 1979.

Böschenstein, Bernhard. "Günter Grass als Nachfolger Jean Pauls und Döblins." *Jahrbuch der Jean-Paul-Gesellschaft* 6 (1971): 86–101.

Boßmann, Timm. *Der Dichter im Schussfeld: Geschichte und Versagen der Literaturkritik am Beispiel Günter Grass*. Marburg: Tectum, 1997.

Botheroyd, Paul. *Ich und Er: First and Third Person Self-Reference and Problems of Identity in Three Contemporary German-Language Novels*. The Hague: Mouton, 1976.

Bourdieu, Pierre. *Male Domination*. Trans. Richard Nice. Stanford: Stanford UP, 2001.

Brandes, Ute. *Günter Grass*. Berlin: Colloquium im Wissenschaftsverlag Volker Spiess, 1998.

Brauner, Sigrid. *Fearless Wives and Frightened Shrews: The Construction of the Witch in Early Modern Germany*. Amherst: U of Massachusetts P, 1995.

Brecht, Bertolt. "The Informer." Trans. Eric Bentley. *The Jewish Wife and Other Short Plays*. New York: Grove, 1992. 41–55.

———. "Von der Jugend." *Werke: Große kommentierte Berliner und Frankfurter Ausgabe*. Vol. 23. Ed. Werner Hecht, Jan Knopf, Werner Mittenzwei, and Klaus-Detlef Müller. Berlin: Aufbau, 1993. 130–31.

Brockmann, Stephen. *German Literary Culture at the Zero Hour*. Rochester: Camden, 2004.

————. *Literature and German Reunification*. Cambridge: Cambridge UP, 1999.

————. "Martin Walser and the Presence of the German Past." *German Quarterly* 75 (2002): 127–43.

————. "Virgin Father and Prodigal Son." *Philosophy and Literature* 27 (2003): 341–62.

Brode, Hanspeter. *Günter Grass*. Munich: Beck, 1979.

————. *Die Zeitgeschichte im erzählenden Werk von Günter Grass: Versuch einer Deutung der Blechtrommel und der Danziger Trilogie*. Regensburger Beiträge zur deutschen Sprach- und Literaturwissenschaft. Bern: Lang, 1977.

Broder, Henryk M. *Jedem das Seine*. Augsburg: Ölbaum, 1999.

Broder, Henryk M., and Michel Lang, eds. *Fremd im eigenen Land*. Frankfurt am Main: Fischer, 1979.

Brooks, Peter. "Narrative Desire." *Reading for the Plot*. New York: Knopf, 1984. 37–61.

Broszat, Martin. "Rotkäppchen vor vierzig Jahren: Zur politischen Satire im dritten Reich." *Süddeutsche Zeitung* 20 Feb. 1977: 79.

Brückner, Wolfgang, ed. *Volkserzählung und Reformation*. Berlin: Schmidt, 1974.

Bulgakov, Mikhail. *The Master and Margarita*. New York: Random, 1996.

Burleigh, Michael. *Germany Turns Eastward: A Study of Ostforschung in the Third Reich*. Cambridge: Cambridge UP, 1988.

Byg, Barton. "Nazism as *Femme Fatale*: Recuperations of Cinematic Masculinity in Postwar Berlin." *Gender and Germanness: Cultural Productions of Nation*. Ed. Patricia Herminghouse and Magda Mueller. Providence: Berghahn, 1997. 176–88.

Cavarero, Adriana. *In Spite of Plato: A Feminist Reading of Ancient Philosophy*. Trans. Serena Anderlini-D'Onofrio and Aine O'Healy. New York: Routledge, 1995.

Cloonan, William. *The Writing of War: French and German Fiction and World War II*. Gainesville: UP of Florida, 1999.

Coury, David. "Transformational Considerations in the Filmic Adaption of Günter Grass' *Die Blechtrommel*." *New German Review* 8 (1992): 74–84.

Cross, Gary. *The Cute and the Cool: Wondrous Innocence and Modern American Children's Culture*. Oxford: Oxford UP, 2004.

Dahn, Felix. *Ein Kampf um Rom: Roman*. Munich: dtv, 2003.

Delaney, Antoinette T. *Metaphors in Grass's Die Blechtrommel*. New York: Lang, 2004.

De Lauretis, Teresa. "Desire in Narrative." *Narratology: An Introduction*. Ed. Susana Onega Jaen and Jose Angel Garcia Landa. New York: Longman, 1996. 262–72.

Deleuze, Gilles, and Félix Guattari. *A Thousand Plateaus: Capitalism and Schizophrenia*. Trans. and introd. Brian Massumi. Minneapolis: U of Minnesota P, 1987.

Diller, Edward. *A Mythic Journey. Günter Grass's Tin Drum*. Lexington: UP of Kentucky, 1974.

Döblin, Alfred. *Alexanderplatz, Berlin: The Story of Franz Biberkopf*. Trans. Eugene Jolas. New York: Ungar, 1976.

Donahue, Bruce. "The Alternative to Goethe: Markus and Fajngold in *Die Blechtrommel*." *Germanic Review* 58.3 (1983): 115–20.

Durzak, Manfred. *Der deutsche Roman der Gegenwart: Entwicklungsvoraussetzungen und Tendenzen: Heinrich Böll, Günter Grass, Uwe Johnson, Christa Wolf, Hermann Kant*. Stuttgart: Kohlhammer, 1979.

Eagleton, Terry. *Literary Theory: An Introduction*. Oxford: Blackwell, 1983.

Eckermann, Johann Peter. *Gespräche mit Goethe in den letzten Jahren seines Lebens*. München: Hanser, 1986.

Eckhardt, Holger. "'Dem Volke unheimlich und merkwürdig': Zum Motiv vom Aasfressenden Aal." *Neophilologus* 83.1 (1999): 115–20.

Eigler, Friederike. *Gedächtnis und Geschichte in Generationenromanen seit der Wende*. Berlin: Schmidt, 2005.

Engdahl, Horace. *Presentation Speech*. Nobel Prize in Literature, 1999. 10 Dec. 1999. 6 Feb. 2007 <http://nobelprize.org/literature/laureates/1999/presentation-speech.html>.

Enzensberger, Hans Magnus. "Wilhelm Meister, auf Blech getrommelt." Loschütz 8–12.

Der ewige Jude. Dir. Fritz Hippler. Deutsche Filmherstellungs, 1940.

"Fall for." *WordNet Search 3.0*. Princeton U. 13 July 2007 <http://wordnet.princeton.edu/perl/webwn>.

Fischer, André. *Inszenierte Naivität: Zur ästhetischen Simulation von Geschichte bei Günter Grass, Albert Drach und Walter Kempowski*. Munich: Fink, 1992.

Foucault, Michel. *Madness and Civilization*. Trans. Richard Howard. New York: Random, 1988.

———. *Society Must Be Defended: Lectures at the Collège de France, 1975–1976*. Ed. Mauro Bertani and Alessandro Fontana. Trans. David Macey. New York: Picador, 2003.

Franke, Reinhold. "Das Märchen vom Däumling in deutscher und französischer Sprache." *Jugendschriftenwarte* 43.11 (1938): 21–25.

Freud, Sigmund. "On Narcissism." 1914. *The Standard Edition of the Complete Psychological Works of Sigmund Freud*. Trans. and ed. James Strachey. Vol. 14. London: Hogarth, 1957. 73–96.

Freytag, Gustav. *Soll und Haben*. Kehl: Swan, 1993.

Frizen, Werner. "*Die Blechtrommel*—ein schwarzer Roman: Grass und die Literatur des Absurden." *Arcadia* 21 (1986): 166–89.

Führer, Maria. *Nordgermanische Götterüberlieferung und deutsches Volksmärchen: 80 Märchen der Brüder Grimm vom Mythus her beleuchtet*. Munich: Neuer Filser, 1938.

Fulbrook, Mary. *A Concise History of Germany*. Cambridge: Cambridge UP, 1990.

Garde, Barbara. "'Die Frauengasse ist eine Gasse, durch die man lebenslang geht': Frauen in den Romanen von Günter Grass." Arnold, *Günter Grass* 101–07.

Geary, Patrick J. *The Myth of Nations: The Medieval Origins of Europe*. Princeton: Princeton UP, 2002.

Geißler, Rolf, ed. *Günter Grass: Ein Materialienbuch*. Darmstadt: Luchterhand, 1976.

Genette, Gérard. *Narrative Discourse: An Essay in Method*. Trans. Jane E. Lewin. Ithaca: Cornell UP, 1980.

————. *Paratexts: Threshold of Interpretation*. Trans. Jane E. Lewin. Fwd. Richard Macksey. Cambridge: Cambridge UP, 1997.

————. *Seuils*. Paris: Seuil, 1987.

Gesche, Janina. *Aus Zweierlei Perspektiven . . . : Zur Rezeption der Danziger Trilogie von Günter Grass in Polen und Schweden in den Jahren 1958–1990*. Stockholm: Almquist, 2003.

Gilman, Sander L. "Is Life Beautiful? Can the Shoah Be Funny? Some Thoughts on Recent and Older Films." *Critical Inquiry* 26.2 (2000): 279–308.

————. *Jewish Self-Hatred: Anti-Semitism and the Hidden Language of the Jews*. Baltimore: Johns Hopkins UP, 1986.

Gockel, Heinz. *Grass' Blechtrommel*. Meisterwerke kurz und bündig. Munich: Piper, 2001.

Goebbels, Joseph. *Michael*. Trans. Joachim Neugroschel. New York: Amok, 1987.

Goethe, Johann Wolfgang. "Blessed Longing." Trans. Michael Hamburger. *German Poetry from 1750–1900*. Ed. Robert M. Browning. New York: Continuum, 1984. 69–71. Trans. of "Selige Sehnsucht." *Werke*. Vol. 2. Hamburger Ausgabe. Munich: dtv, 1994. 18–19, 581–84.

————. *Werke*. Ed. Erich Trunz. 14 vols. Hamburg: Wegner, 1954.

Görtz, Franz Josef. Die Blechtrommel: *Attraktion und Ärgernis: Ein Kapitel deutscher Literaturgeschichte*. Darmstadt: Luchterhand, 1984.

Grass, Günter. *Angestiftet, Partei zu ergreifen*. Ed. Daniela Hermes. Munich: dtv, 1994.

————. *Aus dem Tagebuch einer Schnecke*. Göttingen: Steidl, 1997.

————. *Der Autor als fragwürdige Zeuge*. Ed. Daniela Hermes. Munich: dtv, 1997.

————. *Beim Häuten der Zwiebel*. Göttingen: Steidl, 2006.

————. *Die Blechtrommel: Roman*. 1993. 6th rev. ed. Munich: dtv, 1997.

————. *Der Butt*. Darmstadt: Luchterhand, 1987.

————. *Crabwalk*. Trans. Krishna Winston. New York: Harcourt, 2002.

————. *Die Deutschen und ihre Dichter*. Ed. Daniela Hermes. Munich: dtv, 1995.

————. *Dog Years*. Trans. Ralph Manheim. New York: Harcourt, 1965.

————. *Dummer August*. Göttingen: Steidl, 2007.

————. "Es war mir immer präsent." Interview with Ulrich Wickert. *Der Spiegel* 21 Aug. 2006: 67–68.

————. *The Flounder*. Trans. Ralph Manheim. New York: Harcourt, 1978.

————. *From the Diary of a Snail*. Trans. Ralph Manheim. New York: Harcourt, 1973.

————. *Fundsachen für Nichtleser*. Göttingen: Steidl, 1997.

————. *Gebrannte Erde*. Photographs by Dirk Reinertz. Göttingen: Steidl, 2002.

————. *Hundejahre*. 1963. Darmstadt: Luchterhand, 1985.

————. "Ich klage an." *Essays und Reden I: 1955–1969*. Göttingen: Steidl, 1997. 137–46.

————. *Im Krebsgang: Eine Novelle*. Göttingen: Steidl, 2002.

————. "Der Inhalt als Widerstand." *Essays und Reden I, 1955–1969*. Ed. Daniela Hermes. Frankfurt am Main: Büchergilde Gutenberg, 2004. 16–22.

————. *Katz und Maus*. 1961. Munich: dtv, 1993.

————. *Mein Jahrhundert*. Göttingen: Steidl, 1999. Trans. as *My Century*. Trans. Michael Henry Heim. San Diego: Harcourt, 1999.

————. Personal interview with Pat Brodsky. Mar. 1985.

————. "Rückblick auf *Die Blechtrommel* oder Der Autor als fragwürdiger Zeuge." Geißler 80–85.

————. "Schreiben nach Auschwitz: Frankfurter Poetik-Vorlesung." *Essays und Reden III: 1980–1997*. Göttingen: Steidl, 1997. 235–56.

————. *Der Schriftsteller als Zeitgenosse*. Ed. Daniela Hermes. Munich: dtv, 1996.

————. *The Tin Drum*. 1961. Trans. Ralph Manheim. New York: Vintage Intl., 1990.

————. *Das Treffen in Telgte*. Neuwied: Luchterhand, 1979.

————. *Über meinen Lehrer Döblin und andere Vorträge*. Berlin: Literarisches Colloquium, 1967.

————. "Warum ich nach sechzig Jahren mein Schweigen breche." Interview with Frank Schirrmacher and Hubert Spiegel. *Frankfurter Allgemeine Zeitung* 12 Aug. 2006. 17 Oct. 2007 <http://fazarchiv.faz.net/FAZ.ein>. Path: Archiv.

————. *Werkausgabe*. 16 vols. Ed. Volker Neuhaus and Daniela Hermes. Göttingen: Steidl, 1997.

————. *Werkausgabe in zehn Bänden*. 10 vols. Ed. Volker Neuhaus. Darmstadt: Luchterhand, 1987.

————. *Werkverzeichnis der Radierungen*. Berlin: Dreher, 1979–80.

Grass, Günter, and Harro Zimmermann. *Vom Abenteuer der Aufklärung: Werkstattgespräche*. Göttingen: Steidl, 2000.

Grimm, Jacob, and Wilhelm Grimm. *Brüder Grimm: Kinder- und Hausmärchen*. 3 vols. Leipzig: Reclam, 2001.

————. *Selected Tales*. Ed. and trans. Joyce Crick. Oxford: Oxford UP, 2005.

Grosz, Elizabeth. *Jacques Lacan: A Feminist Introduction*. London: Routledge, 1990.

Guidry, Glenn A. "Theoretical Reflections on the Ideological and Social Implications of Mythic Form in Grass' *Die Blechtrommel*." *Monatshefte* 83.2 (1991): 127–46.

Hake, Sabine. *German National Cinema*. New York: Routledge, 2002.

Hall, Carol. "A Different Drummer: *The Tin Drum*: Film and Novel." *Film and Literature Quarterly* 18.4 (1990): 236–44.

Hall, Katharina. *Günter Grass's* Danzig Quintet: *Explorations in the Memory and History of the Nazi Era from* Die Blechtrommel *to* Im Krebsgang. Bern: Lang, 2006.

Hamelmann, Berthold. *Helau und Heil Hitler: Alltagsgeschichte der Fastnacht 1919–1939 am Beispiel der Stadt Freiburg*. Eggingen: Isele, 1989.

Hamilton, Elizabeth. "Deafening Sound and Troubling Silence in Volker Schlöndorff's *Die Blechtrommel*." *Sound Matters: Essays on the Acoustics of Modern German Culture*. Ed. Nora M. Alter and Lutz Koepnick. New York: Berghahn, 2004. 130–41.

Harsdoerffer, Georg Philipp. *Poetischer Trichter*. Darmstadt: Wissenschaftliche Buchgesellschaft, 1969.

Hauff, Wilhelm, "Die Geschichte von dem kleinen Muck." *Märchen-Almanach auf das Jahr 1826. Project Gutenberg*. 1 Oct. 2004.17 July 2007 <http://www.gutenberg.org/etext/6638>.

———. "Der Zwerg Nase." *Märchen-Almanach auf das Jahr 1827*. Project Gutenberg. 1 Oct. 2004. 17 July 2007 <http://www.gutenberg.org/etext/6639>.

Haug, Wolfgang Fritz. *Die Faschisierung des bürgerlichen Subjekts: Die Ideologie der gesunden Normalität und die Ausrottungspolitiken im deutschen Faschismus*. Hamburg: Materialienanalysen, 1987.

Head, David. "Volker Schlöndorff's *Die Blechtrommel* and the 'Literaturverfilmung' Debate." *German Life and Letters* 36.4 (1983): 347–67.

Herf, Jeffrey. *Divided Memory: The Nazi Past in the Two Germanys*. Cambridge: Harvard UP, 1997.

Herman, Luc, and Bart Vervaeck. *Handbook of Narrative Analysis*. Lincoln: U of Nebraska P, 2005.

Hermand, Jost. "Das Unpositive der kleinen Leute: Zum angeblich skandalösen 'Animalismus' in Grassens *Die Blechtrommel*." Adler and Hermand 1–22.

Hermes, Daniela, and Volker Neuhaus, eds. *Günter Grass im Ausland: Texte, Daten, Bilder zur Rezeption*. Frankfurt am Main: Luchterhand, 1990.

Hille-Sandvoss, Angelika. *Überlegungen zur Bildlichkeit im Werk von Günter Grass*. Stuttgart: Heinz, 1987.

Hilsenrath, Edgar. *Der Nazi und der Friseur*. Cologne: Literarischer, 1977. Trans. as *The Nazi and the Barber*. Trans. Andrew White. New York: Doubleday, 1971.

Hirsch, Marianne. *Family Frames: Photography, Narrative, and Postmemory*. Cambridge: Harvard UP, 1997.

Hitler, Adolf. *Mein Kampf*. Trans. Ralph Manheim. Boston: Houghton, 1943.

Hitlerjunge Quex: Ein Film vom Opfergeist der deutschen Jugend. Dir. Hans Steinhoff. Universum Film, 1933.

Höhn, Maria. "Frau im Haus und Girl im *Spiegel*: Discourse on Women in the Interregnum Period of 1945–1949 and the Question of German Identity." *Central European History* 26.1 (1993): 57–90.

Irigaray, Luce. *Le corps-à-corps avec la mère*. Montreal: Pleine Lune, 1981.

———. *Speculum of the Other Woman*. Trans. Gillian C. Gill. Ithaca: Cornell UP, 1985.

Jahnke, Walter. "'Der weite Rock': Vom Mythos der Höhlen zu den Mutter-Huren." Jahnke and Lindemann 18–29.

Jahnke, Walter, and Klaus Lindemann, eds. *Günter Grass: Die Blechtrommel: Acht Kapitel zur Erschließung des Romans*. Munich: Schöningh, 1993.

Jud Süss. Dir. Veit Harlan. Terra-Filmkunst, 1940.

Jürgs, Michael. *Bürger Grass: Biografie eines deutschen Dichters*. Munich: Bertelsmann, 2002.

Just, Georg. *Darstellung und Appell in der Blechtrommel von Günter Grass: Darstellungsästhetik versus Wirkungsästhetik*. Frankfurt am Main: Athenäum, 1972.

Kacandes, Irene. "Antisemitism, Neo-Nazism, and Xenophobia Today." *The Holocaust: Introductory Essays*. Ed. David Scrase and Wolfgang Mieder. Burlington: Center for Holocaust Studies, U of Vermont, 1996. 207–22.

Kaes, Anton. *From Hitler to Heimat: The Return of History as Film*. Cambridge: Harvard UP, 1989.

————. "The Presence of the Past: Rainer Werner Fassbinder's *The Marriage of Maria Braun.*" Kaes, *From Hitler* 73–103.

Kaltenecker, Siegfried. "Weil aber die vergessenste Fremde unser Körper ist: Über Männer-Körper Repräsentationen und Faschismus." *The Body of Gender, Körper, Geschlechter, Identitäten.* Ed. Marie-Luise Angerer. Vienna: Passagen, 1995. 91–109.

Kamenetsky, Christa. "Folklore as a Political Tool in Nazi Germany." *Journal of American Folklore* 85 (1972): 221–35.

————. "Folktale and Ideology in the Third Reich." *Journal of American Folklore* 90 (1977): 168–78.

Kaufmann, Uri R. *Jewish Life in Germany Today.* Bonn: Inter Nationes, 1994.

Keele, Alan Frank. "Günter Grass." *Contemporary German Fiction Writers.* Ed. Wolfgang E. Elfe and James Hardin. Detroit: Gale, 1988. 69–91. Vol. 75 of *Dictionary of Literary Biography.*

————. *Understanding Günter Grass.* Columbia: U of South Carolina P, 1988.

Kershaw, Ian. *Hitler, 1889–1936: Hubris.* London: Lane, 1998.

Kilborn, Richard. "Filming the Unfilmable: Volker Schlöndorff and *The Tin Drum.*" *Cinema and Fiction: New Modes of Adapting, 1950–1990.* Ed. John Orr and Colin Nicholson. Edinburgh: Edinburgh UP, 1992. 28–38.

Klee, Ernst, ed. *"Euthanasie" im NS-Staat: Die "Vernichtung lebensunwerten Lebens."* Frankfurt am Main: Fischer, 1989.

Klocke, Astrid. "The Concept of Black Humor and Edgar Hilsenrath's Novel *Der Nazi und der Friseur.*" Diss. Indiana U, 2001. *DAI* 61.11 (2001): 4403A.

Kniesche, Thomas. "'Das wird nicht aufhören, gegenwärtig zu bleiben': Günter Grass und das Problem der deutschen Schuld." Adler and Hermand 169–97.

Kolbenhoff, Walter. *Von unserem Fleisch und Blut.* 1946. Frankfurt am Main: Fischer, 1983.

Könecke, Rainer. *Stundenblätter* Die Blechtrommel. Stuttgart: Klett, 1983.

Kontje, Todd. *The German Bildungsroman: History of a National Genre.* Studies in German Literature, Linguistics, and Culture: Literary Criticism in Perspective. Columbia: Camden, 1993.

Koopmann, Helmut. "Der Faschismus als Kleinbürgertum und was daraus wurde." Neuhaus and Hermes 200–22.

Krumme, Detlev. *Günter Grass*: Die Blechtrommel. Munich: Hanser, 1986.

Lawson, Richard H. *Günter Grass.* New York: Ungar, 1985.

Leach, Mary, ed. *Dictionary of Folklore, Mythology, and Legend.* Vol. 1. New York: Funk, 1949.

Levi, Primo. *Se questo è un uomo.* 1947. Turin, It.: Einaudi, 2005. Trans. as *If This Is a Man.*

Lorenz, Dagmar C. G. *Verfolgung bis zum Massenmord: Holocaust-Diskurse in deutscher Sprache aus der Sicht der Verfolgten.* New York: Lang, 1992.

Loschütz, Gert, ed. *Von Buch zu Buch: Günter Grass in der Kritik: Eine Dokumentation.* Neuwied: Luchterhand, 1968.

Lukács, Georg. *The Historical Novel.* Trans. Hannah Mitchell and Stanley Mitchell. London: Merlin, 1962.

———. *Theory of the Novel.* Trans. Anna Bostock. Cambridge: MIT P, 1971.

Madajczyk, Czesław. Introduction. *Generalny plan wschodni: Zbiór dokumentów* [Generalplan Ost: A Collection of Documents]. Ed. Madajczyk. Warsaw: Instytut Historii PAN, 1990. 15–50.

Mandel, Siegfried. *Group 47: The Reflected Intellect.* Carbondale: Southern Illinois UP, 1973.

Mann, Thomas. *Doktor Faustus: Das Leben des deutschen Tonsetzers Adrian Leverkühn.* Stockholm: Bermann, 1947.

Mason, Ann L. *The Skeptical Muse: A Study of Günter Grass' Conception of the Artist.* Bern: Lang, 1974.

Mayer-Iswandy, Claudia. "'Danach ging das Leben weiter': Zum Verhältnis von Macht und Gewalt im Geschlechterkampf: Systemtheoretische Überlegungen zu Günter Grass und Ulla Hahn." *Zeitschrift für Germanistik N.F.* 2 (1997): 303–20.

———. *Günter Grass.* Munich: dtv, 2002.

———. *"Vom Glück der Zwitter": Geschlechterrolle und Geschlechterverhältnis bei Günter Grass.* Frankfurt am Main: Lang, 1991.

McAllester, Matthew. "Germans, Brits Spar over Pope." *Newsday* 22 Apr. 2005: A62.

McElroy, Bernard. "Lunatic, Child, Artist, Hero: Grass's Oskar as a Way of Seeing." *Forum for Modern Language Studies* 22 (1986): 308–22.

Metz, Joseph. "Post-Holocaust Narrative, Postmodernism, and the Gender of Fascism in *Der Vorleser.*" *German Quarterly* 77 (2004): 300–23.

Mews, Siegfried. "Felix Dahn." *Nineteenth-Century German Writers, 1841–1900.* Ed. James Hardin and Mews. Detroit: Gale, 1993. 25–37. Vol. 129 of *Dictionary of Literary Biography.*

Miles, David H. *Günter Grass.* New York: Barnes and Noble, 1975.

———. "Kafka's Hapless Pilgrims and Grass's Scurrilous Dwarf: Notes on Representative Figures in the Anti-bildungsroman." *Monatshefte* 65 (1973): 341–50.

Miller, J. Hillis. "Narrative." *Critical Terms for Literary Study.* Ed. Frank Lentricchia and Thomas McLaughlin. Chicago: U of Chicago P, 1995. 66–79.

Minden, Michael. "A Post-realist Aesthetic: Günter Grass, *Die Blechtrommel.*" *The German Novel in the Twentieth Century: Beyond Realism.* Ed. David Midgley. Edinburgh: Edinburgh UP, 1993. 149–63.

Mitchell, Juliet. *Psychoanalysis and Feminism: A Radical Reassessment of Freudian Psychoanalysis.* London: Penguin, 1974.

Moeller, Hans-Bernhard, and George Lellis. *Volker Schlöndorff's Cinema: Adaptation, Politics, and the "Movie-Appropriate."* Carbondale: Southern Illinois UP, 2002.

Moeller, Robert G. *Protecting Motherhood: Women and the Family in the Politics of Postwar Germany.* Berkeley: U of California P, 1993.

———. "Reconstructing the Family in Reconstruction Germany: Women and Social Policy in the Federal Republic, 1949–1955." *Feminist Studies* 15 (1989): 137–69.

————. "Sinking Ships, the Lost Heimat, and Broken Taboos: Günter Grass and the Politics of Memory in Contemporary Germany." *Contemporary European History* 12.2 (2003): 147–81.

————. *War Stories: The Search for a Usable Past in the Federal Republic of Germany.* Berkeley: U of California P, 2001.

Moeller, Susanne. "Politics to Pulp a Novel: The Fate of the First Edition of Edgar Hilsenrath's Novel *Nacht.*" *Insiders and Outsiders: Jewish and Gentile Culture in Germany and Austria.* Ed. Dagmar C. G. Lorenz and Gabriele Weinberger. Detroit: Wayne State UP, 1994. 224–34.

Moser, Sabine. *Günter Grass: Romane und Erzählungen.* Berlin: Schmidt, 2000.

Mosse, George, ed. *The Image of Man: The Creation of Modern Masculinity.* New York: Oxford UP, 1996.

————. *Nazi Culture: A Documentary History.* New York: Schocken, 1981.

————. *Nazi Culture: Intellectual, Cultural, and Social Life in the Third Reich.* Trans. Salvator Attanasio et al. Madison: U of Wisconsin P, 2003.

Mouton, Janice. "Gnomes, Fairy-Tale Heroes, and Oskar Matzerath." *Germanic Review* 56.1 (1981): 28–33.

Neuhaus, Volker. "Belle Tulla sans merci." Neuhaus and Hermes 181–99.

————. "Das christliche Erbe bei Günter Grass" Arnold, *Günter Grass* 108–19.

————. *Günter Grass.* 2nd rev. ed. Stuttgart: Metzler, 1993.

————. *Günter Grass*: Die Blechtrommel. Oldenbourg Interpretationen mit Unterrichts-hilfen. Munich: Oldenbourg, 1992.

————. *Günter Grass*: Die Blechtrommel. Erläuterungen und Dokumente. Stuttgart: Reclam, 1997.

————. *Günter Grass*: Die Blechtrommel: *Interpretation.* 4th ed. Munich: Oldenbourg, 2000.

————. *Schreiben gegen die verstreichende Zeit: Zu Leben und Werk von Günter Grass.* Munich: dtv, 1997.

Neuhaus, Volker, and Daniela Hermes, eds. Die Danziger Trilogie *von Günter Grass: Texte, Daten, Bilder.* Frankfurt am Main: Luchterhand, 1991.

Øhrgaard, Per. *Günter Grass: Ein deutscher Schriftsteller wird besichtigt.* Trans. Christoph Bartmann. Vienna: Zsolnay, 2005.

"OK City Police Round Up Copies of 'Obscene' Movie Tin Drum." *Los Angeles Times* 27 June 1997: A16.

Oliver, Kelly. *Womanizing Nietzsche: Philosophy's Relation to the "Feminine."* Oxford: Routledge, 1995.

O'Neill, Patrick. *Acts of Narrative: Textual Strategies in Modern German Fiction.* Toronto: U of Toronto P, 1996.

————. *Günter Grass Revisited.* New York: Twayne, 1999.

————. "Implications of Unreliability: The Semiotics of Discourse in Günter Grass's *Die Blechtrommel.*" *Analogon Rationis.* Ed. Marianne Henn and Christoph Lorey. Edmonton: U of Alberta P, 1994. 433–45.

————. "Musical Form and the Pauline Message in a Key Chapter of Grass's *Blechtrommel.*" *Seminar* 10 (1974): 298–307.

Ott, Frederick W. "*Die Blechtrommel: The Tin Drum*, 1979." *The Great German Films.* Secaucus: Citadel, 1986. 288–91.

Ozana, Anna. "Die Situation." *Die Frage der Jugend.* Ed. Rudolf Schneider-Schelde. Munich: Desch, 1946. 69–83.

Parr, Rolf. "Wilhelm Raabe und die Burenkriege, 1899: Deutsche Schriftsteller begeistern sich für die 'Burensache.'" *Mit Deutschland um die Welt: Eine Kulturgeschichte des Fremden in der Kolonialzeit.* Ed. Alexander Honold and Klaus R. Scherpe. Stuttgart: Metzler, 2004. 254–63.

Perrière, Guillaume de la. *Le théâtre des bons engins.* Paris, 1539. Ed. John Horden. New York: Scolar, 1973.

Pflaum, Hans Günther, and Hans Helmut Prinzler. *Film in der Bundesrepublik Deutschland: Der neue deutsche Film—Von den Anfängen bis zur Gegenwart.* Bonn: Inter Nationes, 1992.

Poiger, Ute. *Jazz, Rock, and Rebels: Cold War Politics and American Culture in a Divided Germany.* Berkeley: U of California P, 2000.

Preece, Julian. "The Danger of Reaching Thirty for Franz Kafka, Josef K., and Oskar Matzerath: Kafkaesque Motifs in *Die Blechtrommel.*" *Journal of the Kafka Society of America* 17.1 (1993): 39–50.

———. *The Life and Work of Günter Grass: Literature, History, Politics.* Basingstoke: Palgrave, 2001.

Raabe, Wilhelm. *Der Hungerpastor.* Göttingen: Vandenhoeck, 1966.

Reddick, John. *The Danzig Trilogy of Günter Grass: A Study of The Tin Drum, Cat and Mouse, and Dog Years.* New York: Harcourt, 1974.

Reed, Donna K. *The Novel and the Nazi Past.* New York: Lang, 1985.

Reich, Wilhelm. *The Mass Psychology of Fascism.* New York: Orgone Inst., 1946.

Reimer, Robert C., and Reinhard Zachau. *Arbeitsbuch zu German Culture through Film.* Newburyport: Focus; Pullins, 2006.

Reimer, Robert C., Reinhard Zachau, and Margit Sinka. *German Culture through Film: An Introduction to German Cinema.* Newburyport: Focus; Pullins, 2005.

Remak, Joachim. *The Nazi Years: A Documentary History.* New York: Simon, 1988.

Rentschler, Eric. *The Ministry of Illusion: Nazi Cinema and Its Afterlife.* Cambridge: Harvard UP, 1996.

———, ed. *West German Filmmakers on Film: Visions and Voices.* New York: Holmes, 1988.

Resnais, Alain, dir. *Night and Fog.* 1955. DVD. Criterion, 2003.

Richter, Frank-Raymund. *Günter Grass: Die Vergangenheitsbewältigung in der Danzig Trilogie.* Bonn: Bouvier, 1979.

"Rights Group Sues over a Film Seizure in Oklahoma City." *New York Times* 5 July 1997: 9.

Ripa, Cesare. *Baroque and Rococo Pictorial Imagery.* Trans. Edward A. Maser. New York: Dover, 1974.

Roberts, David. "'Gesinnungsästhetik'? Günter Grass, *Schreiben nach Auschwitz* (1990)." *Poetik der Autoren: Beiträge zur deutschsprachigen Gegenwartsliteratur.* Ed. Paul Michael Lützeler. Frankfurt am Main: Fischer, 1994. 235–61.

Roller, Frank. "Zu *Die Blechtrommel.*" Wertheimer and Allmendinger 100–02.

Romberg, Bertil. *Studies in the Narrative Technique of the First-Person Novel*. Stockholm: Almqvist, 1962.

Roper, Lyndal. *Witch Craze: Terror and Fantasy in Baroque Germany*. New Haven: Yale UP, 2004.

Röpke, Wilhelm. *The German Question*. Trans. E. W. Dickes. London: Allen, 1946.

Rossellini, Roberto, dir. *Germania, anno zero*. Produzione Salvo D'Angelo, 1948.

Rushdie, Salman. "On Günter Grass." *Granta* 15 (1985): 18–85.

Ryan, Judith. "Post-occupation Literary Movements and Developments in West Germany." *Legacies and Ambiguities: Postwar Fiction and Culture in West Germany and Japan*. Ed. Ernestine Schlant and J. Thomas Rimer. Baltimore: Johns Hopkins UP, 1991. 189–206.

———. *The Uncompleted Past: Postwar German Novels and the Third Reich*. Detroit: Wayne State UP, 1983.

Schade, Richard E. "Günter Grass's *Mein Jahrhundert*: Histories, Paintings, and Performance." *Monatshefte* 96 (2004): 409–21.

———. "Layers of Meaning, War, Art: Grass's *Beim Häuten der Zwiebel*." *German Quarterly* 80 (2007): 279–301.

———. "Poet and Artist: Iconography in Grass' *Treffen in Telgte*." *German Quarterly* 55 (1982): 200–11.

Scherf, Rainer. *Das Herz der* Blechtrommel *und andere Aufsätze zum Werk von Günter Grass*. Marburg: Tectum, 2000.

Schilling, Klaus von. *Schuldmotoren: Artistisches Erzählen in Günter Grass' Danziger Trilogie*. Bielefeld: Aisthesis, 2002.

Schirrmacher, Frank. "Abschied von der Literatur der Bundesrepublik." *Frankfurter Allgemeine Zeitung* 2 Oct. 1990: L1–2.

Schlant, Ernestine. *The Language of Silence: West German Literature and the Holocaust*. New York: Routledge, 1999.

Schlink, Bernhard. *Der Vorleser: Roman*. Zurich: Diogenes, 1995. Trans. as *The Reader*. Trans. Carol Brown Janeway. New York: Pantheon, 1997.

Schlöndorff, Volker. Die Blechtrommel: *Tagebuch einer Verfilmung*. Neuwied: Luchterhand, 1979.

Schlöndorff, Volker, and Günter Grass. Die Blechtrommel *als Film*. Frankfurt am Main: Zweitausendeins, 1979.

Schwab, Hans-Rüdiger. "Helden, hoffnungslos: Felix Dahns *Ein Kampf um Rom* als gründerzeitliche Schicksalstragödie." *Ein Kampf um Rom: Historischer Roman*. By Felix Dahn. Munich: dtv, 2003. 1065–129.

Sebald, W. G. *Austerlitz*. Frankfurt am Main: Fischer, 2001.

———. *Luftkrieg und Literatur*. Munich: Hanser, 1999.

———. *On the Natural History of Destruction*. 1999. Trans. Anthea Bell. New York: Random, 2003.

Selbmann, Rolf. *Der deutsche Bildungsroman*. Stuttgart: Metzler, 1994.

Sontag, Susan. "Fascinating Fascism." *Under the Sign of Saturn*. New York: Farrar, 1980. 71–105.

Stafford-Clark, David. *What Freud Really Said*. London: Penguin, 1965.

Stanford, Peter. "From Hitler Youth to Hard Man of the Vatican." *Daily Mail* 20 Apr. 2005: 6.

Stanzel, Franz. *Typische Formen des Romans*. Göttingen: Vandenhoek, 1964.

Steinfeld, Thomas. "Grass ist Deutschland." *Süddeutsche Zeitung* 19–20 Aug. 2006: 4.

Stern, Fritz. "Der Nationalsozialismus als Versuchung." *Der Traum von Frieden und die Versuchung der Macht: Deutsche Geschichte im zwanzigsten Jahrhundert*. Berlin: Siedler, 1988. 164–215.

Stolz, Dieter. *Günter Grass zur Einführung*. Hamburg: Junius, 1999.

Süskind, Patrick. *Das Parfum: Die Geschichte eines Mörders*. Zurich: Diogenes, 1994. Trans. as *Perfume: The Story of a Murderer*. Trans. John E. Woods. New York: Knopf, 1986.

Syberberg, Hans Jürgen. *Vom Unglück und Glück der Kunst in Deutschland nach dem letzten Kriege*. Munich: Matthes, 1990.

Taberner, Stuart. *German Literature of the 1990s and Beyond: Normalization and the Berlin Republic*. Rochester: Camden, 2005.

Tatar, Maria. *Lustmord: Sexual Murder in Weimar Germany*. Princeton: Princeton UP, 1995.

Theweleit, Klaus. *Male Fantasies*. Trans. Erica Carter, Stephen Conway, and Chris Turner. 2 vols. Minneapolis: U of Minnesota P, 1987–89.

Thomas, Noel. *Grass: Die Blechtrommel*. London: Grant, 1985.

———. "Oskar, the Unreliable Narrator in Günter Grass's *Die Blechtrommel*." *New German Studies* 3 (1975): 31–47.

Tighe, Carl. *Gdańsk: National Identity in the Polish-German Borderlands*. London: Pluto, 1990.

Trappen, Stefan. "Grass, Döblin und der Futurismus: Zu den futuristischen Grundlagen des Simultaneitätskonzepts der *Vergegenkunft*." *Euphorion* 96 (2002): 1–26.

Vinocur, John. "After Twenty Years: *The Tin Drum* Marches to the Screen." *New York Times* 6 Apr. 1980, sec. 2.1: 17.

Vognar, Chris. "A Bang-Up Job: Documentary about *Drum* Ban a Worthy Mate to Masterpiece." *Dallas Morning News* 28 May 2004, Entertainment sec.: 8H.

Vormweg, Heinrich. *Günter Grass*. 1986. Überarbeitete und erweiterte Neuauflage. Hamburg: Rowohlt, 2002.

Walby, Sylvia. *Theorizing Patriarchy*. Oxford: Blackwell, 1990.

Walser, Martin. *Ein springender Brunnen*. Frankfurt am Main: Suhrkamp, 1998.

Weisberg, Richard. "Why They're Censoring *The Tin Drum*: Kristallnacht—Reflections on the End of the Epic." *Cardozo Studies in Law and Literature* 10.2 (1998): 161–81.

Weiss, Peter. *The Investigation: Oratorio in Eleven Cantos*. London: Boyars, 1996.

Wells, Larry D. *Handbuch zur deutschen Grammatik*. 2nd ed. Boston: Houghton, 1997.

Welsford, Enid. *The Fool: His Social and Literary History*. New York: Farrar, 1935.

Wertheimer, Jürgen, and Ute Allmendinger, eds. *Günter Grass: Wort und Bild*. Tübinger Poetik Vorlesung und Materialien. Tübingen: Konkursbuch, 1999.

West, Cornel. *Democracy Matters: Winning the Fight against Imperialism*. New York: Penguin, 2004.

Wicki, Bernhard, dir. *Die Brücke*. Fono Film, 1959.

Wildmann, Daniel. *Begehrte Körper: Konstruktion und Inszenierung des 'arischen' Männerkörpers im "Dritten Reich."* Würzburg: Königshausen, 1998.

Wittmann, Jochen. "The GDR and Günter Grass: East German Reception of the Literary Works and Public Persona." *German Literature at a Time of Change, 1989–1990: German Unity and German Identity in Literary Perspective.* Ed. Arthur Williams, Stuart Parkes, and Roland Smith. Bern: Lang, 1992. 273–84.

Wolf, Christa. *Patterns of Childhood*. Trans. Ursule Molinaro and Hedwig Rappolt. New York: Farrar, 1990.

Young, Julian. *Heidegger's Later Philosophy*. Cambridge: Cambridge UP, 2002.

Zemeckis, Robert, dir. *Forrest Gump*. Paramount Pictures, 1994.

Ziolkowski, Theodore. "Günter Grass's Century." *World Literature Today* 74.1 (2000): 19–26.

Zipes, Jack David. *Fairy Tales and the Art of Subversion: The Classical Genre for Children and the Process of Civilization*. New York: Methuen, 1988.

Žižek, Slavoj. *Did Somebody Say Totalitarianism? Five Interventions in the (Mis)use of a Notion*. London: Verso, 2001.

Audiovisual Aids

Die Blechtrommel. Dir. Volker Schlöndorff. 1979. DVD. Arthouse DVD, 2001.

Grass, Günter. *Die Blechtrommel*. Read by Grass. CD. Deutsche Grammophon GmbH, 2004.

———. *The Tin Drum*. Read by George Guidall. Audiocassette. Recorded Books, 2000.

———. *The Tin Drum*. Read by Fred Williams. Audiocassette. Blackstone Audiobooks, 2001.

Selected Web Resources

Danzig

Gdańsk: Morze możliwości. Urząd miejski w Gdańsku. 9 Aug. 2006 <http://www.gdansk .pl>.

Gunter Grass and Gdansk. Gdansk-life.com. 9 Aug. 2006 <http://www.gdansk-life.com/ culture/gunter-grass.php>.

German Film

Film in Herzen Europas. CineGraph. 9 Aug. 2006 <http://www.cinegraph.de/>.

Grass Archives

Günter Grass-Haus: Forum für Literatur und bildende Kunst. 9 Aug. 2006 <http://www .guenter-grass-haus.de>.

Günter Grass Stiftung Bremen. 9 Aug. 2006 <http://www.guenter-grass.de/ggrass/index
.shtml>.

Grass Biographies and Resources

Günter Grass. Universitätsbibliothek der FU Berlin 2006. 9 Aug. 2006 <http://www
.ub.fu-berlin.de/internetquellen/fachinformation/germanistik/autoren/multi_fgh/
grass.html>.

Günter Grass (1927–): Nobel Prize for Literature 1999. About.com. 9 Aug. 2006 <http://
german.about.com/library/blgrass.htm>.

Nobelvorlesung: "Fortsetzung folgt. . . ." Nobel Prize in Literature, 1999. 9 Feb. 2007
<http://nobelprize.org/nobel_prizes/literature/laureates/1999/lecture-g.html>.

Schlöndorff Biographies

Volker Schloendorff. Dirk Jasper. 1994–2005. 9 Aug. 2006 <http://www.djfl.de/entertainment/
stars/v/volker_schloendorff.html>.

Volker Schlöndorff. IMDB. 1990–2006. 9 Aug. 2006 <http://www.imdb.com/name/
nm0772522/>.

Volker Schlöndorff. Reference.com. 9 Aug. 2006 <http://www.reference.com/browse/
wiki/Volker_Schl%F6ndorff>.

INDEX

Modern Language Association of America
Approaches to Teaching World Literature
Joseph Gibaldi, series editor

Shorter Elizabethan Poetry. Ed. Patrick Cheney and Anne Lake Prescott. 2000.
Ellison's Invisible Man. Ed. Susan Resneck Parr and Pancho Savery. 1989.
English Renaissance Drama. Ed. Karen Bamford and Alexander Leggatt. 2002.
Works of Louise Erdrich. Ed. Gregg Sarris, Connie A. Jacobs, and
    James R. Giles. 2004.
Dramas of Euripides. Ed. Robin Mitchell-Boyask. 2002.
Faulkner's The Sound and the Fury. Ed. Stephen Hahn and Arthur F. Kinney. 1996.
Flaubert's Madame Bovary. Ed. Laurence M. Porter and Eugene F. Gray. 1995.
García Márquez's One Hundred Years of Solitude. Ed. María Elena de Valdés and
    Mario J. Valdés. 1990.
Gilman's "The Yellow Wall-Paper" and Herland. Ed. Denise D. Knight and
    Cynthia J. Davis. 2003.
Goethe's Faust. Ed. Douglas J. McMillan. 1987.
Gothic Fiction: The British and American Traditions. Ed. Diane Long Hoeveler
    and Tamar Heller. 2003.
Grass's The Tin Drum. Ed. Monika Shafi. 2008.
Hebrew Bible as Literature in Translation. Ed. Barry N. Olshen and
    Yael S. Feldman. 1989.
Homer's Iliad and Odyssey. Ed. Kostas Myrsiades. 1987.
Ibsen's A Doll House. Ed. Yvonne Shafer. 1985.
Henry James's Daisy Miller and The Turn of the Screw. Ed. Kimberly C. Reed and
    Peter G. Beidler. 2005.
Works of Samuel Johnson. Ed. David R. Anderson and Gwin J. Kolb. 1993.
Joyce's Ulysses. Ed. Kathleen McCormick and Erwin R. Steinberg. 1993.
Works of Sor Juana Inés de la Cruz. Ed. Emilie L. Bergmann and Stacey Schlau.
    2007.
Kafka's Short Fiction. Ed. Richard T. Gray. 1995.
Keats's Poetry. Ed. Walter H. Evert and Jack W. Rhodes. 1991.
Kingston's The Woman Warrior. Ed. Shirley Geok-lin Lim. 1991.
Lafayette's The Princess of Clèves. Ed. Faith E. Beasley and
    Katharine Ann Jensen. 1998.
Works of D. H. Lawrence. Ed. M. Elizabeth Sargent and Garry Watson. 2001.
Lessing's The Golden Notebook. Ed. Carey Kaplan and Ellen Cronan Rose. 1989.
Mann's Death in Venice and Other Short Fiction. Ed. Jeffrey B. Berlin. 1992.
Marguerite de Navarre's Heptameron. Ed. Colette H. Winn. 2007.
Medieval English Drama. Ed. Richard K. Emmerson. 1990.
Melville's Moby-Dick. Ed. Martin Bickman. 1985.
Metaphysical Poets. Ed. Sidney Gottlieb. 1990.
Miller's Death of a Salesman. Ed. Matthew C. Roudané. 1995.
Milton's Paradise Lost. Ed. Galbraith M. Crump. 1986.
Milton's Shorter Poetry and Prose. Ed. Peter C. Herman. 2007.
Molière's Tartuffe and Other Plays. Ed. James F. Gaines and
    Michael S. Koppisch. 1995.

Momaday's The Way to Rainy Mountain. Ed. Kenneth M. Roemer. 1988.

Montaigne's Essays. Ed. Patrick Henry. 1994.

Novels of Toni Morrison. Ed. Nellie Y. McKay and Kathryn Earle. 1997.

Murasaki Shikibu's The Tale of Genji. Ed. Edward Kamens. 1993.

Nabokov's Lolita. Ed. Zoran Kuzmanovich and Galya Diment. 2008.

Pope's Poetry. Ed. Wallace Jackson and R. Paul Yoder. 1993.

Proust's Fiction and Criticism. Ed. Elyane Dezon-Jones and
   Inge Crosman Wimmers. 2003.

Puig's Kiss of the Spider Woman. Ed. Daniel Balderston and Francine Masiello.
   2007.

Pynchon's The Crying of Lot 49 *and Other Works.* Ed. Thomas H. Schaub. 2008.

Novels of Samuel Richardson. Ed. Lisa Zunshine and Jocelyn Harris. 2006.

Rousseau's Confessions *and* Reveries of the Solitary Walker. Ed. John C. O'Neal
   and Ourida Mostefai. 2003.

Shakespeare's Hamlet. Ed. Bernice W. Kliman. 2001.

Shakespeare's King Lear. Ed. Robert H. Ray. 1986.

Shakespeare's Othello. Ed. Peter Erickson and Maurice Hunt. 2005.

Shakespeare's Romeo and Juliet. Ed. Maurice Hunt. 2000.

Shakespeare's The Tempest *and Other Late Romances.* Ed. Maurice Hunt. 1992.

Shelley's Frankenstein. Ed. Stephen C. Behrendt. 1990.

Shelley's Poetry. Ed. Spencer Hall. 1990.

Sir Gawain and the Green Knight. Ed. Miriam Youngerman Miller and
   Jane Chance. 1986.

Song of Roland. Ed. William W. Kibler and Leslie Zarker Morgan. 2006.

Spenser's Faerie Queene. Ed. David Lee Miller and Alexander Dunlop. 1994.

Stendhal's The Red and the Black. Ed. Dean de la Motte and Stirling Haig. 1999.

Sterne's Tristram Shandy. Ed. Melvyn New. 1989.

Stowe's Uncle Tom's Cabin. Ed. Elizabeth Ammons and Susan Belasco. 2000.

Swift's Gulliver's Travels. Ed. Edward J. Rielly. 1988.

Thoreau's Walden *and Other Works.* Ed. Richard J. Schneider. 1996.

Tolstoy's Anna Karenina. Ed. Liza Knapp and Amy Mandelker. 2003.

Vergil's Aeneid. Ed. William S. Anderson and Lorina N. Quartarone. 2002.

Voltaire's Candide. Ed. Renée Waldinger. 1987.

Whitman's Leaves of Grass. Ed. Donald D. Kummings. 1990.

Wiesel's Night. Ed. Alan Rosen. 2007.

Woolf's To the Lighthouse. Ed. Beth Rigel Daugherty and Mary Beth Pringle. 2001.

Wordsworth's Poetry. Ed. Spencer Hall, with Jonathan Ramsey. 1986.

Wright's Native Son. Ed. James A. Miller. 1997.